CONTEXT-SENSITIVITY AN
MINIMALISM

Context-Sensitivity and Semantic Minimalism

New Essays on Semantics and Pragmatics

Edited by
GERHARD PREYER
and
GEORG PETER

OXFORD
UNIVERSITY PRESS

Great Clarendon Street, Oxford OX2 6DP

Oxford University Press is a department of the University of Oxford.
It furthers the University's objective of excellence in research, scholarship,
and education by publishing worldwide in

Oxford New York

Auckland Cape Town Dar es Salaam Hong Kong Karachi
Kuala Lumpur Madrid Melbourne Mexico City Nairobi
New Delhi Shanghai Taipei Toronto

With offices in

Argentina Austria Brazil Chile Czech Republic France Greece
Guatemala Hungary Italy Japan Poland Portugal Singapore
South Korea Switzerland Thailand Turkey Ukraine Vietnam

Oxford is a registered trade mark of Oxford University Press
in the UK and in certain other countries

Published in the United States
by Oxford University Press Inc., New York

First published 2007

British Library Cataloguing in Publication Data
Data available

Library of Congress Cataloging in Publication Data
Data available

Typeset by Laserwords Private Limited, Chennai, India
Printed in Great Britain
on acid-free paper by
Biddles Ltd, King's Lynn, Norfolk

ISBN 978–0–19–921332–0
ISBN 978–0–19–921331–3 (Pbk.)

1 3 5 7 9 10 8 6 4 2

Editors's Preface

We thank our contributors, especially Herman Cappelen and Ernie Lepore; the anonymous referees of the manuscript; and Peter Mometchiloff for his support in realizing the project. This book represents a continuation of the research project in philosophy of language and semantics represented in the journal *Protosociology* at the J. W. Goethe-University, Frankfurt am Main.

G. P. and G. P

J. W. Goethe-University

Contents

Contributors

Jay David Atlas, Department of Philosophy and Department of Linguistics and Cognitive Science, Pomona College, Claremont, United States.

Emma Borg, Department of Philosophy, University of Reading, Great Britain.

Elisabeth Camp, Harvard Society of Fellows, Cambridge MA, United States.

Herman Cappelen, Department of Philosophy, University of St. Andrews, St. Andrews, Scotland.

Lenny Clapp, Department of Philosophy, Illinois Wesleyan University, Bloomington, United States.

Eros Corazza, Department of Philosophy, Carleton University, Ottawa, Canada.

Jérôme Dokic, EHSS and Institut Jean Nicod, Paris, France.

Reinaldo Elugardo, Department of Philosophy, University of Oklahoma, Norman, Oklahoma, United States.

Henry Jackman, Department of Philosophy, York University, Toronto, Ontario, Canada.

Kepa Korta, ILCLI, The University of the Basque Country, Donostia-San Sebasti'n, Spain.

Sarah-Jane Leslie, Department of Philosophy, Princeton University Princeton, NJ, United States.

John MacFarlane, UCB Department of Philosophy, Berkeley, United States.

Ishani Maitra, Department of Philosophy, Syracuse University, Syracuse NY, United States.

Peter Pagin, Department of Philosophy, Stockholm University, Stockholm, Sweden.

Francis Jeffry Pelletier, Department of Philosophy, Simon Fraser University, Burnaby, Canada.

Georg Peter, J. W. Goethe-University, Frankfurt am Main, Germany.

John Perry, Department of Philosophy, Stanford University, Stanford, United States.

Gerhard Preyer, J. W. Goethe-University, Frankfurt am Main, Germany.

Philip Robbins, Philosophy-Neuroscience-Psychology, Washington University, St. Louis, United States.

Ken Taylor, Department of Philosophy, Stanford University, United States.

INTRODUCTION

Semantics and Pragmatics: Some Central Issues

Herman Cappelen

If you vary the context of utterance enough, i.e. vary the audience, the conversational context, the background knowledge, etc., you can get any sentence to communicate different propositions. One central task for those interested in the semantics–pragmatics distinction is to identify and classify such patterns of inter-contextual variability. Having identified such patterns, we develop models that can explain them. In what follows, I first present some versions of three important models: the Semantic Model, the Pragmatic Model, and the Index Model. In the second half of the chapter, I present what I take to be some of the most pressing challenges facing those working in this field.

The goal is to present these issues and challenges, not to defend a theory. In particular, this is not a chapter meant as a defence of Cappelen and Lepore (2004). As this volume of essays clearly shows, the number of powerful objections and alternatives is now so large that responding to all of them would take a new book. This chapter is meant, rather, as a brief overview, written in the light of these criticisms, of how these issues are best structured, and so might serve to frame some of the debates triggered by the book.

There is, however, one small point I will try to promote, at least indirectly: there's no such thing as *the semantics–pragmatics distinction* and looking for it is a waste of time. No such distinction will do any important explanatory work. You can, as I will below, label some level of content 'semantic content', but in so doing no interesting problem is solved and no puzzling data illuminated. To explain inter-contextual variability across different areas of discourse we will need an arsenal of explanatory models and data-gathering procedures. In the light of recent work in philosophy and linguistics, we should be sceptical of any suggestion to the effect that just a couple of such models will do all the work for us. Our bias, I suggest, should be in favour of methodological and explanatory pluralism. I return to this point at the end of the chapter.[1]

1. TERMINOLOGICAL PRELIMINARIES: 'SEMANTIC', 'CONTENT', AND 'CHARACTER'

I will talk about *the semantic content of a sentence relative to context of utterance*, and of *the semantic content of an expression relative to a context of utterance*. By this I will mean, more or less, what David Kaplan (1989) means when he talks about the 'content' of a sentence and an expression. The content of a sentence, S, in a language, L, relative to a context, C, is found by taking the semantic values of the parts of S and combining them in accordance with the semantic and syntactic composition rules of L.

I'll take the semantic values of singular terms to be objects, and assume that properties and functions are the semantic values of other terms, though nothing in what follows will crucially depend on these assumptions. What will matter is how we think of the semantic values of those terms that shift content between contexts of utterance. Kaplan takes terms like 'I' and 'that' as paradigms, and says about them:

> What is common to the words or usages in which I am interested is that the referent is dependent on the context of use and that the meaning of the words provides a rule which determines the referent in terms of certain aspects of the context. (Kaplan 1989: 490)

These rules Kaplan calls 'character'. For example, the rule:

> 'I' refers to the speaker or writer

is, according to Kaplan, the character of 'I'.[2] This rule determines a referent for an occurrence of 'I' relative to a context of use. So, in a context where Tim is the speaker, the content is Tim. When Samantha is the speaker, she is the semantic content. Kaplan sometimes represents characters as functions from contexts of utterance to contents. So understood, indexicals are those expressions that have such non-stable functions as characters. Non-indexical expressions have fixed characters[3] (Kaplan 1989: 506).

[1] In part as a result of this bias, I will have nothing to say about how philosophers have used the words 'semantic' and 'pragmatic' over the last 100 years. Though this no doubt is a fascinating historical topic, it's not one that will be of any use to those of us trying to solve problems in this area.

[2] Kaplan 1989: 505.

[3] So understood, terms that are not semantically context-sensitive, e.g. 'two', have a character, i.e. a function from contexts to contents. This is a stable function, one that yields the same object for all contexts.

Note that while the character of an expression is part of its linguistic meaning, it does not enter into a specification of its semantic content. Characters *determine* semantic contents; they are not *constituents* of semantic contents. The semantic content of, for example, an utterance by A at time t and location l of "I'm here now" is the proposition *that A is at l at t.* The constituents of this proposition are determined by the character of the corresponding lexical elements, but this proposition doesn't in any way 'contain' these rules.

Four points are important to note in connection with the decision to use 'semantic' in this way:

1. Semantic content is determined compositionally and every element in the semantic value of the sentence is syntactically triggered, i.e. is triggered by elements in the syntax of the sentence.
2. The definition remains neutral about whether these syntactic elements are all articulated in the surface grammatical form of the sentences. Some elements in the semantic value of S relative to context C might correspond to syntactic components that occur only in S's logical form.
3. The definition remains neutral about whether semantic contents are propositional. They might be sub-propositional objects (also known as 'propositional skeletons'—more about these below).
4. Finally, the definition remains neutral about whether the semantic content of an utterance, u, is what was said or asserted by u.

Before moving on, it is worth emphasizing the obvious: choosing to use the word 'semantic' in this way is a purely terminological matter. As will become clear below, no interesting issues are settled by this (or any alternative) stipulation.

2. INTER-CONTEXTUAL CONTENT VARIABILITY: SEVEN ILLUSTRATIONS

In what follows, I'll use the expression variability of S's or just 'variability' as a shorthand for talking about some sentence, S, being used in different contexts to express different contents. Talk about 'content variability' is neutral about what *kind* of content varies; it might be semantic content, asserted content, implicatures, or some other level of content. In this section I present some cases of variability and then match them with various explanatory models in §§3–5.

(1) Kiara has had enough

An utterance u of (1) can be used to communicate *that Kiara has had enough pasta*. Another utterance, u′, can be used to communicate *that Kiara has had enough chocolate.*

(2) The kettle is black

An utterance u of (2) can be used to communicate *that the kettle is black on the outside when washed.* Another utterance, u′ of (2) can be used to communicate *that the kettle is black all over before being washed.*

(3) Samantha knows that Tim is in Paris

An utterance u of (3) in a 'high stakes context' might communicate *that Samantha knows by high epistemic standards that Tim is in Paris*. In 'low stakes context', an utterance u′ of (3) might communicate *that Samantha knows by low epistemic standards that Tim is in Paris.*

(4) Sabrina has travelled to Leeds quite often

An utterance u of (4) in response to the question "Does Sabrina have a girlfriend these days?" can succeed in communicating *that Sabrina has a girlfriend in Leeds.* An utterance u′ of (4) in response to the question "Where does Sabrina meet her business partners these days?", can succeed in communicating *that Sabrina meets her business partners in Leeds.*

(5) I'm here now

An utterance u of (5) can be used to communicate *that Nelib was in Florence 29 May 2006*. An utterance u′ of (5) can be used to communicate *that Alex is in Buenos Aires 15 December 2006.*

(6) Every book is in the left corner

An utterance u of (6) can be used to communicate *that every book Alex bought is in the left corner*. Another utterance can be used to communicate the proposition *that every book Nelib wants moved is in the left corner.*

(7) It's raining

An utterance u of (7) can be used to communicate *that it is raining in Buenos Aires.* Another utterance u′ of (6) can be used to communicate *that it is raining in Oxford.*

These are all cases of one sentence being used to express different contents in different contexts of utterance. It is *obvious* that no single theory can explain how this happens. That said, there are various patterns of explanatory models and in what follows I focus on three of them: the Semantic Model, the Pragmatic Model and the Index Model.[4]

3. SEMANTIC EXPLANATIONS (S-EXPLANATIONS)

The variability in (5) is easy to explain: the sentence contains semantically context-sensitive terms and will, as a result, express different semantic contents relative to different contexts of utterance. Not all S-explanations are that simple. S-explanations can differ along two important dimensions: whether they appeal to *obvious* or *non-obvious* indexicality, and whether they appeal to *overt* or *hidden* indexicality. I discuss each in turn.

Obvious vs. Non-Obvious Indexicality

Some terms, like 'I' and 'that', are obviously context sensitive. If you ask for a list of terms that change semantic value between contexts, these would be on anyone's list. Some philosophers claim to find evidence that terms that are not on any initial such list should be. A paradigm is the verb 'know'. Some philosophers claim that a careful study our usage of 'know' reveals that it has a non-stable character so that in this respect it belongs semantically with 'you' and 'I' (this is, for example, one way to interpret, Cohen 1988, 1999, and Lewis 1996). So two utterances of (3) can vary in content because the context of utterance determines different semantic contents for 'know'.

The central challenge for those promoting non-obvious indexicality is to provide evidence that a term which doesn't *seem* to belong with 'I' and 'that' does. One danger here, emphasized in Cappelen and Lepore (2004), is that whatever conditions are specified may over-generate non-obvious indexicality. The relevant evidence must be such that it includes the proponent's favoured cases, but doesn't include every term in the language (unless, of course, you are tempted to conclude that every term in the language is an indexical.

Overt vs. Hidden Indexicality

According to most philosophers and linguists, the *logical form* of a sentence can be radically different from its surface grammatical form. There can be

[4] I don't claim that these are the only important explanatory models. For example, I say nothing here about syntactic ellipsis or about models developed in Dynamic Semantics.

constituents in a sentence's logical form that are not phonologically realized. This opens up the possibility that there can be, so to speak, 'hidden' indexicality in sentences. I'll call this 'hidden indexicality' because you can't hear (or see) these indexicals. Note that these are still S-explanations, given the definition of 'semantic' in §1. (6) provides a much discussed illustration. (6) doesn't seem to contain a context-sensitive component, but it is widely believed that its logical form contains an indexical that refers to a domain. According to this view, the logical form of (6) can be (at least partially) represented by (6.1):[5]

(6.1) Every $\text{book}_{(D)}$ is in the left corner

According to this view, 'D' is an indexical expression that refers to a set (or a property) and the semantic value of "$\text{NP}_{(D)}$" can be thought of as the intersection of the semantic values of 'NP' and 'D'. The variability in content between different utterances of (6) is thus explained by variability in what the 'hidden indexical' refers to.

The central challenge for those promoting S-explanations that appeal to hidden indexicals is to specify what counts as evidence for their existence. As with non-obvious indexicality, there's the danger that the procedure will over-generate. If there are hidden indexicals that refer to domain restrictions, what prevents us from saying there are hidden indexicals in (2) specifying the side on (or way in which) the kettle is black? Again, some might welcome a proliferation of indexicals in logical form, but more moderate proponents of S-explanations will want to avoid over-generation. (For further elaboration on this, see discussion of the binding argument in §6 below.)

I-Explanations and Intentional vs. Non-Intentional Indexicals

One point to note in connection with all S-explanations is that some authors make a great deal out of the distinction between those indexicals that have their semantic values determined by the speaker's intentions and those that are determined solely by the non-intentional features of the context utterance (such as the speaker, time, and place) (see Recanati 2002, 2004; Carston 2004). They argue that this distinction is of enormous significance and insist on using the term 'semantic content' only about those indexicals that have their semantic values fixed non-intentionally. Others (e.g. Cappelen and Lepore 2004: ch 11) argue that this is a paradigm of a pointless dispute about how to use the term 'semantic' and that no substantive or even remotely interesting issue depends on this distinction.

[5] For sophisticated versions and discussions of this idea see Stanley and Szabo 2000; Stanley 2000*a*; Westerstahl 1985.

4. PRAGMATIC EXPLANATIONS (P-EXPLANATIONS)

According to P-explanations of variability, utterances of S communicate distinct non-semantic (that is, pragmatic[6]) contents. For those trying to navigate the current literature on these topics, it might be helpful to classify P-explanations according to the various levels of non-semantic content the variability can be attributed to. Two non-semantic levels can usefully be distinguished: implicatures and asserted content.

Variability in Implicatures

(4) is the paradigm of variability in what Grice called an 'implicature' (Grice 1989*b*). Implicatures, according to Grice, occur when the speaker says that p (or makes as if to say that p) and intends for the audience to recognize that the purpose of the speech act is to communicate something other than what was said. Grice thought of conversations as cooperative enterprises and argued that what enables an audience to derive an implicature is the assumption that the speaker is cooperative. Implicatures are generated when the audience realizes that this assumption is incompatible with the speaker intending to communicate what was said by the utterance. The audience is led to look for some other content the speaker might intend to get across. This other content is the implicature. Consider again the two utterances of (4) in §2. We can assume that both utterances have the same semantic content and that what is said (or made as if to say) is the same proposition. At that level, there is no variability. In both cases, the assumption that the speaker is being cooperative (combined with certain assumptions about what that consists in) leads the audience to figure out that the speaker means for them to interpret the utterance as communicating a content different from what was asserted (or said) by it.

This is the most familiar and generally accepted version of P-explanation. That there are implicatures is generally accepted, but the mechanism through which the audience goes from an utterance to an implicature is more controversial.[7] I'll have some more to say about this in §6 below. First, I turn to another, more controversial type of P-explanation.

Variability in Speech Act Content, i.e. in What Was Said/Asserted

Some P-explanations appeal to variability in what was said or asserted by the utterances. Since P-explanations assume that the semantic content is stable, these

6 I use 'pragmatic' to mean 'non-semantic'.

7 See e.g. Wilson and Sperber 1981; Sperber and Wilson 1986; Davis 1998; Levinson 2000.

explanations must incorporate the view that semantic contents are not (always) asserted. Two versions of this view can be usefully distinguished: according to the first version, the semantic content is not asserted (or said); according to the second, the semantic content is only a part of what is asserted. I discuss these versions in turn.

Version 1

According to Version 1, two utterances u and u′ (of S) can have the same semantic content, *p*, but p is not what was said or asserted by either of them; u asserts that q and u′ that q′. According to some philosophers, (1) provides an illustration: "Kiara has had enough" has as its semantic content a propositional *fragment* or *skeleton*. Let's call it "that Kiara has had enough". This is not asserted by either u or u′. Various non-semantic mechanisms take the audience from the non-propositional semantic content to the asserted proposition; in the example in §2, *that Kiara has had enough pasta* is what u asserts and *that Kiara has had enough chocolate* is what u′ asserts.

Some philosophers go to town on this kind of P-explanation.[8] They think (almost) no semantic values are propositional. If practically no semantic contents are propositional, it is tempting to explain a whole lot of variability in the way just described; there is, after all, no other propositional content around, so variability in what was said (assuming this must be a complete proposition) *must* be given a P-explanation. Such philosophers typically have two primary motivations for denying that semantic values are propositional:

(a) They are unwilling to postulate elements not in the surface syntax of sentence. If, for example, there's no syntactic element corresponding to what Kiara has had enough of in the sentence, "Kiara has had enough", then, by most standards, it is hard to see that semantic composition alone will give you a proposition. If semantic content is non-propositional, it can't account for the variability in content between the two utterances of (1).

(b) They are also typically conservative about what they count as propositions. They often think it is exceedingly hard for a semantic value to reach the level of propositionality. If so, you might think that no matter how many syntactic elements you dump into a sentence's logical form, you won't end up with a proposition. For some classical arguments to this effect, see Travis 1985. For arguments in favour of liberalism with respect to what should count as a proposition, see Cappelen and Lepore 2004; ch 12.

[8] See e.g. Sperber and Wilson 1986; Carston 2002; Recanati 2004. For more moderate appeals to such explanations, see Perry 1986; Crimmins 1992; Bach 1994; Soames forthcoming.

Version 2

Closely related to the previous strategy, but also importantly different from it, is the idea, emphasized in Cappelen and Lepore 1997 and 2004, that an utterance of a sentence can assert a *plurality* of propositions.[9] According to this view, the semantic content could be *one* of these. This opens up the following possibility: two utterances, u and u′, of the same sentence S have the same semantic content, and the semantic content is one of the propositions said/asserted by both. However, other propositions are also asserted and these vary between u and u′.

This strategy can be applied to a wide range of cases. (6) can serve as an example. The semantic content is the unrestrictedly quantified proposition. This is the semantic content of both utterances of (6) and it is asserted by both utterances of (6). It is not, however, *saliently* asserted by either u or u′: u saliently asserts *that every book Alex bought is in the left corner*, u′ saliently asserts *that every book Nelib wants moved is in the left corner*.

P-Explanations and Unarticulated Constituents

In some of the semantics–pragmatics literature there's a lot of talk about 'unarticulated constituents' (see e.g. Perry 1986; Recanati 2002; Stanley 2000). There's debate about what they are and whether they exist. Here is how to place this issue within the framework outlined above: unarticulated constituents refer to elements in what is said (asserted) by an utterance that have no syntactic correlate in S. So understood, to believe in unarticulated constituents is nothing more radical than to think that some cases of variability have P-explanations of Version 1 or 2. Opposition to unarticulated constituents amounts to the claim that no good such explanations are adequate. As I argue in §6 below, given the complexity of these issues, that seems an exceedingly implausible assumption to make. It is also a bit hard to see why so much controversy surrounds this question. If in some cases these explanations turn out to be successful, it's not a big deal.

5. INDEX-EXPLANATIONS (I-EXPLANATIONS)

Some of the basic distinctions from Kaplan are needed to present the idea behind index-explanations. Kaplan says: "we must distinguish possible occasions of use—which I call contexts—from possible circumstances of evaluation of what is said on a given occasion of use"(Kaplan 1989). When defining what it is for an occurrence of a sentence to be true in a context, Kaplan talks about what he calls 'the circumstance of the context'. He says:

[9] A related idea is found in Soames 2002. On one interpretation, this view is also present in Sperber and Wilson 1986.

If c is a context, then an occurrence of ϕ in c is true iff the content expressed by ϕ in this context is true when evaluated *with respect to the circumstance of the context.* (Kaplan 1989: 522; my italics)

According to an I-explanation of variability, two utterances of S, u in C and u′ in C′, can differ in truth-value because the circumstance of C differs from the circumstance of C′. This is compatible with the two utterances expressing the same contents. So, strictly speaking, this is not a model for explaining what I've called 'content variability'; it is, rather, an explanation of the illusion of content variability.

Before showing how this strategy can be put to work, it is worth noting that this is an explanatory strategy that directly contradicts the central claim in the famous passage from Kaplan where he introduces the notion of *content.* Kaplan says, "If what we say differs in truth value, that is enough to show that we say different things" (Kaplan 1989: 500).[10] According to proponents of I-explanations, this is false. We can have variability in truth-value between u and u′ because the circumstances of their respective contexts differ.

Of course, if circumstances of evaluation are just worlds, this won't do any work explaining (away) the cases of variability that I have focused on so far. It becomes a more plausible strategy only when more parameters are added to the circumstance of evaluation.[11] Kaplan 1989 makes one move in this direction. He treats circumstances of evaluation not just as worlds, but as (world, time) pairs. According to this view, an utterance u of "Tim is wearing blue socks" at time t expresses a *temporally neutral* proposition (though as Kaplan points out (1989: 504), this is a potentially misleading label, because such things are not propositions in the classical sense). On this view, u does not express the proposition *that Tim is wearing blue socks at t.* It expresses the temporally neutral proposition *that Tim is wearing blue socks.* Such propositions can be true at some times, and false at others, in the way classical propositions can be true at one world and false at others.

This becomes a general strategy for explaining (away) variability when even more parameters are added to the circumstance of evaluation. Lewis 1980 adds locations and standards of precision as indices of circumstances of evaluation. MacFarlane (this volume) suggests that a 'counts as' parameter be added. According to this latter proposal two utterances of (2) can differ in truth-value, not because they differ in content (they both express the propositional skeleton *that the kettle is black*) but because the circumstances of their respective contexts differ with respect to the *counts as* parameter. We have variability in truth-value, without variability in content.[12]

[10] Remember, for Kaplan, what is said = content.

[11] Lewis 1980 calls the parameters 'indices', hence the somewhat confusing label 'index-model'.

[12] Lewis and Kaplan are moved to this view not because they want to develop an alternative model of variability, but because they think of tense as an operator and they think that requires

Three final remarks about I-explanations:

(*a*) Proponents of I-explanations need an account of the conditions under which parameters can be added to the circumstance of evaluation. As Lewis 1980 points out, we could have a 'person' parameter to fix the value of 'I' or 'you', but we don't. Lewis and Kaplan put strict constraints on when the index-strategy should be invoked. They thought the strategy was acceptable only when an operator could shift the parameter. If that's correct, this model has limited applicability.[13]

(*b*) It is not clear how proponents of I-explanations think of the relationship between semantic contents and speech act content. Consider temporally neutral propositions. It is certainly peculiar to hold that these are said or asserted by utterances of sentences. Some new story about the nature of saying or asserting needs to accompany such views (this point is emphasized in Lewis 1980).

(*c*) The index model is associated with some contemporary versions of relativism. For example, something in the neighbourhood of what has been called 'relativism' results if we introduce people as parameters in the circumstance of evaluation. This would imply that some semantic contents are true only relative to people and worlds (and whatever else goes into the circumstance of evaluation).[14]

6. SIX CHALLENGES

Debates about the context sensitivity of different parts of discourse have a lot in common, but it's dangerous to be seduced by the similarities, and important to pay close attention to the details of each case. To see this, consider the following (far from complete) list of areas where there is currently a lively debate about how to explain variability: quantified noun phrases, focus, adjectives, epistemic terms, vague terms, moral terms, definite and indefinite descriptions, conditionals, names, attitude reports, quotation, tenses, and modals. Understanding each of these will not simply be a matter of finding which explanatory model to dump them into. The patterns of variability will vary from case to case and so will the details of successful explanatory models.

That said, there are a number of connected challenges that face anyone working in this field. I will mention six that seem to me particularly pressing.

postulating a time parameter in the circumstance of evaluation. For an important criticism of this view, see King 2003. For further examples of appeals to I-explanations, see Egan et al., 2005; MacFarlane 2005; Lasersohn 2005. See also discussion in Stanley 2005*b*.

[13] For a useful discussion of this issue, see Stanley 2005*b*.

[14] Some proponents of relativism, e.g. John MacFarlane, claim that this is not relativism *proper*. It becomes relativism *proper*, MacFarlane claims, only when truth is relativized to what he calls 'contexts of assessment'.

Challenge 1: Develop New Diagnostics and Data-Gathering Procedures

Consider someone who proposes an S-explanation to account for the variability of some sentence, S. Such an explanation will appeal either to obvious, non-obvious, or hidden indexicality. For the debate between proponents and opponents of this S-explanation to be constructive, we need diagnostics to help determine when an expression is a non-obvious indexical and when we can legitimately postulate hidden indexicals. We need 'data-gathering procedures' that will help adjudicate between the competing explanations. Similarly, if an S-explanation is ruled out, we need diagnostics to determine which kind of P-explanation we should appeal to.

It's hard to overestimate the importance of trying to develop such diagnostics: if we don't have more or less theory-neutral diagnostics, the prospects of constructive debate between proponents of different explanatory models are dim. Here are three illustrations of the kinds of diagnostics I have in mind:

(*a*) *Grice on cancelability and non-detachability:* Grice proposed two procedures to help distinguish variability in what is said from variability in implicatures: cancelability and non-detachability. According to Grice these are only necessary, not sufficient conditions for being implicatures.[15] Grice's diagnostics have been subject to extensive criticism over the years, but note that even if these tests conclusively established that a certain kind of variability was not at the level of implicatures, that would leave us with a lot of options. It doesn't rule out any of the other P-explanations discussed in §4 nor any of the S-explanations discussed in §3. So even if Grice's tests were necessary and sufficient conditions, they wouldn't take us very far.

(*b*) *Disquotational reporting tests:* A recent development in this field is the proposal that data gathered from so-called 'disquotational reports' can be used to adjudicate between competing explanatory models (see Cappelen and Lepore 2004: ch. 7). Such data play a central role in recent work by various philosophers opposed to S-explanations (e.g. Cappelen and Lepore 2003, 2004; Hawthorne 2003; MacFarlane 2005; Egan et al., 2005). There's already a rather extensive literature on how best to interpret this data. (See e.g. Hawthorne (forthcoming); Cappelen and Lepore (forthcoming *b*); Humberstone 2006; Lesley (this volume).) This is not the place to go into this debate, but one point worth emphasizing is that all those who appeal to such diagnostics are clear on not treating them

[15] The non-sufficiency of the cancelability test is a much-overlooked feature of Grice's view. He says: "unfortunately one cannot regard the fulfilment of a cancelability test as decisively establishing the presence of a conversational implicature" (Grice 1989*b*: 44). Grice's argument for this appeals to what he calls 'loose talk' (see pp. 44–5),

as necessary or sufficient conditions for the applicability of any particular explanatory model. So to object that they fail to *conclusively establish* that one or the other of the other explanatory models applies is a mistake. These diagnostics are devices we use for gathering data. It might be that certain kinds of data patterns are best explained by one of these models (that's the structure of one of the central arguments in Cappelen and Lepore 2004), but the data-gathering procedures alone do not dictate that.

(*c*) *Binding data:* Neither Grice's tests nor the disquotational reporting diagnostics will help us decide when it is acceptable to add hidden indexicals to logical form (LF). Important work on this issue has been done in a series of papers by Jason Stanley (2000*a*, 2000*b*, 2005). According to Stanley, we can use bindability as a diagnostic for when elements should be postulated in LF: if there is data that is best explained by the hypothesis that an element hidden in LF is bound, then we have evidence of its existence. Stanley's view has been subject to much recent criticism.[16] Despite these criticisms, there is no doubt that bindability is an important piece of data and that it will play a significant role in evaluating S-explanations that appeal to hidden indexicals.

As the various debates about (a)–(c) show, there's little agreement on the correct interpretation of, or even the usefulness of, the diagnostics currently on the market. That's a problem. We're unlikely to make any progress on choosing between competing explanations unless someone can come up with improved tests of these kinds. Those unhappy with the diagnostics currently on the table should be hard at work trying to come up with new and less controversial strategies.

Challenge 2: Metaphysics of Propositions

One important issue in many of these debates is how we determine when a semantic value reaches the level of propositionality. As emphasized in §4, a number of P-explanations presuppose that some semantic values are non-propositional. That assumption is also built into all I-explanations. Remember, according to I-explanations, semantic values don't have truth-values *simpliciter*, they are not true or false at worlds and so do not reach the level of propositionality. In the light of this, someone new to these debates might reasonably expect an extensive literature on how we distinguish between semantic values that are propositional and those that are not. That, however, is not the case. It is surprising how little work has been done on developing tests for propositionality.

16 See e.g. Carston 2002; Cappelen and Lepore 2002; Recanati 2004; Marti 2006; Cappelen and Hawthorne 2007; Stanley's reply to some of these criticisms in Stanley 2005.

Challenge 3: Relate Semantic Content and Speech Act Content

In many of the current debates a big fuss is made about how we should think of the relationship between the semantic content of an utterance and what's intuitively asserted or said by that utterance. Some are committed to the view that they practically never come together (Salmon 1991; Cappelen and Lepore 1997), others to the view that they practically always do (Stanley 2000*a*). The issue is connected to a number of other topics mentioned above. Some of the more obvious connections are these:

- Where the line is drawn between propositions and proposition skeletons: if you think that it is really hard for a semantic value to reach the level of propositionality, then many semantic values will be non-propositional, and the semantic value will not be what is said (on the assumption that what is said must be propositional).
- How liberal you are with respect to postulating syntactic elements 'hidden' in LF: the more of these you have, the more likely you are to get close to the intuitive speech act content. How many elements you are willing to postulate in LF will depend on your attitude towards, for example, the binding tests mentioned under Challenge 1 above.
- How you describe the intuitive speech act content: there is no consensus on how we should describe what's said (or asserted) by utterances. If, for example, there's no ***unique*** correct such description (i.e. if there are several distinct equally correct ways to describe what is said by an utterance), as is argued by Cappelen and Lepore 1997 and Soames 2002, then, if there is only *one* semantic value, there will always be a significant gap. If you think what's said can vary from one context of interpretation to another (again see Cappelen and Lepore 2004) and that semantic contents cannot so vary, then once again there will always be a gap.

Note that since this is just the beginning of a long list of issues that will determine how you think of the relationship between semantic contents and speech act content, it is *prima facie* implausible that we will have a unified account of this relationship. We are more likely to find that it will vary from one part of discourse to another. It's not a topic that we'll settle by working on *it*. Rather, patterns might emerge as we get clearer on other issues.[17]

[17] One worry that often comes up in these discussions is a concern about the so-called *cognitive role* of semantic values if these are ***not*** identical to what the speaker said. Sometimes this is raised as a particular concern for those who postulate so-called minimal propositions that are not identical to what was said. Two quick and programmatic comments on that alleged problem: (*a*) this is no more of a problem for those who have minimal propositions as semantic values than it is a problem for those who have non-propositional semantic values (this is important since many of those running this objection to minimal propositions are happy to have non-propositional semantic values all over

Challenge 4: Describe Contextual Mechanisms and Understand the Nature of Contexts

All the explanatory models discussed above are in agreement that context can, in part, contribute to determining content.[18] So all these models need to combine with an account of *how* contexts do what they do. They need an account of the contextual mechanisms that contribute to content. Some illustrations of what I have in mind:

- Proponents of surprise indexicals owe us a story about how their semantic values are fixed in a context of utterance. If, for example, you think 'know' is a context-sensitive term, you need to tell us how that term gets its semantic value in a context of utterance.
- Hidden indexicalists need to tell us how the semantic values of hidden indexicals are fixed in the context of utterance.
- If you are moved by any of the standard criticisms of Grice, appeals to implicatures are in need of an improved account of the contextual mechanism that takes the audience from what the speaker says to what she implicated.
- According to some P-explanations, contexts of utterances help interpreters get from non-propositional semantic values to speech act content. Such explanations need an account of the contextual mechanisms involved.
- I-explanations need an account of how the relevant circumstance of evaluation is fixed in a context of utterance.
- Those who think many propositions are asserted by any utterance (so-called speech act pluralists) need an account of how this plurality of propositions is generated in a context of utterance and how it is related to the semantic value of the sentence uttered.
- Even for the classical, obvious indexicals, it is not at all clear what the reference-fixing mechanisms are. There's no agreement, for example, on the role of demonstrating intentions for demonstratives and on how terms like 'local' and 'left' have their referents determined.

One's view of these issues will have important implications for how other challenges can be met. If, for example, no plausible mechanisms can explain how we get from a non-propositional semantic value to a proposition that is asserted,

the place); (*b*) an assumption underlying this criticism is that we'll have a unified account of the so-called cognitive role of semantic contents—that's an unjustified assumption. A more plausible assumption is that not only will the cognitive role of semantic content vary between sentences, but also between utterances of the same sentence.

18 Of course, this is a bit misleading since, in the case of I-explanations, context contributes to fixing parameters. There is no variation in content.

then certain P-explanations become considerably less plausible. If you think no plausible account can be given of how the semantic value of hidden indexicals are fixed in context, then certain S-explanations will seem considerably less plausible. And so on.[19]

Challenge 5: Explain the Possibility of Shared Content

The thought that we are capable of sharing contents across contexts is a central feature of our self-conception as communicating creatures. This is exhibited in a number of ways, including (a)–(c):

(*a*) We typically think we can understand what someone has said in uttering some sentence S, even if we don't have extensive knowledge of her intentions, context, or audience. So even if we are eavesdroppers, we think we can understand what someone said by uttering "It might be that most linguists read few books". (Hint: she said that most linguists read few books.)

(*b*) We think we can use a sentence, S, in a context, C, to say what someone else said by using that sentence in some other context, C′, even though C and C′ are quite different. For example, if we hear an utterance of "It might be that most linguists read few books" in C′, we think we can use this sentence in some different context, C, to say what the original speaker said.

(*c*) We think disquotational indirect reports often succeed in correctly reporting on what other people said. So we think we can report an utterance of "It might be that most linguists read few books" in C by an utterance of "She said that it might be that most linguists read few books" in C′.[20]

(a)–(c) might seem obvious, but are in constant danger of being undermined by the discovery of various kinds of context sensitivity. By some accounts, "It might be that most linguists read few books" contains five hidden or non-obvious indexicals, and the semantic values of these depends on very complex aspects of the context of utterance. How, then, can someone not familiar with the context of utterance grasp the proposition expressed? How can someone succeed in expressing the same proposition in a very different context?

The idea that we can share content seems to be embedded not just in how we talk about contents. It is also interwoven with important non-linguistic

[19] Closely connected to this is the challenge of saying something precise about what exactly a context is. This is currently an under-explored question. There's a lot of talk about contexts-this and contexts-that, but very little in the way of a precise account of what sorts of things contexts are. See Gauker 1998 and 2003 for interesting discussions of this topic.

[20] Note that while (b) does not rely on our intuitions about indirect reports, (c) does. So, while it might be tempting to explain some (c) phenomena by appeal to special feature of our indirect reporting practices, that strategy does not extend to (b).

practices. When, for example, we hold people responsible for what they have said, we assume that we can grasp what they have said. When we articulate rules, directives, laws and other action-guiding instructions, we assume that people, variously situated, can grasp that content in the same way. When we deliberate over long periods of time, we assume that there is a stable content we deliberate over. Any theory of context sensitivity should have something to say about how these intuitions are preserved.[21]

As Sarah-Jane Leslie points out (this volume, appendix), this is not a problem just for those who postulate a lot of semantic context-sensitive terms in sentences. It is a problem for any theory according to which the speech act content is context-sensitive, even if this content is not identical to the semantic content. Consider again an utterance of "It might be that most linguists read few books". If you hold, as Cappelen and Lepore (2004) do, that what is saliently asserted by such an utterance is context-sensitive, even though the semantic content is not, the assumption of shared content is still threatened.

Challenge 6: Compositionality and the Semantics—Pragmatics Distinction

The way I have set things up in this chapter, semantic values are, by definition, compositionally determined. There are some important advantages to that way of framing these issues. It becomes relatively easy to formulate the central issues, such as: *Is speech act content ever/sometimes/always the semantic content? Is semantic content (i.e. compositionally determined content) always/sometimes/never propositional?*

No matter how you come down on these issues, there remains the challenge of actually working out a compositional semantic theory. How difficult that will be depends, in part, on how you think of the relationship between semantic content and speech act content. The following generalization is roughly correct: if you are willing to have a significant gap between semantic content and speech act content, constructing a compositional semantic theory will be considerably easier than if you insist on keeping them close together. For an illustration consider the semantic for propositional attitude reports. Someone who tolerates a significant gap between semantic content and what speakers intuitively say (and assert) could avoid worrying about how a semantic theory should account for substitution failures in attitude reports. The intuition that substitutions of co-referential terms in such contexts can result in a changed truth-value can be attributed to an effect on non-semantic content. The semantic content stays the same under such substitution, the speech act content (what was said and asserted) changes. On this view, the intuitions that underpin claims about

[21] For further discussion of this view, see Cappelen and Lepore 2006.

substitution failures are intuitions about what speakers succeed in saying, not intuitions that reflect variability in semantic content. The semantics is then pretty straightforward.

The flip side of this is that hard work awaits those who like to keep semantic content close to speech act content. A philosopher with such predilections must, for every contextual variation in content, find a semantic explanation. As a result, she is typically forced to postulate lots and lots of syntactic elements in the LF. That makes doing compositional semantics more complicated.

7. DO WE NEED THE SEMANTICS–PRAGMATICS DISTINCTION?

No, we don't. Philosophers and linguists have used the words 'semantic' and 'pragmatic' in an extraordinarily confusing array of ways over the last 100 years. In part as a result of this, the field is highly susceptible to terminological disputes. The best solution would be for all of us to decide never to use these dreaded words ever again. That, unfortunately, is unlikely to happen.

The danger of thinking that the semantics–pragmatics distinction matters is not just that it leads to terminological disputes because philosophers use these words in different ways. That would be a somewhat serious problem, but not all that hard to get around. More serious, I think, is that it encourages a simplified idea of how to solve the central challenges in this field. Put very simply, it encourages the absurd idea that, if we can just get the semantics–pragmatics distinction right, we will have made progress. Put like this, everyone, I suppose, would agree that it's a mistake. But there's a related idea that's less obviously false. It's the idea that the solutions to a whole range of problems in this field will be aligned—that we can get neat little packages of solutions. In the light of work done by philosophers and linguists on context sensitivity over the last thirty years, the following doesn't seem too bold a conjecture: no neat, general, and grand solutions are likely to succeed. The patterns of usage for various categories of expressions will differ radically and so will the successful explanations.

REFERENCES

Bach, K. (1994), 'Conversational Impliciture', *Mind and Language*, 9: 124–62.

Cappelen, H. (2007), 'Content Relativism', forthcoming in G. Carpintero and M. Kolbel (eds.), *Essays on Relativism*. Oxford: OUP.

—— and J. Hawthorne (2007), 'Locations and Binding', forthcoming in *Analysis*.

—— and E. Lepore (1997), 'On an Alleged Connection between Indirect Quotation and Semantic Theory', *Mind and Language*, 12: 278–96.

—— and —— (2002), 'Indexicality, Binding, Anaphora and *A Priori* Truth', *Analysis* (October): 271–81.

____ and ____ (2003), 'Context Shifting Arguments', *Philosophical Perspectives* 17: *Language and Philosophical Linguistics*, 25–50.

____ and ____ (2005), *Insensitive Semantics: A Defense of Semantic Minimalism and Speech Act Pluralism*. Oxford: Blackwell.

____ and ____ (forthcoming *a*), 'Reply to Critics', *Philosophy and Phenomenological Research.*

____ and ____ (forthcoming *b*), 'The Myth of Unarticulated Constituents', in *Essays in Honor of John Perry*. Cambridge, Mass.: MIT Press.

Carston, R. (2002), *Thoughts and Utterances: The Pragmatics of Explicit Communication.* Oxford: Blackwell.

____ (2004), 'Relevance Theory and the Saying/Implicating Distinction', in L. Horn and G. Ward (eds.), *Handbook of Pragmatics*. Oxford: Blackwell.

____ and ____ (2006), 'Shared Content', in E. Lepore and B. Smith (eds.), *Oxford Handbook of Philosophy of Language*. Oxford: Oxford University Press.

Cohen, S. (1988), 'How to be a Fallibilist', *Philosophical Perspectives*, 2: 91–123.

____ (1999), 'Contextualism, Skepticism, and the Structure of Reasons', *Philosophical Perspectives*, 13: *Epistemology*, 57–89.

Crimmins, M. (1992), *Talk about Belief*. Cambridge, Mass.: MIT Press.

Davis, W. A. (1998), *Implicature: Intention, Convention, and Principle in the Failure of Gricean Theory*. Cambridge: Cambridge University Press.

Egan, A., J. Hawthorne, and B. Weatherson (2005), 'Epistemic Modals in Context', in G. Preyer and G. Peter (eds.), *Contextualism in Philosophy*, pp. 131–70. Oxford: Oxford University Press.

Gauker, C. (1998), 'What is a Context of Utterance?', *Philosophical Studies*, 91 (Aug.): 149–72.

____ (2003), *Words without Meaning*. Cambridge, Mass.: MIT Press.

Grice, P. (1989*a*), 'Logic and Conversation', in *Studies in the Way of Words*. Cambridge, Mass.: Harvard University Press.

____ (1989*b*), *Studies in the Ways of Words*. Cambridge, Mass.: Harvard University Press.

Hawthorne, J. (2003), *Knowledge and Lotteries*. Oxford: Oxford University Press.

____ (forthcoming), 'Reply to Cappelen and Lepore', *Philosophy and Phenomenological Research.*

Humberstone, L. (2006), 'Sufficiency and Excess', *Proceedings of the Aristotelian Society*, 122–98.

Kaplan, D. (1989), 'Demonstratives', in J. Almog, J. Perry, and H. Wettstein (eds.), *Themes from Kaplan*, pp. 481–563. Oxford: Oxford University Press.

King, J. (2003), 'Tense, Modality, and Semantic Value', *Philosophical Perspectives*, 17, ed. J. Hawthorne: *Philosophy of Language.*

Lasersohn, P. (2005), 'Context Dependence, Agreement, and Predicates of Personal Taste', *Linguistics and Philosophy*, 28/6 (Dec. 2005): 643–86(44).

Levinson, S. C. (2000), *Presumptive Meanings: The Theory of Generalized Conversational Implicature*. Cambridge, Mass.: MIT Press.

Lewis, D. (1979), 'Scorekeeping in a Language Game', in *Philosophical Papers*, i. 233–49. Oxford: Oxford University Press, 1983. Originally in *Journal of Philosophical Logic*, 8 (1979): 339–59.

Lewis, D. (1980), 'Index, Context and Content', in S. Kanger and S. Ohman (eds.), *Philosophy and Grammar,* pp. 79–100. Dordrecht: Reidel. Republished in *Papers in Philosophical Logic*, pp. 21–44. Cambridge: Cambridge University Press, 1998.

Lewis, D. (1996), 'Elusive Knowledge', *Papers in Metaphysics and Epistemology*, 74, *Australasian Journal of Philosophy*, pp. 549–67.

Ludlow, Peter (1989), 'Implicit Comparison Classes', *Linguistics and Philosophy*, 12: 519–33.

MacFarlane, J. (2005), 'Assessment Sensitivity of Knowledge Attributions', in Tamar Szabó Gendler and John Hawthorne (eds.), *Oxford Studies in Epistemology*, 1: 197–233. Oxford: Oxford University Press.

Marti, L. (2006), 'Unarticulated Constituents Revisited', *Linguistics and Philosophy*, 29/2: 135–66.

Perry, J. (1986), 'Thought without Representation', in *Supplementary Proceedings of the Aristotelean Society*, 60: 137–52.

Recanati, F. (2002), 'Unarticulated Constituents', *Linguistics and Philosophy*, 25: 299–345.

—— (2004), *Literal Meaning*. Cambridge: Cambridge University Press.

Salmon, N. (1986), *Frege's Puzzle*. Cambridge, Mass.: MIT Press.

—— (1991), 'The Pragmatic Fallacy', *Philosophical Studies*, 63/1 (July): 83–97.

Soames, S. (2002), *Beyond Rigidity: The Unfinished Agenda of Naming and Necessity*. Oxford: Oxford University Press.

—— (forthcoming), 'The Gap between Meaning and Assertion', in Martin Hackl and Robert Thornton (eds.), *Asserting, Meaning, and Implying*.

Sperber, D., and D. Wilson (1986), *Relevance: Communication and Cognition*. Cambridge, Mass.: Harvard University Press.

Stanley, J. (2000*a*), 'Context and Logical Form', *Linguistics and Philosophy*, 23/4: 391–434.

—— (2000*b*), 'Nominal Restriction', in G. Preyer and G. Peter (eds.), *Logical Form and Language*, pp. 365–88. Oxford: Oxford University Press.

—— (2002), 'Making it Articulated', *Mind and Language*, 17: 149–68.

—— (2005*a*), *Knowledge and Practical Interests*. Oxford: Oxford University Press.

—— (2005*b*), 'Semantics in Context', in G. Preyer and G. Peter (eds.), *Contextualism in Philosophy*, pp. 221–54.

—— and Zoltan Szabo (2000), 'On Quantifier Domain Restriction', *Mind and Language*, 15/2: 219–61.

Taylor, K. (2001), 'Sex, Breakfast, and Descriptions', *Synthese*, 128: 45–61.

Travis, C. (1985), 'On What is Strictly Speaking True', *Canadian Journal of Philosophy*, 15/2 (June): 187–229.

—— (1996), 'Meaning's Role in Truth', *Mind*, 100 (Apr.): 451–66.

Westerstahl, D. (1985), 'Determiners and Context Sets', in J. van Benthem and A. ter Meulen (eds.), *Quantifiers in Natural Language*, pp. 45–71. Dordrecht: Foris.

Wilson, D., and D. Sperber (1981), 'On Grice's Theory of Conversation', in P. Werth (ed.), *Conversation and Discourse*, pp. 155–78. New York: St Martin's Press.

PART I

THE DEFENCE OF MODERATE CONTEXTUALISM

1

Content, Context, and Composition

Peter Pagin and Francis Jeffry Pelletier

1. INTRODUCTION

It is traditional, at least since Grice, to make a distinction between what is called *the literal meaning* of an utterance and *what is meant* by that utterance. The former notion is sometimes thought of as "the dictionary meanings of words plus standard semantic effects of the syntactic rules" that were employed in the utterance. The latter notion is often thought of as the "all things considered" information that is conveyed by the utterance in the context it is used. The former is often said to be the "context independent meaning" or "the meaning that is constant across all contexts of use". The latter is often called "what is conveyed in a context". The former is sometimes called "the timeless meaning" or "the meaning-in-the-language" or "the meaning of the linguistic *type* of the utterance". The latter is sometimes called "the meaning of the speech act being performed" or "the meaning of the *token* being uttered".

Intuitively, the former notion allows *no* features of the context in which an utterance is made to enter into its semantic evaluation. The latter notion seems to claim that *every* aspect of the context might be relevant to the evaluation of the utterance.

The notion of *what is said*—as opposed to "the literal meaning" and as opposed to "what is meant"—is a theory-laden notion that is intended to locate an important semantic feature of linguistic communication. The idea is that there is some feature that identifies the *semantic meaning* of an utterance and separates it from its *pragmatic meaning*. Now, these two notions are also theory-laden terms, but there is at least agreement that "literal meaning" is part of semantics while "what is conveyed" is a part of pragmatics. The question has always been: where should the line be drawn? The point where the line is drawn identifies *what is said*, and any further information that might be gleaned in some communicative act will be classified as *what is meant.*[1]

In two recent publications (Recanati 2004, 2005), François Recanati presents a way to organize different theories of language—that is, theories of *what is said*—in accordance with "how much context" the theories will allow as a part of their semantic component. These theories range from "pure literalism"—theories of linguistic semantics that have no use for any kind of contextual information, not even indexicality, and make "what is said" be the same as "literal meaning"—and continue through a series of ever-more-context until we reach "pure contextualism", a theory of the role of semantics that Recanati calls "meaning eliminativism" because "what is said" is entirely a matter of context with no contribution of the "literal meaning". Between these two extremes lie a number of theories that limit the amount of context that is allowed into semantics in one way or another, and are called such things as eternalism, indexicalism, syncretism, quasi-contextualism, and full-blooded contextualism. Recanati notes, for example (2004: 92 n. 20), that these intermediate views come in degrees, so that there are actually a number of different syncretist views, for example.

1.1. Cappelen and Lepore Background

In their recent book, Cappelen and Lepore 2005, Herman Cappelen and Ernie Lepore (CL), propose and defend two views, labeled 'Semantic Minimalism' (henceforth Minimalism) and 'Speech Act Pluralism' (henceforth Pluralism). Generally speaking, Minimalism is the view that Recanati called 'indexicalism'. (We say this despite Recanati's claim that CL's view is syncretic: Recanati 2004: 92.) CL's chief arguments for these views consist in discrediting what they portray as the main alternatives, *radical contextualism* (theories such as full-blooded contextualism that approach Recanati's meaning eliminativism) and *moderate contextualism* (any of Recanati's versions of contextualism "between" indexicalism and full-blooded contextualism). These arguments fall into two categories: on the one hand direct arguments against Radical Contextualism (part 2 of their book), and on the other hand indirect arguments against moderate contextualism (part 1). The indirect ones are arguments that Moderate Contextualism *leads to* Radical Contextualism, and because of that, the arguments against Radical Contextualism will apply to Moderate Contextualism as well. We shall here be concerned with the indirect arguments, those called the Instability Arguments, and will simply accept their arguments against Radical Contextualism. For it is

[1] If one decides that the line should be drawn all the way at the end—at the level of "what is conveyed"—then there are two choices available. One could say that semantics has all of "what is conveyed" in its scope, or that there is no independent semantic theory and "it's all pragmatics". Most of those who hold that this is the only place to draw the line also hold to the position that "it's all pragmatics".

our goal to defend a kind of Moderate Contextualism that does not lapse into Radical Contextualism. But first a couple of terminological explanations.

In order to explain what they mean by 'Semantic Minimalism' CL give a list of expressions that they characterize as 'The Basic Set of Context Sensitive Expressions' (CL 2005: 1–2), comprising the personal pronouns (in their various grammatical forms), demonstratives, the adverbs 'here', 'there', 'now', 'today', 'yesterday', 'tomorrow', '. . . ago', 'hence(forth)', the adjectives 'actual' and 'present', tense and aspect indicators generally, common nouns like 'enemy' and 'foreigner', and adjectives like 'foreign' and 'imported'.

CL immediately point out that the basic set does not contain a number of terms that in recent decades have been given a contextualist analysis, such as 'every' (contextual quantifier domain restriction), 'know' (contextual standards of knowledge), or 'happy' (contextual comparison class).

With reference to the basic set, CL (2005: 2) characterize Minimalism effectively as follows

(i) Only expressions in the basic set ('plus or minus a bit') are accepted as context-sensitive.

(ii) All context sensitivity is grammatically triggered.

(iii) Context has no effect on what proposition an utterance expresses other than to fix the semantic value of these context-sensitive expressions.

Since mainstream natural language semantics provides contextualist analyses of many more expressions (such as those explicitly excluded above) and constructions than CL recognize, Minimalism is a highly controversial position. It also has clearly counterintuitive consequences, in that some sentences that appear context-sensitive, such as

(1) Tipper is ready

(CL 2005: 60; Bach 94*a*, *b*), will not be counted as such. Disregarding the tense ingredient of (1), we would still think that nothing one can say with (1) is fully determined by the sentence itself: Tipper will be ready for some things and not for others, and it has to be understood from the context what Tipper is claimed to be ready for. This is denied by CL (2005: 116), who give the general semantic description

(2) Every utterance *u* of 'A is ready' expresses the proposition *that A is ready*.

Pluralism is introduced as follows:

No one thing is said (or asserted, or claimed, or . . .) by any utterance: rather, indefinitely many propositions are said asserted, claimed, stated. What is said (asserted, claimed, etc.)

depends on a wide range of facts other than the proposition semantically expressed. It depends on a potentially indefinite number of features of the context of utterance and of the context of those who report (or think about) what was said by the utterance. (CL 2005: 4)

Pluralism, too, is both controversial and counterintuitive. A counterintuitive consequence explicitly endorsed by CL is that a speaker can *say* something by a sincere utterance without believing what she says (indeed, while explicitly *dis*believing what she says). For instance by means of an utterance of

(3) That man is shady

the speaker may have *said that* the moronic clown is shady (CL 2005: 202–3), and yet not believe it, since not believing that the man referred to is a moronic clown (in fact, even while *dis*believing that the man referred to is a moronic clown). The indirect discourse attribution is nonetheless correct if the man in fact *is* a moronic clown.

This view is a consequence of CL's very liberal theory about the correctness of indirect discourse attributions, going back to CL 1997. A consequence of this view, and explicitly part of Pluralism, is the nihilistic claim

(N) *There can be no systematic theory of speech act content*

(CL 2005: 190). This claim motivates separating semantic theory from the theory of speech act content (nearly enough[2]), for on their view this is the only way of keeping semantic theory itself systematic. We will return to this general question in §6.

Radical contextualism is in one respect close to being the opposite of Minimalism: the former maximizes the ratio between the pragmatic-contextual and the semantic contribution to any speech act content, while Minimalism postulates (for every utterance) one speech act content for which the ratio is minimal. Radical contextualism is characterized as follows by CL:

(RC1) No English sentence S ever semantically expresses a proposition.[3] Any semantic value that Semantic Minimalism assigns to S can

[2] Although CL argue that there can be no systematic account of whatever else can be said, they do think there can be a systematic account of "semantic content". And since semantic content is always correctly reported as having been said, they say, it follows that there is a systematic account of *part* of what is said. So the separation of semantic theory and speech act content is not total, on their account.

[3] Abstractly, there can be an ambiguity here, between the view that "only people, not inanimate words" can express anything and the view that no (finite) amount of verbiage can completely specify a situation in enough detail so as to be determinately true or false. We think the former of the two views is a mere terminological quibble if it has no support from the second view. For, if it were granted that speakers always express the same proposition by means of uttering a particular sentence *s*, then we could define another relation, *x* schempresses *y*, between expressions and content, and by which *s* schempresses that proposition. So this is not a very interesting proposal, unless it is backed

be no more than a *propositional fragment* (or *radical*), where the hallmark of a propositional fragment (or radical) is that it does not determine a set of truth conditions, and hence, cannot take a truth value.

(RC2) Context sensitivity is ubiquitous in this sense: No expansion of what we are calling the Basic Set of context sensitive expressions can salvage Semantic Minimalism, i.e. however the Basic Set is expanded, the output will never be more than a propositional fragment; something, therefore, not even truth evaluable.

(RC3) Only an utterance can semantically express a complete proposition, have a truth condition, and so, take a truth value. (CL 2005: 6)

As chief representatives of Radical Contextualism, CL designate John Searle (1978, 1980, 1983) and Charles Travis (1985, 1989, 1996).

Contextualism in general, and perhaps the radical variety in particular, is supported by the difficulties of tricky examples, or perhaps better, by intuitions fueled by recognition of these difficulties. The following example (CL 2005: 43, 64) is taken from Travis (1985: 197). The sentence

(4) Smith weighs 80 kg

sounds determinate enough at first blush, but it could be taken as true or as false in various contexts, depending on what counts as important in those contexts. For example, it can be further interpreted as being true if Smith weighs

(4a) 80 kg when stripped in the morning
(4b) 80 kg when dressed normally after lunch
(4c) 80 kg after being force fed 4 liters of water
(4d) 80 kg four hours after having ingested a powerful diuretic
(4e) 80 kg after lunch adorned in heavy outer clothing

The idea is that the literal meaning of (4) does not settle which of these further interpretations (4a–e), or yet others, is relevant in a context, and so fails to determine a propositional content on its own. Looking at a number of seemingly innocent examples in this light gives the impression that no sentence at all expresses a proposition on its own.

Moderate Contextualism does not go that far. Moderate Contextualism is characterized as follows by CL:

up by the claim in the second view. With this backing we would *not* be able to define something like 'schempresses'.

(MC1) The expressions in the Basic Set do not not exhaust all the sources of semantic context sensitivity

(MC2) Many sentences that Semantic Minimalism assigns truth conditions to, and treats as semantically expressing a proposition, fail to have truth conditions or to semantically express a proposition; they express only fragmentary propositions. Such linguistic expressions are described as providing 'incomplete logical forms', 'semantic skeletons', 'semantic scaffolding', 'semantic templates', 'propositional schemas' . . . All of these locutions entail that the expression is not fully propositional; it is incomplete *qua* semantic entity; it is not truth evaluable.

(MC3) For the cases in question, only their utterances semantically express a proposition, and have (interpretive) truth conditions, and so, take a truth value. (CL 2005: 7)

As a typical representative of (one kind of) Moderate Contextualists, CL select John Perry (1986), who made the sentence

(5) It is raining

the paradigm example of so-called *unarticulated constituents* (Perry 1986: 206). The idea is that a speaker of (5) speaks of the weather at some location, even though there is no constituent of (5) that takes location as semantic value. The truth value of the sentence as a whole depends on assignment of a location value, but no part of the sentence *articulates* that dependence. As opposed to location, the tense of the verb articulates the dependence on a *time* value.

On CL's view, there is no unarticulated location constituent in (5). Rather, the content of (5) is given by

(6) 'It is raining' express the proposition *that it is raining* and is true iff it's raining

(CL 2005: 61–3). Although it may seem that adding feature-placing sentences like (5) to the list of context-sensitive expressions is not a drastic addition, it is important for CL to reject it, since according to CL if this is accepted, we would have to accept a lot more. The underlying issue here is that there is no overt syntactic item in (5), or similar sentences, that legitimizes the addition of such features. But if we were to accept Moderate Contextualism of this sort, and give permission to posit additions not tied to anything in the sentence, then we would rationally be led to accepting Radical Contextualism, they say.

On our view, this is not right. In §6 we will endeavor to distinguish various types of contextualism, with the motivation that some of them are not susceptible to the types of considerations that CL employ in their rejection of Moderate Contextualism. The general picture is that we can expand CL's "Basic Set" with certain other words and constructions, such as comparative adjectives and domain restrictions, without having to be a radical contextualist. And as a part of this discussion, we will set out various considerations about compositionality for contextually sensitive terms and sentences. Here we give a framework for characterizing the differences between Recanati's "saturation" and "modulation", and we show by means of examples that it can be coherently applied to support moderate contextualism.

2. CAPPELEN AND LEPORE'S INSTABILITY ARGUMENT

The reason the Moderate position leads to the Radical, according to CL, is that if the *justification* offered for Moderate Contextualism is good enough, it justifies Radical Contextualism as well. This is said to hold of both types of arguments that have been adduced in favor of contextualism: *context shifting* arguments and *incompleteness* arguments.

2.1. Context Shift

The notion of a Context Shifting Argument (CSA) is not given a precise definition in CL, but is characterized as follows.

> One way that philosophers of language [go about in establishing that an expression *e* not in the Basic Set is context sensitive] is to think about (or imagine) various utterances of sentences containing *e*. If they have intuitions that a *semantically relevant feature* of those utterances varies from context to context, then that, it is assumed, is evidence [that] *e* is context sensitive. ... The kinds of features contextualists claim to have intuitions about include
>
> - What is *said* or *asserted* or *claimed* by utterances of sententces containing *e*.
> - The truth condition of utterances containing *e*.
> - The proposition expressed by utterances of sentence containing *e*. (CL 2005: 17–18)

Summing this up, the form of a Context Shifting Argument would be something like

(CS) If a *semantic feature* of utterances of sentences containing *e*, and associated with *e*, changes from context to context, then *e* is context-sensitive.

Now we agree with CL that this is not a good argument form. But (apparently) unlike CL, we think that (CS) can be modified to provide a good argument form, and we will come back to that later, in §6.[4]

As examples of Context Shifting Arguments, CL list alleged evidence for

(*a*) shifts of quantifier domain
(*b*) shifts of comparison class for comparative adjectives
(*c*) shifts of content characterizing notions for belief reports
(*d*) shifts of possible world comparative similarity for counterfactual conditionals
(*e*) shifts of standards for knowledge attributions
(*f*) shifts of content-determining factors for moral evaluations
(*g*) shifts of standards of precision generally
(*h*) shifts of location values for weather reports

To exemplify cases (*a*) and (*b*), consider the sentences

(7) Every bottle is empty
(8) That basketball player is short

An utterance of (7) (from Stanley and Szabó 2000: 219–20) is likely to be concerned with a restricted range of bottles, not with every bottle in the universe. Moreover, which restricted range of bottles it is concerned with depends on context, for instance every bottle on a particular table at some party, or every bottle on a particular shelf in some wine cellar. The intuitive content is then different, and the truth value can well (intuitively) be different, even if the utterances are made at the same time. Hence, by a (CS) argument, there is context sensitivity induced by 'every', or perhaps by 'bottle'.

An utterance of (8) (Stanley 2002: 377) is likely to be concerned with height evaluation in relation to some salient group of objects of comparison. It can be truly said of a basketball player in relation to a group of other, taller, basketball players, but only falsely said of the same basketball player in relation a group of people of average height. Which group is relevant depends on context, and so the truth value of two utterances of the sentence, at the same time, with reference to the same player, can differ. The (CS) conclusion is that there is context sensitivity induced by 'short'.

The main objection by CL against arguments of this kind is spelled out in their principle

[4] As also stressed by our referees, it doesn't follow from the fact that sentences containing *e* are context-sensitive that their sensitivity depends on the meaning of *e*. What we need is a globally well-supported semantic theory that implies this. This remains a task for CL's description of Context Shifting Arguments.

(GEN) With sufficient ingenuity, a CSA can be provided for any sentence whatsoever, and consequently, for any expression.

(CL 2005: 40). In order to establish (GEN), CL provide a series of examples. We shall here briefly recapitulate three of them. First, we have the Travis sentence

(4) Smith weighs 80 kg

and CL present two scenarios (2005: 43). In the first case, a report is made when Smith has just eaten lunch and is fully dressed, but the conversation concerns his recent dieting, and what is relevant is what the scale registered in the morning of the utterance, before breakfast, with naked Smith. In this case, the utterance is true. In the second scenario, on the other hand, it would be false because Smith is about to enter an elevator which can take no more than an extra 80 kg, and the report is intended to be relevant to that. If, at that time, Smith, with clothes, after lunch, weighs more than 80 kg, the consequences are fatal. So two different things are said by (4) in the two contexts, and hence the sentence by a (CS) argument is deemed context-sensitive.

As a second example, CL give the sentence

(9) John went to the gym

(CL 2005: 44–5). In the first context of utterance, the topic of conversation is John's walking habits. In this case the utterance of (9) is true if John walked to the vicinity of the gym. In the second context, the conversation is concerned with John's exercising habits, and the utterance would be true only if John did some workout at the gym. In the third context, John is involved in construction work at the gym, and in this case the utterance is true only if John ended up at the gym and also performed the relevant activity (overseeing the construction of a bathroom).

The third example is provided with the sentence

(10) That's a dangerous dog

(CL 2005: 46–7). In the first context, the conversation is concerned with the disposition of the dog, and is true if the dog is aggressive, false if it is gently disposed. In the second context, the dog is gentle but carries a viral disease that can spread to humans, and in this case the utterance is true.

After giving these and a few more examples, CL think that the reader is able to go on by herself to produce scenarios for context shift for arbitrary sentences. Reflecting on this, one can conclude that any sentence, and thus any expression, is context-sensitive. One must then be a Radical Contextualist, if you give any credence at all to CSAs.

2.2. Incompleteness

The Incompleteness Arguments draw on intuitions that context must contribute something to what is said, since the sentence itself does not have a content that is truth evaluable. CL sum up the nature of Incompleteness Arguments as follows:

A typical Incompleteness Argument, as we think of it, comes in two stages.

> *Stage 1.* A solicitation of an intuition to the effect that the proposition semantically expressed by an utterance of a sentence S (according to Semantic Minimalism) is incomplete, i.e., it is not the kind of thing that can take a truth value.
>
> *Stage 2.* A solicitation of an intuition to the effect that utterances of S have a truth value, i.e., that they can express propositions, and hence, do have truth conditions, and so, can take truth value.
>
> *Conclusion.* Something unaccounted for by Semantic Minimalism must be added in the context to the utterance in order for a complete proposition to be semantically expressed. (CL 2005: 59)

CL add (2005: 60) that we get a more comprehensive argument by adding context shifting intuitions to the conclusion that what is added for getting a complete proposition also shifts between contexts.

Examples of sentences for which incompleteness is claimed include (5) ('It's raining'). It is also claimed by Kent Bach for

(11) Steel isn't strong enough

(from Bach 1994*b*: 269; CL 2005: 34), since the intuition is that to express a full proposition by means of (11), it must be settled in the context of utterance what it is meant that steel isn't strong enough *for*. One naturally asks 'Strong enough for what?'

In a similar vein, Dan Sperber and Deirdre Wilson claim that

(12) Peter's bat is gray

is less than fully propositional, for the possessive construction might refer to many different relations between Peter and the bat; it might be the bat owned by Peter, the bat chosen by Peter, the bat killed by Peter and so on (CL 2005: 35; Sperber and Wilson 1992: 188).

CL deal with the Incompleteness Argument in a way analogous to the way they dealt with the CSAs, by arguing that Incompleteness is ubiquitous—if you allow it to affect the meaning anywhere, it must be allowed to affect it everywhere. And this once again leads to Radical Contextualism. First, the examples they provided for showing context shift in (4), (9), and (10) can also be used for showing that those sentences are incomplete as they stand. For instance, one can ask the questions about (9)

> Went to the gym how? Walked to the vicinity? Did something in the gym? Did what in the gym? For how long? [etc.] (CL 2005: 64–5)

So, these allegedly complete sentences seem to be incomplete by the same criterion that further questions can be asked and further information provided in the context of utterance.

Moreover, further questions can also be asked with respect to alleged completions of the incomplete sentences, such as

(1b) Tipper is ready for the exam.
(11b) Steel isn't strong enough to support the roof.
(12b) The bat owned by Peter is gray.
(5b) It's raining in Palo Alto.

(CL 2005: 62, different numbering). As an example, they take (11b), and claim that it fails to specify truth conditions for (11)

> because it doesn't settle for how long the support must last. Do a few seconds suffice? More than three days? Many years? Why mustn't (11b) also settle whether (11) is false if steel fails to support the roof when placed in temperatures over 390° [etc.]? (CL 2005: 63)

In short, since it seems that further factors can always be added that can settle in context whether the utterance of a sentence is true or false, it appears that if the Incompleteness Argument is good, *any* sentence can with some ingenuity be seen as incomplete, and therefore also context-sensitive.

Before turning to the evaluation of CL's arguments, we shall sketch a framework for handling different kinds of pragmatic additions to semantic content.

3. RECANATI AND SYSTEMATIC THEORY

A natural methodology for justifying a semantic theory S of a natural language L is to see S as part of a more comprehensive theory C of communication by means of L. In each act of successful communicative exchange, one or more thought contents get conveyed by the speaker to the hearer. Speaker and hearer use their communicative abilities to achieve this communicative goal, and part of those abilities consist in making use of properties of the language L itself. A semantic theory of L will then be concerned with special properties of expressions of L by which certain expressions are apt for conveying contents of particular kinds. On such a general strategy, semantics plays a systematic role in a more comprehensive systematic theory of communicated content, or speech act content.

Such a methodology is completely rejected by CL, because of their belief, which we have already mentioned:

(N) *There can be no systematic theory of speech act content*

(CL 2005: 190). By means of a single utterance of a sentence *s*, a speaker says indefinitely many things, including things she is not aware of and does not even believe (CL 2005: 202–3). This is because a speaker says everything she can be correctly reported as saying, and what she can be correctly reported as saying depends on factors of the *reporter's* context that the speaker need not have knowledge of. If there can be no systematic theory of speech act content, then there can be no systematic account of how the meaning of sentences contribute to speech act content.

As we mentioned above, CL do believe, contrary to the claim (N), that there is a correct and systematic partial theory of speech act content, since they hold that the proposition semantically expressed by a sentence *s* is said by means of any utterance of *s*. The speaker *always* says the proposition semantically expressed by the sentence used. This is indeed a systematic theory of speech act content, but not one that is very easy to use to identify what is semantically expressed by a sentence.[5] Rather, one gets the right result only if one has an independent knowledge of what the semantically expressed meaning is. So there is a challenge for CL to explain how the semanticist arrives at the meaning of any linguistic expression.[6]

Still, if the non-systematicity claim (N) is correct, the first mentioned methodology wouldn't work either, because there could not be a systematic theory *C* of communication. Is (N) correct? That question is a big one, and not easily answered. Moreover, the question is not even precise until it is made reasonably clear when to count a theory systematic. We shall here make the assumption

[5] This is so, especially since in some cases what is intuitively conveyed by means of a sentence differs from what it semantically expresses. For instance, the literal meaning of the following sentence

(13) If the elevator stops between two floors, press the alarm button for 20 seconds!

(from a Stockholm University elevator) is such that the injunction is complied with if the elevator stops between the fifth floor and the seventh floor, *on* the sixth floor, and one presses the alarm button for 20 seconds. Discerning the literal meaning from the conveyed meaning (*between two adjacent floors*) is extremely difficult, however. One rather needs an independent grasp of the literal meaning. Once one has that, on the other hand, one can easily see how the conveyed meaning is derived from the literal meaning by means of a free enrichment: the expansion of *two* into *two adjacent*, amounting to a restriction of the determiner meaning.

[6] This is not just equivalent to explaining how one learns a first language: over and above understanding what people say by means of the language, the semanticist must determine what semantic concepts to use and how to apply them, and also be able to justify the choice. The alternative would be to baldly claim to have direct insight into theoretical semantic matters. We take this alternative to be unscientific, or unnaturalistic.

that for literal, non-context-sensitive meaning, the paradigm of systematicity[7] is compositional semantics: a language has a compositional semantics just if

(PoC) The meaning of a syntactically defined whole is a function of the meanings of its syntactic parts and the mode of composition.[8]

The intuitive idea behind the claim that compositional semantics can explain communicative success is that speaker and hearer are able to construct new complexes by means of putting familiar parts together according to familiar patterns. This idea is beautifully expressed in the opening passage of Frege's 'Compound Thoughts':[9]

> It is astonishing what language can do. With a few syllables it can express an incalculable number of thoughts, so that even a thought grasped by a human being for the very first time can be put into a form of words which will be understood by someone to whom the thought is entirely new. This would be impossible, were we not able to distinguish parts in the thought corresponding to the parts of a sentence, so that the structure of the sentence serves as an image of the structure of the thought. (Frege 1923)

The intuitive idea is fairly clear, even though much more is needed to spell it out in detail (cf. especially Pelletier 1994; Pagin 2003). It quickly becomes a lot less clear when we move from literal, context-insensitive meaning to uses of language where context plays an important role. Can the intuitive idea of compositionality be extended or generalized to cover utterance contents that do depend on context in various ways?

In order get a grip on that question we will return to the framework for describing semantic and pragmatic contributions to utterance content developed by François Recanati. As we remarked at the beginning of this chapter, Recanati starts his story with types of "pure literalism", theories of language that have no use for any kind of contextual information, not even indexicality. We need not pause over Recanati's account of why it had no use for indexicality,[10] but instead

[7] As the reader has already noticed, the participants in this discussion are using 'systematicity' in a non-technical sense, not that of e.g. Fodor 1987; Fodor and Pylyshyn 1988.

[8] There are many fine points that are being glossed over here in this statement of compositionality. Some are discussed in Pelletier 1994, others in Pagin 2003, 2005*a*, and still others in Westerståhl 1998, 2004, and Hodges 1998, 2001. We will here mainly leave the exact force of compositionality unspecified, until we need to discuss some specific point.

[9] The general sentiment about the understanding of new sentences and about the infinity of language was much in the air at the time and can also be found in Schlick 1985; Russell 1956; Wittgenstein 1981; all first published between 1918 and 1921. Although some have said that in this quote Frege is ***not*** trying to explain communication, but rather is using the presumed fact that communication is successful together with the considerations of this paragraph to conclude that Thoughts must be structured, to us it seems a more natural interpretation to say that he *is* concerned with communication—especially when taking into account that such a view is present in the contemporaneous works just cited.

[10] Because, according to Recanati, these pure literalists thought that every statement containing an indexical element *said the same thing* as some other statement with no indexicals in it.

we will remark that this is the sort of language that accommodates semantic compositionality very easily. Here the idea is that each of the finitely many primitive elements of the language[11] has a meaning assigned to it, and each of the finitely many syntactic rules that can be used to combine simpler components into longer ones has some specified semantic effect on the meanings of these simpler components.

The next step is to start taking context into account.

3.1. Saturation

Literalism can be modified to allow "pieces of context", according to Recanati. This can be done in two radically different ways, *saturation* and *modulation*, together called "primary pragmatic processes". Saturation is the process of adding semantic values to various parameters associated with simple expressions, so as to get a full proposition, i.e. a truth evaluable entity. It is done in linguistically controlled and mandated ways (Recanati 2004: 7–10). An utterance of

(14) I am in pain

needs saturation by context to fix the reference of 'I' and the time associated with the present tense in order to have a proposition expressed that is true or false. Similarly,

(5) It is raining

needs a time value. According to some theorists, like Perry (1986), (5) also needs a location value, while others, including CL as well as Recanati, disagree.

It is clear that, by Recanati's standards, all the indexical expressions in CL's basic set induce the need for saturation. For instance, both CL and Recanati would count

(15) Yesterday, Phil met a foreigner

as in need of saturation both with respect to time, because of 'yesterday', and with respect to the implicit relatum of 'foreigner' (foreign to what?), as both 'yesterday' and 'foreigner' are in the basic set. CL disagree with Recanati and Bach (and us) about a sentence like

(11) Steel is strong enough

which Recanati and Bach but not CL think is in need of saturation.

[11] Let's just call them 'words' for simplicity, and not worry about subparts of words that might be meaningful and longer phrases that might be primitively meaningful (i.e. idioms). We will consider some of these ideas later.

Setting aside the issue of which sentences are in need of saturation, the present question is whether context sensitivity in the sense of sensitivity to contextually determined saturation can be treated in a systematic manner, i.e. in general accordance with the paradigm that compositionality offers for non-context-sensitive literal meaning. The answer is clearly yes, and the general method, first introduced by Richard Montague (1970*a*, 1970*b*, 1973), and further developed in particular by David Kaplan (1989), is that of distinguishing between two levels of meaning: one a context independent level which is of a functional nature and takes arguments from context, and the other a context dependent level, to which the resulting values of the functions for those arguments belong. In Kaplan's case the higher, functional level is *character*, and the lower level is *content*. In short the *character* of a sentence like (14) is the meaning that belongs to it before saturation is performed, while its content is the lower level meaning that results from contextual saturation, giving a proposition about who is in pain when.

It is clear that such a semantics does or at least can conform to the paradigm of compositionality, since the semantics can have the general property (Principle of Contextual Compositionality) that

(PCC) For any complex expression and context, the meaning-in-context of the complex expression is a function of the meaning-in-context of its parts and the mode of composition.[12]

It should be noted, though, that this is not just a trivial extension of the basic idea of compositionality. For (PCC) can fail in two ways: On the one hand, two expressions can have the same meaning-in-context in a context *c* while substituting the one for the other in a sentence *s* does not preserve the meaning-in-context of *s* in *c*. This would be the case e.g. if synonymy substitution isn't meaning-preserving in belief contexts:

(16) a. Alfred believes he is a pediatrician
b. Alfred believes he is a child doctor

where, on some theories, (16a) can be true and (16b) false if Alfred believes that 'pediatrician' denotes something other than child doctors.

[12] One can imagine that the semantic effects of the syntactic rules might also contain variables that are assigned by context, so that they can have different outcomes in different contexts. While we think this is a live possibility, and might even be useful in accounting for hyperbole and sarcasm, for example, we will not follow this up in our discussion and will instead always talk about the effect of the context just on the meanings of the words and expressions, and not on the rules.

On the other hand, it may be that all the parts of a sentence s have the same meaning-in-context in contexts c and c' while s itself does not. Some theories assume that

(5) It is raining

has no part that specifies a location, but that the sentence as a whole does. In such a theory, two utterances of (5) at the same time t but at different locations l and l' are such that all the parts have the same contextual meaning but the uttered sentence as a whole has different contextual meanings in the two contexts. That would be because the difference in location isn't articulated in any part of the sentence, in accordance with a doctrine of unarticulated constituents.[13] Because of these different variations, we have a distinction between two different notions of contextual compositionality that does not have any counterpart in the context independent case.

Recanati remarks that some of the semantic values of the indexical expressions are determined by speaker intentions, and are not antecedently given, as is suggested by the locution "determination by context". He mentions that the values of demonstratives are really set by what counts as salient and what the speaker intends. Even the value of 'here' and 'now', he says (Recanati 2005: 174), are claimed to be "highly sensitive to speaker's intent". But this, even if true, is not relevant to the particular point under discussion: whether a language with indexicals and demonstratives can in principle be given a compositional semantics. For that issue only concerns the dependence of complex-meanings-in-context on part-meanings-and-structure-in-context, not the mode of determination of part meanings, as we will further discuss in §6.

There is, however, a further question about the order of composition and value assignment. On one view, arriving at the meaning-in-context of a sentence is a bottom–up process where contextual values are assigned to simple expressions, and then the resulting meanings-in-context of simple expressions are combined to reach to meaning-in-context of the syntactic complexes.[14]

The immediate alternative to the bottom–up view of meaning-in-context is the view that we first combine *unsaturated* meanings of parts into a total unsaturated meaning of a complete sentence, and then in a *second* stage assign values to the parameters in the sentence to arrive at the meaning-in-context of the entire sentence.[15]

[13] These matters are discussed in detail in Pagin 2005a. There the location sensitivity is assigned to the meaning of 'rain'. With respect to such an account, there is no context shift failure.

[14] King and Stanley (2005) claim that this is the intuitively correct picture. See also Reimer (2002).

[15] On some views, not all parameters need be given values for a complete proposition to be formed. On these views, such as *temporalism* with respect to time, complete propositions are true

This difference of order does not in itself have much significance, so long as all the operations are defined, as we discuss in §6. However, when Recanati criticizes the bottom–up view, he has a further difference in mind:

> Contrary to what formal semanticists tend to assume, the (intuitive) truth-conditions of our utterances are not compositionally determined by the meanings of words and their semantic arrangement, in a strict bottom–up manner. They are shaped by contextual expectations and world-knowledge to a very large extent. That is true of all utterances, however 'literal' they are (in the ordinary sense). (Recanati 2004: 81–2)

Recanati's alternative view is not just that we don't start by assigning contextual values to simple expressions, but that the *way* a hearer does assign values to parameters proceeds by way of global considerations. The hearer aims at an overall interpretation that makes good sense, and selects contextual values so as to achieve that goal. For instance, to modify an example from Barbara Partee (1989: 275), consider

(17) a. I admire central Europeans. They all speak foreign languages.
b. I am completely lost among central Europeans. They all speak foreign languages.

The intuitively suggested interpretation of (17a) is that of assigning the central European as the relatum of 'foreign', while in (17b) it is the speaker of the discourse. Considerations of this kind seem to be included in what Recanati refers to as "top–down" processes.

However, from the point of view of the compositionalilty of semantics, it does not really matter whether this saturation process is bottom–up or top–down, or some kind of mixture, perhaps differing from case to case. Even when selecting values in a top–down fashion, the hearer can be seen as being guided by the goal of getting a reasonable outcome precisely *by the compositional semantics*. It is because selecting the discourse speaker as relatum to 'foreign' in (17a) results—by the compositional semantics—in a non-intuitive interpretation that this assignment is rejected. So, preferring a top–down view is not in conflict with compositionality, but rather trades on it. Compositionality extended to context dependence clearly contributes to a systematic account of speech act content.

The reason for this indifference is due to the fact that we are talking about *saturation* and therefore about fixing the value of some linguistic item, when the value is present in the (linguistic or non-linguistic) context. Clearly, if *all* values are assigned to words, then top–down and bottom–up will be the same. A difference might come to the fore were we to countenance saturation of items

or false relative to time points, but still constitute the contents of propositional attitudes. See e.g. Richard 1981.

larger than a word, where this saturation could not be accomplished by saturating some subpart of the larger item. For example, if there were a case where an entire verb phrase needed to be saturated but there was no relevant saturation of any of the contained words, then top–down and bottom–up would be different. And perhaps one might think of analyzing referential uses of definite descriptions in this manner also, thinking that there may be no relevant saturation of the descriptive material, but that this descriptive material plays some procedural role in helping the hearer make the correct identification.[16] But these sorts of abstract possibilities have not been mentioned by those who favor such processes as saturation.

Matters are less clear when we switch over to modulation.

3.2. Modulation

Whereas saturation is mandatory, since it is needed to arrive at a full proposition, modulation is optional. Modulations operate on chunks of interpreted material that don't strictly need to be modulated in order to contribute properly. Recanati (2004) distinguishes between three different kinds of modulation: free enrichment, loosening, and semantic transfer.

In free enrichment, semantic material is optionally *added* to what is derived from word meaning and structure. Typical examples are

(18) The table is covered with books

(19) Mary took out her key and opened the door

A normal utterance of (18) would have content like that of

(20) The table *of our living room* is covered with books

but in the case of (18), the addition, i.e. what is expressed by the italicized part of (18), is not articulated, but tacitly added (Recanati 2004: 10). The addition is not needed to have a proposition; it's just that the proposition literally expressed is, by ordinary conventional standards, absurd. The semantically expressed proposition gets freely enriched by the tacit material.

Similarly, in (19), a normal intuitive interpretation adds to the proposition semantically expressed that Mary opened the door *with the key that she took out*, although this is not necessary in order to have a full proposition, for with saturation added concerning 'her key', 'the door', the time etc., (19) expresses a proposition that can be true whether or not Mary used the contextually indicated key to open the contextually indicated door at the contextually indicated time.

[16] A suggestion made by one of the referees of this chapter.

Another kind of modulation is *loosening* (Recanati 2004: 24), as in

(21) The ATM swallowed my credit card

where the verb 'to swallow' has its application conditions *extended* to include the cash machine process referred to.

A third kind of modulation is *semantic transfer*, exemplified by

(22) The ham sandwich left without paying

as said by one waiter to another at a restaurant (the example is due to Nunberg 1979). Here the phrase 'the ham sandwich' is used to refer to the guest who ordered the ham sandwich, rather than to the dish itself. The semantic value has been transferred from the latter to the former.

Modulation is characterized as a top–down process, where the hearer uses his general understanding of the situation to arrive at the interpretation, as opposed to a bottom–up process, where the additions are triggered by elements of the sentence used (Recanati 2004: 18).

Saturation and modulation are what Recanati calls *primary* pragmatic processes. *Secondary* pragmatic processes are distinguished by taking the result of the primary process as input. The secondary processes comprise various kinds of *implicature.* An example of Recanati's combining both kinds is

(23) I've had breakfast

said in reply to the question 'Do you want something to eat?' (Recanati 2004: 8). The speaker of (23) *implicates* the she is not hungry and hence does not want anything to eat. Thereby it exemplifies implicature. It also exemplifies free enrichment, since she communicates not only that she has had breakfast at *some* time or other prior to the time of utterance, which is obviously true in its "literal meaning", but over and above this that she has had breakfast on the very day of the utterance. It is important that the primary process of fixing the day being discussed (to the date of utterance of (23)) must take place *before* the secondary process takes place because the implicature inference cannot be performed without that information. (The hearer can't infer that the speaker is not hungry unless she fixes the time that the speaker had breakfast.)

According to the position Recanati calls 'minimalism' there is a real communicative level of *what is said* that minimally deviates from the literal meaning of the sentence used. The minimal deviation comes from saturation.[17]

[17] There is further view called 'the syncretic view' by Recanati, according to which there are two levels (or two notions) of what is said, the minimal one and a further level that results from modulations. Recanati rejects this position as well (2004: 64).

Recanati rejects minimalism, arguing that the only real level of *what is said* is that delivered by the *combination* of saturation and modulation (Recanati 2004: 21).

More crucially, the rejection of minimalism is backed by the claim that the so-called *minimal proposition*, the result of saturation, is *not*, or at least not in general, computed by the hearer. In the example (22), according to Recanati, the hearer does not first interpret the utterance as an assertion of the absurd proposition that the dish itself left without paying, as minimalism implies, but achieves the semantic transfer locally, i.e. pragmatically reinterprets the phrase 'the ham sandwich' before the combination with the interpretation of the verb phrase is performed (Recanati 2004: 30–1).

Accordingly, on Recanati's picture, semantics, or literal meaning, normally contributes nothing but word meaning to the interpretation process. The interpretation of syntactic complexes takes place on a *pragmatic* level, with *modulated* contents. Modulated contents are composed into contents of larger syntactic units, and this is a purely pragmatic composition. The picture is one of a "bag of word meanings" that gets pragmatically modified and pieced together. In the even more radical picture of meaning eliminativism, words don't really have any meanings at all but only a "semantic potential" (Recanati 2004: 152), and some sorts of "associations" that have been built up by the use of these words in past situations (p. 151). In both cases, semantic compositionality is irrelevant to the communication process, and in the latter case semantics has no role at all; communication rather resembles an "association of ideas" *à la* the old British Empiricists, or to its modern reincarnation as pattern recognition in a conectionist network.[18]

As we see, then, Recanati accepts "more context" in his minimal propositions than what CL accept as being semantically expressed (their minimal propositions). Nonetheless, he rejects the idea that even his minimal propositions play any role in the communication process, except in very unusual circumstances.

Recanati and CL thus agree that semantics cannot play any *systematic* role in accounting for speech act content. According to Recanati, so much the worse for semantics; according to CL, so much the worse for the theory of speech act content.

We disagree with both parties. There is still room for a systematic account of speech act content, where compositionality plays a central role. We shall now proceed to indicate how.

[18] To make our position clear: we do agree with Recanati about the importance of the saturation/modulation distinction, which as he says is a distinction between what is and what is not linguistically controlled. For example, we would find it completely implausible that there be a *linguistic* parameter of 'ham sandwich' that takes *orderer* as value in (22), 'The ham sandwich left without paying'.

4. A SEMANTIC–PRAGMATIC FRAMEWORK

We wish to lay out the structure of a theory that satisfies systematicity by obeying the intuitive content of the Principle of Compositionality and yet also allows for some general theory of language that Recanati would say was "between" pure literalism and radical contextualism (or even his less radical "full-bodied contextualism"). That is, we wish to outline a theory that CL would call a "moderate contextualism". We take our task to have two parts. The first is simply to stake out such a theory, and the second to defend it against CL's instability arguments.

We are moved to this attempted middle ground because we think that there is more to "what is said" than is allowed by CL's minimalist theory, but that "what is said" cannot be so completely unstructured as Recanati's "no meaning" theory (nor maybe even his "full-bodied contextualism"), because then there could be no account that would explain how conversational participants can produce or understand novel utterances.

The middle ground can be occupied by an account that integrates semantic composition and modulation. There is reason to think that the two *can* be integrated, for if we look at the examples given of modulations, it seems they are pretty much controlled by semantic structure. First, in the standard modulation examples given, the semantic *category* of the original meaning is preserved under modulation. That is, if the original meaning is a concept of an action, the modulated content will be a concept of an action. If the original meaning is a sortal concept, then the modulated concept will be a sortal concept as well, and so on.[19]

Second, the composition function, by which simpler contents are mapped onto more complex contents, is simply taken over from the semantics. If the speaker starts out with a subject-predicate construction, semantically interpreted as a concept applying to an object, the modulated combination will again correspond to the subject-predicate construction, with some concept (perhaps a different one) applying to some object (again perhaps a different one).

Third, the structural *role* of a modulated part in determining the modulated proposition will be the same as the structural role of the unmodulated part in determining the minimal proposition. The enriched interpretation of a

[19] There are partial exceptions to this, as when you say, after Oscar has been accidentally squashed ('Oscar' was the proper name given to a tomato), that "There was Oscar all over the floor". In that case the concept of an object is mapped onto the concept of a stuff; but in this case too, the composition function is taken from the linguistic construction, and the non-category-preserving modulation of an object concept is required by the semantic composition.

grammatical direct object will again be the interpretation of the grammatical direct object, and so on.

These regularities could be explained syntactically, if modulation were a syntactic phenomenon, where a syntactic operation is performed that does not leave any trace on the surface string, but introduces ellipsis at an underlying level. However, *pace* Stanley (2002), we do not find this syntactic hypothesis to be plausible. We see it rather, as on Recanati's picture, that modulations are content operations, and as such they should be seen as controlled by a *conceptual structure*, on which they operate. Those are the immediate reasons for the account below.

The main idea, then, is to combine a more basic immediate output of the semantics—here called a 'conceptual structure'—with pragmatic modulation operations that modify the transition from the conceptual structures to standard propositional representations. We shall operate with the familiar homomorphism format of compositionality from the Montague and Hodges traditions. We shall not set out the machinery with full precision, but only as far as is required to articulate the idea.

To start, we have a language L consisting of a set of atomic expressions A_L, a set of syntactic operations Σ_L, and a set of expressions E_L (we shall drop the subscripts from now on). E is the set that can be produced from A by means of the operations in Σ. Now we have a *meaning function* μ that maps structured syntactic entities, like syntactic trees or terms, onto meanings.[20]

Together with the meaning function μ there is a *general composition function* ρ. ρ takes as argument a syntactic operation $\sigma \in \Sigma$, and gives as value a *particular composition function* $\rho(\sigma)$. The particular composition function $\rho(\sigma)$ in turn maps meanings of the parts of a complex expression onto the meaning of the complex expression itself.

This gives us the formalized counterpart to (PoC):

$$(\mathcal{PC}) \quad \mu(\sigma(t_1, \ldots, t_n)) = \rho(\sigma)(\mu(t_1), \ldots, \mu(t_n))$$

where the $t_1, \ldots, t_n$ are the syntactic trees or terms that are the immediate syntactic constituents of the complex $\sigma(t_1, \ldots, t_n)$. $\mu(t_1), \ldots, \mu(t_n)$ are of course the meanings of the parts.

To this we can now add context dependence, by letting each constituent have a context argument. A context can be represented formally as a sequence of contextual values, like *time* or *place*, in the simplest cases. Certain operations on contexts, like $T(c)$ to pick out the time of context c, provide what is relevant to

[20] It is important that the meaning function is defined on expressions that are syntactically unambiguous. That is why it cannot in general be defined on ordinary expressions, since in natural language ordinary (surface) expressions are often ambiguous.

the expression in question, and for an atomic expression, this will be specified in its basic semantic clause.

With the addition of context ($\mathcal{PC}$) can be modified into

$$(\mathcal{PC}_c) \quad \mu(\sigma(t_1, \ldots, t_n), c) = \rho(\sigma)(\mu(t_1, c), \ldots, \mu(t_n, c))$$

where the contextual meaning of the complex depends on the contextual meanings of the parts and the mode of composition.[21] To have a complete context semantics we would also have to specify how the meanings on the higher, context independent level relate to the contextual meanings, by the normal methods involving λ-abstraction and λ-conversion. Since our aim here is to give a way of handling modulation, we will leave this part out.

Normally, we would take the output of the meaning function to be a standard representation of states of affairs, of what things are like, say a proposition, where we think of a proposition as something without internal structure, a *flat* representation.[22] If that is what we think the saturated content of an utterance is, and as well what the saturated and modulated content of an utterance is, then we would want the end-result of the formal interpretation process to be a proposition. But the immediate output of the semantic function need not be a proposition. Rather, for the purpose of providing material for further operations, a *structured output* is more suitable.

What we suggest, therefore, is an alternative meaning function μ' which, instead of delivering the result of applying the particular composition function onto the part meanings, delivers instead the ordered n-tuple of the particular composition function and the (alternative) part meanings. That is, we define μ' as follows:

$$(\mathcal{PC}'_c) \quad \text{(i)} \quad \mu'(t, c) = \mu(t, c), \text{ if } t \text{ is atomic}$$

$$\text{(ii)} \quad \mu'(\sigma(t_1, \ldots, t_n), c) = \langle \rho(\sigma), \mu'(t_1, c), \ldots, \mu'(t_n, c) \rangle$$

Note that the general composition function ρ' that is thereby defined for μ' is such that for a given n-place syntactic operation σ

$$(25) \quad \rho'(\sigma) = \langle \rho(\sigma), \xi_1, \ldots, \xi_n \rangle$$

(with the ξ_i marking the argument places).

21 We get a different version of contextual compositionality by adding a context argument to the particular composition function:

$$(24) \quad \mu(\sigma(t_1, \ldots, t_n), c) = \rho(\sigma)(\mu(t_1, c), \ldots, \mu(t_n, c), c)$$

This weaker alternative corresponds to the idea that the sentence 'It is raining' (see above) can have different contextual meanings in two contexts even if all the parts have the same meaning in both contexts.

22 See Cresswell 2002 for an argument that propositions don't have structure.

If we have a complex expression with iterated applications of syntactic operators, the output of μ' will be a tree structure, where every constituent of an $n+1$-tuple, except the first, is the vertex of a sub-tree.

For a simple example, consider the sentence

(26) a. Alfred loves Elsa

b. $[_{S} [_{NP}$ Alfred $][_{VP} [_{VT}$ loves $][_{NP}$ Elsa $]]]$

(where we employ a standard phrase structure as given in (26b)). Let σ_1 be the operation that combines a VT and an NP into a VP, and σ_2 the operation the combines an NP and a VP into an S. Then, given μ and ρ, the output of μ' will be

(27) $\mu'(\sigma_2(\text{Alfred}, \sigma_1(\text{loves}, \text{Elsa}))) =$
$\langle \rho(\sigma_2), \mu(\text{Alfred}), \langle \rho(\sigma_1), \mu(\text{loves}), \mu(\text{Elsa})\rangle\rangle$

(since μ' coincides with μ on atomic expressions). The third element of the top triple is itself a triple.

The output of μ', a "conceptual structure", is taken as the primary output of the semantics. The primary output is then transformed into a standard output by means of an *evaluation* function E that takes a conceptual structure as argument and gives a standard interpretation as value. The definition of E is straightforward:

(E) (i) $E(\mu'(t)) = \mu'(t)$, for atomic t

(ii) $E(\langle \rho(\sigma), \mu'(t_1, c), \ldots, \mu'(t_n, c)\rangle) = \rho(\sigma)(E(\mu'(t_1, c)), \ldots, E(\mu'(t_n, c)))$

So the application of E to an $(n+1)$-tuple simply consists in applying the first element of the tuple, which is an n-place function, to the E-values of remaining n elements. By an elementary induction proof it can be shown that

(28) $\mu(t) = E(\mu'(t))$

for any term t for which μ is defined.

Although it seems that this is merely an alternative way to arrive at the same result that a standard semantic theory would generate, the point of introducing conceptual structures and their evaluations into ordinary interpretations is that we can identify the evaluation step as the step where pragmatic modulations enter the process. To illustrate, the *modulated evaluation*, E_m, of an utterance of (22)

(22) The ham sandwich left without paying

in a context c can be said to be achieved by means of applying the function *the orderer of* . . . to the part of the conceptual structure that is given by μ' (the ham sandwich). Skipping the syntactic details below the NP-VP structure, we have conceptual structure with the topmost triple

(29) $\langle \rho(\sigma_2), \mu'$ (the ham sandwich, c), μ' (left without paying, c)$\rangle$

We then have the contextual modulated evaluation:

(30) $E_m(\langle \rho(\sigma_2), \mu'$ (the ham sandwich, c), μ' (left without paying, c)$\rangle$, c)
$= \rho(\sigma_2)(O(E_m(\mu'$(the ham sandwich, c))), $E_m(\mu'$(left without paying, c)))

where O is the *orderer of* function.

We can here see the modulation as an operation that *replaces* the standard evaluation function by a modified evaluation function E_m in the step from conceptual structure to standard interpretation. An alternative is to give a slightly more liberal definition of the standard evaluation function E so that modulation enters as a function from immediate conceptual structure to modulated conceptual structure. The idea is to add a third schema to the definition so that

(E') (i) $E(\mu'(t)) = \mu'(t)$, for atomic t
(ii) $E(\langle \rho(\sigma), \mu'(t_1, c), \ldots, \mu'(t_n, c)\rangle) = \rho(\sigma)(E(\mu'(t_1, c)), \ldots, E(\mu'(t_n, c)))$
(iii) $E(f(\mu'(t))) = f(E(\mu'(t)))$

for arbitrary non-semantic function f. Then we can say instead that

(31) $E_m(\langle \rho(\sigma_2), \mu'$(the ham sandwich, c), μ'(left without paying, c)$\rangle$, c)
$= E(\langle \rho(\sigma_2), O(\mu'$(the ham sandwich, c)), μ'(left without paying, c)$\rangle$)

If we suppose that E_m in context c gives us all the modulation information, i.e. the information of all the modulating operations performed on the conceptual structure, we can provide the general format as follows:

(E_m) (i) $E_m(\mu'(t)) = \mathcal{M}(E(\mu'(t)))$, for atomic t
(ii) $E_m(\langle \rho(\sigma), \mu'(t_1, c), \ldots, \mu'(t_n, c)\rangle, c)$
$= \mathcal{M}(E(\langle \rho(\sigma), E_m(\mu'(t_1, c), c), \ldots, E_m(\mu'(t_n, c), c)\rangle))$

where $\mathcal{M}$ is the modulation performed at the topmost level of the structure or substructure under consideration. $\mathcal{M}$ might be the *null*-modulation, in case no non-trivial modulation is performed at that level.[23] Each application of E_m gives an output of the same format, with an initial modulation, possibly the null-modulation, followed by applying the basic evaluation function E to the following structure.

In this way a well-defined structure is the immediate output of the semantics, and the primary pragmatic processes (as opposed to implicatures and other secondary operations) can be defined as operations on this semantic output. This shows that acknowledging modulations as primary pragmatic processes isn't in conflict with accepting a central role for compositional semantics.[24]

It is important to keep in mind that although the E_m function applies in the familiar recursive way, there is as yet no good reason to regard it as a *compositional* function in the ordinary sense. For this to be adequate, we would need to treat E_m as a *universal* function that delivers a particular modulation $\mathcal{M}$ as value for particular conceptual + contextual arguments. So far, however, we have no conception of the *contextual elements* that are apt to trigger, for example, the semantic transfer modulation *the orderer of*. Rather, it seems to be a matter of global interpretational features of the context (i.e. what Recanati calls a top–down process) that cannot easily be coded as contextual elements. We will return in §6 to the question of whether this precludes a *systematic* account of the choice of selection of modulation function in the interpretation process.

5. THE INSTABILITY ARGUMENTS REVISITED

In the previous section we showed that modulations can be happily combined with a compositional semantics. We shall now try to show that a consistent application of the semantics/modulation distinction will defuse the CL instability arguments.

So consider first our man Smith

(4) Smith weighs 80 kg

[23] There is a complication that has to be accounted for somehow. Considering a sentence like

(32) The ham sandwich liked the ham sandwich

we would want an interpretation where the interpretation of the first occurrence of the definite description gets modulated by the *orderer of* function while the second doesn't. So it is not just the overall E_m-function and the argument that determines the modulation. Either we need a more fine-grained notion of context, or else a more fine-grained notion of a modulated evaluation function. We shall here leave the difficulty unresolved.

[24] That is the main point of Pagin 2005*b*, where this way of combining compositional semantics with modulations is first suggested.

and let's assume that 'weighs' is a genuinely present tensed transitive verb, true of a pair of an object and a pair of number and weight unit, at a particular time.[25] In that case we have a straightforward true application in the cases when Smith weighs

(4a) 80 kg when stripped in the morning

if the sentence is uttered in the morning and intended to concern the time of utterance. The same holds in the cases where Smith weighs

(4c) 80 kg after being force fed 4 liters of water

(4d) 80 kg four hours after having ingested a powerful diuretic

It might of course be the case that the speaker who makes the utterance of (4) at a time when Smith has been force fed 4 liters of water does intend Smith's normal morning weight. But that is easily treated as a case of modulation. For instance, the speaker might intend the addition of temporal quantification, together with a replacement of a reference to the present time by a morning-restricted time variable, perhaps with a further free enrichment concerning eating conditions:

(4a′) [It is normally the case that] Smith weighs 80 kg [in the morning before breakfast]

where the added material is represented within square brackets. This result can be achieved by means free enrichment and perhaps also semantic transfer (for the time reference). In the case of

(4e) 80 kg after lunch adorned in heavy outer clothing

the result is again easily achieved by means of a modulation that can be classified in various ways:

(4e′) Smith [together with his clothes] weighs 80 kg

And so on. The various propositions that might normally be intended by (4) are fairly easily accounted for by means of reference to modulations. These modulations account for context shift features, as well as for a possible impression

[25] We leave it open whether there is also a separate lexically coded *habitual* or *iterative* present tense, i.e. a coded aspect relating a pair not at a particular time but with respect to some time interval, and true of the pair if the number gives something like the average weight of the object during the interval.

of incompleteness that might be evoked by the context shifts. The extra material does not add to something that is inherently incomplete, but, as Recanati says, maps a (complete) proposition onto another proposition.

Let's consider the case of

(9) John went to the gym

and assume that standardly, 'went to' is true of a pair consisting of a moving object and a place, at a time, just in case the the object at the time had traveled along some trajectory and reached the boundary of the place. Then, when the topic of conversation is John's walking habits, the content of the utterance would be straightforwardly accounted for by another enrichment

(9′) John went to [the vicinity of] the gym

In the other two cases, where we are concerned with John's exercise or construction work, then no modulation is needed. It is simply an implicature under the Gricean maxim 'Be relevant' (Grice 1989: 27). If the topic of conversation is John's work activities, and it is common knowledge that construction work is going on at the gym, then we have a violation of the relevance maxim if the speaker simply meant that John went to the gym to work out or admire the building. The speaker might have meant literally that John reached the boundary of the gym, without having any further information, in which case any stronger claim would violate the quality maxim 'Do not say that for which you lack adequate evidence' (Grice 1989: 27). Again, the further interpretations are easily derived. In this case, too, both context shift and the accompanying impression of incompleteness are accounted for.

The case of

(10) That's a dangerous dog

is even easier, since the speaker need not even intend to inform the hearer, *by means of that particular utterance*, of the *explanation* of why the dog is dangerous. Similarly, when CL ask about (9) 'Went how to the gym?', this concerns further information about different ways (9) might be made true. No pragmatic process, neither primary nor secondary, is needed. It is not a case of propositional incompleteness at all.

These examples contrast strikingly with the proposed paradigmatic examples of incompleteness

(1) Tipper is ready

(11) Steel isn't strong enough

where there simply is *no* candidate available for being the proposition expressed without modulation or implicature. We simply don't know what it is to be ready, or strong enough, *simpliciter*. It cannot be that (1) is true just in case a condition obtains that is common to all the contexts in which it is correct to assert (1). For what is common is that there is something for which Tipper is ready. Then, by parity of reasoning,

(33) Tipper is not ready

is true just if there is something for which Tipper is *not* ready. By these explanations it would hold that Tipper is both ready and not ready, in case there is something for which Tipper is ready and something for which Tipper is not ready.[26]

CL's defense of the completeness claim is the instability argument itself, i.e. the argument that the intuitions by which (1) and (11) are deemed *incomplete* can be used equally well against the alleged completions (CL 2005: 62–3). We have by means of a number of examples tried to make it plausible that this strategy does not work, as the various cases differ in important respects.

Some of CL's examples are of course problematic. As regards the sentence

(11b) Steel isn't strong enough to support the roof

CL are right to say (2005: 62) that it is not so clear what the truth conditions of an utterance are meant to be. As they ask, for how long, and under what condition? Nevertheless, it is clear that at a time t such that there is some temporal neighborhood of t under which the roof is supported by a steel construction,[27] the sentence

(34) Steel supports the roof

would be literally true. By the same token, with respect to t it would be equally true to say

(35) Steel is strong enough to support the roof

No completion is necessary. As a matter of fact, we would not use (11) to make nor interpret an utterance of (11) as making such a weak claim, presumably because it would violate a relevance requirement. What is relevant is rather that there is support during a foreseeable future, and under fairly bad but not necessarily extreme conditions. Of course it is vague what to count as foreseeable

[26] A similar point is made in Borg 2006: §iii.

[27] That is, the construction undergoes only negligible decay during that time span.

and what to count as extreme conditions, but that is beside the point, since vagueness is a separate problem. The relevant issue is rather that the qualifications about time span and conditions can be seen as added by way of modulation.

All in all, the appeal to modulation, and sometimes even implicature, seems adequate to deal with the examples that are used by CL to show that any sentence can be seen as semantically incomplete and context dependent. As far as we can make out, the CL instability arguments fail.

6. CONCLUDING REMARKS

As we have remarked at various places in this chapter, there are further issues that are relevant to our attempt to employ semantic compositionality in our explication of how we might arrive at a moderate contextualism. Our professed strategy, recall, was to invoke systematicity, but to explain that notion by using compositionality as a prototypical case of systematicity. (Cf. n. 7 above.) It is time now to consider just how well we think compositionality fares on its own as an account of the systematicity that is required to counter the instability arguments that are used by both CL and Recanati in their denials of the viability of a moderate contextualism.[28]

We start with some comments about compositionality, briefly surveying the extent to which it is successful by trying to give as strong a case as possible for employing compositionality in this realm. In the end we decide that compositionality, strictly understood, is not adequate for the job, and that we need to make an appeal to some wider notion of systematicity of the sort employed in §4. We follow this with a more general discussion on the prospects for a systematic theory. Further comments on this can be found in Pagin (2005*b*).

6.1. Reflections on Compositionality

One central topic concerning whether compositionality can be the entire content of systematicity is the issue concerning the appropriate manner to accommodate contextual information even when it is believed that the information *is* susceptible of a compositional account—a topic we considered in subsection 3.1. Consider for example the "first step" along Recanati's "ever more context" pathway—explicit indexicals. In such a case we have a sentence containing some "ordinary" words that have their ordinary meanings and some indexical words that have a "meaning" but still need to have a semantic value specified for them. One way to proceed here, a way suggested by Kaplan's character–content

[28] CL's argumentative strategy was to endorse the radical contextualist's employment of the Incompleteness and Context Shifting arguments. Both sides here deny that there is a stopping point that can give moderate contextualism a home.

distinction, would be to compute the meaning of the sentence in accordance with a compositional mechanism (giving us the character of the sentence) and then to specify the content of the sentence by letting context specify the values of the indexicals (by "saturation"). Compositionality here works on character, or as one might say, on the literal meaning of the words and phrases: the literal meaning of the sentence (its character) is compositionally derived from the literal meanings of its parts and the syntactic manner in which these parts are combined. Saturation then occurs at the sentence level to generate an occasion meaning.

But another way could be to saturate the indexical words—giving them their occasion meanings[29]—and thereupon employing the compositional mechanism on these occasion meanings to generate the occasion meaning of the sentence. Here compositionality takes the occasion meanings of the parts and compositionally generates the occasion meaning of the sentence.

Although we discussed this sort of case in subsection 3.1, where we distinguished a Principle of Compositionality (PoC) from a Principle of Contextual Compositionality (PCC), we think that a few more words are in order. Even given the sort of simplicity we are imagining in the realm of indexicals (and demonstratives?), the two compositional methods are not equivalent. In subsection 3.1 we mentioned issues of substitution and of "unarticulated constituents". A question for compositionalists then is to determine whether these sorts of differences lead to any important differences in accounting for communication.

The example given above concerns explicit indexicals. One question is whether this can be extended to other words that a moderate contextualist might wish to embrace, such as *foreigner* and *enemy*.[30] As we explained in 3.1, there is an important difference between seeing the compositionality principles as *descriptive* characterizations of the language (as made by a linguist, say) versus as a *psychological* mechanism employed by the participants of a communicative act. In the former case, the character–content distinction could once again be invoked, with (it seems) pretty much the same results as we found for the indexicals. But the case is somewhat different when considered as a psychological mechanism employed by conversational participants. In this interpretation it is natural to think of the participants as engaging in Recanati's "top–down processing"; and some theorists (including Recanati) seem to think that this cannot support compositionality, with its commitment to literal meaning. However, even here (as we noted in 3.1) we can view the psychological interpretation as being guided by trying to employ the descriptive compositional semantics.

And so a moderate contextualist who wished to rely solely on compositionality would wish to make the descriptive–psychological distinction in the case of *all* context-sensitive words (presumably even indexicals). As we said in 3.1, there is no barrier to a conversational participant using top–down processing or

[29] In this picture, the occasion meaning of non-indexical words would be their literal meaning.
[30] Or *different*, as in the Partee example we mentioned in 3.1.

bottom–up or a mixture of the two, so long as the descriptive compositional structure is in place.

As stated, the PCC method is only defined for cases where an individual *word* is to be saturated, as with the indexicals, or tense, or the other context-sensitive words. We earlier raised the question of whether saturation ever *needs* to be done on units that are larger than a word, where this effect cannot be achieved by saturating any individual words in the unit. For example, can there be noun phrases or verb phrases that require saturation to get their occasion meaning but where there is no subcomponent of that phrase which can be saturated to get the same effect. In 3.1 we gave the example of an utterance of *It is raining*, which some might argue needs to be saturated by a location, but also argue that there is no item in the sentence that can be thus saturated. (The question before us now is not a sentence saturation, but of a phrasal saturation that has no component word saturation.) It is not so clear to us that the *is raining* (or: *to rain*) really can accept a location saturation, but we acknowledge that this sort of idea remains a possibility that could be developed in a more complete theory.

The preceding was a defense of using "pure compositionality" as an account of how saturation might be dealt with. But a compositionalist might have something different to say concerning Recanati's use of the various types of modulation, but especially the processes of *loosening* and *enrichment*. As a first pass, a committed compositionalist would deny that certain of the argumentative strategies that Recanati employs (and which CL then take advantage of in their Instability considerations) are even required. Consider, for example

(18) The table is covered with books

(19) Mary took out her key and opened the door

(21) The ATM swallowed my credit card

where Recanati claims that "what is said" by (18) includes *table in our living room*, that "what is said" by (19) includes that *the door was opened by the key* (both cases of enrichment), and that the meaning of *swallowed* in (20) has been extended from its literal meaning. The committed compositionalist might dispute these presumed data, and claim that they should instead be seen as cases of *generality*. Why, the compositionalist might cry, should we think that 'swallowed' in (21) has been "loosened"? What has been added to the dictionary meaning *to envelop or take in*? If Recanati has at the forefront of his mind something about *taking through the mouth and esophagus into the stomach* when he utters 'swallow', the correct response by the compositionalist will be that this confuses generality with difference in meaning. The sentence

(36) Kim Johnson is a fine person

simply does not have two different meanings, depending on whether the speaker "has a picture in mind" of a woman or of a man. The noun 'person' is *general* and applies to both. Why, a compositionalist asks, is the case with (21) any different? Similarly, why would one wish to say that 'the table' in (18) has been enriched? Although the speaker may "have in mind" the table in their living room, this can seem irrelevant to the compositionalist. (And in fact it does seem irrelevant to some such theorists, as in Lepore (2003).) The fact that sentences like (19) allow for cancellation of the *with the key* seems to show that this is not a case of enrichment (a primary pragmatic process, in Recanati's terms) but rather an implicature (a secondary pragmatic process).

At any rate, those are the sort of things that a committed compositionalist might appeal to in an attempt to use compositionality as the touchstone for constructing a moderate contextualism. We think, however, that in the "strict" reading of compositionality there are some issues that need further embellishment, and it was for that reason we shifted our attention to the wider notion of systematicity. So, we should turn to the question of how well such a theory can be expected to perform in our search for a moderate contextualism.

6.2. The Prospects of a Systematic Theory

By showing how to integrate a compositional semantics of the sort indicated in §4 with primary pragmatic processes we have shown how it is possible to account for speech act content, up to secondary pragmatic processes, in a way that is systematic in one respect: it shows for a particular interpreted utterance how the interpretation is arrived at by means of the contextual meaning of parts, the mode of composition, and the modulation function. However, in another respect the account is not fully systematic.

Compare standard compositional semantics. The interpretation of a complex expression is determined completely by the syntactic build-up of the sentence and the meanings of the atomic expressions. There is scope for variation to the extent that there is semantic or syntactic ambiguity, for then the interpreter needs to choose between different syntactic/semantic readings. In this case, however, all the possible readings can be extracted from the syntax and semantics alone.

When we add indexicals, a further element of uncertainty is added. So-called 'pure' indexicals, in Kaplan's sense, like 'I', 'you', 'now', normally get their contextual reference determined by a simple function from the context, for example, 'I' is assigned *the speaker of* the context. It is more difficult with demonstratives, including demonstrative uses of pronouns. For example, in case of an utterance of a sentence like

(37) She was late yesterday

the hearer needs to figure out which female the speaker has in mind. That will be the female that is most *salient* for the speaker at the time of utterance, which may and may not coincide with the female that is most salient for the *hearer* at that time.

In the case of possessive constructions like 'Peter's bat' in (12) above, the hearer needs to figure out which *relation* between Peter and the bat is the most salient one.

As far as we are aware, there is so far no general and successful theory that tells us how to *predict* what will be most salient to a speaker or hearer on an occasion.[31] We do have some simple rules of thumb, like the rule that things become salient by being mentioned, and by being visually or audibly different from their environment in conspicuous ways, but not much more than that. To the extent that we cannot predict the salience profile of a context from more overt elements, there is a limit to our ability to account for communicative success. We may know that usually the same things are salient to both speaker and hearer, but lack a general theory for predicting what it will be.

Still, when it comes to interpreting an utterance of (37), we can say in general, for example, the utterance is *true* provided the most speaker-salient female of the context of utterance was late to something or other on the day before the day of the utterance. That is, we know exactly how the interpretation depends on the salience profile of the context. The fact that Elsa (say) is the most speaker-salient female can be treated as one element of the context, similar to the fact that, say, Alfred, is the *speaker* of the context. Since we know how context-sensitive utterances like (37), or

(38) I was late yesterday

depend on the contextual parameters, we can specify the interpretation in terms of them.

In the case of modulations, the difficulties are greater. Given that we know the target interpretation of, for example,

(9′) John went to [the vicinity of] the gym

and we know the saturated but non-modulated meaning of the sentence (9), we can account for how to get the former from the latter. But to have a fully

[31] It does seem that, by default, what is salient to the speaker is what the speaker believes is salient to the hearer, and vice versa. In some cases, which deserve a closer study, a discrepancy arises. For instance, global considerations about reasonable interpretation might motivate a hearer to change her assumption about the identity of the female that is most salient to the speaker. This will make the new candidate (if there is one) most salient to the hearer.

systematic account, we should also be able to predict the interpretation from the context, i.e. predict which modulation to apply *without* making use of independent knowledge of the target interpretation.

To some extent, selecting the right modulation, given some contextual information, is like selecting the right referent of a demonstrative: in both cases some pragmatic skill, or representation of pragmatic skill, is required. But there is also a difference, for the appeal to salience in the demonstrative cases is an appeal to a contextual parameter that is independent of the interpretation itself. That is, to be the most speaker-salient female is a property that depends on speaker psychology, irrespective of interpretation.

By contrast, it is at least not obvious that there is some particular contextual parameter whose value in a context *c* determines the function *the vicinity of* as the right modulation of the interpretation of the NP 'the gym' in (9′). Rather, it seems to be something arrived at by means of general pragmatic skill, taking into account the topic of conversation, the current focus, the established conversational score, and perhaps further features of speaker psychology or speaker idiosyncrasies. It seems to depend on *global* interpretational considerations rather than individual parameters. If this is right, is there any hope of giving a correct, systematic account of the selection of modulations? Or must we ultimately agree with the CL thesis (N) that there cannot be a systematic theory of speech act content? If a modulation simply is a function mapping propositions onto propositions, without any further restriction, there is just no limit to how random and strange modulations can be.

Although this is not the place even to *start* an investigation into the systematic nature of modulations, let us express some optimism. We think that much of the work done in pragmatics in recent decades, for example, within Relevance Theory (Sperber and Wilson 1992) or within the theory of impliciture (Bach 1994*a*), contributes to the understanding of these processes. The modulations that do occur seem to be fairly simple transformations of propositions or of parts of the conceptual structures that evaluate into propositions. They typically restrict, enlarge, or offset reference in small doses. They often add reference to assumed *causes* of events that are explicitly referred to.[32] Probably, there is a fairly small set of normal *types* of modulation, even if we go beyond the division into loosening, free enrichment, and semantic transfer. Identifying modulations seems

[32] This phenomenon was noted already by in Frege 1892, where Frege considers the sentence

(39) Napoleon, who recognized the danger to his right flank, personally led his troops against the enemy's position

noting that what seems to be expressed includes a third proposition, that the recognition of the danger was the reason for the action.

to be a process motivated by standard considerations of relevance, clarity, and simplicity. There is reason to be optimistic about progress in mapping it out.[33]

REFERENCES

Bach, K. (1994*a*), 'Conversational Impliciture', *Mind and Language*, 9: 124–62.

—— (1994*b*), 'Semantic Slack: What is Said and More', S. Tsohatzidis (ed), *Foundations of Speech Act Theory*, pp. 267–91, London: Routledge.

Borg, E. (2006), 'Minimalism vs Contextualism in Semantics', in G. Preyer and G. Peter (eds.), *Content and Context: Essays on Semantics and Pragmatics*. Oxford: Oxford University Press.

Cappelen, H., and E. Lepore (1997), 'On an Alleged Connection between Indirect Quotation and Semantic Theory', *Mind and Language*, 12: 278–96.

—— and —— (2005), *Insensitive Semantics: A Defense of Semantic Minimalism and Speech Act Pluralism*. Oxford: Blackwell.

Cresswell, J. M. (2002), 'Why Propositions have No Structure', *Nous*, 36: 643–62.

Feigl, H., and W. Sellars (eds.) (1949), *Readings in Philosophical Analysis*. New York: Appleton-Century Croft.

Fodor, J. (1987), *Psychosemantics*. Cambridge, Mass.: MIT Press.

—— and Z. Pylyshyn (1988), 'Connectionism and Cognitive Architecture', *Cognition*, 28: 3–71.

Frege, G. (1892), 'Über Sinn und Bedeutung', *Zeitschrift für Philosophie und Philosophische Kritik*, 100: 22–50. Tr. Herbert Feigl as 'On Sense and Nominatum', in Feigl and Sellars 1949: 85–102.

—— (1923), 'Compound Thoughts', *Mind*, 72: 1–17, tr. R. Stoothof, and published in *Mind* (1963).

Grice, H. P. (1989), *Studies in the Ways of Words*. Cambridge, Mass.: Harvard University Press.

Hodges, W. (1998), 'Compositionality is Not the Problem', *Logic and Logical Philosophy*, 6: 7–33.

—— (2001), 'Formal Features of Compositionality', *Journal of Logic, Language and Information*, 10: 7–28.

Kaplan, D. (1989), 'Demonstratives', in J. Almog, J. Perry, H. Wettstein (eds.), *Themes from Kaplan*. Oxford: Oxford University Press.

King, J., and J. Stanley (2005), Semantics, Pragmatics, and the Role of Semantic Content, in Z. Szabó (ed.), *Semantics vs. Pragmatics*. Oxford: Oxford University Press.

Lepore, E. (2003), 'An Abuse of Context in Semantics: The Case of Incomplete Definite Descriptions', in A. Bezuidenhout and M. Reimer (eds.), *Descriptions and Beyond: An Interdisciplinary Collection of Essays on Definite and Indefinite Descriptions and Other Related Phenomena*. Oxford: Oxford University Press.

Montague, R. (1970*a*), 'Universal Grammar', *Theoria*, 36: 373–98.

[33] We are grateful to comments from two anonymous referees. We have also benefited from discussions of the themes of the paper with François Recanati and Mike Harnish. Work on this paper has been supported by a grant from the Swedish Research Council (for Pagin) and the Canadian NSERC (for Pelletier).

——(1970*b*), 'English as a Formal Language', in B. Visentini (ed.), *Linguaggi nella Società e nella Tecnica*, pp. 189–224. Milan: Edizioni di Comunità.

——(1973), 'The Proper Treatment of Quantification in Ordinary English', in J. Hintikka, J. Moravcsik, and P. Suppes (eds.), *Approaches to Natural Language*, pp. 221–42. Dordrecht: Reidel.

Nunberg, G. (1979), 'The Non-Uniqueness of Semantic Solutions: Polysemy', *Linguistics and Philosophy*, 3: 143–84.

Pagin, P. (2003), 'Communication and Strong Compositionality', *Journal of Philosophical Logic*, 32: 287–322.

——(2005*a*), 'Compositionality and Context', in G. Preyer and G. Peter (eds.), *Contextualism in Philosophy*, pp. 303–48. Oxford: Oxford University Press.

——(2005*b*), 'Semantic and Pragmatic Composition', paper presented at the semantics–pragmatics workshop in Context 05.

Partee, B. H. (1989), 'Binding Implicit Variables in Quantified Contexts', in C. Wiltshire, B. Music, and R. Graczyk (eds.), *Papers from CLS 25*, pp. 342–56. Chicago: Chicago Linguistics Society. Repr. in Partee 2004: 259–81. Page references to the reprint.

——(2004), *Compositionality in Formal Semantics: Selected Papers by Barbara H. Partee.* Oxford: Blackwell.

Pelletier, F. J. (1994), 'The Principle of Semantic Compositionality', *Topoi*, 13: 11–24, expanded version reprinted in S. Davis and B. Gillon (eds.) (2004), *Semantics: A Reader*, pp. 133–57. New York: Oxford University Press.

Perry, J. (1986), 'Thought without Representation', *Proceedings of the Aristotelian Society*, 60: 263–83.

Recanati, F. (2004), *Literal Meaning*. Cambridge: Cambridge University Press.

——(2005), 'Literalism and Contextualism: Some Varieties', in G. Preyer and G. Peter (eds.), *Contextualism in Philosophy*, pp. 171–96. Oxford: Oxford University Press.

Reimer, M. (2002), 'Do Adjectives Conform to Compositionality?', *Nous*, 16: 183–98.

Richard, M. (1981), 'Temporalism and Eternalism', *Philosophical Studies*, 39: 1–13.

Russell, B. (1956), 'The Philosophy of Logical Atomism', in R. Marsh (ed.), *Bertrand Russell: Logic and Knowledge, Essays 1901–1950*, pp. 175–281. London: Unwin Hyman; 1st publ. 1918.

Schlick, M. (1985), *General Theory of Knowledge*. Peru, Ill.: Open Court, 1st publ. 1918.

Searle, J. (1978), 'Literal Meaning', *Erkenntnis*, 13: 207–24.

——(1980), 'The Background of Meaning', in J. Searle, F. Kiefer, and M. Bierwisch (eds.), *Speech Act Theory and Pragmatics*, pp. 221–32. Dordrecht: Reidel.

——(1983), *Intentionality*. Cambridge: Cambridge University Press.

Sperber, D., and D. Wilson (1992), *Relevance: Communication and Cognition*, 2nd edn. Oxford: Blackwell.

Stanley, J. (2002), 'Making it Articulated', *Mind and Language*, 17: 149–68.

——and Z. Szabó (2000), 'On Quantifier Domain Restriction', *Mind and Language*, 15: 219–61.

Travis, C. (1985), 'On What is Strictly Speaking True', *Canadian Journal of Philosophy*, 15: 187–229.

——(1989), *The Uses of Sense*. Oxford: Oxford University Press.

——(1996), 'Meaning's Role in Truth', *Mind*, 100: 451–66.

Westerståhl, D. (1998), 'On Mathematical Proofs of the Vacuity of Compositionality', *Linguistics and Philosophy*, 21: 635–43.

—— (2004), 'On the Compositional Extension Problem', *Journal of Philosophical Logic*, 35: 549–82.

Wittgenstein, L. (1981), *Tractatus Logico-Philosophicus.* London: Routledge & Kegan Paul; 1st publ. 1921.

2

A Little Sensitivity Goes a Long Way

Kenneth A. Taylor

1. INTRODUCTION

In *Insensitive Semantics*, Cappelen and Lepore do several things and they do them with great rhetorical flourish. They distinguish radical from moderate contextualism. They argue that moderate contextualism collapses into radical contextualism. But radical contextualism, they claim, is a crazy and inconsistent doctrine. On the positive side, they defend the combination of semantic minimalism and speech act pluralism. In my estimation, hardly any of it succeeds. They've shown neither that moderate contextualism collapses into radical contextualism nor that radical contextualism is inconsistent. Their defense of semantic minimalism is unsuccessful. What they call speech act pluralism is either old news or false. But truth is not the sole virtue and falsity not the sole vice. There are interesting ways of being mistaken and uninteresting ways of being right. Cappelen and Lepore have the virtue of being mistaken in quite interesting ways, ways that help us see what is really at stake in a sometimes difficult to untangle thicket of argument. So despite the fact that I mostly disagree with their premises, their conclusions, and their arguments, I find myself considerably provoked by their book.

Although my disagreements with Cappelen and Lepore are pretty thoroughgoing, they are not utter and complete. They have glimpsed part of the truth about the underappreciated phenomenon of *modificational neutrality*. A predicate, for example, is modificationally neutral when it expresses a property or relation that is neutral with respect to the class of (metaphysically) possible modifications of that property or relation. For example, there are many ways for a thing to be red.[1] A thing can be red by being a particular shade of red. Or it can be red

[1] In *one* sense, *every* predicate may be thought to be "modificationally neutral". But it is important to distinguish two different things—the indefinite *grammatical* modifiability of a predicate and the, as it were, *metaphysical* modifiability of a full-blown but neutral property. Even semantically incomplete predicates, predicates that express no fully determinate property, are indefinitely grammatically modifiable. Some grammatically unmodified, but still indefinitely

by having some salient part or surface that is colored partly, mostly, or wholly red. Moreover, standards of redness vary with the type of object in question. Red dirt must be *through and though* red, but it suffices for the redness of a table that its upward-facing surface be red enough. Being scarlet, being cardinal, being through and through red, and having an upward-facing surface that is predominately red might be thought of as four different ways of being red. We might quite naturally ask what determinate way of being red is required for the truth of an instance of the scheme:

(1) x is red.

Since standards of redness apparently vary from object to object, one might be tempted to think that what proposition an instance of scheme (1) expresses will depend partly on exactly what noun phrase we replace the 'x' with. We typically express something different about the table when we call it red from what we express about dirt when we call it red. Even if we hold the object fixed but vary the context, standards of redness seem to vary as a function of our purposes and intentions. An object with a surface that is not red enough to count as red taken in isolation may count as *the red one* when it is redder than any of the alternatives.

Some may conclude that 'red' is semantically incomplete, that we must supply standards of redness in "context", that different standards may be operative in different contexts. There are many semantically incomplete predicates, but 'red' is not one of them. 'Red' is rather what I call modificationally neutral. Though there are many ways of being red, many metaphysical modifications of redness, the predicate 'red' expresses a property that is neutral with respect to *all* such modifications. More generally, a modificationally neutral assertion to the effect that x is P expresses the weakest possible positive proposition about the P-ness of x. If 'red' is modificationally neutral, then an instance of scheme (1) typically will not be strictly equivalent to any instance of scheme (2):

(2) *x* is *m-ly* red.

In many conversational settings, modificationally neutral assertions will be minimally informative and of minimal conversational relevance. However, speakers who make modificationally neutral assertions may pragmatically convey something more informative and less neutral by their words. That fact has led many to mistakenly see semantic incompleteness where there is only modificational neutrality. One who infers semantic incompleteness from data that support only a conclusion of modificational neutrality has committed what I

modifiable predicates may fail to express *any* determinate property until modified. Such a predicate would not ipso facto count as modificationally neutral. Modificationally neutral predicates express full-blown properties, just very undiscriminating, easy to instantiate properties.

call a fallacy of misplaced modification (Taylor 2007). Fallacies of misplaced modification lead many to believe that sentences with perfectly determinate, though modificationally neutral semantic contents stand in need of semantic supplementation. All forms of so-called radical contextualism are, I suspect, founded on fallacies of misplaced modification. Even some forms of moderate contextualism succumb locally to such fallacies. On this score, Cappelen and Lepore and I are in broad agreement. Indeed, their book is, in one way, really a sustained polemic against fallacies of misplaced modification. Unfortunately, they vastly overestimate the prevalence of modificational neutrality and are thereby led astray in their arguments against moderate contextualism.

2. LEPORE AND CAPPELEN AGAINST MODERATE CONTEXTUALISM

Lepore and Cappelen (2005: 7) define moderate contextualism by the following theses:

MC1. The expressions in the Basic Set do not exhaust all the sources of semantic context sensitivity [where the basic set is the set of indisputably context-sensitive expressions].
MC2. Many [syntactically well-formed] sentences . . . fail to have [complete] truth conditions or to semantically express a [complete] proposition.
MC3. For the cases in question, only their utterances semantically express a proposition, and have (interpretive) truth conditions, and so, take a truth value.

Against moderate contextualism, Cappelen and Lepore offer a collapsing argument. Since the moderate contextualist rejects radical contextualism, they will be home free if their collapsing argument succeeds. There is, of course, a facial difference between moderate and radical contextualism. The moderate contextualist claims that only *some* expressions outside the basic set are context-sensitive and/or semantically incomplete, while the radical contextualist claims that every expression or construction outside the basic set is context-sensitive.[2] If the moderate contextualist is to resist the collapsing argument, she owes us a principled way of augmenting the store of context-sensitive linguistic expressions and/or linguistic contexts by some but not all the expressions that fall outside the basic set. Cappelen and Lepore seem to hold that the moderate contextualist can't have that principled basis and that the contextualist's own methodology prevents her from doing so.

Consider the two currently extant forms of argument on behalf of moderate contextualism—arguments from incompleteness and context-shifting arguments. Context shifting arguments purport to show that what is (strictly,

[2] This isn't quite fair. The radical contextualist typically thinks that there are content generating processes of a pragmatic nature. It's not a fact about expressions taken one by one.

literally) said by an utterance *u*′ of some target sentence *S* need not be identical to what is (strictly literally) said by a distinct utterance *u*′ of *S*. Arguments from incompleteness purport to show that some sentences are such that, although they are syntactically well-formed and contain no expressions from the basic set, only *utterances* of the relevant sentence express complete propositions. Such a sentence, taken on its own, expresses no complete proposition, independently of context. Moderate contextualism is an attempt to explain the source of incompleteness and variability.

Now Cappelen and Lepore claim that as the arguments of the moderate contextualist actually go, they would suffice to show that some expression or construction not in the basic set is context-sensitive, only if they sufficed to show that *every* expression or construction not in the basic set is context-sensitive. All that prevents the moderate contextualist from seeing this, they claim, is a simple failure of imagination. As they put it, "Moderate contextualists are unimaginative radical contextualists."

Let's look more closely at the details of this claim. As construed by Cappelen and Lepore, the contextualist's context-shifting arguments are breathtaking in their simplicity.[3] A theorist imagines, perhaps in the company of some audience, uttering a sentence *S* in a certain context (more or less fulsomely described). She then imagines uttering *S* in some different context (also more or less fulsomely described). She produces in herself the "feeling" that the two imagined utterances say or express different propositions. The theorist concludes, apparently solely on the basis of this feeling, that the sentence is contextually variable. So, for example, I might imagine myself standing on a corner in San Francisco, sometime in late March. I might imagine myself producing an utterance *u* of "It's raining rather heavily." I might also imagine myself attending a conference in St Louis in late April and producing a distinct utterance *u*′ of "It's raining rather heavily." The contextualist intuition is that *u* and *u*′ express different propositions: *u*′ expresses a proposition about the weather in St Louis (at the time of the utterance); *u* expresses a proposition about the weather in San Francisco (at the time of the utterance). Given that, except for verb tense, our expression contains no *obviously* context-sensitive construction, the contextualist wonders how *u* and *u*′ manage to express propositions about entirely different places. Contextualists are not of a single mind. Jason Stanley posits unpronounced variables present in the "logical form" of the sentence (Stanley 2000). John Perry posits unarticulated constituents that somehow get introduced into the expressed proposition without being the value of any either explicit or suppressed constituent of the relevant sentence (Perry 1986). I have appealed to the subsyntactic basement of the lexicon (Taylor 2001). Substantive and methodological issues divide these and

[3] Cappelen and Lepore do distinguish what they call the inadequate context-shifting arguments of the contextualists from real context-shifting arguments. I discuss one of their three tests below.

other forms of moderate contextualism one from another.[4] Cappelen and Lepore are not interested in such internecine debates. They reject not so much the further substantive and methodological positions associated with this or that brand of moderate contextualism. They reject the starting intuition shared by all forms of contextualism. They deny that *u* and *u*′ express propositions about different places. On their view, holding the time of utterance fixed, the sentence "It's raining" (strictly literally) expresses one and the same proposition, no matter where it is said.[5]

To see why context-shifting arguments prove too much, if they prove anything at all, we are asked to consider cases in which the moderate contextualist denies, but the radical contextualist asserts, the presence of contextual variability. By the moderate contextualist's own standards of evidence, claim Cappelen and Lepore, the radical contextualist wins in every case.[6] Consider two different utterances of:

(3) Smith weighs 80kg

and consider two different scenarios:

> Scenario 1. Smith has been dieting for the last eight weeks. He steps on the scale one morning, naked, before breakfast (but after having gone to the bathroom) and it registers 80kg.
>
> Scenario 2. Smith is exactly as above. But (3) is uttered just as Smith is about to enter an elevator with a capacity of no more than an extra 80kg. Moreover, Smith is wearing a heavy overcoat and carrying a briefcase full of books.

Now we are supposed to have the intuition that, as uttered in scenario 1, (3) expresses a proposition about the weight of Smith's naked body, but as uttered in the second scenario, it expresses some proposition about the combined weights of Smith's body, his clothing, and his briefcase.

Or consider a case of a slightly different kind. What it takes for someone to count as having gone to the gym also turns out to be a variable matter. For consider an utterance of:

(4) John went to the gym

[4] It is worth noting that the class of views that counts as forms of moderate contextualism, by Cappelen and Lepore's lights, is quite a motley crew. It includes not only thinkers like Jason Stanley, but also thinkers like François Recanati. In defending one form of "moderate contextualist", I do not mean to defend all such views.

[5] Cappelen and Lepore's speech act pluralism does allow them to say that the total set of speech acts performed by distinct utterances of the same sentence may vary from context to context even if the narrowly semantic contents of distinct utterances remain the same.

[6] Of course, that victory turns out to be pyrrhic, since radical contextualism collapses of its own weight. But never mind those arguments here. I come to defend moderate contextualism, not radical contextualism.

as it occurs in three different speech situations:

1. It is common ground that John walks nightly for exercise and that he typically does so only after the gym has closed.
2. You are discussing John's exercise and diet routines with his trainer, who asks you about John's exercise today.
3. You are at a meeting of a construction company planning on putting down some hardwood floor at the local gym. The boss asks who went over to the gym to supervise the construction of a bathroom in its basement.

Again, Cappelen and Lepore claim that an utterance of (4) expresses something different in each of these speech situations. In the first scenario, it expresses a proposition that can be true even if John never entered the gym. In the second, it expresses a proposition that is false if John merely arrived in the vicinity of the gym, but never entered it. And in the third, it expresses a proposition that is false if John failed to engage in supervisory activities while inside the gym.

Now Cappelen and Lepore seem to believe that with enough imagination an intuition of shiftiness of the sort prompted by scenarios like these can be produced for just about any sentence. And they apparently think that the methodology employed by the moderate contextualist commits her to conceding on the basis of such examples that if context-sensitivity is anywhere (outside the basic set) then it's everywhere (outside the basic set). They enshrine this conviction as a principle:

> (GEN) With sufficient ingenuity, a Context Shifting Argument can be provided for any sentence whatsoever, and consequently for any expression.

3. SPEECH-SITUATIONAL SENSITIVITY VS. CONTEXT-SENSITIVITY

Before responding to these last claims, I distinguish two different flavors of sensitivity. I distinguish what I call speech-situational sensitivity from context sensitivity. By a context, I mean more or less what David Kaplan means (Kaplan 1989). We may take a context to be some collection of more or less objective features of a speech situation. Following Kaplan again, let us allow that context-sensitive expressions have "characters", understood as functions from Kaplanian contexts to contents. But there is another class of sensitive expressions that exhibit not Kaplanian context sensitivity, but sensitivity of another kind namely, what I call *speech-situational sensitivity*. An expression is speech-situationally sensitive, roughly, when its semantic contribution to the (narrowly) semantic content of the utterance in which it occurs is determined by the speech situation in which that utterance is produced. A speech situation may contain a Kaplanian context as a proper part, but speech situations typically contain more than is countenanced in a Kaplanian context. Though speech situations have many objective features—they happen at a place, over a span of time, in a possible world, and involve various participants—a speech situation should not be thought of primarily as abstract bundles of such features. A speech situation is primarily a locus of action. As such, it falls less to *logic* and more to *the theory of action* to study their effects on meaning. Moreover, it is important to stress that speech-situationally sensitive expressions should not be construed as pure indexicals. They are expressions of an entirely different semantic nature from the pure indexicals made prominent by Kaplan.[7]

My talk of the theory of action rather than logic will immediately suggest to some that speech-situational sensitivity lives not on the pristine pastures of semantics but in the untamed wilderness of pragmatics. But that reaction betrays a misunderstanding of both the reach of pragmatics and the nature of the so-called semantic–pragmatic interface. As I have argued in detail elsewhere and hope to demonstrate further in this chapter, there is no such interface (Taylor, in progress). There is no one place where the work of semantics ends and that of pragmatics begins. Pragmatics and semantics are everywhere intertwined because pragmatics happens everywhere. To say this is not to say that the semantic collapses into the pragmatic. It is not to deny that there is a distinction in both concept and principle to be had between the semantic and the pragmatic. It is, however, meant to suggest that some of what falls squarely within the domain of the semantic is enmeshed with the pragmatic from the very start. In fact, I have argued elsewhere that the lexicon itself often directly "licenses" the "intrusion" of the pragmatic into the determination of narrowly semantic content (see Taylor 2002, 2003, in press, in progress). Indeed, this is precisely what happens with expressions that exhibit speech-situational sensitivity.

I illustrate with an example. Consider:

(5) The cat is on the couch again.

I take (5) to be syntactically complete in the sense that it is a perfectly well-formed sentence, missing no syntactically mandatory elements. Despite its syntactic completeness (5), just taken on its own, independently of speech situation, appears to be semantically incomplete. Taken on its own it fails to express any fully determinate proposition. It no more expresses the proposition that the one and only cat in the universe is once again on the one and only couch in the universe than it expresses the proposition that the one and only cat owned

7 Kaplan erred, I think, in treating demonstratives and indexicals as members of a more or less uniform semantic category. I would argue that while indexicals are context-sensitive, demonstratives are speech-situationally sensitive. Indeed, in his discussion of the role of directing intentions in determining reference for demonstratives (1989) Kaplan himself comes close to grasping the difference.

by Ken Taylor is on the one and only couch on Ken Taylor's patio.[8] That is because neither the quantifier phrase 'the cat' nor the quantifier phrase 'the couch' has a fully determinate quantificational significance on its own, independently of speech situation. But once (5) is uttered in an appropriate speech situation, more or less determinate domains of quantification for the quantifier phrases 'the cat' and 'the couch' may be determined.

It is an interesting and significant question just *how* speech situational determination works. I cannot tell a detailed story about that here. I have argued elsewhere that quantifier phrases, and some limited array of other expressions, are associated with "suppressed" parameters of various sorts. I have conjectured that such parameters hang out in what I call the subsyntactic basement of the lexicon and are present more as what I call *subconstituents* of certain *words or phrases* rather than *constituents* of the *sentences* in which the relevant words or phrases occur. On this approach, an adequate *lexical* representation of an expression may need to specify certain sententially suppressed parameters such that:

1. The values of those parameters are to be speech-situationally determined.
2. The lexicon constrains the kind of value the relevant parameter can take and determines what contribution the value will make, once determined, to the proposition expressed by an utterance of any sentence in which the "master" expression will occur, typically by assigning the value of the suppressed parameter a theta-like role in the "argument structure" of the relevant expression.
3. The values of such parameters are typically not straightforwardly determined by objective features of the context, but by the speaker's intentions.
4. The speaker is free, in effect, to "load" a speech-situationally appropriate value onto the relevant parameter.
5. The relevant "parameter" need not be expressed as a *sentence level constituent* of any sentence in which the relevant expression occurs, though it may show up as a separable constituent of the expressed proposition.
6. As subconstituents rather than constituents, such parameters will, in the general case, be "below" the reach of sentence level quantifiers and so should *not* be thought of as occupying bindable positions in logical form.

[8] Cappelen and Lepore would, I suspect, agree with the claim that (5) does not express either the proposition that the one and only cat in the universe is on the one and only couch in the universe or the proposition that the one and only cat owned by Ken Taylor is on the one and only couch on Ken Taylor's patio. But they would explain this not by appeal to semantic incompleteness but by appeal to what I—but not they—call modificational neutrality. They would say that (5) expresses the proposition *that the cat is on the couch again*. Full stop. And asked for a further characterization of just what proposition that proposition is and when it is true, they would refuse to offer any such thing. Their minimal propositions are, in short, only pleonastically specifiable, it seems.

Points 1–6 need substantial further spelling out and more defense than I can afford to give them here. For present purposes, 3 and 4 are the important ones. They capture the thought that a speaker who chooses an expression with a suppressed parameter of the sort outlined above takes on a double burden—one semantic, one pragmatic. In particular, she takes on the semantic burden of loading a value of the requisite kind onto the suppressed parameter. And she takes on the communicative burden of making it mutually manifest to her communicative partners what value she intends to load. A speaker typically cannot rely on any merely objective feature of the surrounding context to do the value loading for her. Value loading is something that *she* must do. That is why the kind of sensitivity that such parameters display is *not* a form of *context sensitivity* but a form of *speech-situational sensitivity*. When expressions are speech-situationally sensitive, the content determining role falls not to "objective" features of the context, but to agents, the semantic and communicative burdens they undertake, and the actions they perform in discharging those burdens. It is right to think of the discharging of lexically generated semantic burdens as a bit of pragmatics. Typically, the pragmatics involved in the discharging of lexically generated semantic burdens involves what I call pre-propositional pragmatics. Pre-propositional pragmatics plays a decisive role in generating and making manifest what below I call the narrowly or purely semantic content of an utterance in a speech situation.

4. TOTAL UTTERANCE CONTENT VS. NARROWLY SEMANTIC CONTENT

I claimed above that there is no such thing as *the* semantics/pragmatics interface because there is no one place where semantics ends and pragmatics begins. Nonetheless, I grant that there is a distinction between *what is strictly, literally said* by an utterance and *what is merely pragmatically conveyed*, somehow or other, by that utterance. This distinction in fact turns out to be highly relevant to Cappelen and Lepore's collapsing arguments against moderate contextualism. Cappelen and Lepore offer up various scenarios in which what is communicated by a given form of words varies from situation to situation. They insist that for any form of words such variation is always possible. But if mere variation suffices to establish context sensitivity, moderate contextualism quickly collapses into radical contextualism. But this line of reasoning presupposes that the moderate contextualist can have no principled basis for distinguishing two different sorts of situational or contextual variation—variation in what is strictly literally said or expressed by an utterance and variation in what is merely pragmatically conveyed by an utterance, even as what is said remains fixed.

Cappelen and Lepore seem tacitly to concede that some such strategy is available to the moderate contextualist. They grant, for example, that their intuition pumps are effective against moderate contextualism only if the pumped intuitions can be shown not to be due to "ambiguity, syntactic ellipsis, polysemy, non-literality, or vagueness". To that list, they might have added Gricean conversational implicatures, Searlean indirect speech acts, or what I have elsewhere called pseudo-assertion rather than assertion (Taylor 2000). Curiously, they claim that the range of cases they have chosen is "obviously not explicable by any of these irrelevant factors". They add that "As far as we know, no one has suggested the examples we will now utilize can be so explained." Consequently, they apparently feel no need to even try out alternative explanations. This is a puzzling argumentative strategy. Either the moderate contextualist will contest their particular examples or she will not. If she does not, they can't be used to make any point against moderate contextualism and in favor of radical contextualism. There might still be dividing issues about the source and nature of the alleged context sensitivity in such cases. But such issues are irrelevant to any argument of Cappelen and Lepore's. On the other hand, if the cases *are* contested, then Cappelen and Lepore must be accusing the moderate contextualist of missing the obvious. But is it really "obvious" in each case that no alternative explanation of the sort a moderate contextualist would want to give of the pumped intuitions is available?

Now Cappelen and Lepore apparently do think that it is obvious that the speaker *asserts* something different, something non-minimal, in each of the imagined alternative speech situations. In this, I think, they side with the radical contextualist against the moderate contextualist. Of course, against the radical contextualist, Cappelen and Lepore claim that there is also something constant but minimal *asserted* in the two scenarios. By contrast, a moderate contextualist who would deny the presence of any surprise sensitivity in (3) above, for example, might say that by an utterance of (3) at t a speaker strictly, literally asserts the non-minimal proposition that Smith's body weighs 80kg at t.[9] And he might

[9] I am setting to one side here delicate issues raised by the fact that we now know that weight (as opposed to mass) is relative to gravitational field. It is worth noting, though, that the discovery that weight, as opposed to mass, is relative to a gravitational field, even though the relation expressed by the verb 'weighs' in our language has no explicit argument place for gravitational field, raises interesting semantic and pragmatic issues not at all addressed by Cappelen and Lepore. Theories that posit such things as unarticulated constituents or processes like free enrichment are in part motivated by cases like these. On such approaches, there is *no* claim that the verb 'weighs' is itself a context-sensitive expression. Nor is the claim that sentences containing this verb have hidden indexical elements or suppressed argument places or anything of that sort. Perry claims e.g. that *speakers* may introduce unarticulated constituents into a proposition even when that constituent turns out not to be the value of *any* constituent of the relevant sentence—though he does sometimes say that an expression or construction may "call for" the introduction of an unarticulated sentence. His approach is not entirely dissimilar to Recanati's appeal to "free enrichment". Though free enrichment is viewed by Recanati as a primary and therefore mandatory pragmatic process, it does not require that some either explicit or hidden *constituent* take the enriched content as its own value. It is fair to wonder for both Perry and Recanati what a sentence is doing semantically expressing a proposition some of whose constituents are not values of any constituent of the relevant sentence. But that is a question for another setting. I make this point because there is a quite natural-seeming

insist that the truth or falsity of this proposition depends, in each scenario, entirely on how things are by Smith's body. He might say, moreover, that if we hold time fixed, then we get the very same non-minimal proposition expressed in both scenario 1 and scenario 2. When it comes to explaining the felt *communicative* difference between the two scenarios, the moderate contextualist need simply distinguish the *total utterance content* of an utterance from the *purely or narrowly semantic content* of an utterance. The purely or narrowly semantic content of an utterance will be the proposition or propositions, if any, that are determined by a sentence's syntactic structure and the combination of lexically, contextually, and speech-situationally determined semantic values of its semantically valued constituents. The total utterance content of an utterance is the totality of contents conveyed in the uttering of the relevant sentence in the relevant speech situation. That which is part of total utterance content, but not part of the narrow semantic content of the utterance, I call pragmatic externalities of the relevant utterance. On just about anybody's theory, the act of uttering a sentence will almost always produce some pragmatic externality or other, sometimes many such externalities. To this extent we are all descendants of Grice. But there are many proposals about just what sorts of propositions (or non-propositions) count as pragmatic externalities of an utterance. Curiously, Cappelen and Lepore canvass none of them. I am thinking not just of Gricean conversational implicatures, but of Perryesque reflexive propositions, of propositions made inferentially salient by the explicit adding of some proposition or other to the ever developing common ground, of propositions generated by accommodation, and of propositions generated by what I have called one and half stage pragmatics.

Since it may be the least familiar, let me focus briefly on the latter. Start by recalling my earlier claims about the semantics of

(5) The cat is on the couch again.

way of reading Cappelen and Lepore in which their view is more or less a notational variant on views like Perry's and/or Recanati's, despite rhetorical abuse to which they subject such views. After all, Cappelen and Lepore claim that what we strictly literally say in making an utterance goes beyond—and typically far beyond—the "narrow" semantic content of the utterance. Like Perry and like Recanati they agree, in particular, that once you've fixed the meanings of all the words and have provided values for all the explicit indexicals, you still need not have the full content in the sense of "what is said" of the speech act performed in making an utterance. Moreover, they agree with Perry and with Recanati that the additional ingredients of what is said that are somehow generated in a speech situation need not and typically are not the semantic values of any either suppressed or explicit constituents of the uttered sentence. So far then it looks as though Cappelen and Lepore may have simply rediscovered the radical contextualism against which they so intently rail. As far as I can tell all that is supposed to *save* them from this charge is their quite implausible claim that an expression like 'tall' expresses on its own, independently of context, a determinate (but apparently only pleonastically specifiable) property had by all tall things and no non-tall things. But this claim is quite frankly incredible, so much so, that one wonder if its only job is to prevent their view from collapsing into radical contextualism. And I say this as one who believes that they have dimly glimpsed a part of the truth about what I call the modificational neutrality of some predicates.

I suggested that a speaker who utters (5) in a speech situation takes on a double burden—the semantic burden of loading a domain of quantification onto a suppressed parameter and the communicative burden of making the loaded value mutually manifest. But *taking on* semantic and communicative burdens in a speech situation does not ipso facto entail successfully and openly *discharging* them. A speaker may fail to have a determinate domain of quantification in mind when she uses a phrase like 'the cat' or 'the couch'. Even if she does have a determinate domain in mind, she may fail to make it mutually manifest. But such failures are often the stuff of which further communication can be made. Suppose, for example, that Cottontail, the cat, and the green couch on Ken Taylor's patio are highly salient in a speech situation in which I utter (5) to my wife, Claire. Suppose that it is common ground between Claire and Ken that Cottontail frequently sleeps on that very couch and common ground that she is not allowed to do so. In that speech situation, my utterance of (5) may convey to my wife the pragmatically external singular proposition that Cottontail is on that very couch. And it may do so, I have argued elsewhere, even if I never discharge my semantic burden of loading a value onto the suppressed domain of quantification parameters associated with 'the cat' and 'the couch'. Indeed, we may say that it is *by* failing to discharge my burdens and by doing so openly that I generate the relevant pragmatic externality. I call externalities generated in this way one and half stage externalities to indicate that they are generated as we make the journey from sentence meaning to narrowly semantic utterance content. One kind of speech act we perform in the course of generating a one and half stage externality is what I have called *pseudo-assertion*. Pseudo-asserting a proposition is a way of putting forth a proposition as true, not by strictly literally asserting it in the course of what I below call an immediate speech act; nor by implicating it via a "post-propositional" conversational implicature. Pseudo-asserting happens on the way toward a flat out assertion and can happen whether the assertion itself comes off or fails to come off because of the failure to discharge the required semantic burdens.

The existence of one and half stage externalities underlines the myriad levels at which pragmatics plays a role in generating total utterance content. Again, pragmatics happens everywhere. Pragmatics plays a decisive role in completing semantically incomplete sentences, in ways constrained but not fully determined by the lexicon. During the lexically constrained journey from sentence meaning to narrowly semantic content, pragmatics often generates one and half stage externalities along the way. Nor is pragmatics done when the journey from sentence meaning to narrowly semantic content is complete. Suppose, for example, that I say to my son, who is in the kitchen as I enter and start preparing breakfast for myself "Have you had much breakfast?" I have done several things. I have *presupposed* that he has already had some breakfast. If he *accommodates* that presupposition, I have added a proposition to our common ground. I have *directly asked* him whether he has had much breakfast and have *indirectly offered* to make more if he wants it. The fact that I can offer by asking depends partly on the content of my question and partly on the Searlean background. Consider a parallel question asked in a therapist's session with a couple experiencing marital difficulties. The couple has had an initial consultation. They are back for a follow-up visit. The therapist asks the couple. "Have you had much sex?" Whatever else she is doing, she is clearly not *offering* them sex. She is not even *inviting* them to engage in sex together.

We do *lots* of things, many of them content generating, in making an utterance. One way to say this is to say that we are liable to perform *many speech acts* in any *one act of uttering*. The diverse speech acts we perform in a single uttering may have *many different contents*. If this sounds like a version of what Cappelen and Lepore call speech act pluralism, perhaps it is. But if so, then speech act pluralism is an unremarkable doctrine, one that is endorsed, in some form or other, by just about *everybody* who has ever been concerned with the semantics and pragmatics of communication. But if that is right, it's hard to see why Cappelen and Lepore are convinced that their collapsing argument does any work at all against moderate contextualism. My guess is that they think such strategies as I gestured toward are legitimate only if they are accompanied by a solution to the demarcation problem. By the demarcation problem, I mean the problem of demarcating, in a principled way, that which belongs to narrowly or purely semantic content of an utterance "neatly" from that which is a pragmatic externality of the utterance. In addition to the demarcation problem, there is also what I call the generation problem. That is the problem of explaining how the externalities of an utterance are generated by facts about the speech situation. The demarcation and the generation problems may be conceptually distinct, but they are likely to be methodologically intertwined. I suspect that the best way to demarcate the pragmatic externalities of an utterance from the narrow semantic content of the utterance is to show how each is generated. And it is arguable that any purported solution to the demarcation problem that left it entirely mysterious how the demarcated externalities were generated would, for that reason alone, be unsatisfying.

Theorists of various stripes have offered up solutions to both the demarcation problem and the generation problem. But Cappelen and Lepore *seem* to believe that the very methodology employed by the moderate contextualist makes it impossible for her to provide any principled solution to the demarcation problem. Such desperate and forlorn attempts as have been attempted amount to either stubbornly digging in the heels in denial or unrealistically insisting that introspectable qualities decisively settle what belongs to semantic content and what counts as a pragmatic externality or working piecemeal on clever local fix after clever local fix, while missing the global shape of the problem. What underlies these desperate attempts to draw a boundary that apparently cannot be drawn—at least not by any methods plausibly available to the moderate contextualist—is supposed to be the "blind adherence" to the mistaken assumption that:

> A theory of semantic content is adequate just in case it accounts for all or most of the intuitions speakers have about speech act content, i.e. intuitions about what speakers say, assert, claim, and state by uttering sentences. (Cappelen and Lepore 2005: 53)

The key to semantic progress, Cappelen and Lepore claim, is to abandon this blind adherence and to recognize that "there is no close and immediate connection between speech act content and semantic content".

This claim is rather startling. The very distinction introduced above between narrowly semantic content and total utterance content already takes something rather like Cappelen and Lepore's proposed corrective more or less fully on board. Moreover, I have stressed only a few of the myriad ways in which pragmatic externalities may be generated and how greatly those externalities may diverge from the narrow semantic content of the utterance. Cappelen and Lepore may mean by "speech act content" something different from what I mean by "total utterance content". It is plausible, though not undeniable, that for every sentence *s*, there is at least one speech act *a* performed in the uttering of *s* such that *a* more or less directly "inherits" its content from *s*, as *s* occurs in the relevant context and speech situation. Call any such *a*, an *immediate speech act* performed in the uttering of *s* and say that the *immediate speech act content(s)* of an utterance is (are) the content(s) of the immediate speech act(s) performed in the uttering of *s*. Immediate speech act contents are, by definition, identical to narrowly semantic contents. In effect, radical contextualists deny that there are immediate speech acts, but Cappelen and Lepore do not. They are quite explicit that *one* of the things that gets asserted in a pluralistic speech act is a minimal proposition. Moderate contextualists, on the other hand, can certainly allow that there are both immediate speech acts and mediate speech acts. But notice also that, on my own brand of moderate contextualism, which makes room for one and half stage pragmatic externalities, a speaker can perform a contentful speech act even if she performs no immediate speech act. Recall, for example, the notion of pseudo-assertion introduced briefly above. I have argued elsewhere that a speaker who utters the sentence 'Santa Claus isn't coming tonight' directly *asserts* no fully determinate and truth-evaluable proposition (Taylor 2000). 'Santa Claus' is an empty name. Empty names are, in a sense, devices of direct reference "in waiting." Because of the emptiness of 'Santa Claus' there is no complete proposition, but at best a "gappy" propositional frame, to serve as an immediate speech act content for an utterance of this sentence. Nonetheless, a speaker may *pseudo-assert*, via one and half stage pragmatics, a complete proposition via such an utterance. She may pseudo-assert something like the proposition that no jolly, bearded man, wearing red, who lives at the North Pole is coming tonight by such an utterance.

Given the variety of ways that speech act contents can be generated and the variety of ways they relate to narrowly semantic content, Cappelen and Lepore must be assuming that the moderate contextualist is committed to thinking that *only* immediate speech acts count as assertings or claimings. That is, they must be assuming that for the moderate contextualist no pragmatically external proposition, however generated, can be the content of any asserting or claiming. It is certainly true that the moderate contextualist is likely to hold that not all speech acts performed in the uttering of a sentence are immediate speech acts and not all speech act contents are immediate speech act contents. But she may or may not want to reserve titles like 'assertion' or 'claim' for immediate speech acts. For all Cappelen and Lepore have to say about "assertion" the question of which of the many speech acts performed in an utterance act deserves the title 'assertion' would seem to rest on nothing deeper than arbitrary linguistic legislation. To say the least, it is hard to see why they think any particular decision on this issue is supposed to lead the moderate contextualist into troubled waters.

I do not mean to suggest that in fact settling which speech acts deserve the title 'assertion' must be an altogether trivial matter. I do not doubt that the title 'assertion' properly belongs to some privileged class of speech acts. And I suspect that there may be some robust principle on the basis of which we might hope to pick out that privileged class. Assertion is plausibly distinguished from other speech acts partly by what we might call its commitive force. To assert that p is, at least in part, to stake out, via an utterance, a commitment to it being the case that p. One can, perhaps, imagine an argument to the effect that the pragmatic externalities of our utterances do not carry anything like the commitment characteristic of full-bore assertion. If that were so, it would give us some principled grounds for reserving the title 'assertion' for propositions directly expressed via immediate speech acts. Such issues are worthy of further exploration and they may yield something deep and revealing both about the nature of assertion and about the difference between immediate and non-immediate speech acts. But as far as I can tell, Cappelen and Lepore have nothing at all to say that might illuminate such issues. Absent further analysis of the very idea of an assertion on their part, it is quite premature of them to conclude anything at all about how much of the many things we do in making an utterance should count as assertions.[10]

10 A great deal of philosophical work remains to be done on the notion of assertion, and on the relationship between the narrowly semantic content of an utterance and its assertoric content. But a start has been made. For some illumination, see Soames (2004, forthcoming). Though Soames is inclined to reject a form of moderate contextualism that posits hidden indexicals in LF, his views seem entirely consistent with the form of contextualism I have been at pains to defend in this chapter. See also Stojanovic (2003). She offers an illuminating discussion of just how complex the relation can be between what a speaker *says* by uttering a sentence and the semantic content of that sentence. See also Bach (2004): he does not think of himself as a moderate contextualist, but many of his observations about the gap between semantic content and assertoric content can be taken on by moderate contextualism. But the main point here is that nothing at all prevents moderate contextualism from fully acknowledging that the relationship between assertoric content and narrowly semantic content is complex and multifarious. Indeed, it strikes me as just a mistake to say, as Cappelen and Lepore do, that the moderate contextualist seeks to load all that is asserted by an utterance into the narrowly semantic content of the utterance. Certainly, *this* moderate contextualist

5. INDIRECT REPORTS AND SPEECH SITUATIONAL SENSITIVITY

In this section, I explore more fully the theoretical significance of the distinction between speech-situational and context sensitivity. I begin by considering one of the three tests proposed by Cappelen and Lepore for detecting "genuine" context sensitivity. They claim that context-sensitive expressions typically block what they call inter-contextual disquotational indirect (ICDI) reports. Suppose that Smith makes the following utterance on Tuesday:

(6) Jones will come home tomorrow.

And suppose that on Wednesday, Black wants to report what Smith said on Tuesday. She can't do so simply by disquoting, as in:

(7) Smith says that Jones will come home tomorrow.

Rather, if Black wants to stick with an indexical in her report, she must switch indexicals, as in:

(8) Smith said that Jones would come home today.

Now Cappelen and Lepore admit that there are prima-facie exceptions to the apparent regularity that context-sensitive expressions block ICDI reports. That is perhaps why they say only that context-sensitive expressions *typically* block ICDI reports. As they put it,

> Sentences containing 'I' cannot be disquotationally indirectly reported (*except by self-reporters*); utterances of 'now' cannot be disquotationally reported (*except by simultaneous reporters*); utterances containing the demonstrative expression 'that' cannot be disquotationally reported (*except by co-demonstrating reports*) and so on for each member of the basic set. (Cappelen and Lepore 2005: 108–9; emphasis added)

Arguably, however, such apparent exceptions to the rule are directly predictable from semantic character of the relevant expression and consequently are untroubling. Suppose that in context C I, Ken Taylor, utter:

(9) I [Ken Taylor] am hungry.

has not attempted to do so. To be sure, there is an issue that does separate moderate from radical contextualist on this score. Radical contextualists tend to view the mechanisms that somehow bridge the gap, when there is one, between narrowly semantic content and assertoric content as in some sense unconstrained. On my view, the generation of assertoric content is *semantically constrained without being semantically determined.*

As long as I am the speaker in C′, I can disquotationally report in C′ what I said in C without switching indexicals, as in:

(10) I [Ken Taylor] said that I [Ken Taylor] am hungry.

That is because an occurrence of 'I' denotes the speaker whether it occurs in embedded or unembedded position. To run truly afoul of Cappelen and Lepore's ICDI test, we would need a context C′ in which someone other than me could report by using 'I' in C′ what I said by using 'I' in C. That is something that can't be done. But only such a context would count as "relevantly different" for the purposes of our current test for context sensitivity. As Cappelen and Lepore put it:

> Suppose you suspect, or at least want to ascertain, whether *e* is context sensitive. Take an utterance *u* of a sentence S containing *e* in context C. Let C′ be a context *relevantly different from* C (i.e. different according to the standards significant according to the contextualists about *e*). If there is a true disquotational* indirect report if *u* in C′, then that's evidence S is context insensitive. (Disquotational* just means you can adjust the semantic values of components of S that are generally recognized as context sensitive, i.e., we just test for the controversial examples.) (2005: 89)

To be sure, they concede that, even when two contexts C and C′ are relevantly different, a context-sensitive expression *e* may still turn out to have the same value in both C and in C′. But they insist that when this happens it is a mere accident that it does. They say:

> So, if *e* is a context sensitive expression and Rupert uses *e* in context C, and Lepore uses it in context C′, and the relevant contextual features change, then *it will be just an accident if their uses of e end up with the same semantic value.* In particular, if Lepore finds himself in a context other than Rupert's and wants to utter a sentence that matches the semantic content of Rupert's utterance of sentence with *e*, he can't use *e* i.e. he can't report Rupert's utterance disquotationally. (Ibid.; emphasis added)

To appreciate the full significance of these caveats, it will help to consider a few other examples drawn from the basic set. Take the case of 'we'. At first glance, it may appear that 'we' sometimes does and sometimes does not block ICDI reports. For consider the following examples:

(11) We [S, S_1] had a good time. (Said by S, to S_1 and S_2)
(12) S said that we[S_1, S] had a good time. (Said by S_1 to S_2)
(13) S said that we [S_2, ?] had a good time. (Said by S_2 to S_1.)

S_1 can utter (12) truly as a way of reporting what S said to S_1 and S_2. But S_2 cannot utter (13) truly by way of reporting what S said. If S_2 wants to report what S said, he has to utter something like:

(14) S said that *you* [S, S_1] had a good time. (said by S_2 to S_1)

Now one might suppose that we have three different contexts for 'we' here.

A: S is speaking, addressing S_1 and S_2, and referring to S and S_1.
B: S_1 is speaking, addressing S_2, and referring to S and S_1.
C: S_2 is speaking, addressing S_1, and referring to [S_2, ?].

If just *any* difference in who is speaking or who is being addressed counts as a *relevant* difference in context for 'we', it would seem to follow directly that 'we' is equivocal with respect to the ICDI test.

But some caution is required here. It is open to Cappelen and Lepore to claim that only the shift from context A to context C is relevant to the question whether 'we' blocks ICDI reports. It is entirely unsurprising that in shifting from A to B 'we' does not block ICDI reports. S_1 is a member of the reference set for 'we' in A. Since S_1 is speaking in B, S_1 is guaranteed to be a member of the reference set for 'we' as it occurs in context B. These facts guarantee that the reference set for 'we' in B overlaps with, and may possibly be identical to, the reference set for 'we' in A. On the other hand, since S_2 is *not* a member of the reference set for 'we' in A and since S_2 is guaranteed, in virtue of the fact that S_2 is speaking, to be a member of the reference set for 'we' in C, the reference set for 'we' in A and the reference set for 'we' in C are guaranteed to be different. And that is why, Cappelen and Lepore will no doubt say, the shift from A to C is, but the shift from A to B is not, relevant to the ICDI test. That is, we can read Cappelen and Lepore as insisting that a context shift from C to C′ is ICDI relevant, as we might call it, for 'we' just in case the reference set for 'we' shifts from C to C′. One way to guarantee this result is simply to stipulate that a context must "contain" a reference set for 'we' and that contexts that contain different reference sets are ipso facto different contexts.

I have no particular objection to taking the reference set for 'we' to be one constituent of context among others. But notice that if we have a sufficient basis for making that move in the case of 'we' we will also have a sufficient basis for making a similar move for various other members of the basic set. We can't stop there. There is no basis for confining this strategy to members of the so-called basic set. Indeed, I shall argue that we pretty quickly get to a point where we begin to lose hold of any principled distinction between expressions within the basic set and expressions without the basic set.

To begin to appreciate why this is so, notice that, although S_1 *can* truly report in B what S says in A via an embedded use of 'we', nothing merely linguistic guarantees that S's use of 'we' will co-refer with S_1's use of 'we'. All that is linguistically guaranteed is that S_1 refers to at least herself by her use of 'we'. From a purely linguistic perspective it is *always* an "accident" of usage if two tokens of 'we' co-refer. That is, there is no purely linguistic relation between pairs of contexts, *x* and *y*, such that an occurrence of 'we' in x co-refers with an occurrence of 'we' in *y* that would serve to distinguish such pairs from pairs of contexts x^*, y^* in which occurrences of 'we' fail to co-refer. That is because who, if anyone, besides the speaker herself is included in the reference set for 'we' is entirely up to the speaker and her contingent referential intentions. Where a speaker S_1 does not use 'we' with the same referential intention as S, then S_1 cannot indirectly report what S said via an embedded use of 'we'. Where S and S_1 do use 'we' with the same referential intentions, S_1 can indirectly report what S said via an embedded use of 'we'.

We find a similar regularity for other members of the basic set as well. Consider, for example, 'that'. Suppose that S utters the following:

(15) That [shirt A] is a lovely shirt.

Suppose that S_1 intends to report what S has said. In the right sort of "context" S_1 can do so by uttering:

(16) S said that that [?] is a lovely shirt.

What counts as a context of the right sort? The answer is obvious. Any "context" in which S_1 refers to shirt A by her use of 'that' will suffice. And any context in which she does not refer to shirt A will not suffice. Once again, nothing merely linguistic guarantees that S's use of 'that' and S_1's use of 'that' will co-refer in the requisite way. Once again, we may stipulate for the purposes of ICDI testing that *only* contexts in which the referent of 'that' shifts are ICDI relevant. And once again, it is only this stipulation that preserves the claimed regularity that expressions in the basic set one and all block ICDI reports.[11]

[11] Consider the case of so-called contextuals like 'foreign'. Suppose that I'm in France, surrounded by a bunch of locals. And suppose that I look puzzled upon observing some local custom. Picking up on my look, François utters:

(a) You are a foreigner who doesn't understand our customs.

Now suppose that I am back in America and Claire wants to inform me about what François says. She might utter something like:

(b) François says that you are a foreigner who doesn't understand their customs.

At first glance, it looks as though Claire can disquotationally* report in America what François said in France using 'foreigner'. But mere disquotation leaves it open whether Claire intends by her embedded use of 'foreigner' to represent Francois as attributing the property of being foreign to America or foreign to France to me. Nothing merely linguistic settles this issue. It is settled by Claire's intentions and only her intentions. Once again, from the linguistic point of view it is merely an accident if one speaker's use of 'foreign' is indexed to the same country as another speaker's is. And once again it follows that if we want 'foreign' to comport with the ICDI test we simply have to stipulate that only in contexts in which different index countries are intended does 'foreign' block

I will not try to decide whether there is a principled basis, independent of Cappelen and Lepore's prior commitment to ICDI, for construing ICDI relevance in just the requisite way. Some will no doubt see the relevant stipulation as arbitrary and question-begging. But I am not certain. If one assumes that the ICDI test enjoys a certain prima-facie warrant, one can use it as a defeasible heuristic for determining what the context must be for various candidate context-sensitive expressions. Given an intuitively context-sensitive expression, one asks what the context must be if the relevant expression is to systematically pass the ICDI test. This is not to deny the possibility that one may decide either to abandon the ICDI test or revise one's intuitive judgements of context-sensitivity by a process of semantic reflective equilibrium. But I will not explore such issues further at present. That is because I shall argue that, whether one regards ICDI relevance as arbitrary and stipulative or as a well-motivated heuristic, it turns out that *whatever* one wants to say about expressions like 'that' or 'we' or 'foreigner'—expressions supposedly contained within the basic set—one should *also* say about expressions like 'ready' that supposedly fall outside the basic set. That is to say, once one has restricted the notion of context in ways that make the expressions of the basic set comport with the ICDI test, it turns out that, if we make similar restrictions for expressions outside the basic set, they too comport with ICDI.

Consider 'ready'. Cappelen and Lepore claim that sentences like (6) stand in sharp contrast with sentences like:

(17) John is ready.

To see why, consider two different speech situations:

S1. In a conversation about exam preparation, someone raises the question of whether John is well prepared [for the exam]. Nina utters (17).

S2. Three people are about to leave the apartment; they are getting dressed for heavy rain. Nina utters (17).

Cappelen and Lepore intuit that 'ready' does not block inter-contextual disquotational indirect reports. They claim that a speaker in a third context can straightforwardly and truly assert each of the following:

(18) Nina said that John is ready. (With respect to (17) as uttered in S1)

(19) Nina said that John is ready. (With respect to (17) as uttered in S2)

(20) In S1 and S2, Nina said that John is ready.

ICDI reports. And once again, one way to implement this suggestion is to make the indexed country an ingredient of "context". Of course, the way a country gets to count as the indexed country is not simply by being the country in which the speaker is speaking, or the country in which the speaker is located, but only by being the country to which the speaker intends to index her use of 'foreign'.

Now I do not deny that a speaker *can* utter 'Nina said that John is ready' and thereby either pragmatically convey or strictly literally assert something true in each of the imagined scenarios. The interesting questions concern *what* a speaker who utters this sentence in various speech situations says or conveys, *how* she manages to say or convey that very thing, and *whether* the situation in which the indirect report is made plays any role in determining what is said by the relevant utterance. Cappelen and Lepore apparently believe that an utterance of this sentence will express or convey at least some merely minimal—or as I prefer to call it modificationally neutral—proposition. In addition, they apparently believe that the speech-situation or context plays no role in determining what is strictly literally said by the utterance of such a report. But there is, I shall argue, no direct evidence to support either of these claims and ample evidence in support of the claim that the relevant indirect reports are themselves speech-situationally sensitive. Indeed, it turns out that 'ready' behaves very much like 'that' or 'we' in the context of inter-contextual disquotational indirect reports.

Notice to begin that an utterance of 'Nina said that John is ready' can itself at least convey a non-minimal proposition. Moreover, such an utterance conveys different non-minimal propositions in different speech situations. Suppose, for example, that John, Bill, Nina, and Sally are planning to go to the theater together. Suppose, moreover, that Sally is in the middle of writing. She tells the others that she will stop writing and get ready (to leave for the theater) when, and only when, John is ready to leave. Addressing Bill, who cannot see for himself that John is ready, Nina utters:

(21) John is ready. Go tell Sally.

Bill complies. Addressing Sally, he utters:

(22) Nina says that John is ready.

He might want to make explicit the relevance of his report of what Nina said to the broader conversational purposes. One way for him to do so would be to utter:

(23) Nina says that John is ready. So let's get going.

It seems undeniable that at least the total utterance content of (22) as uttered in the imagined scenario includes some non-minimal, non-neutral proposition—in particular, the proposition that Nina says that John is ready *to leave*. But the pressing question is whether the total utterance content of (22) also includes, as the narrowly semantic content of the utterance, the modificationally neutral proposition that Nina said that John is, as it were, barely ready. Moreover, it is fair to wonder whether we in any way cognize that modificationally neutral proposition, if there is one, in the course of cognizing the non-neutral content that would evidently be communicated if our imagined scenario were actual.

Before answering, suppose that we vary the case. Sally, Nina, and Bill are about to have dinner. Sally wants to keep working until dinner is ready (to eat). When it is ready, she will stop working and come to the table. Addressing Bill, Nina, who is cooking the pork, the last part of the meal, utters:

(24) The pork is ready. Go tell Sally.

Bill complies. Addressing Sally, he utters:

(25) Nina says that the pork is ready.

If Bill wants to make more fully explicit the relevance of his report of Nina's assertion, he might report that assertion as follows:

(26) Nina says that the pork is ready. So let's eat.

Again, it is clear that a certain non-minimal proposition, the proposition that Nina says that the pork is ready *to eat* is *somehow* conveyed by the utterance of (25) and/or (26) in the imagined scenario.

Now lets combine our two earlier scenarios into a third scenario. John is about to leave and the pork is about to be served. Sally has made it clear that she wants to be told both when the pork is ready to be served and when John is ready to leave for the airport. She intends to have dinner with Nina and Bill when the pork is ready and intends to say goodbye to John when he is ready. Addressing Bill, Nina utters:

(27) John is ready and the pork is ready. Go tell Sally.

Bill, addressing Sally, utters the following:

(28) Nina says that John is ready and that the pork is ready.

Again, it seems intuitively obvious that, at the bare minimum, at least the total utterance content of (28), as uttered in the imagined scenario, contains the non-neutral proposition that Nina says that John is ready *to leave* and the pork is ready *to eat*. Cappelen and Lepore predict that there will also be a reading of (27) in which Bill's report ascribes to Nina the assertion that bare readiness holds of both John and the pork. Any further attribution to Nina of a predication of a modification of readiness communicated by Bill's utterance must, on their view, be part of the total utterance content of Bill's utterance, but not part of its narrowly semantic content.

I suspect that Cappelen and Lepore would support this claim by arguing that from (28) something else follows, namely:

(29) Nina says that both John and the pork are ready.

And I'm guessing that they will say that (29) *does* have a modificationally neutral reading. They may even insist that (29) *must* have a modificationally neutral reading. After all, (29) seems intuitively true in the imagined scenario. But only on the modificationally neutral reading of 'ready' could (29) be true, they are likely to claim.

This last claim seems mistaken, however. It is true that in uttering (29) Bill *utters* only one token predicate. But if he speaks truly, *what he says* by uttering the one token predicate must involve two distinct predications of readiness—one with respect to John, the other with respect to the pork. Bill represents Nina as predicating readiness twice over, but he uses only one token of 'ready' to do so. With respect to the pork, he represents Nina as predicating readiness to be eaten. With respect to the John, he represents Nina as predicating readiness to leave.[12] Or so it seems to me. At the bare minimum, it seems clear that the total utterance content of Bill's utterance in the envisioned speech situation does contain two such predications. It would be a further, more complicated step to show that the narrowly semantic content of the utterance involves a double predication. It would also be a further step to show that the narrowly semantic content of Bill's utterance does not involve a double predication. I don't propose to settle that issue. There is, however, no antecedent reason to think that the presence of a single token predicate in a sentence implies that the content of the sentence can contain only a single predication. In (29) we have *two* embedded subjects that need not be taken collectively. Indeed, it seems clear that readiness is predicated of the subjects severally rather than collectively. Since the embedded subjects need not be taken collectively, the sentence need not represent Nina as predicating *the same modification of readiness* to the two subjects. Explaining exactly how a double predication of readiness, with each involving a different modification of readiness, gets introduced into either the

[12] Notice that in (29) John and the pork are differently thematically related to the states for which they are implicitly represented as being ready. John is the *agent* of the implicit act of leaving, while the pork is the *theme* of the implicit act of eating. This is further evidence that (29) is not after all modificationally neutral. But this observation raises an intriguing further issue. Just how do we explain the thematic variability of 'ready'. It seems inadequate to suggest that 'ready' has a subsyntactic parameter in my sense with a singled, fixed theta-role. A more initially tempting hypothesis is that 'John is ready [to leave]' and 'The pork is ready [to eat]' are derived from two different underlying syntactic structures. Going this route would suggest that apparently elliptical examples like 'John is ready [to leave] and the pork is [ready to eat] too' should be unacceptable. Unfortunately, I lack the space to explore this matter further here. Thanks to anonymous referee for raising this intriguing issue, which I gather is discussed in a great deal more detail by at least one paper in the current volume.

narrowly semantic or total utterance content of an utterance of (29) is a slightly delicate matter. Whatever the exact details, it seems clear that Cappelen and Lepore have not yet discharged their burden of showing that an utterance like (29) is strictly literally true *only* on a minimal or modificational neutral reading of 'ready'.

I have been exploiting speech situations in which any supposed minimal or modificationally neutral reading of 'ready' is either minimally salient or entirely inaccessible. Cappelen and Lepore will no doubt insist that we need also to consider contexts in which the minimal or neutral reading is the *only* accessible and/or natural reading. Are there such situations? Consider reports made in ignorance. Nina intends to tell John that the students in her class all seem well-prepared for an upcoming exam. She utters:

(30) The students in my class are all ready.

Sally overhears Nina and John talking. She mistakenly thinks that Nina and John are discussing the school field trip. Unbeknownst to Sally, Nina's class isn't going on the field trip at all. Now Sally and Bill are trying to figure out which classes are ready for the field trip. Sally says to Bill:

(31) Nina said that the students in her class are ready.

It seems intuitively obvious that a certain false and non-neutral proposition—the proposition that Nina said that the students in her class are ready *for the field trip*—is an element of at least the total utterance content of Sally's utterance of (31). Is there a true neutral proposition associated with the utterance as its narrowly semantic content? I see no reason to think so.

Of course, Sally is not merely *ignorant.* She is *mistaken.* Perhaps it's her mistaken, hasty assumption, and not her ignorance, that serves to somehow raise the non-neutral proposition to salience. Suppose that Sally simply doesn't know and makes no hasty assumption about what exactly Nina's students are ready for. In what speech situations, if any, Sally would feel entitled to utter (31)? Suppose, for example, that Sally and Bill are again trying to determine which classes are ready to leave for the field trip. Sally cannot straight out utter (31) and leave it at that, at least not if she intends to be a cooperative conversational partner to Bill. Sally's uttering (31) in the imagined scenario would, at a minimum, invite the inference that Nina said that the students in her class are ready for the field trip and would, at the maximum, flat out assert that proposition. Sally is in no position either to offer such an invitation or to make such a flat out assertion. There are assertions that Sally can make in the imagined scenario that would neither invite inferences that Sally is in no position to invite nor make an assertion stronger than Sally is in a position to make. Sally could say:

> (32) I overheard Nina say that the students in her class are ready. But I couldn't tell, from what I heard, what she was saying they are ready for. She might, for all I know, have been talking about the field trip.

Even here there is no reason to assume a modificationally neutral reading of 'ready'. A more natural interpretation is that Sally is reporting that Nina says that her students are ready *for something or other*. That is not precisely what Nina herself originally said. But sometimes an indirect discourse report functions only as a *partial characterization* of what another says. In such cases, the ascribed content need not be identical to the content originally expressed. This fact alone gives us reason to refrain from drawing hasty inferences from premises about the felt content of an indirect discourse use of 'ready' to conclusions about the content of an unembedded use of 'ready'.

As Cappelen and Leppore themselves point out, the property of being ready *for something or other* comes about as close as one can get, within a parameterized approach, to "bare readiness". The property of being ready for something or other is, after all, a property shared by anyone who enjoys any modification of readiness whatsoever. Indeed, they claim that anyone who thinks that *every* occurrence of 'ready' expresses such a property has, in effect, endorsed the minimalist reading of 'ready'. But it simply does not follow from the fact that *some* uses of ready—especially in the context of indirect discourse reports—may take on an "abstract" non-specific value for the suppressed parameter in a given situation, that 'ready' is, therefore, speech-situationally insensitive. We have just examined a plethora of cases in which no such reading of ready seems salient, accessible, or relevant. Moreover, it takes a quite peculiar discourse setting to render such a reading salient, accessible, or relevant at all.

Strikingly Cappelen and Lepore seem to hold that *all* instances of 'John is ready' must have an "abstract" narrowly semantic content, if *any* instances do. Though they allow that some occurrences of 'ready' may also express some *additional* non-neutral content specifically tied to the peculiarities of the speech situation, they insist that any additional non-neutral content is *always* a pragmatic externality of the relevant utterance. Given the cases we have just considered, they have not discharged the burden of argument they have taken on in making this claim. Moreover, if one keeps the notion of a one and a half stage pragmatic externality clearly in mind, it should be clear that they could not discharge their explanatory burdens merely by adducing the kinds of considerations and examples they put on offer. Recall that such externalities may be generated even if the speaker manifestly *fails* to discharge her semantic burdens. Semantic failure may, in fact, play the decisive role in making such externalities communicatively salient. Imagine, for example, a speaker who utters (31) with no particular modification of readiness in mind in such a way as to render no particular modification of readiness salient or accessible. If ready is parameterized, then she has failed to say anything fully propositionally determinate. Nonetheless, if the dialectical setting is right, she may still succeed in communicating something about Nina's assessment of the state of readiness of her class. She may, for example, communicate that Nina takes her class to be ready for something or other. And she may do so, even if she hasn't managed to make that very proposition the narrowly semantic content of her utterance.

Cappelen and Lepore's disquotational test for context sensitivity thus leaves the moderate contextualist completely free to maintain that, in virtue of the parameterized lexical character of 'ready', any speaker who utters 'Nina said that John is ready' by way of indirectly reporting an utterance of (17) above has herself taken on the semantic burden of semantically "completing" her use of 'ready' by loading a semantic value onto a suppressed parameter. Never mind for the moment where in syntax or subsyntax such a parameter might sit. And never mind for the moment the exact semantic function of the suppressed parameter. A speaker who selects a speech-situationally sensitive expression takes on not only a semantic burden but also the communicative burden of making it mutually manifest what value she intends to load onto the relevant parameter. Though such burdens are not difficult to discharge, they are not discharged automatically, merely through the device of disquotation. Nothing in the scenarios described by Cappelen and Lepore suffices to show otherwise. Indeed, it seems clear that a speaker who utters either (18) or (19) as a way of reporting (17) without loading a value onto the parameter for 'ready' has failed to ascribe a fully determinate propositional content to Nina. She has thus failed to discharge the semantic burden that she has taken on in electing to use 'ready'. But we have seen that pragmatics may step in to fill the communicative gap by generating one and half stage externalities even when semantics falters. This is a fact that no moderate contextualist need deny. And given that, it is hard to be moved by Cappelen and Lepore's various arguments against the lexically driven speech-situational sensitivity of 'ready' and other such expression.

In this connection, it is easy to see that 'ready' fares much the same as 'that' or 'we' or 'foreign' with respect to Cappelen and Lepore's disquotational test for context sensitivity. We have already seen, for example, that 'that' appears to "block" ICDI reports only where a shift in "context" involves a shift in reference. Where reference is preserved, 'that' does not block such reports. To preserve the intuitive context sensitivity of 'that' as measured by the ICDI test, we stipulated that only where reference is not preserved do we have an ICDI relevant context shift for 'that'. One way to implement this stipulation is simply to take the demonstrated object of the demonstration as itself an ingredient of context for 'that'. This makes it automatic that, where reference shifts, context has shifted in an ICDI relevant way. But it is surely open to the contextualist to say much the same about 'ready'. The contextualist can hold, that is, that an ICDI relevant context shift for 'ready' must involve a shift in the intended respect of readiness. One way to implement this suggestion is to take respects of readiness themselves to be ingredients of context for uses of 'ready'. But now when context shifts in an ICDI relevant way, 'ready' will also block ICDI reports. So the take-home message is that Cappelen and Lepore's disquotational test so far does nothing to distinguish 'that' from 'ready'. 'Ready' is no more or less context-sensitive than 'that' is. Either both are context-sensitive or neither is. But however one decides that issue, the contextualist wins. If 'ready' turns out to be on a semantic par, more or less, with 'that', 'we', 'foreign', and many other expressions in the so-called basic set, the contextualist has shown all that she has set out to show.

6. SEMANTICS VS. METAPHYSICS

I turn to one last charge leveled by Cappelen and Lepore against contextualists—both of the radical variety and of the moderate variety—namely, viz., that contextualists of all stripes have confused semantics and metaphysics. Charging the contextualist with conflation of metaphysics and semantics is, in large measure, a defensive move. It is designed to ward off the charge that their own minimal propositions are metaphysically incoherent. They have ample reason to be defensive. They claim, for example, that the proposition that *x is tall* can be true or false simpliciter, without any relativization to a standard of height or any reference class of heights. They claim, moreover, that there is nothing more they need to say about the truth conditions of this proposition than is expressed by the T-sentence " 'x is tall' is true if and only if x is tall". They don't even attempt to say just what it takes to be tall simpliciter. And when pressed, they protest that it's the business of metaphysics, not of semantics, to answer such questions. Crucially, they claim that incompleteness arguments rest on an illegitimate conflation between semantics and metaphysics. The moderate contextualist who insists that a sentence like 'John is tall' is semantically incomplete, on the basis of the felt intuition that nothing can be tall simpliciter, is really asking the semanticist for something that he has no obligation to provide—at least not qua semanticist. He is demanding a metaphysical analysis of what all tall things share.

Now I confess to having deep sympathy for the project of keeping semantics as disentangled from metaphysics as possible. Moreover, some arguments for contextualism do conflate metaphysics and semantics. For example, in defense of the claim that utterances of sentences like

(33) It is raining.

express propositions containing unarticulated constituents, John Perry likes to say things such as the following:

> In this case, I say that the place is an *unarticulated constituent* of the proposition expressed by the utterance. It is a constituent *because, since rain occurs at a time in place, there is no truth evaluable proposition unless a place is supplied.* It is unarticulated, because there is no morpheme that designates that place. (Perry 2001: 45; emphasis added)

But it simply does not follow from the fact that rain occurs at a time and in a place that an utterance of 'it is raining' fails to express a complete proposition unless a place is supplied. Consider, for example, certain other apparently necessary properties of rainings. Whenever it rains, it rains a certain amount and for a certain duration. But we can express a fully determinate proposition by an utterance of 'it rained' without having to specify how much rain fell or over what span of time the rain fell.

Let me hasten to add that I agree with Perry, and disagree with Cappelen and Lepore, that unless a place is supplied we don't yet have a truth evaluable proposition. So the question naturally arises just *why* we must specify *where* it is raining in the case of the present tense 'it is raining' if we are to express a complete proposition, but we need not specify *how much* it rained or for *how long* it rained in the case of the past tense 'rained' in order to express a complete proposition. A confused semanticist, of the sort against whom Cappelen and Lepore rail, might be tempted by another distinction of Perry's—that between the argument *roles* of relation*s* and the argument *places* of predicates. Let us stipulate, for the space of the argument, that the verb 'rain' has fewer argument places than the raining relation has argument roles. I claim that a bare mismatch between the adicity of the predicate and the adicity of the expressed relation does not directly entail the semantic incompleteness of the relevant predicate. Moreover, there need be no deep metaphysical difference between those argument roles that are associated with some argument place and those that are not.

If one were antecedently convinced of the need to import deep metaphysical distinctions into one's semantics, one might attempt to enforce something like the adjunct/argument distinction, not at the level of verbs and predicates, but at the level of relations themselves to explain why some roles are realized as argument places and other roles are not. This strategy is unpromising in the extreme. It really would bog semantics down in the metaphysical muck. For any relation in *n* arguments with a claim to be the unmodified raining relation, there will be other relations in *m* arguments, for *m* distinct from *n*, that appear to have no less of a claim to being *the* or at least *a* raining relation. There is a relation that holds between a place, a time, and a velocity just in case it is raining at the time, at that place, with that velocity. There is another, less "articulated" relation that holds between a time and a place just in case it is raining at that time at that place. Does one or the other of these relations have more of a claim to being *the* raining relation? Is the former relation merely a modification of the latter? If these questions are supposed to be purely metaphysical questions about relations rather semantic questions about verbs and predicates, then I confess to not having the foggiest clue how to answer them.

If incompleteness arguments for moderate contextualism rested squarely on such metaphysical questions, Cappelen and Lepore would have a point. But incompleteness arguments shouldn't be construed as arguments about the metaphysics of relations. They are really arguments about the semantics of verbs and other argument-taking expressions. I claim it is a fact about the verb 'to rain', and not a fact about the metaphysics of the raining relation, that it demands contextual provision of a place, but not contextual provision of an intensity, amount, or duration. In particular, I claim, and have argued at length elsewhere, that the verb 'to rain' has a lexically specified, but syntactically suppressed parameter that is theta-marked **THEME**, that takes places as values. I will not elaborate on this proposal further here except to say that the fact that the verb demands a location as its theme endows location with a semantic privilege, but not a metaphysical one.

We may contrast 'to rain' with 'to dance' in order to illustrate that some verbs fail to semantically privilege the place where the relevant goings-on happen. There can't be a dancing that doesn't happen somewhere or other. For all the semanticist has to say, it may be that the place where a dancing happens is metaphysically on a par with the place where a raining happens. But they are clearly not on a par semantically speaking. Suppose a speaker utters:

(34) Laura danced the tango until she could dance no more.

without saying where Laura danced. The speaker has left nothing out required for the semantic completeness and full truth-evaluability of her utterance. One can say something fully determinate, something fully truth evaluable, by uttering (34) even if the speech situation makes manifest no place as the place where the dancing happens. I have hypothesized that the difference between (33) and (34) depends entirely on the differences in the way 'to dance' and 'to rain' relate to the places where rainings and dancings happen. Unlike 'to rain', 'to dance' does not mark the place where a dance happens as the theme or undergoer of the dance. The theme or undergoer of a dancing is the dancer herself. The place where a dancing "takes place" is merely the place where the dancer dances. When Laura is dancing in a place, it is not the place that undergoes the dancing. This fact about the verb 'to dance' explains why, despite the fact that one cannot dance without dancing somewhere or other, a sentence containing 'to dance' can be semantically complete, even if the place where dancing happens is not situationally provided. That a dancing must take place somewhere or other is a (mutually known) metaphysical fact about the universe—a fact that supervenes on the nature of dancing and the structure of space-time. But that metaphysical fact is not explicitly reflected in the argument structure of the verb 'to dance'.

These remarks are intended to show only that, contrary to Cappelen and Lepore, arguments from semantic incompleteness need not conflate semantics and metaphysics. But if that point is granted, it follows directly that their defensive maneuvers are entirely unavailing. They make the highly counter-intuitive claim, supported by no evidence that I have seen, that objects can be barely tall, that is, tall without relativization to any reference class or standard of tallness. They admit this to be an incredible claim, endorsed as far as I can tell, by exactly two philosophers. About the best that they can do by way of defending this claim is to insist that qua semanticists they have no burden of explaining what all barely tall objects share. And to insist that semantics does bear such a burden, they claim, is to conflate semantics with metaphysics. We don't have to take any stand on whether there is or is not such a property as bare tallness in the order of things to show that no expression of our own language expresses such a property. It is a better bet that the lexical meaning of 'tall' determines that 'tall' applies not to heights directly but only to heights as measured by some variable standard or as compared to some variable reference class. It is also a good bet that the lexicon explicitly represents that standards of tallness are to be speech-situationally determined and not fixed once and for all by the lexicon itself. If that is right, the lexicon itself licenses pragmatic intrusion into the business of semantics from the very start.

REFERENCES

Bach, K. (1994), 'Conversational Impliciture', *Mind and Language*, 9: 124–62.

—— (2001*a*), 'Speaking Loosely: Sentence Nonliterality', *Midwest Studies in Philosophy*, xxv. *Figurative Language*, ed. Peter French and Howard Wettstein, pp. 249–63. Oxford: Blackwell Publishers.

—— (2001*b*), 'You Don't Say', *Synthese*, 128: 15–44.

—— (2004), 'Context ex Machina', in Z. Szabo (ed.), *Semantics vs. Pragmatics*, pp. 356–82. Oxford: Oxford University Press.

Barwise, J., and J. Perry (1983), *Situations and Attitudes*. Cambridge, Mass.: MIT Press/Bradford Books.

Cappelen, H., and E. Lepore (2005), *Insensitive Semantics*. Oxford: Blackwell.

Carston, R. (2002), *Thoughts and Utterances: The Pragmatics of Explicit Communication*. London: Blackwell Publishers.

Kaplan, D. (1989), 'Demonstratives', in J. Almog, J. Perry, and H. Wettstein (eds.), *Themes from Kaplan*. New York: Oxford University Press.

Lepore, E., and H. Cappelen (2007), 'Unarticulated Constituents and Hidden Indexicals: An Abuse of Context in Semantics', in M. O'Rourche and C. Washington (eds.), *Situating Semantics: Essays in Honor of* John Perry. Boston: MIT Press.

Perry, J. (1986), 'Thought without Representation', *Supplementary Proceedings of the Aristotelean Society*. Repr. in Perry (2000). Page numbers refer to reprinted version.

—— (2000), *The Problem of the Essential Indexical and Other Essays: Expanded Edition*. Stanford, Calif.: CSLI Publications.

—— (2001), *Reference and Reflexivity.* Stanford Calif.: CSLI Publications.

Recanati, F. (2001), 'What is Said', *Synthese,* 128: 75–91.

—— (2003*a*), 'What is Said and the Pragmatics/Semantics Distinction', in Claudia Bianchi and Carlo Penco (eds.), *The Semantics/Pragmatics Distinction*, Stanford, Calif.: CSLI Publications.

—— (2003*b*), *Literal Meaning: The Very Idea.* Cambridge: Cambridge University Press.

Soames, S. (2004), 'Naming and Asserting', in Z. Szabo, *Semantics vs. Pragmatics,* pp. 356–82. Oxford: Oxford University Press.

Soames, S. (forthcoming). 'On the Gap Between Meaning and Assertion', in Martin Hackl and Robert Thornton (eds.), *Asserting, Meaning, and Implying.* Oxford: Oxford University Press.

Sperber, D., and D. Wilson (1995), *Relevance: Communication and Cognition.* London: Blackwell Publishers.

Stanley, J. (2000), 'Context and Logical Form', *Linguistics and Philosophy*, 23: 391–434.

Stojanivic, I. (2003) 'What to Say on What is Said', in P. Blackburn, C. Ghidini, and R. Turner (eds.), *Modeling and Using Context.* Berlin: Springer-Verlag.

Taylor, K. (2000), 'Emptiness without Compromise: A Referentialist Semantics for Empty Names', in T. Hofweber and A. Everett (eds.), *Empty Names: Fiction and the Puzzles of Non-Existence.* Stanford, Calif.: CSLI Publications. Reprinted in Taylor 2003.

—— (2001), 'Sex, Breakfast, and Descriptus Interruptus', *Synthese*, 128/1*a*2: 45–61. Reprinted in Taylor 2003.

—— (2002), 'De Re and De Dicto: Against the Conventional Wisdom', *Philosophical Perspectives: Language and Mind*, 16: 225–65.

—— (2003), *Reference and the Rational Mind.* Stanford, Calif.: CSLI Publications

—— (2007), 'Misplaced Modification and the Illusion of Opacity', in M. O'Rourke and C. Washington, *Situating Semantics: Essays in Honor of John Perry.* Boston: MIT Press.

—— (in progress), 'Pragmatics Everywhere'.

3

Radical Minimalism, Moderate Contextualism

Kepa Korta and John Perry

1. INTRODUCTION

Cappelen and Lepore's (hereafter, "CL") book *Insensitive Semantics* faces issues involved in reconceptualizing the nature of and boundaries between semantics and pragmatics in the light of the phenomenon often called "pragmatic intrusion". The received theory might have been expressed this way. Semantics determines *what is said*; that is, the proposition that is expressed by an utterance is determined by the conventional meanings of the words used and compositional rules for combining words. Pragmatics takes as its input what is said and, taking into consideration facts about the particular utterance (and possibly some other conventions), determines what has been conveyed and what speech acts have been performed, largely by considering the communicative and other perlocutionary intentions of the speaker.

The classic picture of pragmatic intrusion is that we often need to reason about the intentions of the speaker in order to determine what is said; semantics doesn't get us the whole way. Authors like Bach (1994), Carston (1988, 2002), Recanati (1989, 2004), Sperber and Wilson (1986), and others point to a variety of cases: comparative adjectives, quantifier expressions, weather reports, etc.

CL seek to develop a concept of semantics that does not countenance pragmatic intrusion. They alter the received picture by disengaging the "output" of semantics, the "semantic content", from the intuitive concept of "what is said". The semantic content can be determined without regard to intrusive pragmatic elements. Pragmatics plays a role in getting us to what is said, but since what is said is beyond the border of semantics, it isn't intrusion. Thus their "semantic minimalism". But CL have further ambitions about the concept of what is said; they want not only to demote it from the role of being the terminus of semantics, but also to undermine the idea that it is an important, central, and robust concept of pragmatics. Thus their "speech act pluralism".

We are sympathetic to the project of keeping semantics free of pragmatic intrusion, but we pursue a somewhat different strategy, that we see as both more radical than that of CL, and closer to their motivating ideas. On the issue of what is said, however, we differ; we think what is said, or some theoretical explication of it, has a central and honorable role to play in pragmatics.

This chapter began as a contribution to a symposium on *Insensitive Semantics* for *Philosophy and Phenomenological Research.* In order to meet the page limits, the second part of our case, concerning pragmatic pluralism, had to be cut. At the invitation of Gerhard Preyer we include the entire original paper here, with such changes as the passage of time and the accumulation of wisdom have dictated.

2. TERMINOLOGICAL PRELIMINARIES

First, there is the "content" of an utterance, more commonly called "the proposition expressed". The question is how much pragmatics is involved in determining it. Literalists say none. Contextualists say a lot. Moderates say something in between. But this concept of semantic content is basically a conflation of two quite different concepts. We'll call these *locutionary content* and *semantic contribution.*

Locutionary content is rooted in such common locutions as "what X said", and "what X said by uttering (saying, writing, signing) so and so". They surface in Austin, Grice, and the "new theory of reference". There the *theoretical* concept of *the proposition expressed* is motivated by intuitions mined with the help of these common-sense concepts. This is most explicit in Kaplan's *Demonstratives* (1989), in the crucial Peter–Paul argument (pp. 512–13).

Our working definition of "locutionary content" is the conditions the truth of an utterance of a declarative sentence puts on the objects it is about. This is called "referential content" in Perry (2001). The locutionary content is, we think, *normally* what is said, but not in those cases for which Grice used "make as if to say" instead of "say". There are also other cases, such as informative identity statements, where we might not identify what is said with the locutionary content (see Perry 2001). Thus we agree with CL and others that "what is said" is a rather complicated concept, but we find more order in this complexity than they do.

The second root of the concept of content is "semantic contribution". Meaning is commonly assumed to be a property of simple and complex expressions that derives from conventions that pertain to the meaning of simple expressions, found in a lexicon, and conventions about modes of combination. This is what the semantic component of model-theoretic or other formal analyses of languages assign to expressions. It is also what philosophers and cognitive scientists take to be a central aspect of knowledge of language, of "semantic competence".

"Content" is a semi-technical expression. The philosophy of language has been heavily influenced by Kaplan's use, where paradigmatic content primarily is assigned to utterances, or uses of declarative sentences, or, as officially in his formal development, pairs of such sentences and contexts, where contexts are quadruples of agent, location, time, and world (Kaplan 1989). Declarative sentences are the model, and the content is taken to be a proposition that incorporates the truth-conditions of an utterance, use, or sentence in context. We will reserve the use of "content" for utterances, uses, and sentences in context, and "meaning" for types of expressions, following Kaplan, whose approximation to meaning is called "character". So, in Kaplan's system, the content of a sentence in context is a function of the character of the sentence and the context. We'll use the term "semantic contribution" for the property of sentences that CL seem to be after.

In our terms, CL maintain that the semantic contribution of a sentence is not as tightly linked to the locutionary content of an utterance of the sentence as might be thought. Locutionary content is a concept that belongs to pragmatics, semantic contribution belongs to semantics. With this we agree. Thus there are two questions instead of one:

> How much pragmatics is involved in determining the locutionary content of an utterance?
>
> How much pragmatics is involved in determining the semantic contribution of a sentence used in a standard way in an utterance?

We are contextualists with regard to the first question, and minimalists as regards the second, and so in broad agreement with CL. We are more moderate than they on the first question, which we pursue in sections 5 and 6. We start with the second, where our complaint is that CL are not minimalist enough. But, before that, a remark on the epistemology of language.

3. A NOTE ON EPISTEMOLOGY.

The word "pragmatics" brings to mind two sorts of facts that are connected with particular utterances. First are narrow contextual facts: the speaker, audience, time, and place of the utterance. Second are matters of the intentions of the speaker (and perhaps relevant mental states of other participants in the conversation). The paradigms of such intentions are the sort that Grice emphasized in his study of implicature: intentions to convey something beyond, or in place of, what is literally said. But in fact the discovery of intentions is involved at every stage of understanding utterances.

Herman says to Ernie, "I am tired". Ernie learns that Herman is tired. Knowledge of different kinds is involved here. First, there is the knowledge Ernie has as a semantically competent user of English. We take this to be the knowledge of the meanings of the words of English and how to interpret the modes of combination one finds in complex English expressions. This, *and this alone*, seems to us to be semantic, at least from a *minimalist* perspective. And this does *not* depend on anything about the utterance; Ernie's knowledge of the semantics of the English sentence "I am tired" was in place before Herman said anything, and the same knowledge would be involved in his understanding of anyone's utterance, or Ernie's own production of such an utterance.

Then there is perception of the public factors involved in Herman's utterance. Ernie hears the words Herman uses, and recognizes them as sounds that could be used as words of English. He also sees that Herman is the speaker.

Then there are Herman's intentions. If, as we assume, Ernie knows no Norwegian, he might briefly entertain the possibility that the sounds he hears are being used as Norwegian words. But why would Herman say something in Norwegian to Ernie? So he concludes Herman is speaking English, a fact about Herman's intentions in producing the noises he does. Notice that Ernie's knowledge of the semantics of "I am tired" will likely play a role here. If Herman emits some sounds which sound like "Albuquerque is probably pregnant," his knowledge of Herman's likely intentions and the semantics of "Albuquerque is probably pregnant" would instead argue for the utterance not being in English.

Having established that Herman intends to be speaking English, another layer of thinking about intentions comes up with the word "tired". Probably Herman realizes he is not an automobile, and means to use "tired" in the sense in which people who would like to nap are tired. There is the issue of exactly what Herman counts as "tired". Consistent with English he might mean to say that he is tired as opposed to being full of vim and vigor, or that he is dead-tired, barely able to lift a pencil. More intentions. Then, finally, there is the question of what Herman is trying to convey, to implicate, by saying what he does. That he needs a coke? That he needs a nap? That he needs a vacation? That battling with the absurdity of life and language has driven him to a deep and unshakeable ennui? More intentions.

Our point is that the understanding of particular utterances requires a great deal of knowledge in addition to semantic knowledge, properly so-called, and knowledge of intentions saturates every aspect of understanding in every transaction. The picture that semantic knowledge, in any reasonable sense, gets us very far by itself is untenable. In particular, the idea that simply by knowing the meanings of English expressions and modes of composition we can get to the locutionary content, and only after that, in figuring out implicatures, to what we need to discover and reason about intentions, is certainly false.

4. MINIMALISMS

In Kaplan's theory, philosophical arguments about what is said guide the choice for what the content of an utterance is taken to be, suggesting that content is *what is said*, in a fairly robust and intuition-rich sense of that phrase, which, in the limited sort of cases Kaplan considers, is or is very close to locutionary content in our sense. Character is semantic contribution. Content is determined by character and context. This gives us two possible, Kaplan-inspired, minimalisms:

(i) Minimal semantic contribution should be like Kaplan's *content*: it is determined by character *plus* context (agent, location, time, world).

(ii) Minimal semantic contribution should be like Kaplan's *character*; it is the same for every utterance of a sentence.

Minimalism (i) seems to be a non-starter. In Kaplan's system, *content* is what *varies* from utterance to utterance, even though the semantics—everything Kaplan's theory tells us about the sentence, everything in the lexicon and the compositional rules—stays the same. Minimalism (ii), on the other hand, seems quite promising; it identifies minimal semantics with exactly the sort of facts that semantic theories like Kaplan's provide, and the usual meaning of "semantics", namely, the meaning of expressions as determined by the conventions of the language to which they belong.

CL explain their basic idea as follows:

> The idea motivating Semantic Minimalism is simple and obvious: The semantic content of a sentence S is the content that all utterances of S share. It is the content that all utterances of S express no matter how different their contexts of utterance are. It is also the content that can be grasped and reported by someone who is ignorant about the relevant characteristics of the context in which an utterance of S took place. (p. 143)

CL emphasize their broad agreement with Kaplan, so this use of "content" is rather odd; for Kaplan the content is what *changes* with context; the character remains the same and is what is grasped by someone ignorant of context. If the *contents* of all utterances of a sentence S were the same, their truth-value would also be the same: a bullet no one wants to bite. At this point one might suppose that minimalism (ii) fits everything in the basic idea so well that this use of "content" must just come to "contribution". Thus we would have:

> There is a *semantic* contribution that all utterances of a sentence S make to contents of the utterances, which is the same for all utterances whatever the context and is what someone who is ignorant of the relevant characteristics of the context grasps.

However, having given us this basic idea of semantic minimalism, CL almost immediately replace it with another conception; they call it an "elaboration", but it is really nothing of the sort. It is a move from something prima-facie coherent like (ii) to something prima-facie incoherent like (i). They list seven theses of what we shall call CL Semantic Minimalism. The heart of the matter is their thesis 5, which gives us our next concept of minimalism:

(iii) CL minimalism (pp. 144–145)

In order to fix or determine the proposition semantically expressed by an utterance of a sentence S, follow steps (a)–(e):

a) Specify the meaning (or semantic value) of every expression in S (doing so in accordance with your favorite semantic theory . . .).
b) Specify all the relevant compositional meanings rules for English (doing so also in accordance with your favorite semantic theory . . .).
c) Disambiguate every ambiguous/polysemous expression in S.
d) Precisify every vague expression in S.
e) Fix the semantic value of every context sensitive expression in S.

What are clauses (c) through (e) doing in an exposition of semantic *minimalism*, a description of the "content" that all utterances of a sentence *share*? The clauses (c), (d), and (e) all pertain to factors that *differentiate* the content of English sentences as used by different people at different times, or with different intentions about which meanings of ambiguous expressions they wish to employ, and the standards of precisification for vague expressions. Something has gone awry, and the basic idea of semantic minimalism has slipped away.

5. KP MINIMALISM

We will propose two forms of minimalism that are more in accord with CL's basic idea—more pure—than CL minimalism. We will call them "Kosher and Pure minimalisms" or "KP minimalisms" for short.

Both forms of KP minimalism result from eliminating parts of CL minimalism. The first form eliminates (d) and (e); the second form eliminates (c) as well.

For this purpose we use the concept Content_M from Perry (2001). In general, the content of an utterance is what the world has to be like for the utterance to be true, taking certain things about the utterance as fixed. Let **u** be an utterance of "I am tired" in English, the meanings of the words and the mode of composition involved are given, but not the speaker, time, etc. The Content_M of *u* is:

(1) That the speaker of *u* is tired at the time of *u*.

(1) is what we call a *reflexive* content of *u*, since it puts conditions on **u** itself. Content_M gets at the vision behind CL's basic idea: it is what all utterances of the same sentence have *in common*.

Of course, two utterances, *u* and *u′* of "I am tired" by different people will not have the same *content*, reflexive or locutionary, and they may differ in *truth-value*. This difference is reflected in the difference between (1) and (2):

(2) That the speaker of *u*′ is tired at the time of *u*′.

Suppose you find a note **n** that reads "I am tired". You don't know who wrote it, or when, but you assume it is written in English. On the CL account you *do not* grasp the semantic contribution of the sentence, for you do not have the information necessary, on their theory, to grasp "the proposition semantically expressed". But of course you do, and you can report it:

Note **n** is true iff the person who wrote it was tired at the time he wrote it.

Suppose Tom wrote the note at noon Wednesday. If you knew that you could say,

Note **n** is true iff Tom was tired Wednesday.

The proposition that Tom was tired Wednesday is what we call the locutionary content of the note; the Content$_C$ or the referential content in Perry (2001). It is what is required of the world for the note to be true given *not only* that it was written in English, *but also* that it was written by Tom on Wednesday. With the sentence "Tom was tired Wednesday" you can actually *express* the proposition Tom expressed with the note. Without that information you cannot *express* that proposition, but you can give an *utterance-bound* or *reflexive* characterization of it.

The requirement that to grasp the *semantic* content of an utterance you need to know the contextual facts, so that you can *express* the locutionary content, as opposed to merely providing an utterance-bound description of it, is unmotivated by CL's basic idea, and by the general truth-conditional and compositional approach to semantics.

If one looks at a formal theory, such as Kaplan's in "Logic of Demonstratives", the compositional clauses work at the level of utterance-bound meaning; that is, they quantify over contexts, and thus contextual factors. One can grasp the contribution that parts make to wholes, on Kaplan's account, without having any idea who made the utterance and when (or what the context of a sentence–context pair is).

Consider, for example, a note:

(3) Because I ran a marathon yesterday, I am too tired to fix the car today, so I'd better wait until tomorrow, so you can't use it to go to the store until then.

We can grasp the utterance-bound truth-conditions of (3) if we grasp the utterance-bound truth-conditions of the parts; we don't need to know who said it, and when, and to whom.

This is not a point that simply pertains to indexicals. Suppose the note is "I'll fix the car soon." What does the speaker mean by "soon"? It is a vague expression. CL would claim that we don't grasp the semantic "content" unless we can fix what counts as "soon". But surely we do grasp the utterance bound truth-conditions:

> The note is true iff the author of the note fixed the car he is referring to within the length of time that counted as upper bound of what counted as "soon" according to his intentions.

Suppose you get an email from Gretchen that says, "David has made an amazing discovery." There are a lot of Davids. You don't know which one Gretchen is referring to with her use of "David": David Kaplan, David Hills, David Israel? You respond, "David Who?" Your response can be understood precisely because you *do* grasp utterance-bound truth-conditions of the email:

> This email is true if the David the author it was referring to with "David" has made a great discovery.

By recognizing the fact that the *common* semantic contribution of sentences of English is at the level of utterance-bound truth-conditions, we can provide a conception of semantic contribution and semantic content that is much more in accord with CL's basic idea:

> KP-1
>
> The semantic contribution of an English sentence is determined by the meanings of the expression in the sentence in English and the English rules for modes of combination, plus a disambiguation of any ambiguous expressions. The semantic content of an utterance of the sentence is the reflexive truth-conditions of the utterance, where contextual factors, the reference of nambiguous[1] names, and standards of precisification are not fixed but quantified over.

We also propose a more radical rendering of semantic minimalism, limited to (a) and (b) on CL's list.

> KP-2
>
> The semantic contribution of an English sentence is determined by the meanings of the expression in the sentence in English and the English rules for modes of combination. The semantic content of an utterance

[1] 'Nambiguous' is Perry's (2001) neologism for names with multiple bearers. This phenomenon is quite different from ordinary lexical ambiguity. See Perry (2001: ch. 6).

> of the sentence is the reflexive truth-conditions of the utterance, where contextual factors, the meanings of ambiguous expressions, the reference of nambiguous names, and standards of precisification are not fixed but quantified over.

This is the conception of semantic contribution needed by the working epistemologist of language or cognitive scientist. Consider Grice's example (1967) "He was in the grip of a vice." What does someone know, who hears this sentence uttered, and recognizes the expressions, based merely on his knowledge of the meanings of words and the grammar of English? We suggest, following Grice rather closely, something like this:

> This utterance is true iff the speaker is using "in the grip of a vice" to mean "has a particularly bad habit or moral failing", if the person the speaker uses "he" to refer to has a particularly bad habit or moral failing, or if the speaker is using "in the grip of a vice" to mean "held by a clamping vise" and the person he is referring to is held by a clamping vise.

The material to the right of the "iff" provides us with an utterance-bound truth-condition. This is a complicated proposition that is ultimately about the utterance itself. This proposition fits very well with CL's basic idea, for it is what a semantically competent speaker of English grasps simply in terms of that semantic competence, with no additional knowledge of the intentions of the speaker beyond that of speaking English.

Perhaps we need to emphasize that utterance-bound contents are ***not*** our candidates for what is said, or *the* proposition expressed, or locutionary content. The utterance-bound content of an utterance *u* of "I am tired" is the proposition that the speaker of *u* is tired. This is certainly *not* what is said. The speaker was not *saying* something about his or her own utterance, but about him or herself.

We believe that once either of these truly—radically—minimalist conceptions of semantics is adopted, many of CL's arguments against the presence of pragmatically or contextually determined elements in locutionary content, such as unarticulated constituents, lose whatever force they may have had. But for now we turn to CL's 'Speech Act Pluralism'.

6. PLURALISM AND CONTEXTUALISM

Both minimalists and contextualists must face the question:

> How much pragmatics is involved in determining the locutionary content of an utterance? (For the moment, you can take 'locutionary content' just as our technical term for 'what is said'.)

Once CL have separated locutionary content from the output of semantics, they are free to agree with contextualists: a lot of pragmatics is involved in getting to what is said.

This is not their only coincidence with contextualism. They share with many contextualists the assumption that for the generation of implicatures it is necessary to have what we called an expressive description of a certain proposition, not what is said, but the (enriched) explicature (in Carston's terminology) or the contextually shaped what-is-said (in CL's terminology, pp. 179–81). We argue elsewhere[2] that this is a mistake; one can reason about the likely intentions of a speaker on the basis of a very utterance-bound description of what he has said.[3]

But what is most surprising and puzzling to us is that, concerning what is said, now distinguished from both the semantic content and the enriched explicature, CL defend a contextualism virtually without limits. That is, they appear to deny that the utility of what is said, or theoretical concepts based on our intuitions about what is said, play a significant role in shaping the enterprise of semantics and pragmatics.

In our view CL's 'Speech Act Pluralism' is the collection of three different theses that we will call 'content pluralism', 'the relativity of what is said', and 'pragmatic indiscernibility'. The first we accept; the second leads to a theoretical pessimism we don't want to share; the third we reject; it goes directly against Grice's fundamental distinction between what is said and implicatures, and, ironically, combined with the second, threatens to undermine any motivation for CL's version of semantic minimalism. Let's consider them one by one.

6.1. Content Pluralism

Content pluralism concerns the quantity of contents of an utterance; it claims that any utterance has a variety of them. We have already argued for the existence, for any utterance, of at least a minimal content corresponding to the semantic contribution of the sentence uttered, a locutionary content which can be considered for our current purposes more or less as what is said, and a bunch of more or less utterance-bound or reflexive contents somehow 'in between'. Each of these contents is available for the hearer when understanding an utterance. We (theoreticians) can represent them as different propositions, with different truth-conditions. Contrary to what is common usage among philosophers and linguists, then, it is misleading to talk of *the* content of an utterance—or equivalently about *the* truth-conditions of an utterance. We think there is a

[2] See Korta and Perry (2006).

[3] It is true that relevance theorists admit mutual adjustments of explicatures and implicatures, so the former need not be determined *before* the latter. Our point, anyway, is that the expressive description of the proposition need not be determined either *before* or *after* the determination of implicatures; an utterance-bound description will often do either as the input for an inference or as the result of mutual adjustment. Thanks to one of the referees for raising this point.

plurality of contents, of sets of truth-conditions, of an utterance. We agree with CL on this point. We are pluralist on contents.

However, assuming that any of these contents can equally be considered *as said* is an error too, and so also that they can be called "the proposition expressed", where that bit of technical terminology is introduced, as is common, in terms of the intuitive concept of what is said.

As we pointed out, we do not ordinarily consider the utterance-bound truth-conditions of an assertion as what is said or even part of what is said. If OJ's utterance *u* is of "I am innocent", he has not said that there is a unique speaker of *u* and that person is innocent. He hasn't said anything about *u* at all. Someone who heard *u*, but didn't hear who said it, would know its utterance-bound truth-conditions, but not what was said. Probably, he could figure out who said it, and thus what was said, if he knew enough about the trial he was attending.

Another sort of pluralism that must be acknowledged has to do with the plurality of *descriptions* or other designations available for any particular proposition. If one takes propositions to be abstract objects, then, like any objects, there will be innumerable ways of designating them. There is a special, perhaps canonical, way of designating propositions in (philosophical) English: embed a sentence that expresses the proposition from the speaker's context in a that-clause. Among the innumerable ways of designating propositions will be ordinary ways open to competent language users:

> that OJ is innocent
>
> What OJ just said
>
> Whatever OJ just said (I didn't hear him clearly)

as well as ways that are used by theorists, in the context of a certain way of modeling propositions:

> {w | OJ is innocent in w}, that is, the set of possible worlds in which OJ is innocent;
>
> << λx[x is innocent]>,OJ>, that is, the ordered pair consisting of the property of being innocent and OJ

The plurality of descriptions of what OJ said, does not, of course, imply a plurality of things OJ said.

Finally, we ordinarily count the subject-matter-preserving entailments and near-entailments of what a person said as among the things they said. So OJ said he was innocent, then he said that he wasn't guilty; that he didn't do the deed; and so forth. If he said he wore shoes and socks and a coat that day, then he said he wore shoes and he said that he wore socks and a coat.

Another complication, and the primary reason we think it is worth developing a semi-technical concept, *locutionary content*, as an explication of what is said, is that the latter concept has a heavy *forensic* aspect, that is tied to its daily use in not only describing utterances but assigning responsibility for their effects, but isn't helpful for theoretical purposes.

Consider a variation of one of CL's examples. Suppose L and C are with some worshipful graduate students in the philosophy lounge. Looking at famous philosopher X, affectionately called "that moronic clown" by C and L, L says, somewhat carelessly since others are listening, "That moronic clown just published another book." Our concept of locutionary content (still in development) would zero in on the proposition L believed, and intended to communicate to C, namely, that X just published another book. Something like Donnellan's concept of referential uses of descriptions would help get to that content. We wouldn't want the moronic attributes, real, or imagined, or merely ascribed affectionately with some sort of pretence, to be part of the locutionary content. But suppose one of the graduate students spreads the word that L thinks X is a moron. Called to account by L, the student says, "But that's what you said." We would have at least great sympathy with the student's claim. L was responsible for the effects of his careless utterance. This forensic aspect of what is said is partly responsible for the sense that what is said is so contextually relative as to be theoretically useless.

The concept of what is said that partly motivated the "new theory of reference" comes close to what Perry calls the "referential content" of an utterance. It is the proposition that captures the requirements the truth of an utterance places on the objects referred to. In a wide variety of cases, preserving these requirements with a different form of words will count as "saying the same thing". And in a wide variety of cases, the counterfactual possibilities to which an utterance directs our attention will involve those objects and requirements, and not other requirements involved in referring to them in the actual world. So "Aristotle might not have been named "Aristotle" " and "I might not be speaking, or might not even exist" make perfectly good sense.

But in some cases, it is clear that the information one intends to communicate is not the referential content, but something that involves the conditions of actual world reference. If K says to a confused P, "Donostia *is* San Sebastian", he intends to convey that "Donostia" is another name, or perhaps one should say, the real name, of the Basque city of San Sebastian. He does not merely intend to honor that city with an attribution of self-identity. In such cases, the ordinary use of what is said may track the information conveyed, rather than the referential content.[4]

These complications with the ordinary use of "what is said" do not imply that it cannot be the basis of a robust and useful theoretical concept; and of course it has been just this, in at least two quite different traditions, Gricean pragmatics

[4] See Perry (2001: 118 ff.).

and the new theory of reference of Donellan, Kripke, Kaplan, and others. The considerations raised by CL fall far short of showing otherwise.

6.2. The Relativity of What is Said

CL jump from content pluralism plus the observation that it is sometimes difficult to determine what is said and the claim that there are a lot of descriptions or reports, indefinitely many, about what is said, to the conclusion that no one description or report is more correct than any other, and therefore, any of them counts as said by the utterance. Their 'first thesis of Speech Act Pluralism' is:

> No one thing is said (or asserted, or claimed, or . . .) by any utterance: rather, indefinitely many propositions are said, asserted, claimed, stated, etc. (p. 199).

There is no compelling argument for this conclusion. While it is sometimes difficult to determine exactly what is said, for reasons just surveyed, it is often very easy to identify what is said; as easy as it is *to say the same thing*. Take one of CL's examples. OJ uttered:

(4) At 11:05 p.m. I put on a white shirt, a blue Yohji Yamamoto suit, dark socks, and my brown Bruno Magli shoes.

Knowing English, the identity of the speaker, and the day of the utterance, there is no difficulty in identifying what was said. JP can do it and can also say the same thing uttering (referring with 'he' to OJ, and talking about the same day):

(5) At 23:05 he put on a white shirt, a blue Yohji Yamamoto suit, dark socks, and his brown Bruno Magli shoes.

KK could also say it uttering:

(6) Gaueko 11k eta 5ean, alkandora zuria jantzi zuen, eta Yohji Yamamoto traje bat, galtzerdi ilunak eta bere Bruno Magli zapatak marroiak.

This is one of the most amazing properties of linguistic action. It is possible for different people, OJ, JP, and KK for instance, to say the same things, in different places, different contexts, in different languages. CL should accept that these three utterances express the same proposition, and constitute no argument for the relativity of what is said. They would also agree, we think, that one can correctly report what OJ said uttering:

(7) OJ said that at 11:05 p.m. (the day of the offense) he put on a white shirt, a blue Yohji Yamamoto suit, dark socks, and his brown Bruno Magli shoes.

But one could also report it as

(8) OJ said that at shortly after 11:00 p.m. (the day of the offense) he put on a shirt, a Yohji Yamamoto suit, socks, and his Bruno Magli shoes—he mentioned the colors, but I don't remember them.

The that-clause does not provide a *canonical* description, for the sentence that follows the "that" does not express the proposition in question. It does identify some of the constituents of the proposition (OJ, suit, socks, Bruno Magli shoes) and delimits accurately if incompletely others (the colors of the suit, socks, and shoes, and the exact time). Similarly with

(9) OJ said that he put on his clothes—I don't remember which—at 11.00 p.m.—more or less.

Finally, one can just say,

(10) What OJ said

to designate the proposition in question.

This plurality of descriptions in no way implies the existence of a plurality of propositions *said* by OJ's original utterance. All of them are true descriptions of what OJ said, although only (7) is a canonical, *expressive description.* (8)–(10) are less and less informative and do not claim to express the same proposition OJ did—(10) is of course sub-sentential, so doesn't express a proposition at all.[5]

Even when there is some relativity to context in what is said, there is not the radical sort of relativity required to undermine the utility of what is said as a basis for theoretical work. As we noted, if L says "That moronic clown just wrote another book", forensic issues may introduce a certain amount of relativity. Those issues aside, whether one wants to maintain that L said that X just wrote another book, which, assuming X is not both a moron and a clown, would require a Donnellan-like treatment of descriptions, or rather maintain that L managed to convey the information that X just wrote another book to C, not by saying it, but by saying something else, obviously false or without truth-value, and thereby implicating that X just wrote another book, would depend on one's overall theory. But theorists, in debating this, would be using and developing what is said as a central theoretical concept, not abandoning it.

[5] Sometimes by making sub-sentential utterances speakers do express full propositions (see Carston 2002: 152–7), but this is not the case with (10).

6.3. Pragmatic Indiscernibility

CL go further than content pluralism and the relativity of what is said. They claim that, given some facts that should be mutually known, the following would also be true descriptions of what OJ said:

(11) He said that he dressed up in some really fancy clothes late in the evening.

(12) He said that he changed his clothes right after 11 p.m.

(13) He said that he stopped exposing himself to the neighbors right after 11 p.m.

(14) He said that he gave the sign at 11:05.

All of these examples are naturally regarded as falling into one or both of two categories. They may be what one might call incremental implications of what OJ said. That is, what OJ said, together with certain assumptions, as for example that Bruno Magli shoes and Yohji Yamamoto suite are pretty posh duds, implies that he dressed up in fancy clothes. Or they may be regarded as implicatures: why else would OJ tell us of these brands, if he didn't want to impress us with what a fancy dresser he was?

Most authors would consider (11)–(14), in the right context, as reports of putative implicatures—stronger or weaker, following Sperber and Wilson's (1986) distinction—of OJ's sayings. They could only be considered as reports of what he said, as CL do, if one ignores the Gricean distinction between what is said and what is implicated by an utterance. And this is what CL do. Contrary to what they seem to assume when defending (their version of) semantic minimalism,[6] CL just end up erasing the Gricean theoretical distinction between what is said and what is implicated by an utterance:

> There is no fundamental theoretical divide between sayings and implicatures. They are both on the side of speech act content. Whatever mechanisms might generate implicatures are also all used to generate what speakers say. (p. 204)

This is really puzzling. CL's greatest enemies, confessed radical contextualists such as relevance theorists for instance, do admit that the same kind of pragmatic processes are involved in the derivation of both what-is-said (explicatures, in their terminology) and implicatures;[7] but neither they nor other radical contextualists

[6] Here for instance: "We agree with her [Carston] that you need a contextually shaped content to generate implicatures in all of the cases she discusses . . . What's needed in order to derive the implicature in these cases is a contextually shaped content, i.e., a contextually shaped what-is-said" (p. 180).

[7] Recanati (2004) makes a distinction between primary and secondary pragmatic processes in order to distinguish the (non-inferential) pragmatic processes involved in getting at 'what is said' and pragmatic processes involved in the inference of implicatures. Relevance theorists think that the

like Recanati, Searle, or Travis are ready to blur the distinction between what-is-said and implicatures. CL are. And thus, they go not only against what everybody else accepts in pragmatics nowadays (this we don't consider bad in itself; we sympathize with defenders of unpopular causes), but they go also, we are afraid, against their own version of semantic minimalism.

7. SEMANTIC MINIMALISM DEFEATED

Consider the following premises, both quoted from CL:

(a) 'There is no fundamental theoretical divide between sayings and implicatures' (p. 204).

(b) 'One of the many propositions asserted by an utterance [i.e. one of the sayings] is the semantic content of the utterance (the proposition semantically expressed)' (p. 200).

Ergo—one can be led to conclude:

(c) There is no fundamental theoretical divide between the proposition semantically expressed, sayings and implicatures.

So we are asked to believe that, on the one hand, there is a minimal proposition called the 'semantically expressed proposition', that results from the sentence's conventional semantic meaning plus pragmatic processes of reference fixing, disambiguation, and precisification, that plays a crucial role in a theory of understanding and communication. On the other hand, this proposition is only one, among indefinitely many others. What is so important about it? It isn't what is said. Even if it were, it would only be one of indefinitely many "sayings". Why are the factors, specific to the utterance, that resolve ambiguities, the reference of demonstratives and names, worthy of elevation into the well-guarded realm of semantics, while other utterance specific factors are not? The relativity of what is said seems to undermine any story that would account for what is special about their "semantic content".

CONCLUSION

Our main contentions, then, are as follows:

- We agree with CL in a minimalist conception of semantics. Semantics is the study of the conventional meanings of types of expressions and modes of combination.

same kind of (inferential) pragmatic processes are involved in the derivation of both explicatures and implicatures.

- We disagree that the suitable conception of semantic contribution, given the minimalist perspective, is their conception of semantic content, which incorporates into semantics not only the objective contextual facts that resolve the reference of indexicals, but also a number of factors that depend on the intentions of the speaker and perhaps also other mental facts about the participants in the conversation in questions: the resolution of demonstratives, the reference of names, and precisification of vague terms.
- We instead maintain that, insofar as semantics needs to reason about contents (propositions) rather than merely about meanings (or characters), the appropriate vehicle is the utterance-bound content, which quantifies over contextual and intentional factors.
- That said, we do not maintain that such minimal semantic contents are what is said, and we claim that determination of what is said inevitably depends on factors typically inferred by pragmatic methods. Here we agree with CL.
- We disagree, however, with their skepticism about the theoretical usefulness of what is said. We are confident that a theoretically useful concept of what is said, explicated as locutionary content, can be developed that will play more or less the roles contemplated by both Grice and the new theorists of reference.
- We do not claim to have provided such a concept here, but only to have made some progress towards developing it.[8]

REFERENCES

Bach, K. (1994), 'Conversational Implicitures', *Mind and Language*, 9: 124–62.

Cappelen, H., and E. Lepore (2005), *Insensitive Semantics*. Oxford: Blackwell.

Carston, R. (1988), 'Implicature, Explicature, and Truth-Theoretic Semantics', in R. Kempson (ed.), *Mental Representations: The Interface between Language and Reality*, pp. 155–81. Cambridge: Cambridge University Press.

—— (2002), *Thoughts and Utterances: The Pragmatics of Explicit Communication*. Oxford: Blackwell.

Grice, H. P. (1967), 'Logic and Conversation', in Grice, *Studies in the Way of Words*, pp. 22–40. Cambridge, Mass.: Harvard University Press, 1989.

Kaplan, David (1989), 'Demonstratives', in J. Almog, J. Perry, and H. Wettstein (eds.), *Themes from Kaplan*, pp. 481–563. Oxford: Oxford University Press.

Korta, K., and J. Perry (2006), 'Three Demonstrations and a Funeral', *Mind and Language*, 21/2: 166–86.

[8] The first author thanks the University of the Basque Country (9/UPV 00I09.I09-14 449/2002) and the Diamond XX Philosophy Institute for support. The second author thanks Stanford University and the Diamond XX Philosophy Institute for support. Both authors thank the editors and the anonymous referees for their valuable comments and suggestions.

Perry, J. (2001), *Reference and Reflexivity*. Stanford, Calif.: CSLI Publications.
Recanati, F. (1989), 'The Pragmatics of What is Said', *Mind and Language*, 4: 295–329.
____ (2004), *Literal Meaning*. Cambridge: Cambridge University Press.
Sperber, D., and Deirdre W. (1986), *Relevance: Communication and Cognition*, Oxford: Blackwell; 2nd rev. edn., 1995.

4

How and Why to be a Moderate Contextualist

Ishani Maitra

1. INTRODUCTION

Much recent work in the philosophy of language has focused on the extent to which what linguistic expressions express depends upon context. It is (relatively) uncontroversial that some expressions are context-sensitive, for instance, indexicals like 'I', and demonstratives like 'this'. But there is little agreement beyond this point. On some views (the Minimalist views), there is not much context-sensitivity in the language that goes beyond these uncontroversially context-dependent expressions. On other views (the Radical Contextualist views), context-sensitivity is everywhere in language. And on yet other views (the Moderate Contextualist views), the truth lies somewhere in between these extremes. (I shall offer more precise renderings of these views in what follows.)

In an influential book, Herman Cappelen and Ernie Lepore have argued against both Moderate and Radical Contextualism on a variety of grounds (Cappelen and Lepore 2005). In particular, they argue that Moderate Contextualism in fact collapses into Radical Contextualism, that any attempt (on the part of the Moderate Contextualist) to resist Radical Contextualism must result in either inconsistency or arbitrariness. In addition, Cappelen and Lepore also argue that Radical Contextualism is unable to explain how speakers and hearers regularly succeed in communicating. Here, they suggest that if there were as much context-sensitivity as Radical Contextualists think there is, it would take a miracle for a speaker and a hearer to ever successfully communicate. (This argument, which I label the *Miracle of Communication Argument*, or *MCA* for short, will be explained in more detail later in this chapter.) Given the instability of Moderate Contextualism, and the failure of Radical Contextualism to explain successful communication, Cappelen and Lepore conclude that both views must be rejected.

In this chapter, I defend Moderate Contextualism against the charges described above. But I approach this conclusion in a somewhat roundabout way. In the next section (§2), I begin with a characterization of what's at issue in the debate between Moderate and Radical Contextualists. As will become clear later in the chapter (§3), this way of characterizing what's at stake between the two camps differs from Cappelen and Lepore's characterization, but has the advantage of being able to resist the latter's 'collapse' arguments, i.e. arguments to the effect that Moderate Contextualism just collapses into Radical Contextualism. Next (§4), I describe the Miracle of Communication Argument, and offer an initial assessment of the problem raised by that argument for Contextualists of all kinds. Then (§5), I describe a Moderate Contextualist view (in my sense) that can answer the challenge posed by the MCA. Finally (§6), I conclude by drawing attention to the major consequences of my argument for current debates about context-sensitivity.

2. WHAT MAKES A CONTEXTUALISM MODERATE?

It will be useful to begin by fixing some terminology. Following Richard Heck (2002), and Jeff King and Jason Stanley (2005), I shall say that the conventional meaning of an expression is its *standing meaning*. The standing meaning of an expression is invariant across contexts. However, expressions differ in whether they pick out (or express) the same thing in different contexts, when used according to their standing meanings. I shall say that what an expression picks out (or expresses) in a particular context when used according to its standing meaning is its *semantic content* in that context. Some expressions (e.g. 'Boston') pick out the same object in every context, and so have the same semantic content in every context, whereas others (e.g. 'I', 'this') pick out different objects in different contexts, and so have different semantic contents in different contexts. Finally, I shall say that an expression is *context-sensitive* if its semantic content varies from context to context.

Next, given any expression *e*, I shall say that a Contextualist view about *e* is any view according to which *e* is context-sensitive. This is obviously a very broad characterization of Contextualism. One (perhaps counter-intuitive) consequence of this characterization is that Cappelen and Lepore's positive semantic view—namely, Semantic Minimalism—turns out to be Contextualist about several expressions, namely, the expressions in their Basic Set.[1]

On my usage, all Contextualist views (of both Moderate and Radical persuasions) are Contextualist about some expression or other. As already suggested in

[1] For Cappelen and Lepore, the Basic Set consists of the following members: personal and demonstrative pronouns in their various cases and number, the adverbs 'here', 'there', 'now', 'today', 'yesterday', 'tomorrow', 'ago', 'hence(forth)', the adjectives 'actual' and 'present', tense indicators, and contextuals like 'enemy' and 'foreign' (2005: 1–2).

the Introduction, what divides Moderates from Radicals is *how much* context-sensitivity each recognizes. To spell out this idea, we need some way of gauging the extent of context-sensitivity recognized by any Contextualist view.[2] Describing a framework for doing this will be the main project of the current section.

To begin: on most Contextualist views, the standing meaning of any context-sensitive expression plays some role in determining its semantic content in a context. For example, if the standing meanings of indexicals are their characters, in the sense of Kaplan (1989), then the standing meaning of 'I' can be represented as a function that takes any context to the speaker in that context.[3] On this picture, the standing meaning of 'I' constrains its possible semantic contents: for example, it makes it the case that I cannot use the expression to pick out a chair in my current context.

But even among those who agree that the standing meanings of expressions play some role in determining their semantic contents, there is disagreement about how great that role is. To illustrate, consider the following toy example. Let *e* be a context-sensitive expression, and let *C* and C_{Macro} be a pair of Contextualist views about *e* which disagree about its standing meaning. According to *C*, the standing meaning of *e* may be represented as a function from contexts to objects; moreover, on this view, for any object whatsoever, there are (perhaps merely possible) contexts in which *e* can be used to pick out that object. According to C_{Macro}, the standing meaning of *e* may be represented as a function from contexts to *macroscopic* objects. Then, *C* and C_{Macro} differ on the extent to which the standing meaning of *e* constrains its possible semantic contents. By imposing greater restrictions on the range of possible semantic contents for *e*, C_{Macro} attributes a greater (i.e. more constraining) role to the standing meaning of *e* than *C* does.[4]

In categorizing Cappelen and Lepore's positive view as Contextualist, I do not mean to suggest that there are no important differences between Contextualist views and Minimalist views. However, part of the point of this chapter is to argue that one putative difference between the two classes of views—namely, that Minimalist views can explain various facts about successful communication that Contextualist views cannot—is not a genuine difference. More on this in §§4–5.

[2] There is, of course, more than one way to gauge how much context-sensitivity a view recognizes. As will be discussed in §3, Cappelen and Lepore's way has to do with determining how many sources of context-sensitivity the view in question recognizes. In this section, I will outline a different approach to gauging context-sensitivity.

[3] I focus on this simple way of representing standing meanings for illustrative purposes only. It seems likely that this way of representing standing meanings will not be adequate for all theoretical purposes. I think, however, that it is possible to make sense of the idea of standing meaning constraining semantic content on alternative accounts of standing meaning as well, though I cannot consider such alternative accounts here.

[4] The standing meaning of an expression depends, in part, on its syntax. One way (but not the only way) in which standing meaning can constrain semantic content is by restricting the effect of context on content to that which is syntactically triggered.

The discussion in the preceding paragraphs gives us one dimension along which Contextualist views about a particular expression might differ. There is a further dimension of difference as well. Most Contextualist views agree that the effect of context on semantic content is rule-governed. But there is disagreement about how rule-governed that effect is. To illustrate, consider another toy example. Let $C_{Salient}$ and $C_{Speaker}$ be two versions of the Contextualist view C mentioned above. Being versions of C, both $C_{Salient}$ and $C_{Speaker}$ agree that the standing meaning of *e* can be represented by a function from contexts to objects. But they disagree about what the relevant function is. According to $C_{Salient}$, the semantic content of *e* in a particular context is whichever object is most salient in that context. According to $C_{Speaker}$, the semantic content of *e* in a context is whichever object the speaker in that context intends to pick out. Let's assume (as I think is plausible) that how salient an object is in a given context depends on a number of factors about that context, including (but not limited to) the intentions of the speaker in that context. Moreover, $C_{Salient}$ does not specify how the various factors should be added together to determine salience. Because it allows a strictly greater range of contextual factors to play a role in determining the semantic contents of *e*, and because it doesn't offer a recipe for combining these factors, $C_{Salient}$ takes the effect of context on content to be *less* rule-governed than does $C_{Speaker}$.[5]

To sum up the discussion thus far: given any expression *e*, Contextualist views about *e* can differ with respect to how they answer the following questions:

> To what extent does the standing meaning of *e* constrain its semantic contents?
>
> To what extent is the effect of context on the semantic contents of *e* rule-governed?

The first is a question about the contribution that standing meaning makes to the semantic contents of an expression, while the second is a question about the contribution that context makes to those semantic contents. I shall label the first the *Meaning Question*, and the second, the *Context Question*. The two questions correspond to two dimensions along which Contextualist views about any expression can differ.[6]

[5] To say that the effect of context on content is more rule-governed according to one Contextualist view than another is not necessarily to say either (i) that the first view specifies rules governing that effect while the second does not, or (ii) that the first view specifies more rules governing that effect than the second. Rather, the notion of rule-governedness that I have in mind is roughly the following: the more rule-governed the effect of context on content, the easier it is for the hearer to work out the semantic content of the expression in a given context by using the rules. Thus e.g. the effect of context on content for automatic indexicals (in Perry's sense) is more rule-governed in my sense than the effect of context on content for other indexicals (Perry 1997).

[6] Some theorists might be inclined to say that the rules governing the effect of context on semantic content are just part of standing meaning. In that case, the Context Question would be

With this set-up, I am now in a position to characterize what makes a Contextualist view about a particular expression more or less Moderate (or equivalently, less or more Radical) than others. Here's the idea. I said earlier that Moderates and Radicals differ about how much context-sensitivity each recognizes. The two dimensions distinguished above provide a way of spelling out this thought. For any Contextualist view, how much context-sensitivity it recognizes varies inversely with (i) how constraining a role it assigns to standing meaning, and (ii) how rule-governed it takes the effect of context to be. The more constrained and rule-governed the semantic contents of an expression are on a given Contextualist view, the less context-sensitive that expression is taken to be. And the less context-sensitivity a view recognizes, the more Moderate (less Radical) it is.

To make things slightly more precise: let *e* be a context-sensitive expression, and let *C*1 and *C*2 be a pair of Contextualist views about *e*. With respect to the Meaning Question, *C*1 is more Moderate (less Radical) than *C*2 if *C*1 assigns a more constraining role to standing meaning than *C*2 does. Similarly, with respect to the Context Question, *C*1 is more Moderate (less Radical) than *C*2 if *C*1 regards the effect of context on content to be more rule-governed than *C*2 does. Putting this together, if *C*1 is more Moderate along both dimensions than *C*2, then it is a more Moderate (less Radical) Contextualist view about *e* than *C*2.

A few points of clarification may be useful here. First, I have thus far been focusing on what it is for a Contextualist view *about a particular expression* to be more or less Moderate than another Contextualist view about the same expression. But the account can be extended to Contextualist views about *classes* of expressions. I will say that a Contextualist view about some class of expressions is more Moderate (less Radical) than a second Contextualist view about the same class if the first view is more Moderate about each expression in the class than the second view. In the case in which the class includes all expressions in the English language, I shall say that the first view is just more Moderate (with no further qualification) than the second.

Second, there are some tricky cases that are not covered by the account as developed thus far. For instance, given two Contextualist views about a particular expression, it is possible that one is more Moderate along one dimension (say, with respect to the Meaning Question), but more Radical along the other dimension, than the second. In that case, taking the two dimensions together, what should we say about which of the views is more Moderate?[7] Similarly,

part of the Meaning Question. The family of views that Recanati labels *Conventionalism* might be committed to such a conception of standing meaning (Recanati 2005). However, the point of distinguishing the Context Question from the Meaning Question is to note that it is possible to think that the effect of context on content is very rule-governed without committing oneself to such an expansive view of standing meaning.

[7] This question arises for demonstrative like 'this' and pronouns like 'it', which allows for somewhat Radical answers to the Meaning Question, but very Moderate answers to the Context

given two Contextualist views about several classes of expressions, it is possible that one is more Moderate about some of the classes, but more Radical about the others, than the second. Again, taking all the classes together, what should we say about which of the views is more Moderate? The account thus far does not answer either of these questions. There is more than one way of extending the account to cover these tricky cases. Since these details do not matter for my main argument, I shall not consider the relative merits of the possibilities. Still, it seems reasonable to suppose that a good answer to these questions should take into consideration *how* Moderate (or Radical) each view is along each dimension (or with respect to each of the classes in question).

Finally, the account I have developed here yields a comparative notion of moderation (and radicalization). That is to say, on this account, whether a Contextualist view is Moderate (or Radical) is really a matter of degree, a matter of how it compares to other Contextualist views. At first glance, this looks like a significant difference between my account and Cappelen and Lepore's (to be discussed in the next section). However, I will argue that this is merely a prima-facie difference: given Cappelen and Lepore's way of setting things up, they too should recognize degrees of moderation (and radicalization). Moreover, though introducing degrees of moderation adds a measure of complexity to the discussion, this is necessary to do justice to the current debates about context-dependence in the philosophy of language. I shall return to this point in the next section.

3. MODERATE CONTEXTUALISM AND THE COLLAPSE ARGUMENTS

As I've already mentioned, my account of what makes a Contextualism Moderate (or more accurately, more Moderate than other Contextualist views) differs from Cappelen and Lepore's. In this section, I shall compare the two accounts, and offer some reasons for preferring mine.

Moderate and Radical Contextualism, in Cappelen and Lepore's sense, are each families of views, all members of which recognize that some expressions are context-sensitive. More specifically, it is common ground among members of these families that the expressions in the Basic Set are context-sensitive.[8] Where the two sides differ is with respect to how much context-sensitivity they recognize *beyond* this Basic Set.

Radical Contextualists (in Cappelen and Lepore's sense) believe, first, that every sentence of the English language (and perhaps, every single expression

Question. Here, it may turn out that, on the best view of these expressions, the answers to the Context Question are *so* Moderate that we're inclined to be Moderates about these expressions overall.

[8] See n. 1 for a description of the Basic Set.

as well) is context-sensitive, and second, that no sentence expresses a complete proposition (2005: 6). By contrast, Moderate Contextualists (also in their sense) believe, first, that members of the Basic Set are not the only "sources of context-sensitivity", and second, that for many sentences, their context-sensitivity can be traced (at least in part) to sources other than the expressions in the Basic Set (2005: 7). On this view, then, Radical Contextualists see context-sensitivity everywhere, whereas Moderate Contextualists see context-sensitivity in many places.

Three features of Cappelen and Lepore's view need to be highlighted for my purposes. First, as they see things, the crucial difference between Moderate and Radical Contextualism has to do with how the following question is answered:

> To what extent do the sources of context-sensitivity outstrip the members of the Basic Set?

I shall label this the Sources Question. Regarding this question, Moderate Contextualists think that the sources of context-sensitivity go some moderate distance beyond the members of the Basic Set, but do not include all expressions of the language. Radical Contextualists, on the other hand, believe that the sources of context-sensitivity go far beyond the Basic Set, perhaps all the way to including all expressions in the language.

Second, though they do not speak this way, Cappelen and Lepore's account readily admits of a comparative notion of moderation (and radicalization). We can say that one Contextualist view is more Moderate (less Radical) than another if the first holds that the sources of context-sensitivity constitute a lesser expansion of the Basic Set than the second does. This way of speaking has the advantage of avoiding the awkward conclusion that there is a sharp dividing line between Moderate and Radical Contextualist views, and that, consequently, Contextualist views that differ on only a few expressions must be placed on different sides of that line.

Third, and most importantly for my purposes, it is possible for a Contextualist view to be Radical in Cappelen and Lepore's sense, but Moderate (or among the more Moderate) in my sense. To illustrate, imagine a Contextualist view according to which every (or nearly every) expression is context-sensitive, but the semantic contents of each context-sensitive expression are both heavily constrained by their standing meanings, and determined in very rule-governed ways by contexts. The converse is also possible, i.e. a Contextualist view that is Moderate in Cappelen and Lepore's sense, but among the more Radical in my sense. These possibilities will prove crucial in what follows.

In the remainder of this section, I will offer two reasons for preferring my account of what makes a Contextualist view Moderate over Cappelen and Lepore's. A third reason will be mentioned briefly below, and then discussed in more detail later (§5).

First, Cappelen and Lepore's way of drawing the distinction makes it hard to capture some important differences among views that are relevant to the current debates on context-dependence. To see this, consider the following kind of Contextualist view, modeled on Stanley (2002). (I'm not claiming that Stanley would or should endorse this position. I'm merely describing a position that is taxonomically interesting.) According to the sort of view I have in mind, (nearly) every expression in the language contributes a variable to the logical form of any sentence containing it. The values of these variables are fixed by context, via a few simple rules. Context makes no further contribution to semantic content beyond fixing the values of these variables. The standing meaning of every expression tightly constrains its possible semantic contents, in part by narrowly circumscribing the possible values that the associated variable can assume. Given all of this, it is a fairly easy task to figure out the semantic contents of most expressions in most contexts.

The type of view described above is a very Moderate Contextualist view in my sense, since the semantic contents of all expressions are highly constrained by their standing meanings, and the effects of context on semantic contents are highly rule-governed. However, this kind of view gets classified as an extremely Radical Contextualist view in Cappelen and Lepore's sense, since almost every term in the language is context-sensitive. But intuitively, this position is much closer to the positions of the paradigmatic Moderate Contextualists (such as King and Stanley 2005; Perry 1998; Stanley 2000, 2002; Szabó 2001; Taylor 2001) than to those of the paradigmatic Radical Contextualists (such as Bezuidenhout 2002; Carston 1988, 2002; Recanati 1989, 2004; Sperber and Wilson 1986; Travis 1996, 2000). Part of the debate, indeed a large part of it, between the philosophers I just described as Moderates and those I classified as Radicals is whether *anything like* the kind of Contextualist view described above can capture all of the context-sensitivity in language, with the Moderates saying "Yes", and the Radicals saying "No". Given the wide divergence of views within both camps, there are of course a number of ways to slice the debate at its joints. But any slicing that puts the sort of view just described in the Radical camp obscures a large part of what is at issue here.

Second, Moderate Contextualism in my sense is a stable position. In particular, Moderate Contextualists (on my account) can resist Cappelen and Lepore's 'collapse' arguments, which purport to show that Moderates can refuse to embrace Radical Contextualism only on pain of arbitrariness or inconsistency.

Here's a brief sketch of one of Cappelen and Lepore's arguments for this collapse. Moderate Contextualists often rely on what they label *Context Shifting Arguments* (or *CSA*s for short) to defend their views. A CSA attempts to establish the context-sensitivity of a sentence S by showing that it is possible to construct two relevantly similar contexts C and C' such that an utterance of S in C says something different (has a different truth value) from an utterance of S in C'. Cappelen and Lepore object that "with sufficient ingenuity", CSAs can be constructed for any sentence whatsoever (2005: 40). Therefore, if a CSA suffices to show that a particular sentence is context-sensitive, other CSAs can be used to show that every sentence is context-sensitive. But then, Radical Contextualism follows.[9]

Whatever the merits of this argument, it is easy to see that it does not put pressure on Moderate Contextualists in my sense. CSAs only serve to show that particular sentences (and expressions within them) are context-sensitive. They leave open *how* context-sensitive any expression is in my sense. That is, they leave open how the Meaning and Context Questions should be answered for any particular context-sensitive expression. But, on my view, moderation (and radicalization) is a matter of how the latter questions are answered. Even if a CSA can be constructed for every expression whatsoever, that does not tell us how standing meanings and contexts combine to determine their semantic contents. Accordingly, even if this collapse argument succeeds, it does not put any pressure on a Contextualist to become more Radical (in my sense).[10]

Third, and finally, moderation in my sense helps explain certain facts about successful communication that would be puzzling otherwise. To build up to this third point, it will be useful to take a detour through Cappelen and Lepore's Miracle of Communication Argument. In the next section, I shall sketch that argument, and assess the challenge it poses for Contextualist views. Then, in §5, I shall show how moderation in my sense helps to answer this challenge.

4. THE MIRACLE OF COMMUNICATION ARGUMENT

The Miracle of Communication Argument (or MCA) purports to show that Radical Contextualism (in Cappelen and Lepore's sense) cannot explain how speakers and hearers regularly succeed in communicating with each other. Here's the argument. Radical Contextualists believe that a hearer needs to know several things about a context in order to work out the semantic content of any sentence

[9] Cappelen and Lepore also offer a second argument for this collapse, which focuses on what they label the *Incompleteness Arguments* for Moderate Contextualism. On their view, Incompleteness Arguments, like CSAs, over-generate: that is, if any such argument succeeds in showing that some sentence is context-sensitive, then arguments of the same type can be used to show that every sentence is context-sensitive (2005: 61).

[10] An analogous point applies to Cappelen and Lepore's other collapse argument, mentioned in n. 9. Space considerations prevent me from spelling out this point further here.

What I have said here leaves open the possibility that Cappelen and Lepore's collapse arguments might succeed in putting pressure on a Contextualist who is Moderate in my sense to become more Radical in *their* sense, even if such arguments fail to put pressure on such a Moderate to become more Radical in my sense. And that, Cappelen and Lepore might say, is bad enough, for Radical Contextualism (in their sense) is vulnerable to a number of problems, including those posed by the Miracle of Communication Argument. In the remainder of this chapter, I shall argue that a Contextualist view that is sufficiently Moderate in my sense can survive the challenge posed by that argument, regardless of how Radical it is in Cappelen and Lepore's sense. I shall not be able to address their other objections to Radical Contextualism here.

in that context. This includes all of the following bits of knowledge (listed by Anne Bezuidenhout):

(i) knowledge that has already been activated from the prior discourse context (if any);
(ii) knowledge that is available based on who one's conversational partner is and on what community memberships one shares with that person;
(iii) knowledge that is available through observation of the mutual perceptual environment;
(iv) any stereotypical knowledge or scripts or frames that are associatively triggered by accessing the semantic potential of any of the expressions currently being used;
(v) knowledge of the purposes and abilities of one's conversational partners (e.g., whether the person is being deceitful or sincere, whether the person tends to verbosity or is a person of few words, etc.);
(vi) knowledge one has of the general principles governing conversational exchanges (perhaps including Grice's conversational maxims, culturally specific norms of politeness, etc.). (Bezuidenhout 2002: 117, quoted in Cappelen and Lepore 2005: 123–4)

Now consider a speaker who utters even a simple sentence, such as:

(1) Philosophy is fun.

If Radical Contextualism were true (say Cappelen and Lepore), a hearer might need to have all of (i)–(vi) in order to figure out what is expressed by (1) in this context. More specifically, the hearer would need this information to figure out what counts as philosophy in this context, as well as what property 'fun' expresses here. Hearers generally do not have all of the information mentioned on Bezuidenhout's list regarding any particular context. Therefore, if Radical Contextualism were true, it would take a miracle for the hearer to successfully work out the content of (1) on this occasion. But hearers do regularly figure out semantic contents, and there are no miracles. So, Cappelen and Lepore conclude, Radical Contextualism must be false.[11]

Does the MCA succeed? A major worry about the argument (upon which I shall elaborate below) is that, *regardless* of whether Radical Contextualism is true,

[11] Cappelen and Lepore also mention a related argument against Radical Contextualism, which focuses on how someone in a context other than the speaker's can work out the semantic content of an utterance of (1) in the speaker's context. The worry here is that those not located in the speaker's context generally know even less about that context than those who are located there. Yet, those not in the speaker's context can regularly work out the semantic contents of sentences uttered by the speaker in the speaker's context. If Radical Contextualism were true, Cappelen and Lepore conclude, such inter-contextual communication is even harder to explain that intra-contextual communication. The problem raised by this second argument against Radical Contextualism is closely related to the problem raised by the (apparent) ease of inter-contextual indirect reports of semantic contents. I consider the latter problem briefly in n. 13.

much of our ordinary communication makes use of (i)–(vi) on Bezuidenhout's list. Therefore, either the argumentative strategy employed in the MCA can be extended to show that all of this ordinary communication is regularly unsuccessful as well (which seems implausible), or else, *contra* Cappelen and Lepore, the success of communication that relies on (i)–(vi) need not be miraculous.

To illustrate this worry, consider some of the different ways in which information is communicated. First, it is uncontroversial that much of what is communicated is communicated implicitly, for example, via conversational implicatures. Consider the following conversation:

(2) *Annie*: Do you want a glass of milk?
Bianca: Milk puts me to sleep.

In saying what she does, Bianca implicates something, but what she implicates depends upon the context. If, for instance, it is night-time, and it is well-known that Bianca is an insomniac, then she implicates that she does want milk. If, on the other hand, it is clear that Bianca is working on a project that will require several more hours to complete, she implicates that she does not want milk. In either case, Annie will succeed in working out Bianca's implicature only by relying upon at least (i)–(iii), and (v)–(vi). Working out other implicatures will require even more information. But if speakers and hearers regularly succeed in communicating implicatures (as surely they do), then communication that relies upon several of the items on Bezuidenhout's list need not be miraculous.

Second, on Cappelen and Lepore's own view, what is said (or asserted) by any utterance goes far beyond its semantic content. They illustrate this view with the following utterance (produced by O. J. Simpson during his trial):

(3) At 11:05 p.m. I put on a white shirt, a blue Yohji Yamamoto suit, dark socks, and my brown Bruno Magli shoes.

According to Cappelen and Lepore's Speech Act Pluralism, what a speaker says (or asserts) depends upon a variety of factors, including (but not limited to) facts about the speaker's intentions and beliefs, facts about the conversational context of the utterance, other facts about the world, and logical relations (2005: 193–4). Thus, depending on what the context of utterance is like, Simpson might assert all of the following in uttering (3):

(4) He dressed up in some really fancy clothes late in the evening.
(5) He changed his clothes right after 11 p.m. (If uttered in a context

in which it is shared knowledge that he was wearing different clothes before 11 p.m.).

(6) He gave the sign at 11:05. (If uttered in a context in which it is shared knowledge that putting on brown shoes is a sign of some significance or other.) (2005: 196)

Given this expansive view about what is said, Cappelen and Lepore are committed to the consequence that much of the information on Bezuidenhout's list is relevant for determining what a speaker has asserted. Nevertheless, surely hearers regularly work out what speakers assert. So, once again, communication that relies upon the information mentioned on Bezuidenhout's list need not be miraculous.[12]

This is not to deny that hearers sometimes fail to figure out what has been asserted, or, for that matter, what has been implicated. As Cappelen and Lepore point out, some of what is asserted (on their view) will be difficult for the hearer to grasp, for example, if he is unaware of relevant facts about the speaker. But this is compatible with thinking that hearers do regularly work out (much of) what speakers assert and implicate, and that this is a crucial part of ordinary communication.

At this juncture, Cappelen and Lepore might admit that communication that relies on (i)–(vi) can be regularly successful (and non-miraculous). But they might protest that there is nevertheless some significant difference between what is communicated implicitly or by merely being asserted, and what is communicated by being semantically expressed. For example, they might suggest that a hearer can be more confident about what is communicated via semantic contents than about what is communicated in other ways.[13] Then, the problem for Radical Contextualism is not that reliance on the items on Bezuidenhout's list is incompatible with regular successful communication, or that it renders

[12] There is a stronger point to be made here. Both (2) and (3) are cases in which hearers must make *extensive* use of the items on Bezuidenhout's list to work out implicatures and assertoric contents. Moreover, this is true of many such contents. So, even successful communication that relies heavily upon (i)–(vi) need not be miraculous.

[13] Relatedly, Cappelen and Lepore might also say that it is easier to make inter-contextual indirect reports of semantic contents than of what is communicated in other ways. For example, whereas a hearer would need to know quite a lot about context in order to report O. J. Simpson as having asserted (4), (5), or (6) in uttering (3), he (the hearer) would not need to know much about context in order to report my utterance of "It's warm in Syracuse" as "Ishani said that it's warm in Syracuse." My response to this imagined reply has two parts. First, the data regarding inter-contextual indirect reports is rather complicated, in ways that make it quite difficult to spell out the sense in which it is *easier* to make inter-contextual indirect reports of semantic contents than of other contents. To illustrate this point, consider the contexts in which Charlie's utterance (in front of his fridge) of "There's no beer" can be truly reported by "Charlie said that there's no beer". Second, moderation in my sense helps explain how semantic contents can be correctly (or at least, approximately) indirectly reported in contexts other than the original context of utterance, as well as how hearers in such contexts can come to know (or at least approximately know) the semantic contents of the original utterances via such indirect reports. Unfortunately, due to space considerations, I am unable to elaborate on these points here.

communication miraculous, but rather, that such reliance is incompatible with certain further facts about communication, including facts about differences between what is communicated via semantic contents, and what is communicated in other ways.

Unfortunately, this is still not right, because even on Cappelen and Lepore's view, hearers have to rely on the items on Bezuidenhout's list to work out semantic contents as well. Consider the following sentences:

(7) That is pretty. (Said when the speaker is pointing towards a collection of objects).

(8) We need a ride. (Said when the speaker is standing with a group of friends).

Both 'that' and 'we' are members of the Basic Set. In order for a hearer to work out the semantic contents of either of these sentences in particular contexts, he must know the contents of these expressions in those contexts. To figure this out, the hearer needs much of the information on Bezuidenhout's list. Take 'that': depending on one's favored theory of demonstrative reference, the semantic content of the occurrence of 'that' in (7) might be determined by the speaker's intentions, the speaker's demonstration, the salience of some object in the perceptual environment, the salience of some object in the prior discourse context, or (most plausibly) some combination of all of the above. In other words, in order to work out the content of some occurrence of 'that', a hearer might need to appeal to at least (i)–(iii). Similar points apply to 'we'. Thus, (at least some) communication via semantic contents relies on the items on Bezuidenhout's list, just like other forms of communication. So, even if it is true that hearers are more confident about what is communicated via semantic contents than about what is communicated in other ways, that difference cannot be explained by the supposition that communication via semantic contents does not rely on the items on Bezuidenhout's list.

Here again, Cappelen and Lepore might admit this last point, but maintain that, since the sources of context-sensitivity are so few on their view, semantic contents are *generally* easier to work out than implicatures and assertoric contents. Thus, hearers can *generally* be more confident about what is communicated via semantic contents than about what is communicated in other ways.[14] This,

[14] Spelling out this thought remains tricky. Here's one formulation that cannot be right: hearers can be more confident about what is communicated via semantic contents of *most* sentences than about what is communicated in other ways. The difficulty for this formulation is that most sentences are tensed. Even on Cappelen and Lepore's view, tense is a source of context-sensitivity. To work out the semantic content expressed by "It was raining in New York", a hearer must know quite a bit about the context in which the sentence is uttered, including (again) several of the items on Bezuidenhout's list. If Cappelen and Lepore allow that hearers can be sufficiently confident about the semantic contents of tensed sentences despite this context-sensitivity, then they should allow

then, is a fact about communication that requires explanation.[15] But since Radical Contextualists believe that (nearly) every sentence (and expression) is context-sensitive, no explanation of this fact would be forthcoming if Radical Contextualism were true. So, the problem for Radical Contextualism (and, for that matter, for Moderate Contextualism) is not that *any* reliance on the items on Bezuidenhout's list is incompatible with facts about regular successful communication, but rather, that *too much* reliance on such items is incompatible with those facts. That is the challenge posed by the MCA.

In the next section, I shall argue that some more Moderate Contextualist views can answer this challenge. Before turning to that response, however, it is worth emphasizing that there is some indeterminacy in what is required to answer this challenge. That is to say, if I am right in suggesting that the MCA raises a problem for Contextualist views that entail too much reliance on contextual information, then that immediately invites the question: how much is too much? Without a somewhat determinate answer to that question, the nature of this challenge remains unclear.

5. EVERYTHING IN MODERATION

I argued in the previous section that the challenge raised by the MCA is really this: how can a Contextualist view explain why hearers are *generally* more confident about what is communicated via semantic contents, than about what is communicated in other ways? My response will proceed in two stages. First, I will sketch a fairly Moderate Contextualist view (in my sense), and show that it alleviates much of the worry raised by the MCA. Second, I will argue that what remains of that challenge can be answered by paying attention to what is required for successful communication. Note that it is not my aim in this section to establish the truth of the sort of Moderate Contextualist view I describe: though I think that such a view is plausible, the task of offering a full defense is beyond the scope of this chapter. Rather, my aim is to argue for the following conditional claim: *if* a Moderate Contextualist view of this type were true, that would be sufficient to answer the challenge posed by the MCA.

To focus the discussion in this section, it will help to concentrate on one class of expressions. I shall focus on comparative adjectives, such as 'tall', 'fast', 'rich', and 'young'. However, much of what I say about expressions in this class, at least

that hearers can be equally confident about other sources of context-sensitivity that are constrained in similar ways.

[15] Actually, it is not at all clear to me that this is indeed a fact. Nevertheless, for the purposes of this chapter, I shall assume that this is true, and argue that its truth would pose no problem for at least some varieties of Contextualism.

with respect to answering the challenge posed by the MCA, will generalize to other classes as well.

Recall that, on my account, moderation (and radicalization) depend on how the Meaning and Context Questions are answered. Let's begin with the Meaning Question. How Moderate a Contextualist view is with respect to this question depends on how much the standing meanings of the expressions in question constrain their semantic contents. According to the sort of view I have in mind, the standing meanings of comparative adjectives contribute relations to their semantic contents. In so doing, these meanings do not fully determine semantic contents, for the latter also depend on comparison classes (to be discussed below). But they do rule out a lot of possibilities. For example, given its standing meaning, 'fast' can never express the relation that obtains between an object and a class when the object is large compared to the objects in that class, or the one that obtains when the object is red compared to the objects in the class. Thus, on such a view, the standing meanings of comparative adjectives eliminate many relations as possible semantic contents.

Next, let's turn to the Context Question. Consider the following sentences, in which the comparative adjectives are used predicatively:

(9) Sammy is fast. (Said in a context in which Sammy the snail is salient.)

(10) That basketball player is short. (Said of a basketball player who is six feet tall.)

A natural reading for (9) is that Sammy is fast for a snail, not that he is fast for any creature whatsoever. Similarly, a natural reading for (10) is that the basketball player in question is short for a basketball player, not that he is short for any entity (or even any person) whatsoever. In each case, on the sort of view I have in mind, the context provides as a comparison class some salient kind K that is instantiated by the individual (Sammy, the basketball player) of which the comparative adjective is predicated.[16]

It is easy to see that the comparison classes mentioned above for (9) and (10)—the class of snails, the class of basketball players—are not the only ones that a context could provide. Among other things, (9) could be used to express that Sammy is fast for all living creatures (e.g. in a context in which Sammy is known to have acquired super-powers), or that Sammy is fast for snails that have recently eaten (e.g. in a context in which we have just watched Sammy eat). So, the natural reading mentioned above is by no means the only semantic content that (9) can express. However, what is noteworthy about these additional

[16] I focus on this simple account of what context contributes to the semantic contents of comparative adjectives for illustrative purposes only. The argument in this section can be reformulated to fit alternate accounts of how context affects the semantic contents of expressions in this class.

(non-natural, or less natural) contents is that they require setting up in a way that the natural reading does not: whereas the latter is available in a wide variety of contexts, the former are only available in some particular contexts. Other readings, for example, that Sammy is fast for snails that have eaten a pound of leaves within the last forty minutes, are rarer still, though perhaps in principle available. Relatedly, even if it is possible to use (9) to express that Sammy is fast for snails that have eaten a pound of leaves within the last forty minutes, using (9) in this way is (to put it mildly) unusual.

How Moderate a Contextualist view is with respect to the Context Question depends on how rule-governed it takes the effect of context on content to be. According to the kind of Contextualist view I want to consider, some comparison classes that can be provided by context will result in natural readings (in the sense described above) of sentences like (9), while others will not. Recognizing that there are such natural readings, and putting significant constraints on the values of K that result in such readings, constitutes one way (though not the only way) in which the effect of context on content can be rule-governed on a Contextualist view. Such a view may thus fall on the Moderate end of the spectrum regarding the Context Question, the more so when the constraints on natural comparison classes (i.e. comparisons classes that result in natural readings) are more significant.

Putting all of this together, a more Moderate Contextualist view about comparative adjectives can be described as follows. First, on this view, the standing meanings of comparative adjectives constrain the range of semantic contents they can express. Though these meanings do not fully determine these semantic contents, they do rule out many candidates. Second, all comparative adjectives require comparison classes, to be provided by context. However, some of the classes that context can provide will result in natural readings (i.e. readings that are available across a wide variety of contexts, and ones that are expressed frequently), while others will not.

With this view in mind, let us return to the challenge posed by the MCA. What does this view say about what a hearer has to do in order to work out the semantic contents of sentences containing comparative adjectives? For the hearer, most of the work to be done in working out the semantic contents of sentences like (9) or (10) consists in figuring out the comparison class contributed by the context. In principle, this could be any class at all that contains the subject. But to say this is not to say that all candidate comparison classes should be treated equally. In the absence of special cues to the contrary, a hearer can infer that one of the natural comparison classes has been used, and thereby significantly narrow down the possibilities regarding the semantic content in question.[17]

[17] Of course, for most sentences, more than one comparison class will yield a natural reading in my sense. But deciding between even a handful of comparison classes is a much easier task than deciding among infinitely many.

Even if it is true that any of indefinitely many classes could in principle be the comparison class provided in a given context, this appears to be the same sense of 'in principle' according to which an interlocutor who appears, on the basis of visual experience, to be an old friend could in principle turn out to be a cleverly disguised impostor. My belief that I am speaking to my friend is surely justified, and can even qualify as knowledge, even though I might have been fooled by an impostor. Analogously, a hearer's belief that a speaker has expressed a particular semantic content, involving a natural comparison class, may be justified, and can even qualify as knowledge, even though the hearer might have made a mistake had the speaker expressed some other semantic contents. The fallibilism involved here would be objectionable only if communicative success required infallible knowledge. But such a view of communicative success—i.e. as requiring infallible knowledge—seems implausible.

On the picture I am suggesting, a more Moderate Contextualist view of the sort I have sketched can answer the challenge posed by the MCA as follows. On such a view, hearers can generally be more confident about what is communicated via semantic contents than about what is communicated in other ways because semantic contents are more heavily constrained (both by standing meanings and by the rules governing the effect of context on content) than assertoric contents, implicatures, and the rest. As I argued in the previous section, reliance on contextual information, including the items on Bezuidenhout's list, needn't make regular successful communication miraculous. Here, I have been arguing that reliance on contextual information needn't make it impossible (or miraculous) for hearers to come to *know* the semantic contents of sentences in a wide range of contexts, though this might be fallible knowledge.

Picking up on a thread running through Cappelen and Lepore's collapse arguments, it may be objected here that the Moderate Contextualist cannot help herself to the sorts of comparison classes I've mentioned above, especially the natural comparison classes. Consider again the following sentence:

(9) Sammy is fast. (Said in a context in which Sammy the snail is salient.)

I said above that a natural comparison class for (9) is the class of all snails. But there are many ways of being fast for a snail. For example, Sammy could be fast for a snail moving over a flat surface, or for a snail moving over a rough surface. Further, Sammy could be fast for a snail moving over a flat surface that is very hot, or fast for a snail moving over a flat surface that is cool. And so on. According to the current objection, a Moderate Contextualist must say that comparison classes for (9) are always maximally specific kinds, i.e. kinds for which these questions about different ways of instantiating the kind do not arise. Unless she does so, she has not provided a truth-evaluable semantic content for the sentence. Since the class of all snails is not the extension of any such maximally specific kind, it is ruled out as a possible comparison class. But if only these maximally specific kinds can serve as comparison classes, then it seems implausible that there are natural comparison classes in the sense I've been discussing above. Or so the objection goes.

To see why this is misguided, consider two possible motivations for the objection. One motivation is that there is no such thing as being fast for a snail *simpliciter*, only fast for a snail moving over a fast surface under some maximally specific condition *C*. Whatever the merits of this motivation, it is not one that would move Cappelen and Lepore. After all, on their own Semantic Minimalism, there is such a thing as being fast *simpliciter*, which is the property predicated of Sammy by (9). Accordingly, they should say that there is also a property of being fast for a snail *simpliciter*, which is presumably the property predicated of Sammy by the following sentence:

(11) Sammy is fast for a snail.

But to allow that there is such a thing as being fast for a snail *simpliciter* is to disavow the motivation mentioned above.

A second (and more plausible) motivation for this objection is the thought that anything short of a maximally specific kind will give rise to intuitions of semantic incompleteness in the sense at issue in the Incompleteness Arguments.[18] So, anyone who is moved to embrace Contextualism by such arguments should only recognize maximally specific kinds as comparison classes. Here, I'll happily concede that once a Contextualist starts appealing to intuitions about semantic incompleteness, it *is* tempting to think that only maximally specific comparison classes yield semantic contents that are complete in the relevant sense. But this objection gets no grip against a Contextualist who is moved by (for example) CSAs, rather than Incompleteness Arguments, since CSAs are compatible with the view that in most contexts, the comparison classes are easily specified.

Finally, to close out this section, it is worth considering what the Moderate Contextualist view I have described can say about cases in which hearers make mistakes about what is expressed, because they do not know some of the pertinent facts about the contexts in question. In such cases, of course, communication will not be entirely successful. But if a Contextualist view is Moderate enough, then it is still possible that communication will be partially successful. And partially successful communication will be sufficient for many practical purposes.

To illustrate the notion of partially successful communication, consider an utterance of the following sentence:

(12) John only plays the banjo.

[18] See n. 9.

Suppose that (12) is uttered in the vicinity of two hearers, Andy and Ben. Andy hears the utterance, but doesn't know what a banjo is. He only knows that it is some kind of stringed instrument. Ben, on the other hand, doesn't hear the last word of (12). While Andy does not know precisely was said, he does come to know, as a result of this utterance, that John doesn't play the trumpet, or the drums, or the fool. That's more than Ben comes to know. Thus, though the speaker in this case didn't succeed in communicating perfectly with either Andy or Ben, her attempt to communicate is more successful with respect to Andy than with respect to Ben. Even this partially successful communication between the speaker and Andy will be enough for a variety of practical purposes. For example, if Andy has been wondering whether he should give John a set of drums for his birthday, he is in a position to infer, on the basis of this utterance, that that might not be such a good gift.

Given this notion of partially successful communication, let's consider again cases in which hearers do not know the semantic contents expressed in certain contexts, because they do not know some relevant facts about the contexts in question. On a Contextualist view that is Moderate with respect to the Meaning Question, even fairly dramatic ignorance about the context is compatible with good (but approximate) knowledge of the semantic content of the sentence uttered, for the hearer will know that the content expressed must be one of those permitted by the standing meaning of the sentence. That is good enough for partially successful communication. Further, on a Contextualist view that is also Moderate with respect to the Context Question, a hearer who knows *roughly* what the context is like—and so, is in a position to approximate the comparison class used—will have even better (but still approximate) knowledge of the semantic content of the utterance. A Contextualist view that is Moderate along both dimensions (as I think the best view about comparative adjectives must be) makes it very easy for hearers to have good but approximate knowledge of semantic contents in pretty much every actual context. Moreover, for many (though not all) practical purposes, this approximate knowledge on the part of the hearer, and the resulting partially successful communication, will be sufficient.

In this section, I've defended a fairly Moderate Contextualist view about comparative adjectives against the challenge posed by the MCA. That is, I've argued that *if* such a view were correct, that would be enough to answer the challenge posed by the MCA. To decide whether the same can be done for Moderate Contextualist views about other classes of expressions, we would have to go case by case through these other classes. And I don't want to pretend that that is an easy task. In fact, if most expressions in the language are context-sensitive (as is compatible with Moderate Contextualism in my sense), then finding the correct Contextualist view about every such class will be no easier than constructing a complete semantics (and metasemantics) for the language. But provided that the correct theory turns out to be Moderate with respect to both the Meaning and Context Questions, it will not be subject to the challenge posed by the MCA, regardless of how it answers the Sources Question.

6. CONCLUSION

I began this chapter with the observation that Moderate and Radical Contextualists differ with respect to how much context-sensitivity there is in language. I suggested a way of making this thought more precise: how much context-sensitivity a Contextualist recognizes depends on how she answers the Meaning and Context Questions. As we've seen, this is not the only way of measuring context-sensitivity. But I've also argued that there are advantages to my approach: among other things, it allows us to construct a response to the MCA.

The core of my response to the MCA is the thought that what matters for communicative success is moderation with respect to the Meaning and Context Questions. That is to say, as long as both standing meanings and the rules governing the effect of context on content impose substantial constraints on the semantic contents of every expression, communicative success need not be miraculous.

Unfortunately, as a matter of fact, we don't know much about how to answer the Context Question for most classes of expressions. It is striking that most Contextualists, even the ones who are most Moderate on the Meaning Question, don't have much to say with respect to the Context Question (though there are some exceptions). So it may be thought that my optimism regarding the feasibility of constructing Contextualist views that are Moderate in this respect is ill-founded. I think that this is a reasonable worry, and one that cannot be fully addressed here. But at the same time, until it can be shown that such moderation is impossible, we also have no reason to think that communicative success is rendered miraculous on every Contextualist view.[19]

REFERENCES

Bezuidenhout, A. (2002), 'Truth-Conditional Pragmatics', *Philosophical Perspectives*, 16: 105–34.

Cappelen, H., and E. Lepore (2005), *Insensitive Semantics: A Defense of Semantic Minimalism and Speech Act Pluralism*. Oxford: Blackwell.

Carston, R. (1988), 'Implicature, Explicature, and Truth-Theoretic Semantics', in *Mental Representations: The Interface between Language and Reality*, pp. 155–81. Cambridge: Cambridge University Press.

[19] I would like to thank Brian Weatherson, Ernie Lepore, Herman Cappelen, John Hawthorne, Kent Bach, two anonymous advisers for Oxford University Press, and audiences at the Context and Content Workshop in Oslo and at the University of Texas, Austin, for helpful feedback regarding this chapter.

Carston, R. (2002), *Thoughts and Utterances: The Pragmatics of Explicit Communication*. Oxford: Blackwell.

Heck, Jr., R. G. (2002), 'Do Demonstratives have Senses?', *Philosophers' Imprint*, 2: 1–33.

Kaplan, D. (1989), 'Demonstratives', in J. Almog, J. Perry, and H. Wettstein (eds.), *Themes from Kaplan*, pp. 481–563. Oxford: Oxford University Press.

King, J. C., and J. Stanley (2005), 'Semantics, Pragmatics, and the Role of Semantic Content', in Z. G. Szabó (ed.), *Semantics vs. Pragmatics*, pp. 111–64. Oxford: Oxford University Press.

Perry, J. (1997), 'Indexicals and Demonstratives', in B. Hale and C. Wright (eds.), *A Companion to the Philosophy of Language*, pp. 586–612. Oxford: Blackwell.

—— (1998), 'Indexicals, Contexts, and Unarticulated Constituents', in A. Aliseda, R. van Glabbeek, and D. Westerståhl (eds.), *Computing Natural Language*, pp. 1–11. Stanford, Calif.: CSLI Publications.

Recanati, F. (1989), 'The Pragmatics of What is Said', *Mind and Language*, 4: 295–329.

—— (2004), *Literal Meaning*. Cambridge: Cambridge University Press.

—— (2005), 'Literalism and Contextualism: Some Varieties', in G. Preyer and G. Peter (eds.), *Contextualism in Philosophy*, pp. 171–96. Oxford: Oxford University Press.

Sperber, D., and D. Wilson, (1995), *Relevance: Communication and Cognition*, 2nd edn. Oxford: Blackwell.

Stanley, J. (2000), 'Context and Logical Form', *Linguistics and Philosophy*, 23: 391–434.

—— (2002), 'Nominal Restriction', in G. Preyer and G. Peter (eds.), *Logical Form and Language*, pp. 365–88. Oxford: Oxford University Press.

Szabó, Z. G. (2001), 'Adjectives in Context', in I. Kenesei and R. M. Harnish, (eds.), *Perspectives on Semantics, Pragmatics, and Discourse*, pp. 119–46. Amsterdam: John Benjamins.

Taylor, K. (2001), 'Sex, Breakfast, and Descriptus Interruptus', *Synthese*, 128: 45–61.

Travis, C. (2000), *Unshadowed Thought: Representation in Thought and Language*. Cambridge, Mass.: Harvard University Press.

—— (1996), 'Meaning's Role in Truth', *Mind*, 105: 451–66.

5

Moderately Sensitive Semantics

Sarah-Jane Leslie

1. INTRODUCTION

What is context sensitivity? What tests are reliable indicators of this phenomenon? Here I shall take up and develop some themes of Herman Cappelen and Ernie Lepore's book *Insensitive Semantics*, in order to better understand the phenomenon, and the tests that reveal it. If we eschew such tests, and rely on intuitions about what is said, then, Cappelen and Lepore argue, it is hard to resist the conclusion that all of language is contextually sensitive. While most semanticists take themselves to be Moderate Contextualists—who hold that natural language contains a broad but limited stock of context-sensitive items—Cappelen and Lepore claim that Moderate Contextualism is an unstable position. The same intuitions that lead semanticists to espouse Moderate Contextualism should lead them to instead espouse Radical Contextualism—which is the view that context sensitivity is so rampant, no natural language sentence ever semantically expresses a proposition independent of context. The phenomenon of what is said is so unconstrained that, if we try to capture it semantically, we shall be forced to adopt Radical Contextualism. Since, Cappelen and Lepore claim, the arguments for Moderate Contextualism hinge on the desire to account for what is said, there is a slippery slope from Moderate Contextualism to Radical Contextualism.

Cappelen and Lepore level three main objections against Radical Contextualism, and thus, if their slippery slope stands, against Moderate Contextualism. They claim that the contextualist classifies as context-sensitive items that fail their three tests, which is an unacceptable result. They then argue that, if Radical Contextualism were true, we would be unable to communicate with each other with the ease and reliability that we, in fact, routinely employ. Finally, they claim that Radical Contextualism is internally inconsistent.

In what follows, I shall defend Moderate Contextualism against both Cappelen and Lepore's slippery slope argument and their claim that Moderate Contextualism posits context-sensitive items that fail their three tests. Specifically, I will argue that the Inter-Contextual Disquotation/Real Context Shifting Argument test classifies more items as context-sensitive than Cappelen and Lepore suggest. In addition to the basic set, I shall argue that the ICD/RCSA test itself indicates that there is a range of items that are also contextually sensitive. I will refer to this set of contextually sensitive items that are not included in the basic set as the intermediate set. The intermediate set, which *is* determined by Cappelen and Lepore's ICD/RCSA test, is quite restricted; it excludes many of the items that the Radical Contextualist would count as context-sensitive. For example, the intermediate set includes "tall", "ready", "enough", and "every", among others, but does not include "weighs 80 kg", "is red", and "is tall for a pregnant giraffe that is standing up straight". Thus if we take the ICD/RCSA test seriously, as I think we should, it provides the Moderate Contextualist with a way of blocking Cappelen and Lepore's slippery slope argument. The ICD/RCSA test gives us a means of investigating contextual sensitivity without relying on intuitions about what is said. We have a sober and restricted means of determining when a given item is contextually sensitive, and this means tells in favor of Moderate Contextualism.

I shall then consider the other two tests in light of these considerations. I will argue that ICD/RCSA is not negotiable as a test of context sensitivity, and so we should look to understand how the items in the intermediate set could appear to fail the other two tests, despite their being context-sensitive. I provide an account of how the members of the intermediate set behave in 'says that' reports and collected predications that explains their apparent failure on the Report and Collection tests. My account proceeds by first considering how the semantic values of items including "then", "there", "local", "nearby", "left", and "right" are determined in reports and collected predications, and then simply extending this account to the intermediate items. The investigation sheds some light on the complex phenomenon of non-indexical context sensitivity.

Since I am only concerned with defending Moderate Contextualism, I shall not address Cappelen and Lepore's charge that Radical Contextualism is internally inconsistent. As Moderate Contextualism is in fact a stable position, this criticism does not apply; the charge is specific to Radical Contextualism, as it rests on the claim that every sentence is contextually sensitive. I will also not address the claim that contextualism cannot account for our ability to communicate with each other across contexts in the main body of the chapter, though I have included an appendix in which I discuss the matter. I argue there that Cappelen and Lepore's positive view, Semantic Minimalism, cannot explain our communicative practices any better than Moderate or even Radical Contextualism.

Although it may appear that I thoroughly disagree with the view presented in *Insensitive Semantics*, this is not so. Cappelen and Lepore's main point concerns semantic methodology, in particular, our unwarranted reliance on intuitions about what is said. On this point, I am in full agreement with them. Their point is an important one, and should be recognized as such. Unfortunately, this point—their main point—has been overlooked because of the provocatively small size of their "basic set". If I am right, however, this is no more than an artefact of their misapplication of their own tests, and not itself reflective of the quality and plausibility of their position. I hope that this chapter will help to clarify this point, and so allow us to see how valuable Cappelen and Lepore's *real* contribution is to the debate.

2. MODERATE CONTEXTUALISM AND REAL CONTEXT SHIFTING ARGUMENTS

Let us begin with Cappelen and Lepore's (henceforth CL) third test, which concerns Inter-Contextual Disquotation and 'Real' Context Shifting Arguments. This test is, I believe, the most important and the most telling. CL note that:

> It is a constitutive mark of a context sensitive expression *e* that it can be used with different extensions (semantic values) in different contexts of utterance . . . it follows from this constitutive fact alone that for any context sensitive expression *e* our use of *e* in *this* context . . . with whatever extension it takes on in this context need not be the same as whatever extension it takes on in another context. There can be no denying that this is so.
>
> Based on this constitutive fact about context sensitivity, the following test recommends itself for judging whether *e* behaves as it should by actually *using* *e* in a context of utterance . . . and simultaneously describ[ing] another use of *e* with a distinct semantic value in another context.
>
> Since *e* is not context sensitive unless its semantic values can shift from context to context, and since the semantic values *e* takes in, say, *this* context of utterance . . . can be distinct from the semantic value it takes in some other context, to test whether *e* is context sensitive or not, simply use *e*; in order to use *e*, put it in a sentence S and then use S. *e* is context sensitive only if there is a true utterance of an instance of the following schema for Inter-Contextual Disquotation (ICD for short, where S contains *e*):
>
> (ICD) There are (or can be) false utterances of "S" even though S. (2005: 104–5)

CL claim that the members of their basic set pass this test with ease. Consider, for example, the following obviously true remark: there are false utterances of "I am female" even though I am female. The ICD test has a sister test; if an item passes ICD, we should be able to construct a Real Context Shifting Argument (RCSA) for the item, and vice versa. An RCSA is essentially an ICD, but with the contextual details explicitly supplied, rather than left to the interpreter's imagination. We may think of ICD and RCSA as two sides of the same test.

We might, for example, construct the following RCSA for "then":

> *Then* Let's think back to the year 2000. Barry lived in California then. The other day, Gideon and I were talking about last summer. He said "Barry lived in California then", but that was false because Barry was living in Princeton last summer. This is so even though, thinking back to 2000, Barry lived in California then.

Such an RCSA helps us fill out the otherwise awkward "there are false utterances of 'Barry lived in California then' even though Barry lived in California then". It should be clear that RCSAs simply function to flesh out the bare bones of the ICDs; the difference between an RCSA and an ICD is only one of packaging.

The ICD/RCSA test is a convincing test of context sensitivity. If an item can be shown to pass it, it is hard to deny that it is context-sensitive. On the other hand, if an item does not pass ICD/RCSA, then this is good evidence that it is not contextually sensitive, and any data or intuitions to the contrary should be reconsidered. CL describe the test as reflecting a constitutive fact about what it is to be context-sensitive; I have no quarrel with this claim, but rather embrace it. This test should be taken seriously.

2.1. Do the Items in the Intermediate Set Really Fail This Test?

Let us consider just which items pass ICD/RCSA. CL write as though all items that lie outside their basic set fail ICD/RCSA, though in providing examples of such failures, they focus exclusively on items that only a Radical Contextualist would consider context-sensitive—predicates such as "knows", "is red", and "weighs 80 kg". Many a Moderate Contextualist would deny that these expressions are contextually sensitive, while maintaining that the basic set is too restrictive. At this point in their argument, it is understandable why CL would focus exclusively on these items; they have already argued that there is no such stable position as that which the Moderate Contextualist would endorse—there is only their position, which acknowledges no semantic context sensitivity outside of the basic set, or Radical Contextualism. This argument proceeds by way of claiming that the Moderate Contextualist cannot embrace the intuitions that lead to his moderate case without also embracing those that lead to a radical one. There is alleged to be a slippery slope between Moderate and Radical Contextualism, so that the Moderate Contextualist has no principled way of drawing the line between his items and those of the Radical Contextualist.

Since CL take themselves to have established this, they may suppose there is no reason why they cannot object equally well to the Moderate's position by focusing on the more radical items. Thus they focus on whether items such as "knows" and "weighs 80kg" fail their tests. This transition is too hasty, however. All the Moderate Contextualist needs is some way or other to resist the slide down the slippery slope, and she cannot be held responsible for the Radical Contextualist's failings. If there is some limited range of items outside the basic set that pass ICD/RCSA, then the Moderate Contextualist will have found the firm footing she needs along the slope to Radical Contextualism. She will have found a principled way to draw the line between the items she takes to be context-sensitive, and the multitude that the Radical Contextualist classifies as such.

I will argue in what follows that there is a set of items that is intermediate between the tiny basic set and the Radical Contextualist's teeming horde. These intermediate items easily pass ICD/RCSA, while items like "knows", "weighs 80 kg", and "is tall for a pregnant giraffe that is standing up straight" do not. Since passing this test is a matter of our having intuitions about the truth or acceptability of various stories or utterances, I have informally polled people who are not involved in this debate, and have found that their intuitions accord with mine. My informal poll is a far cry from a controlled experiment, and such an experiment might prove useful here; it would certainly trump my poll, were the results found to ultimately differ. A poll, however informal, is valuable in that it keeps the debate from reducing to SJ's-intutions-versus-CL's. The purpose of the poll is to reflect that I am not alone in construing the data this way. (Nor are my opinions only shared by Moderate Contextualists with a stake in the debate. Most of the people I spoke with were either not philosophers of language, or were not philosophers at all.)

Consider the following Real Context Shifting Arguments for various intermediate items.[1]

Enough

> I've just moved apartments, and I'm hanging a picture in my living room. It's pretty light, so a small picture hook is strong enough. But yesterday, my friend was helping me hang a 25lb mirror, and he said "Oh, a small picture hook is strong enough". That was false (and I have a cracked mirror to prove it), even though, given how light this picture is, a small picture hook is plenty strong enough.

Ready

> John is woefully unprepared from his APA interviews, and is about to pass out from nerves. He really needs more time before his interviews; he is simply not ready. There is an evangelist hovering around the convention, looking to see whether there are any lost souls for whom the time is right to accept Jesus Christ as their Personal Saviour. Spotting John, the evangelist says "Ah, *he's* ready!" This is true; as it turned out the evangelist managed to convert John, in large part thanks to his looming interviews, coupled with the fact that he just wasn't ready.

Every

> Princeton has really clamped down on grade inflation. I'm teaching Intro to Logic this semester, and it is definitely not the case that every student will get an A. I'm going to make sure of that, or else the administration

1 See Hawthorne (2006) for more examples of RCSAs for items not found in the basic set.

> will get ticked off with me. My friend Des has a lot more guts about these things than me, though. He was telling me about his Kant class the other day, and said "My students are great. I don't care what the administration says. Every student will get an A!" That was true, too—I saw his grade sheet—but as for my class, it's decidedly false that every student will get an A.

It's raining

> I'm in New Jersey right now, and the weather is beautiful. It's one of those clear spring days, and it's definitely not raining. My poor grandmother called me from Scotland this morning though, and one of the first things she told me was, "it's raining". She was right—I checked the weather report for Scotland. Anxious to make sure the day would remain nice, I looked outside. No worries; it wasn't raining.

Tall

> Seeing as how he measures 6′3″, Tom is tall. He plays basketball from time to time, and once he called me from the court, because he was feeling nervous before the game. To reassure him, I said "well, it'll help that you're tall". He replied "are you kidding me? You should look at the guys I'm up against. I'm not tall at all!". He was right (the other guys were approaching 7′!), even though at 6′3″, Tom is definitely tall.

These scenarios are perfectly intelligible, and as natural as anything else in this debate. And as far as I am able to tell, they all count as RCSAs. In each of them, the sentence in question is *used* in the context (twice in fact—once at the beginning, and again at the end), and mentioned in another, where it receives a different truth value. By CL's own standards, "enough", "ready", "every", "tall", and "it's raining" pass their RCSA test for context sensitivity.

There are two objections to the validity of these RCSAs that I can imagine that CL might raise, but they each turn out to be non-starters since they also apply to RCSAs for non-indexical members of the basic set such as "then". The first is that, when we use the sentence a second time at the end of the RCSA, we need a brief remark to 'bring us back' to the original context. For example, in *Enough* we have:

> I've just moved apartments, and I'm hanging a picture in my living room. It's pretty light, so a small picture hook is strong enough. But yesterday, my friend was helping me hang a 25lb mirror, and he said "Oh, a small picture hook is strong enough". That was false (and I have a cracked mirror to prove it), even though, *given how light this picture is*, a small picture hook is plenty strong enough.

The italicized phrase makes a significant contribution to the naturalness of the RCSA. Now, we do not need to supply such a phrase in giving an RCSA for an indexical. For example, I might simply write "I am female. The other day Bill said "I am female". This was false, even though I am female". No phrase, however minimal, is needed to bring us back to our context. This, however, is not so with those members of the basic set that are not pure indexicals. Consider the RCSA we gave for "then", for example:

> Let's think back to the year 2000. Barry lived in California then. The other day, Gideon and I were talking about last summer. He said "Barry lived in California then", but that was false because Barry was living in Princeton last summer. This is so even though, *thinking back to 2000*, Barry lived in California then.

Removing the italicized phrase here undermines the RCSA for "then" as much (if not more) than removing the corresponding phrase from *Enough*. We cannot insist that an RCSA be no more complex than is needed for a pure indexical or we will rule out items such as "then".

The second challenge to the validity of my RCSAs might hold that, for an RCSA to be successful for a predicate "is F", we must be able to remark in the RCSA that the relevant utterance is false because the speaker was not concerned with F-hood. CL end their unsuccessful RCSA for "weighs 80 kg" by writing "If someone were to utter "Rupert weighs 80 kg" her utterance would be false, even though he weighs 80 kg. *The utterance would be false, not because Rupert's weight has changed, but because the speaker is concerned with something other than what Rupert weighs, for example with what a scale registers were he to step on it fully clothed*" (2005: 111; my emphasis). Now, one *can* end an RCSA for a pure indexical in such a manner, for example, "Bill's utterance of "I am female" is false because Bill was concerned with something other than whether I am female". But we cannot so amend our RCSA for "then", on pain of incoherence:

> Let's think back to the year 2000. Barry lived in California then. The other day, Gideon and I were talking about last summer. He said "Barry lived in California then", but that was false because Gideon was concerned with something other than what Barry was doing then.

This amended RCSA is clearly unacceptable; it is every bit as bizarre as CL's proffered RCSA for "weighs 80kg". Again, unless we are to decide that items such as "then" are not contextually sensitive, we cannot require that an RCSA for an expression *e* contain a remark that the false utterance of ". . . *e* . . ." was false because its speaker was not concerned with *e*. This cannot be a constraint on a successful RCSA. I will thus take myself to have met CL's challenge, and have provided RCSAs for the intermediate items above.

A question that now arises is whether we can construct successful RCSAs for just about any item, as the Radical Contextualist might hope, or whether only a modest collection of items are amenable to RCSAs. It is not a trivial matter to construct an RCSA for an item, and it seems to me that there are many items that do not pass the RCSA test. For example, the RCSA that CL attempt to provide for "knows" (i.e. their *Known Rupert*) is decidedly awkward, and I'm not convinced that mine is much better:

Knows

> Right now I'm writing a paper on semantics, and am not thinking about epistemology. I know a lot of things right now, including that I have hands. But earlier today, Jim called me, and we talked about epistemology—in particular about the possibility of being a brain in a vat. I said "Wow, I guess I don't know that I have hands!" That was true, since I can't rule out the possibility of my being a brain in a vat. But now that I'm back to writing my semantics paper, I know that I have hands.

This RCSA is considerably less natural, to my ear at least, than the ones above. Perhaps a better one could be constructed, or perhaps "knows" is just not context-sensitive, as various leading theorists have argued (see Stanley 2005; Hawthorne 2004, for example). Insofar as some putatively context-sensitive expressions pass RCSA while others fail it, the Moderate Contextualist has found her way off CL's slippery slope.

I am myself neutral on the question of whether knowledge attributions are contextually sensitive, but I would very much like to be sure that Moderate Contextualism does not lead inexorably to Radical Contextualism. CL argue that the intuitions that tell us that "is tall" is context-sensitive should also tell us that "is tall for a giraffe" is context-sensitive. They ask: Are we talking about pregnant giraffes? (Pregnancy, they tell us, affects giraffes' necks in ways that are relevant to determining their height.) Once we have decided whether or not we have in mind pregnant giraffes, the questions arise: Are the giraffes in question standing up straight? Have they just taken a bath? (CL inform us that bathing makes a difference to a giraffe's height.) CL claim that all these further factors are ones that start to seem contextually relevant, once we start down the contextualist road. (Why this is so is not wholly apparent; to me these seem more like cases of vagueness or perhaps mere determinability, but let us put that aside.)

The challenge to the Moderate Contextualist is then to provide a principled way of acknowledging the context sensitivity of "is tall" without allowing that "is tall for a pregnant giraffe that is standing up straight" is also context-sensitive. Here, CL's RCSA test is most helpful. Consider the following (decidedly odd) RCSA:

Tall for a pregnant giraffe that is standing up straight

> Georgina is simply not tall for a pregnant giraffe that is standing up straight. No one who saw her would claim that she was. But the other day, we were talking about pregnant giraffes that are standing up straight but have just taken a bath. I said "Georgina is tall for a pregnant giraffe that is standing up straight!" What I said was true, because taking a bath shrinks giraffes by a small amount. Of course, now that I am just looking at a dry Georgina, she is definitely not tall for a pregnant giraffe that is standing up straight.

There is a clear difference in acceptability and plausibility between the RCSA above, and *Tall*, reprinted below:

> Seeing as how he measures 6′3″, Tom is tall. He plays basketball from time to time, and once he called me from the court, because he was feeling nervous before the game. To reassure him, I said "well, it'll help that you're tall". He replied "are you kidding me? You should look at the guys I'm up against. I'm not tall at all!". He was right (the other guys were approaching 7′!), even though at 6′3″, Tom is definitely tall.

The Moderate Contextualist, it seems, *can* distinguish between "is tall" and "is tall for a pregnant giraffe that is standing up straight"; and she can do so using CL's own test for context sensitivity! Whether one can construct as RSCA for a term then, seems a robust and theoretically well-grounded test. I fully agree with CL that it is an important test for context sensitivity, though of course I disagree with them about which terms pass it. As CL emphasize throughout their book, though, their main concern is with semantic methodology, rather than with defending the boundaries of their basic set. Inasmuch as predicates such as "is tall for a pregnant giraffe that is standing up straight" are not amenable to RCSAs, the introduction of the RCSA as a benchmark is an extremely valuable contribution to the debate.

RCSA's sister test, ICD, is also very helpful in this regard. My intuitions, and the intuitions of the neutral parties polled, are that the following ICDs are easily heard as true:[2]

> *I* There are false utterances of "I'm female" even though I'm female.
>
> *Now* There are false utterances of "Jason is reading an email now" even though Jason is reading an email now.
>
> *Ready* There are false utterances of "SJ is ready" even though SJ is ready.

[2] As I say, I did not conduct a controlled experiment, but the people I spoke to were instructed to hold fixed tense/time of evaluation, facts about the world, and the referents of proper names.

Enough There are false utterances of "steel is strong enough" even though steel is strong enough.

It's raining There are false utterances of "it's raining" even though it's raining.

No one I spoke to had any difficulty hearing the above group (*I*, *Now, Ready, Enough*, and *It's raining*) as true.

One or two people found the following ones unnatural, though they reported that they were able to hear them as true if they thought about them:

Then There are false utterances of "John went to the store then" even though John went to the store then.

Tall There are false utterances of "Tom is tall" even though Tom is tall.

Every There are false utterances of "every student got an A" even though every student got an A.

It is important to note that while *Tall* and *Every* were less natural than *Ready, Enough,* and *It's raining,* so was the basic set member *Then. Tall* and *Every* were not *more* difficult for people to hear than *Then.* And remarkably enough, *Ready, Enough*, and *It's raining* struck people as more natural than even *Then*!

Overwhelmingly, however, people could not hear the following ones as true:

Tall for a pregnant giraffe that is standing up straight There are false utterances of "Georgina is tall for a pregnant giraffe that is standing up straight" even though Georgina is tall for a pregnant giraffe that is standing up straight.

Red There are false utterances of "Clifford is red" even though Clifford is red.

Weighs 80kg There are false utterances of "Smith weighs 80kg" even though Smith weighs 80kg.

Of these, *Red* was the only one that anyone even wondered whether they could hear as true. It turned out, though, that this had do to with the vagueness of "red"—not with the possibility of our being concerned with the color of, say, Clifford's innards, to take CL's example. Everyone was confident about the falsity of the ICDs containing "weighs 80kg" and "is tall for a pregnant giraffe that is standing up straight". People were confident that these statements could not be true.

These intuitions are exactly those that the Moderate Contextualist would predict, and they accord well with naturalness of the corresponding RSCAs. Thus if we grant CL's methodology of testing items for context sensitivity in this manner, and embrace ICD/RCSA as a valid and accurate test, then Moderate

Contextualism emerges as the leading view. Minimalism wrongly predicts that many items that easily pass will in fact fail, and Radical Contextualism wrongly predicts that items that fail will in fact pass. Moderate Contextualism makes the correct predictions. This test also serves to rescue the Moderate Contextualist from CL's slippery slope. Thus, adopting CL's methodology seems to vindicate Moderate Contextualism.

3. THE OTHER TWO TESTS

The ICD/RCSA test is not the only test that CL offer. They suggest that we adopt two additional tests for context sensitivity, which I will refer to as the Report test, and the Collection test. The Report test concerns inter-contextual disquotation. An item is context-sensitive, they claim, only if it "typically blocks inter-contextual disquotational indirect reports" (2005: 88). They write:

> Suppose you suspect, or at least want to ascertain whether, *e* is context sensitive. Take an utterance *u* of a sentence S containing *e* in context C. Let C′ be a context relevantly different from C (i.e. different according to those standards significant according to contextualists about *e*). If there's a true disquotational* indirect report of *u* in C′, then that's evidence that S is context insensitive. (To be 'disquotational*' just means you can adjust the semantic values of components of S that are generally recognized as context sensitive, i.e., we just test for the controversial components.) (2005: 89)

CL argue that the members of their basic set pass this test with flying colors. If Bill utters "I am male", Mary cannot correctly report him by saying "Bill said that I am male". In contrast, they claim that items that are context-sensitive according to the contextualist often fail this test. If Nina utters "John is ready" in the course of discussing an exam he is to take, CL, in the context of writing their book at a café, can correctly report her by saying "Nina said that John is ready".

The next test, the Collection test, concerns so-called collected predications. On this test they write:

> If a verb phrase v is context sensitive . . . then on the basis of merely knowing that there are two contexts of utterance in which "A v-s" and "B v-s" are true respectively, we *cannot* automatically infer that there is a context in which 'v' can be used to describe what A and B have both done . . . On the other hand, if for a range of true utterances of the form "A v-s" and "B v-s" we obviously *can* describe what they all have in common by *using* 'v' . . . then that's evidence in favor of the view that 'v' in these different utterances has the same semantic content, and hence, is not context sensitive. (2005: 99; original emphasis)

An indexical such as 'yesterday' clearly passes this test; if there is a true utterance of "John left yesterday", and a true utterance in another context of "Bill left yesterday", we cannot 'automatically assume' that there is a context in which "John and Bill left yesterday" is true. In contrast, they suggest, from a true utterance of "John is ready", and a true utterance of "Bill is ready", then, as they put it, the following collective description is perfectly natural: "Both John and Bill are ready".

Given that the intermediate items pass ICD/RCSA while apparently failing the other two tests, we appear to have a tension in CL's own theory. Whatever CL's personal convictions may be, it seems that people overwhelmingly have the intuitions that suggest the intermediate items pass ICD/RCSA. On the other hand, it does appear that the intermediate items fail the Report and Collection tests.

One option is to reject ICD/RCSA as a test for context sensitivity. This option seems to me to be the least attractive, for reasons independent of my favoring Moderate Contextualism. The ICD/RCSA test captures a constitutive feature of context sensitivity. CL themselves insist on this:

> it is a constitutive mark of a context sensitive expression *e* that it can be used with different extensions (semantic values) in different contexts of utterance . . . It follows from this constitutive fact alone that for any context sensitive expression *e* our use of *e* in *this* context . . . with whatever extensions it takes on in this context need not be the same as whatever extension it takes on in another context. There can be no denying this is so. (2005: 104)

They go on to notice that it is the truth of an ICD statement containing *e* that guarantees the inadequacy of a disquotational T-statement for *e*. If 'S' contains *e* and there can be false utterances of 'S' even though S, then clearly the following biconditional cannot hold: 'S' is true iff S. CL point out that ICD is precisely what shows us that the biconditional '*"I am female" is true iff I am female* is false. There can be false utterances of "I am female" even though I am female, so this biconditional is false, and therefore unusable in a T-schema, or any similar semantic framework. If an item passes ICD, then we cannot give its truth conditions disquotationally, for doing so would result in a biconditional that is false, precisely because we have not recognized the item's context sensitivity. If an item passes ICD, and relatedly, RCSA, it must be recognized as contextually sensitive.[3] I see no way of denying this fact, and I do not believe that CL would care to deny it either.

Since it is hard to see how an item could pass the ICD/RCSA test but not be contextually sensitive, let us try to understand how the intermediate items could appear to fail the Report and Collection tests despite their being contextually

[3] CL speak at times as if none of their three tests were necessary, nor jointly sufficient, for establishing that an item in contextually sensitive. It seems to me quite possible, though, that a true ICD is sufficient for an item to be counted as contextually sensitive, provided that the truth of the ICD cannot be traced to vagueness, ambiguity, or such factors. Constructing a corresponding RCSA for the item is important in ruling out those factors; the minimal ICD might be heard as true for such extraneous reasons, but in producing an RCSA we can ensure that we are paying attention only to relevant differences between contexts. If an ICD for an item is true, and its truth cannot be traced to vagueness, ambiguity, etc, then it hard to see how that item could fail to be context-sensitive. Certainly, the truth of the ICD guarantees that we cannot give a disquotational T-schema for the sentence.

sensitive. I will argue that once we have a better understanding of the nature and behavior of context-sensitive items *other than the pure indexicals*, it will become clear how some context-sensitive items might seem to fail these two tests. In what follows, I will discuss how the semantic values of context-sensitive items such as "then", "there", "nearby", "local", "left", and "right" are determined when they occur in the scope of 'says that' reports, and in collected predications. I offer an account of how their values are determined in such constructions, and argue that the account extends naturally to the intermediate items. The account allows us to see why the intermediate items appear to fail the Report and Collection tests, thereby resolving the theoretical tension generated by their passing ICD/RCSA while failing the other two tests.

The account I will offer is not intended as a full-fledged theory, but is rather somewhat schematic in nature. I do not doubt that there is more to be said about the items in question. I have also tried to remain neutral between the various moderate theories of context sensitivity, and have not tied my account to any particular one.

Let us begin to develop our account by noting that the intermediate items are *not* always amenable to being disquotationally reported, or collected. It is not difficult to construct a scenario in which such reports and collections are unacceptable. Consider the following scenario, for example (adapted from Leslie 2004):

John's APA Nightmare

> John is on the job market, and about to be interviewed for his dream job. Unfortunately, he hasn't prepared for the interview at all. He can barely even remember what his thesis is about, and is unbelievably nervous.
>
> Now, the night before John's APA nightmare, he was very hungry. People were going out for dinner, and inquired if John was in a position to eat dinner right then. He was indeed ready to eat dinner, and appropriately responded, "Yes, I'm ready".
>
> John's classmate Mary, on the other hand, is very well prepared for her interviews. She has her dissertation summary down pat, has her syllabi memorized, and is well equipped to answer any questions thrown at her. Her friend takes one look at her confident demeanor and remarks "I gotta hand it to you. You are ready".

Report test

> The interviewing committee decides that they will allow John to reschedule, if his thesis advisor agrees that he needs to take more time to prepare. The thesis advisor disquotationally* reports John's utterance by saying "Hey, he said himself last night that he's ready". The report is simply false under these circumstances.

Collection test

> The interviewing committee reacts with surprise when they hear this, since John looks to them to be woefully unprepared, especially in contrast to Mary. The thesis advisor collects the two true utterances that attribute readiness to John and Mary, and remarks in response: "Nope, they're both ready". The collection is false as described.

If there is some salient activity to be ready for, disquotational reports and collections only strike us as true if they pertain to that salient activity. Parallel situations are easily produced for the other intermediate items. This is not to say that the intermediate items pass the Report and Collection tests after all. Recanati (2006) discusses examples such as my example above, but CL (2006*b*) reply that the existence of such scenarios does not count against their view. In particular, they note that the existence of *some* contexts in which the relevant reports and collections may take place, despite relevant contextual differences, is all that they require. We still need an account of why we are able to *ever* disquotationally report and collect in the face of relevant differences in context.

In their recent article "Shared Content", Cappelen and Lepore suggest that our intuitions in scenarios such as the one above are tracking speech act content rather than semantic content; the salience of the APA interview leads us to focus on expressed propositions that are relevant to it, and thereby 'blind us' to the minimal, shared semantic content (2006*c*). They encourage us to look to contexts of 'ignorance' and 'indifference': contexts in which we might, for example, say "John said he was ready" without knowing or caring exactly what activity was under discussion at the time of John's utterance. The ignorance and indifference constitute relevant differences between the contexts, yet such differences do not render disquotational reports or collections unacceptable.

Of course, it is vital that the reports and collections we consider occur in contexts that are "relevantly different" from the contexts of the original utterances. Clearly, it is irrelevant to consider reporting and collecting contexts in which the relevant contextual factors are the same as in the original context. As CL note in their reply to Hawthorne, "we can disquotationally report uses of 'I' *if the right circumstances are in place*, i.e. if the reporter is identical to the original speaker" (2006*a*). The question then becomes: under what circumstances are two contexts 'relevantly different' from each other?

3.1. The Report Test

CL themselves clearly do not think that there is an easy answer to this question; that this is so becomes clear in the course of their response to Hawthorne (CL 2006*a*). Hawthorne (2006) notes that 'nearby' and 'left' seem to fail the Report test. Hawthorne writes:

Let us try 'left' and 'nearby'. Suppose Ernie is in New York City and I am in Birmingham. Ernie says 'A nearby restaurant has good Vietnamese food'. I can report this by saying 'Ernie said that a nearby restaurant has good Vietnamese food,' even though I am far away from him. Suppose that Ernie is facing me. A car goes to Ernie's left and my right. Ernie says 'The car went left'. I can say 'Ernie said that the car went left', even though my orientation is radically different to his. (2006)

In their reply, CL defend the claim that "nearby" and "left" are context-sensitive, and argue that Hawthorne's example does not show them to fail the Report test. They argue as follows:

For the test to be applicable, it is essential that the contexts of the report and the reportee be *relevantly different*, i.e. that the relevant contextual features should be different in the contexts of the report and the reportee.

So what are the contextually relevant features for, say, 'nearby'? Maybe the answer is something like this: the character of 'nearby' determines that an utterance of 'nearby' in a context C refers to a location salient in C, but that location needn't be the location of C (i.e. it needn't be the location where the speech act occurs). It is whatever location is salient in C, and that could be the location of the reportee—if, for example, that location is made salient in indirectly reporting her.

Hawthorne's examples can then be understood as examples in which we can disquotationally report utterances containing 'nearby' because the relevant contextual features in the two contexts (i.e. the salient location) are the same. If this is the correct diagnosis, all the examples show is that when the same location is salient in two context, C and C′, you'll be able to disquotationally report utterances of sentences containing 'nearby' from C to C′ (or the other way around). But this is no more surprising than being able to disquotationally report utterances of sentences containing the first person pronoun when the reporter is the same as the reported speaker. (2006*a*)

CL go on to adduce support for this claim by noting:

According to this suggestion, 'nearby' refers to whatever location is salient in the context of utterance, and if your intuition is that Hawthorne's disquotational reports are true, that is because the location of the reportee has become salient in the context of the report. Further support for this diagnosis is provided by imagining examples in which the salient locations differ in the context of the report and the context of the reportee, and hence blocks the disquotational report. Consider this variation in Hawthorne's example (i)–(ii):

i. Ernie says to John, walking on 7th street in NY looking for a restaurant: *A nearby restaurant has good Vietnamese food.*

ii. John, walking around Birmingham looking for a restaurant, reports Ernie's utterance to his friends by saying: *Ernie says that a nearby restaurant has good Vietnamese food.*

(ii) is intuitively false, and the above account provides an explanation: in the context of (ii) it is the location of the report (i.e. the location where the indirect report is uttered) that is salient—the search for a restaurant in Birmingham has made Birmingham the salient location. (2006*a*)

These observations concerning "nearby" are quite analogous to my observations concerning the intermediate items such as "ready". As evidenced by *John's APA*

Nightmare, disquotational reports of ascriptions of readiness are false if there is a salient activity to be ready for, and the reported utterance did not concern that activity. If John's thesis adviser says "John said himself that he was ready", on the basis of John's saying in connection with dinner "I'm ready", this report is false. If there is a salient activity to be ready for in the context of the report, then we cannot disquotationally report readiness ascriptions, unless they pertain to that activity. Similarly, if there is a salient location in the context of the report, then we cannot disquotationally report utterances containing "nearby", unless, of course, they pertain to the same salient location.

But in the case of "ready" and other intermediate items, CL direct us to consider only contexts of ignorance and indifference, and thus to set aside such scenarios as *John's APA Nightmare*. It is those contexts that are relevant to the Report and Collection tests. Should not the same advice apply to Hawthorne's examples? Hawthorne's examples seem to be prime cases of reports under ignorance or indifference, but in case we are unconvinced, let us borrow an example directly from CL's reply to Hawthorne. (The example is offered in response to Hawthorne's suggestion that the reports contain mixed quotation, but it is well suited to our purposes here.) They write:

> Consider an example involving 'nearby': Imagine answering a ringing payphone on the street, and a woman's voice says: 'There's a river nearby', then she hangs up. Asked what the caller said, you reply: 'The woman on the phone said there is a river nearby' It seems perfectly possible that the speaker intended to *use* 'nearby' and not to talk about "nearby" *and that in so doing, she succeeded in saying something true* (if our earlier diagnosis (of the character of 'nearby') is correct, that's what we would expect). (2006*a*; my emphasis)

The reporting context described here is clearly one of ignorance and indifference, in that the reporter does not know or care where the woman was calling from. CL claim that ignorance and indifference are factors that lead us to focus on semantic content rather than speech act content. Yet even in these circumstances of ignorance and indifference CL agree that we are able to disquotationally report an utterance containing "nearby", a term that they take to be contextually sensitive.[4] Presumably they take it that, as in Hawthorne's example, the woman's location becomes salient, *just in virtue of our reporting her utterance*. That is, no precursor is needed to render salient the location; it is enough for the reporter to utter "The woman on the phone said there is a river nearby", for the woman's location to be made sufficiently salient. It is also not in any way a necessary condition for the report that the reporter know *what or where the location is*. He may be completely ignorant of this. Both the reporter and the

[4] Ernie Lepore suggested to me (pers. comm.) that perhaps only predicative uses of "nearby" are contextually sensitive, and that when it is used as a modifying adjective, it is not. I will return to this issue below, but it is important to note here that the utterance that is disquotationally reported is one in which "nearby" occurs predicatively.

audience understand "nearby" to operate on the woman's location, *whatever it may be.*[5]

It appears then that "nearby", which even CL (probably) recognize to be contextually sensitive, behaves like the intermediate items on the Report test. That is, we can disquotationally report utterances containing "nearby" in contexts of ignorance and indifference, just as we can disquotationally report utterances containing the intermediate items in such contexts. If, however, the context of the report is not one of ignorance and indifference, and there is a salient value for the item in the context of the report, then a disquotational report will be unacceptable (unless, of course, that same value was salient in the context of the original utterance). CL point out that this is the case for "nearby"; if the context of the report is one in which Birmingham is a salient location, we cannot say "Ernie said that a nearby restaurant has good Indian food" if Ernie said this while discussing eateries in New York City. Similarly, if a particular activity is salient in a context, we cannot disquotationally report utterances of the form "x is ready" if they were made in contexts where a different activity was salient. We saw this in *John's APA Nightmare*; John's adviser cannot say to the interviewing committee, "John said he was ready" on the basis of John's having said "I'm ready" in connection with the previous night's dinner. It is not hard to see that the same holds for the other intermediate items. (Consider, for example, the Real Context Shifting Arguments given above. If we place ourselves in the context of those stories, unqualified disquotational reports of the utterances mentioned in the stories are false.) The intermediate items behave exactly like "nearby" in this respect. We can disquotationally report utterances containing them in contexts of ignorance and indifference, but not in contexts in which a different value for the context-sensitive item is salient.

There are other similarities between "nearby" and the intermediate items. Consider what happens if we preface our disquotational report with a brief description of the context in which the original utterance occurred. Including such a preamble allows us to disquotationally report utterances containing "nearby" and the intermediate items, even if the context of the report includes a contextually salient value for the item in question, which would otherwise prohibit us from disquotationally reporting. In the case of "nearby", suppose we are in Birmingham and looking for a good Indian restaurant there, as per CL's example, but instead of uttering out-of-the-blue "Ernie said that there was a

[5] Not everyone finds such disquotational reports as acceptable as CL do. One may well doubt that the reporter could properly report the woman's utterance as above. Similarly, in the case of 'ready', one could reasonably be skeptical that, if we had no idea what John was said to be ready for, we could unqualifiedly report Bill's utterance of 'John is ready' by saying 'Bill said that John was ready'. Many people feel that, in such circumstances, we would be obliged to add 'but I don't know what for', or some such qualification. Of course if this is correct, this casts doubt on the claim that items such as 'ready' actually pass the Report test. I'm sympathetic to this position, but I will not pursue it here. I will rather grant CL their data, and show that, even if it is correct, it does not mean that items such as 'ready' are not contextually sensitive.

really good Indian restaurant nearby", I say instead, "when we were in Princeton and talking about restaurants in NJ, Ernie said that there was a really good Indian restaurant nearby". This little preamble of mine makes it clear that in the context of Ernie's utterance, Princeton, not Birmingham, was salient, and so "nearby" should be interpreted accordingly. With this small preamble, we can override the contextually salient location of Birmingham—the salience of which is enough to render false a disquotational report that does not follow such a preamble.

The same pattern is to be found among the intermediate items. If John's thesis adviser says to the interviewing committee, "John said he was ready" with no preamble, his report is false. If, however, he begins with a preamble, he can successfully offer a disquotational report: "when we were talking about dinner last night, John said that he was ready". As is the case with "nearby", a little preamble allows us to disquotationally report the utterance.

CL do not discuss preambles, but in keeping with their earlier treatment of "nearby", I imagine that they would understand the preamble as making salient another location—in my above case, the preamble makes Princeton salient, and so "nearby" is interpreted relative to this.

I propose that, if we simply extend this model to encompass the intermediate items, we will eliminate the tension between the ICD/RCSA test and the Reporting test. If an item such as "nearby" occurs in a 'says that' report, its semantic value depends on (*a*) the location that was salient in the context of the original utterance, as introduced by a preamble or some such means; if no such location is available then it will depend on (*b*) a location that is salient in the reporting context, and if there is no such location, then (*c*) it will be understood as dependent on some location or other that was salient in the context of the original utterance, even though the reporter and his audience are ignorant as to which location this may be.[6] This last case, case (*c*) includes contexts of ignorance and indifference, and if "nearby" operates in the manner here described, we can understand how it can be contextually sensitive, while permitting disquotational reports in contexts of ignorance and indifference.

What we, in effect, have is a pattern of cascading defaults, which determine the semantic value of a contextually sensitive item figuring in a report.

The intermediate items can be assimilated to this schema. As *John's APA Nightmare* suggests, the predicate "is ready" operates in a parallel fashion. If the predicate "is ready" occurs in a 'says that' report, its extension depends on (*a*) the salient activity in the context of the original utterance, as introduced by a preamble or some such means; if no such activity is salient, then it will depend on (*b*) an activity that is salient in the reporting context, and if there is no such activity, then (*c*) it is understood as dependent on *some activity or other that was salient in the context of the original utterance.* The reporter and her audience

[6] This is not, of course, intended as a full description of how "nearby" operates. I do not doubt there is far more to say than has been said here.

need not have any clue as to the nature of this activity, any more than they need know which location was salient in the original context when reporting utterances containing "nearby". These conditions hold, *mutatis mutandis*, for the other intermediate items, as far as I am able to tell. It is this pattern of cascading defaults that allows us to disquotationally report the intermediate items under conditions of ignorance and indifference.

It should be noted that we can find members of the basic set exhibiting this behavior, at least to some extent. We can, contra CL, sometimes use such items in 'says that' reports under conditions of ignorance and indifference. Suppose, for example, that I am talking to Rachel while she is on her cell phone. I have no idea where she is calling from, and I don't bother to ask. In the course of the conversation, Rachel remarks "It's raining here". I can report Rachel by saying "Rachel said that it's raining there".[7] This report is not, of course, strictly disquotational—there is a mandatory switch from "here" to "there"—but nonetheless a member of the basic set is used in a report made under conditions of ignorance. We have no trouble interpreting the occurrence of "there" as picking out Rachel's location, *wherever that may be.*

When members of the basic set that are not pure indexicals occur in 'says that' reports, they are also sensitive to the occurrence of preambles that describe the context of the original utterance. Such a preamble can easily override whatever values may be salient in the reporting context. Consider, for example:

> I had a great conversation with John the other day. The sun was shining then, and we were both in a good mood. We got to talking about Plato's Greece, and John said that philosophy was done so much better then.

The reporting context contains a salient value for "then"—namely the day that the reporter spoke to John—and it is this value that the first occurrence of "then" picks up. On the basis of the minimal preamble "we got to talking about Plato's Greece", we easily understand the second occurrence of "then" as referring to the time of Plato's Greece. It is important to notice how easily we obtain the value of the second "then" on the basis of this minimal information. Nothing in the preamble "we got to talking about Plato's Greece" contains a reference to the *time period* of Plato's Greece, yet we automatically extract such a time as a value for "then". Clearly, we can extract values for contextually sensitive items

[7] Even if one does not think that this is the most natural report possible, it is no less natural than disquotationally reporting an utterance by Rachel of "There is a restaurant nearby" under the same conditions. For that matter, it is not clear that our intuitions are as firm as CL would have us believe when it comes to disquotational reports of the moderate items under ignorance and indifference. It is not very natural to utter "Nina said that John is ready" if one has no idea of what Nina took John to be ready for. If one feels a temptation to amend the report "Rachel said that it's raining there" by adding "but I don't know where she is", consider whether one does not also feel that it would also be more natural to say "Nina said that John is ready, but I don't know what for", or "Rachel said there is a restaurant nearby, but I don't know where she is".

on the basis of minimal and oblique preambles, and such values override other potentially salient values in the reporting context. If the members of the basic set behave in this way, it is not surprising that the intermediate items do too.

My reader may be wondering why I have separated out values made salient by a preamble from ones that are otherwise salient in the context. Could not both be treated under the banner of salience? Preambles affect the context by making a particular value salient; they are one among many ways by which a value may become salient in a context. I don't think there is anything wrong with this way of thinking, but it is helpful to separate out values that are salient *in the reporting context*, and those that become salient *only in connection with the context of the original utterance*. The preambles I have been discussing thus far function to make values salient in the latter way. The distinction is helpful when we consider multiple, collected reports, to which we now turn.

Multiple, collected 'says that' reports are possible with members of the basic set, such as "then". We might say, for example, "The other day, I spoke to John about Plato's Greece, and Barry about Shakespeare's England. Both said that intellectual standards were much higher back then". Here the preamble does not serve to render salient one single value for "then", but rather makes salient one value for John's utterance, and another for Barry's. We understand the collected report to attribute one utterance to John in which the time of Plato's Greece determines the extension of "then", and another to Barry in which the time of Shakespeare's England determines the extension of "then". These different attributions are possible even though we choose to report the utterances with a collected 'said that' report. The preamble (again, minimal and oblique) is enough to allow us to interpret the report as attributing assertions to John and Barry in which "then" takes on different respective values.

We do not always even require a preamble for such a distributive interpretation. Distributive interpretations, it seems, are possible even under conditions of ignorance and indifference. To see this, let us elaborate CL's scenario in which one answers the phone only to hear a woman mysteriously utter "there is a river nearby" and then hang up. Let us imagine that, immediately after the woman hangs up, weirdly enough, a man calls, also utters "there is a river nearby", and promptly hangs up. If asked what the callers said, one might reply "The woman and the man both said that there is a river nearby". This report is as natural as the single report CL describe. One might offer this collected report even if one had no idea where the speakers were calling from, and one certainly need not assume that they are calling from the same location to offer it. We easily understand "nearby" as tied to each speaker; we understand the report distributively, as equivalent to "the woman said there is a river nearby, and the man said there is a river nearby", where the semantic value of the first occurrence of 'nearby' depends on whatever location is salient in the woman's context, while the semantic value of the second depends on whatever location is salient for the man.

Given that we can collect 'says that' reports for items that are contextually sensitive, and can even do so under conditions of ignorance, it is no surprise that we can also do this for the intermediate items, as CL point out:

We're thinking about different utterances of "John is ready". We're imagining the following two contexts of utterance of (1):

(1) John is ready.

Context of Utterance C1 In a conversation about exam preparation, someone raises the question of whether John is well prepared. Nina utters (1).
Context of Utterance C2 Three people are about to leave an apartment; they are getting dressed for heavy rain. Nina utters (1).
. . . In (1.1) we report on her utterance in C1, in (1.2) her utterance in C2:

(1.1) Nina said that John is ready
(1.2) Nina said that John is ready.
(1.3) In both C1 and C2, Nina said that John is ready. (2005: 90–1)

It should be clear that the possibility of these reports does not count against the context sensitivity of "ready". The behavior of "ready" is not different from that of "nearby" or even "then" in this regard. (To make the parallel with "then" even more explicit, consider: *The other day, I spoke to John about Plato's Greece, and then later about Shakespeare's England. In both contexts, he said that intellectual standards were much higher back then.*)

So far it seems that the behavior of the intermediate items in reporting contexts does not differ in unacceptable ways from the behavior of items that are clearly contextually sensitive. Once we understand their behavior on the model I have proposed—a model that is required to account for the behavior of contextuals such as "nearby", and perhaps even Kaplanian adverbs such as "there" and "then"—it becomes clear why the intermediate items appear to fail the Report test, despite their being contextually sensitive. We have seen that, for all these items, a minimal preamble lets us understand the value of the context-sensitive item in a 'says that' report as dependent on what was salient in the context of the original utterance. The value is thus dependent on the context of the original utterance, as opposed to the reporting context, and further, this can be so across multiple, collected reports—even if the various reported utterances occurred in very different contexts. We have seen that this is so for "then" and "nearby", as well as for the intermediate items.

If we find ourselves in a context of ignorance and indifference—that is, if no preamble is given and nothing relevant is known about the original context, and the reporting context does not provide the relevant value needed to determine the item's semantic value—then we can nonetheless disquotationally report utterances containing "nearby", and in some circumstances, even "there". We simply understand the relevant, required value to be *what it was in the original context, whatever that may have been.* I see no reason why we cannot understand reports containing intermediate items in contexts of ignorance and indifference in the same way. We understand out-of-the-blue utterances of "Bill said that John was ready" to mean roughly that *Bill said that John was ready for some activity or other that was salient in the context of Bill's utterance.*

Let us bolster this last claim by considering the following report. Imagine that we do not have any particular activity in mind, and we do not know what activities were salient in the original contexts. Then consider the following report:

> Tom said that John was ready. Later, Barry said that John wasn't ready, but that was in another context, so he and Tom didn't disagree.

Such a report may well be true. Tom can say that John was ready, while Barry can say that John wasn't ready, and yet Tom and Barry need not contradict each other. For CL, however, "John is ready" and "John is not ready" are contradictories—"is ready" is an invariant predicate, and so either John possesses the property it expresses or he does not. Barry and Tom would have to be in disagreement, since they predicated contradictory things of John. CL must claim that our intuition that the above report might be true is based on our tracking speech act content, rather than semantic content, since the semantic content of the complements of the reports are contradictories. It is not clear why we would be tracking speech act content here, though, given that we are tracking semantic content in the scenarios they use for their Report test.

The proposal I have outlined, however, offers a natural rendering of the above report. Since this is a context of ignorance and indifference, we understand the initial report "Tom said that John was ready" to mean roughly that *Tom said that John was ready for something or other that was salient in the context of Tom's utterance*, and we understand the second report "Barry said that Tom wasn't ready" to mean roughly that *Barry said that John wasn't ready for something or other that was salient in the context of Barry's utterance.* Since we are told that the two contexts differed, it is easy to see how the two reports could be true, and yet Tom and Barry fail to disagree. The contents of the reports are not contradictories on the view proposed here, which fits well with our intuitions concerning scenarios such as this.

3.2. The Collection Test

We have seen how we might reconcile the results of the ICD/RCSA test with those of the Report test. It is not difficult to extend the model described above to also help us reconcile the results of the ICD/RCSA test with those of the Collection test. Consider "nearby" and "local". Both appear to fail the Collection test, as the following example illustrates:

> John lives in St Louis, and Bill lives in San Francisco. Both John and Bill buy their food from local farmers. And last night, both John and Bill went to a nearby restaurant for dinner.

We can collect predications containing "local" and "nearby" across relevantly different contexts. That means both items apparently fail the Collection test. The situation here, though, is not too different from the one we faced when dealing with collected 'says that' reports. There, we understood the context-sensitive elements to be indexed to their respective contexts, so that they might have different semantic values in each of the multiple reports that were collected. For example, if we say "I spoke to John about Plato's Greece, and then later on about Shakespeare's England. In both contexts, he said that intellectual standards were much higher back then", we understand that two utterances are being reported, and the semantic value of "then" in the first is the time of Plato's Greece, and in the second it is the time of Shakespeare's England. An analog of this approach is appropriate here: we understand "local" in the collected predication above as meaning *local w/r/t John and Bill respectively*, and "nearby" as meaning *nearby John and Bill respectively*.

But now consider simple, non-collected predications such as "John went to a nearby restaurant". Here, I propose that "nearby" may receive either a 'subject-based' interpretation, i.e. *nearby John*, or a 'context-based' interpretation, which is relative to a salient location in the context of utterance. If there is such a salient location in the context of utterance, then the item is most naturally interpreted relative to that location; otherwise it is interpreted relative to the subject, so long as that is appropriate. (I will discuss these conditions of appropriateness below.) Thus, if one utters out-of-the-blue "John went to a nearby restaurant last night", "nearby" can be naturally interpreted as meaning *nearby John*, and so the utterance may be true even if John is in New York, while the utterer is in Birmingham. If, however, one is trying desperately to find a restaurant in Birmingham, and one's friend says "John went to a nearby restaurant last night", "nearby" is here interpreted as *nearby the location of the speaker*, and so is false.

Having drawn the distinction between these two ways in which the semantic value of "nearby" may be determined, we can notice that not all sentences lend themselves to the subject-based interpretation. Consider, for example "John is nearby". This sentence can only be interpreted to mean that John is near the location of the utterer (or at least near some location that is salient in the context of the utterance). A subject-based interpretation of "nearby" here would yield the unacceptable *John is nearby John*, and so is not available as an interpretation of that sentence. Only the context-based interpretation is acceptable here.

If collected predications drawing on different contexts are only acceptable when the context-sensitive item receives a subject-based interpretation, then we would predict that sentences in which the subject-based interpretation is not available could not be collected. This is indeed the case: if Bill utters in San

Francisco "John is nearby", and Barry utters in Princeton "Shanna is nearby", we cannot conclude that both John and Shanna are nearby. The collection is unacceptable.

I believe that this treatment explains Hawthorne's otherwise puzzling observation that some collected predications of "nearby" and "left" are permissible, while other are not. Hawthorne writes:

> Suppose in Birmingham, I say, 'I am going to a nearby restaurant' and Ernie, in New York, says 'I am going to a nearby restaurant'. We can certainly 'collect' with 'John and Ernie are going to nearby restaurants'. But suppose Ernie says 'There is good Vietnamese food nearby' and I say, 'There is good Indian food nearby'. We cannot 'collect' with 'There is good Vietnamese food and Indian food nearby.'
>
> A similar pattern holds for 'left'. Suppose Ernie turns to his left, saying 'I am turning left', and I turn to my left, saying, 'I am turning left'. I can collect: 'We are both turning left'. I can also use verb phrase ellipsis: I turned left and Ernie did too. But suppose Ernie and I are facing each other. Noticing a ball rolling to from his right to his left, Ernie says 'The ball is moving left'. Noticing a balloon moving from my right to my left, Ernie says 'The balloon is moving left'. I cannot collect with 'The ball and the balloon are moving left'. Relatedly, I cannot say 'The ball moved left and so did the balloon'. This particular pattern of success and failure cries out for some kind of explanation. (2006)

With "there is good Vietnamese food nearby" and "there is good Indian food nearby", there is no subject-based interpretation available. For these sentences, the 'dummy' subject "there" does not support a subject-based interpretation. If we consider, say, "good Indian food" to be the dislocated subject of the sentence, as many syntacticians do, this does not help matters; the sentence would then mean *Good Indian food is nearby*, which does not allow for a subject-based interpretation, just as "John is nearby" does not. As my treatment predicts, because there is no subject-based interpretation available, we cannot collect these predications.

In the case of "left", it matters whether the subject determines a frame of reference appropriate for right and left. People determine such frames, so it is possible to interpret "John and Ernie both turned left" as *John and Ernie both turned left from the point of view of John and Ernie respectively*. Balls and balloons, however, do not determine such frames—there is no such thing as left from the point of view of a balloon. Only the context-based interpretation is possible in such cases, and we cannot collect these predications.

Ernie Lepore (pers. comm.) has suggested to me that perhaps "nearby" is ambiguous between a context-sensitive predicative sense, as in "John is nearby", and a context-insensitive adjectival sense, as in "John went to a nearby restaurant". The suggestion is ingenious, and would capture the data described thus far, without recourse to subject-based interpretations. I think, however, that it is not adequate to draw the distinction between predicative and adjectival uses, for there are some adjectival uses that also block collection. Consider, for example "John is in a nearby restaurant". Let us suppose that Bill in St Louis utters "John is in a nearby restaurant" and Mary in Portland utters "James is in a nearby restaurant". We cannot conclude that both John and James are in nearby restaurants. The simple change of verb from "went to"/"is going to" to "is in" suffices to block the collection. "Nearby" here can only be interpreted as nearby a location salient in the context of utterance. It is, however, occurring in adjectival form. This shows that the situations in which "nearby" does not allow for collection are not limited to ones in which "nearby" occurs as a predicate. Whether we use "to be in" rather than "to go to" makes the difference between predications with "nearby" that can be collected and ones that cannot. It is hard to see how this could be explained by positing ambiguities in "nearby".

The model here described predicts this outcome; while one can *go to* a restaurant that is near one's location, one cannot *be in* a restaurant that is near one's location, since one is located *in* the restaurant. An item cannot be near another item if the former is located within the latter. In "John is in a nearby restaurant", "nearby" cannot mean *nearby John*; John is *in* the restaurant, and so cannot be *nearby* the restaurant. The subject-based interpretation is unavailable, and so cannot be invoked in interpreting the sentence. Collection, as in "John and Bill are both in nearby restaurants", is therefore unacceptable. My account lets us see why the small change in verb can make the difference between collected predications being acceptable or unacceptable.

The distinction between subject-based interpretations and context-based ones, then, is an important one. If we posit that context-sensitive items such as "nearby" and "left" can receive subject-based interpretations when such interpretations are acceptable, we are able to explain why some collections are permissible, while others are not. I take this to be good reason to assume that some context-sensitive items can receive these subject-based interpretations, and that collected predications across different contexts are permissible only when the items receive subject-based interpretations.

There is no reason to suppose that the intermediate items do not behave similarly.[8] I suggest that the intermediate items sometimes receive subject-based interpretations, and that we can collect predications containing them only when they receive these subject-based interpretations. As we have seen, there are circumstances under which we cannot collect intermediate items such as "ready". If a particular activity is salient in a context, then we cannot collect predications of readiness, unless of course they pertain to that activity. We saw this in *John's APA Nightmare*; in the context of that scenario, we cannot collect the true utterance of "John is ready" (said in connection with dinner) and the true utterance of "Mary is ready" (said in connection with APA interviews) to obtain *John and Mary are both ready*. Such a collection is impermissible in that context. This, I claim, is because the context-based interpretation of "ready" is favored, since the context of the collection supplies a salient activity. Similarly, if

[8] Stanley (2000, 2002) offers an important and detailed treatment of intermediate items such as "tall" along these lines.

we are hungrily seeking a restaurant in Birmingham, we cannot say "both John and Bill went to nearby restaurants last night" unless the restaurants in question are near to our current location.

If, however, the context is one of indifference, where no salient value for the context-sensitive item is provided, then we can collect predications containing intermediate items, such as "ready" and "tall". Since we have established that *some* context-sensitive items permit subject-based interpretations, I propose that we understand the intermediate items to allow subject-based interpretations where appropriate. Just as with "nearby", we can collect predications containing intermediate items across different contexts *only* when those items receive a subject-based interpretation. So, for example, we understand the collection "both John and Bill are ready" to mean roughly that *both John and Bill are ready for activities that are salient for John and Bill respectively.*[9]

Notice that we can collect predications containing "nearby" even in contexts of ignorance, so long as the subject-based interpretation is available. If Tom utters "John went to a nearby restaurant last night", and George utters "Bill went to a nearby restaurant last night", then I might collect the two utterances and say "Both John and Bill went to nearby restaurants last night". I might do this even if I have no idea where either John or Bill happen to be. My collection is understood as meaning *Both John and Bill went to restaurants that are nearby their respective locations, whatever those may be.* I suggest that we understand collected predications containing intermediate items in contexts of ignorance and indifference in a similar way. If Tom utters "John is ready" and George utters "Bill is ready", then I might collect these and say "Both John and Bill are ready", even if I have no idea what they are ready for. We understand the collection to mean that John and Bill are ready for activities that are salient for them both respectively, *whatever those activities may be.*

In general, the intermediate items are no worse off than items such as "nearby" with respect to the Report and Collection tests.

In short, once we recognize the possibility of subject-based interpretations of context-sensitive items, we need not think that the possibility of collection counts against an item's being contextually sensitive. We should not assume that, just because we might say *A and B are F*, this means that we are predicating the very same property of both A and B. This would be akin to arguing that we predicate the same property of every girl when we say "every girl loves her mother" (Stanley 2005), or arguing that John and Bill must desire the same thing if we are to be able to say "both John and Bill want to be department chair".

[9] Just as in the Report test, not everyone is as confident of the data as CL are. One might reasonably doubt that such collects really are acceptable. I will once again respond to CL on their own terms, however, and show how, even if these data are correct, items such as 'ready' may nonetheless be contextually sensitive.

As a final remark on the possibility of collecting the intermediate items, it should be noted that the predicate "is ready" does not allow collection in all cases. Consider, for example, the impermissibility of the following collection:

> My guests have arrived for dinner, and are very hungry. I ask them if they are ready to eat, and they reply "yes, we are ready". I call into the kitchen to check on the status of the beef tenderloin, and the cook replies "it is ready". Wonderful, I think to myself. My guests and the tenderloin are both ready.

We cannot collect in these circumstances. "My guests and the tenderloin are ready" is no more acceptable than the zeugma "Mary left in a huff and a taxi". As linguists have long noted, "ready" allows for both 'tough' readings and 'control' readings', hence the ambiguity of "the goose is ready to eat'. On the control reading, the subject "the goose" controls the unpronounced subject of "to eat"; this is the interpretation according to which the goose is ready to eat, in the same sense that one's guests may be ready to eat. On the so-called tough reading,[10] the subject is identified with the unpronounced object of "to eat"; in this sense, the goose is ready to eat in the way that a beef tenderloin may be ready to eat. Just as we cannot accept "my guests and the beef tenderloin are ready to eat" (except on an interpretation that calls to mind Hannibal Lecter and the like), we cannot accept "my guests and the beef tenderloin are ready". The explanation of the failure of collection when the infinitival clause is articulated is straightforward: we cannot collect predications that differ so in their underlying syntax. Since collection fails in exactly the same way when the infinitival clause is not articulated, this suggests that we are nonetheless at some level representing the infinitival clause and its dependence relations to the subject. This suggests that there is no such predicate as "is ready, period"—there is always some completion required, though not always articulated. The syntactic nature of the completion determines whether collection is permissible.[11]

This point is, of course, specific to "ready". It is telling, though, since these data strongly suggest that we represent the object of the readiness, even if we do

[10] So-called because sentences such as "John is tough to please" are only interpreted in this way. "John is tough to please" can only mean that it is tough for the arbitrary person to please John; it cannot mean that it is tough for John to please the arbitrary person.

[11] The point is made most clearly when we try to collect predications of readiness across people and inanimate objects. This is because inanimate objects almost invariably occur with tough interpretations; it is hard to imagine cases in which we might say of an inanimate object that it is ready to itself undertake an action. People, on the other hand, are usually said to be ready to do such-and-such a task. The failure of collection can occur when all the subjects are people, however. Consider: "John is ready to run a marathon. Bill is ready to shoot a basket. George is ready to fall down. They are all ready." This collection strikes us as a sort of bad joke, a sign of zeugma.

not articulate it. If this is so, then the Report and Collection tests are misleading in the case of "ready"; CL use these tests to argue that there is a simple, invariant predicate "is ready", which predicates a single property of its subject, no matter the context. The syntactic data above suggest this cannot be so, thus these tests cannot be trusted. Instead, we should rely on the ICD/RCSA test, which correctly characterizes "ready" as contextually sensitive.

4. CONCLUSION

Cappelen and Lepore's *Insensitive Semantics* forces us to think carefully about the phenomenon of semantic context sensitivity. What are our standards for counting an item as contextually sensitive? Are they so lax that all of natural language turns out to be context-sensitive? And how do we explain the behavior of context-sensitive items in a variety of linguistic constructions, across a variety of contexts?

I have argued that Cappelen and Lepore's ICD/RCSA test should be a benchmark for context sensitivity. It reflects basic, constitutive facts about the nature of context sensitivity, and it sets the bar high enough that only a limited range of items are able to pass it. With that test in hand, we are able to draw a principled distinction between those items that are context-sensitive and those that are not. We are no longer in no danger of sliding down the slope into Radical Contextualism.

Since the ICD/RCSA test should be taken seriously, a challenge emerges. There are a fair number of items that pass the ICD/RCSA test, and yet can occur in disquotational reports and collected predications, both across different contexts. How is this possible, if these items are contextually sensitive? I have tried to sketch out how this might happen, and in doing so, I hope to have shed some light on the phenomenon of non-indexical context dependence. Cappelen and Lepore are right to point out to us the prima-facie incompatibility of an item's being contextually sensitive, yet amenable to disquotation and collected predication. It is no simple matter to understand how this is possible, and we are indebted to Cappelen and Lepore for pointing out that this is a phenomenon in need of explanation.

Finally, as a meditation on semantic methodology, *Insensitive Semantics* reminds us time and again that intuitions about what is said are poor guides to semantic content. This point, so often overlooked, is an important one for semanticists to take on board. I have attempted here to extend Cappelen and Lepore's work so as to provide tests and standards for context sensitivity that do not depend on intuitions about what is said. On the importance of developing and adhering to such tests, I am in full agreement with Cappelen and Lepore. I differ from them only on exactly which items pass the tests.

5. APPENDIX: MINIMALISM AND COMMUNICATION

Cappelen and Lepore level three charges against the contextualist: they argue that she classifies items that fail their three tests as context-sensitive, that she cannot account for the ease with which we communicate with each other, and that her theory is internally inconsistent. In the main body of this paper, I argued that Moderate Contextualism is indeed a stable position, contra CL, and that it does not count any items as context-sensitive if they do not pass their ICD/RCSA test. I also provided an account of non-indexical context sensitivity that explains why some of the Moderate Contextualist's context-sensitive items might appear to fail the Report and Collection tests. Thus I take myself to have answered CL's first objection to contextualism, namely that it counts items that fail their tests as context-sensitive. I will not address their third objection—that contextualism is internally inconsistent—because the objection applies only to theories that hold that all sentences are contextually sensitive. That is, it is only an objection to Radical Contextualism, not to Moderate Contextualism, and my concern here is only to defend Moderate Contextualism.

In this appendix, I will consider CL's claim that only their view, Semantic Minimalism, is able to explain how we can successfully communicate across contexts, or perhaps even within a given context. I will argue that Semantic Minimalism is hard pressed to account for our communicative practices. Simply put, the minimal proposition[12] that is semantically expressed is far too minimal to be what we care about in communication. If Semantic Minimalism was the correct view of semantics, then it would follow that we would almost never be concerned with semantic content in communication, but rather with speech act content. On CL's view, a huge range of propositions are expressed by every utterance, though only one of those propositions is the semantic content of the utterance, while the others constitute the remainder of its speech act content. If their view was correct, our intuitions about even the truth and falsity of an utterance would often fail to track the truth value of the proposition semantically expressed, and would rather track one of the many propositions that are merely said, not semantically expressed. Since our intuitions about the truth and falsity of an utterance may often fail to track its semantic content, the minimal proposition that is semantically expressed does not explain our ability to communicate with one another in the way that CL claim it does.

CL introduce their objection to contextualism by writing:

[12] The minimal proposition expressed by a sentence "S" is the semantic content of "S", and if "S" does not contain any members of the basic set, then the minimal proposition expressed by "S" is just the proposition *that S*.

If RC [Radical Contextualism][13] were true, it would be miraculous if people ever succeeded in communicating across diverse contexts of utterance. But there are no miracles; people do succeed in communicating across diverse contexts of utterance with boring regularity. So, RC isn't true.

Only slightly more elaborated, it goes like this: If RC were true, then *what's said by an utterance* by a speaker A in context of utterance C depends, at least in part, on very specific features of C . . . In sum, if RC were true, it would be a miracle if speakers in different contexts were ever able to agree, disagree, or more generally, share contents. (2005: 123; my emphasis)

It is not easy to understand exactly what the objection is here, since on their own view *what is said* by a given utterance depends on specific features of the context of the utterance (93). (In fact, what is said by a given utterance even depends on features *outside* the context of the original utterance; see their rejection of 'Original Utterance Centrism'.) CL devote the entire last chapter of their book to describing and emphasizing how varied and unconstrained speech act content, or what is said, turns out to be, once we look closely. What is said, on their view, depends heavily on features of the context of utterance, among other things.[14]

How, then, do CL envision their objection applying to contextualism, but not to their own view? It is their minimal proposition that they suppose gives their account an advantage over its alternatives. This minimal proposition *that S*—the proposition that is semantically expressed by an utterance of "S"—is *always* among the indefinitely many propositions expressed by an utterance of "S" (2005: 205). It is the availability of this context-invariant proposition that allows us to communicate with each other across contexts. They write:

Semantic Minimalism, and no other view, can account for how the same content can be expressed, claimed, asserted, questioned, investigated, etc. in radically different contexts. It is the semantic content that enables audiences who find themselves in radically different contexts to understand each other, to agree or disagree, to question and debate with each other. It can serve this function simply because it is the sort of content that is largely immune to contextual variations. (2005: 152)

Since it is their minimal proposition that CL believe enables us to communicate across contexts, let us consider the nature of these minimal propositions, so as

[13] Remember that CL take themselves to have established that Moderate Contextualism collapses into Radical Contextualism; that is why they are addressing their objection only the Radical Contextualist.

[14] They write: "What's crucial to notice here (and in general) is that our intuitions about what speakers say with their utterances are influenced by, at least, the following sorts of considerations: (1) *Facts about the speaker's intentions and beliefs* . . . (2) *Facts about the conversational context of this particular utterance* . . . (3) *Other facts about the world* . . . (4) *Logical Relations*" (193). They also state that "there's no reason to think that [these factors] exhaust all the factors that influence our intuitions about what speakers say" (194). Finally, it's important to note that they "take our non-theoretic beliefs about intuitions about what speakers say, assert, claim, etc, at face value" (191).

to see whether they can indeed serve this purpose. In particular, let us consider the proposition that CL believe is semantically expressed by sentences containing the intermediate items, such as "John is ready". CL hold that "John is ready" expresses the proposition *that John is ready*, which is true iff John is ready (2005: 155). The question that naturally arises is, what is the nature of the property of *being ready*? When does a person or object posses this property?

CL are adamant that a semanticist should not have to answer such metaphysical questions. Nonetheless, they sketch how they imagine an analysis of this property would proceed:

> Think about what metaphysicians do. For at least the last two millennia, metaphysicians have been asking *What-Do-they-Have-in-Common-Questions* (CQ, for short). Suppose you're curious about what it is to be G. Then you ask (this is at least one of the questions you ask):
>
> (CQ) What do all G things have in common?
>
> . . . Think about what people who are ready have in common. To make this vivid, imagine A's being ready to commit a bank robbery, B's being ready to eat dinner, and C's being ready to take an exam.
>
> Thinking about A, B and C, you've got two options:
>
> a) You might think, as we do: Well, they have a common relation they stand in to their respective projects: There's something in common between A's relation to the bank robbery, B's relation to the dinner and C's relation to the exam. What they have in common is that they are all *ready*.
> b) Alternatively, you might think that there's *nothing* these people have in common. The fact that we would describe them as all being ready for their various projects doesn't mean that they have anything whatsoever in common. There's no state of readiness that they share with respect to their respective tasks.
>
> We find (a) overwhelmingly plausible. It's not just a pun that we feel comfortable describing them all as being ready. They really are all *ready*. That's different from their all being *done with* the tasks, or *excited about* them, or *prepared for* them, or *good at* them, etc. (159–67)

So CL conclude it is this shared property that 'is ready' expresses. A has it in virtue of being ready to rob a bank, B has it in virtue of being ready to eat dinner, and so on. Generalizing, we have that *being ready* is a property that one possesses in virtue of being ready to do some task or other. Any time A is ready to do X, for any X at all, then A is ready.

One should wonder that this does not make it very easy to be ready. CL are aware of this, and though they do not specifically address this question with respect to readiness, they say of their corresponding claim concerning "enough":

> The following concern might now be raised: Doesn't that make it very easy to have had enough? If that's all it takes, haven't we all had enough all of the time? Suppose the answer is 'yes' (though we have no idea whether this is correct or not; presumably it all depends on doing more serious metaphysics, but suppose it's correct). When you think

real hard [sic.] about enoughness, maybe that's all it takes. If so, then it's not that hard to have had enough. (168 fn.)

Thus while CL hedge slightly in their parenthetic remarks, they are quite open to the above metaphysical analysis of properties such as *being ready*. Let us for now assume that this is indeed their intended account of the property of *being ready*, and therefore that the proposition *that John is ready* is co-extensive with the proposition *that John is ready for something*.[15] The question now arises: is this proposition the one that we care about in communication?

CL intend this minimal proposition to be one that is communicated by all utterances of "John is ready". Now, it is not in dispute that all utterances of "John is ready" communicate that John is ready for something. (CL sometimes write as though the contextualist would deny this, but I do not see why this would be so.) Even if contextualism is true, the truth of "John is ready" entails that John is ready for something—i.e. if John is ready for some contextually salient activity, then he is ready for something. It is quite reasonable to think that a proposition that is at least co-extensive with CL's minimal proposition is communicated by all utterances of "John is ready", no matter which view of semantics one adopts.[16]

But what are we to make of utterances of "It's false that John is ready"? Surely the proposition semantically expressed by "it's false that John is ready" is the negation of the proposition expressed by "John is ready". But if "John is ready" semantically expresses a proposition that is co-extensive with *John is ready for something*, then "it's false that John is ready" must semantically express a proposition that is co-extensive with *not: John is ready for something*. This proposition is false if there is anything at all that John is ready for. But is it reasonable to think that we communicate such a proposition with every utterance of "it's false that John is ready"? Surely this is not so. We simply do not interpret utterances of "it's false that John is ready" as communicating anything this

[15] These propositions (and the properties that figure in them) are co-extensive, but not identical. I assume that CL adopt a structured approach to propositions so that this is possible.

[16] CL repeatedly argue as though the contextualist should want to deny that this is so, and claim that there is nothing in common between people who are all ready for their respective tasks. I must confess that I do not understand why they anticipate this line of objection. Clearly, there are many, many things that two people who are ready for different tasks have in common—they are both self-identical, both complex material objects, both human beings, and of course, both ready to do something. No one would deny that there is something in common between two people who are ready to perform different tasks. The question is not whether there are some commonalities between these people, the question is whether we semantically predicate a common property of them when we say that A and B are both ready. Consider e.g. girls who all love their respective mothers. There are many properties shared in common between girls who love their mothers—they are all self-identical, they are all girls, they all love someone, and so on. This observation has no bearing on the semantics of "each girl loves her mother". We do not conclude from the fact that these girls share common properties that we are semantically predicating one of these common properties of all of them when we say "each girl loves her mother". That there are many properties shared between the objects of thought and talk is an observation that is completely orthogonal to issues concerning semantic context sensitivity.

strong. We do not intend to convey this information by uttering such a sentence, and we do not glean this information from utterances of the sentence. Since CL urge us to take our pre-theoretic intuitions about what is said at face value, it is hard to see how such a proposition could be among those that are said by *any* utterance of "it's false that John is ready", let alone one that is said by *every* such utterance.

Even if we were to be somehow convinced that this proposition is always among those that are said by an utterance of "it's false that John is ready", it is *clearly* not the proposition that we care about in communication, since we are not even aware that we are communicating it to one another.

Minimal propositions are poorly suited for the communicative work for which CL intend them. They are rarely, for example, our objects of disagreement. I discussed this point in Leslie (2004), and Hawthorne (2006) also makes this point. Let us return to *John's APA Nightmare* to see this more clearly.

Disagreement

Recall that poor John is on the job market, and is thoroughly unprepared for his interviews. Looking at him, his thesis advisor says: "Well, at least John's ready." The department chair appropriately responds: "Are you out of your mind? He's clearly not ready!" In other words, the chair adamantly disagrees with the advisor's claim that John is ready. What is the basis for this disagreement? It is surely not that the chair takes John not to be ready for *anything*. He may well think John is ready to do a variety of things: pass out, bolt from the APA, etc. But:

> If the chair thinks John is ready to bolt from the APA,
>
> And if being ready to do something is sufficient for having the property *being ready*,
>
> And the property of *being ready* is what is semantically predicated of John by and utterance of 'John is ready',
>
> And if disagreements are over semantically expressed propositions,
>
> Then the chair would have no grounds to disagree with the thesis advisr.

It is clear that the minimal proposition that CL endorse is not sufficient to explain disagreements. A corollary is that the minimal proposition is also not our object of debate and deliberation, since these notions are intimately tied to disagreement. When the department chair questions the advisor's judgment, he is not questioning the truth of a proposition that is co-extensive with *John is ready for something*. It is simply not true that "it is the semantic content that enables audiences who find themselves in radically different contexts to understand each other, to agree or disagree, to question and debate with each other" (152). The semantic content does not even serve this purpose *within* a context.

In their paper, "Shared Content", Cappelen and Lepore provide a variety of other purposes that shared content serves. I shall not go through every purpose they cite, but it is clear that their minimal proposition is simply not up to task. Consider, for example, the following two additional purposes:

Responsibility

Responsibility is another phenomenon that CL claim is based on shared content. Again the minimal proposition is not sufficient to bear the burden. If the interviewers ask John's thesis advisor if John would like to take more time and reschedule the interview and the advisor responds, "No, he's ready", then John may hold his advisor responsible for the consequences of this. It is no defense on the part of the thesis advisor that the proposition semantically expressed was true in virtue of John's being ready to bolt from the APA.

Reasons for Action

CL point out that what others say often provides us with reasons for action. If John's thesis advisor says "no, John's ready", the interviewing committee takes this as a reason for them to go ahead and interview John right away, rather than rescheduling his interview. The advisor's utterance would not provide them with a reason to do this if it was not understood to mean that John is ready *to be interviewed.* If the advisor could truly utter "John's ready" in virtue of John's being ready to bolt from the APA, then his utterance would not provide the interviewing committee with a reason to go ahead with the interview.

The minimal proposition clearly cannot explain the communicative phenomena that CL wish it to explain. The minimalist is no further forward than the Radical Contextualist in explaining communication.

We might wonder to what extent the difficulties we raised for the minimal proposition depend on the particular metaphysics of *being ready* that CL seem to adopt. I believe that any invariantist account of *being ready* will face similar difficulties. Let us adopt a different analysis of *being ready*—let us say that x is ready iff x is ready for the activity that is most salient to x.[17] Then the minimal proposition expressed by "John is ready" will be co-extensive with *John is ready for the activity that is most salient to him.* In *John's APA Nightmare*, this activity is clearly his APA interview, so "John is ready" here expresses a proposition that is co-extensive with *John is ready for his APA interview.* Notice that this is an invariant property; in every context, an utterance of

[17] CL suggest an analogous analysis of *being tall* (171), so it is not a stretch to imagine that they might adopt such an account of *being ready.*

"John is ready" expresses this same property, so "John is ready" is not context-sensitive on this picture. This account offers a much better rendering of the situation described above; an utterance of "John is ready" will be false, and any disagreement over whether John is ready amounts to disagreement over whether he is ready for his interview, and so on. It seems that we have the correct result so far.

Unfortunately, it is easy to replicate the difficulties we encountered earlier. Imagine, for example, that two evangelists are hovering around the APA, looking for lost souls that are ripe for conversion. They discreetly observe John, and it is manifestly clear to them that he is not ready for his interview. Neither of them doubts this fact. The evangelists come to discuss whether the time is right to approach John to discuss his accepting Jesus Christ as his Personal Savior. Is John ready to be saved, they wonder? The first evangelist says, "Take one look at him. He's lost and bewildered. This guy is definitely ready." The second expresses doubt, saying "I disagree. Let's wait and see how things unfold. If his interview goes badly—as it surely will—then he'll be ready. Right now, I just don't think he's quite ready." The evangelists are in disagreement over whether John is ready, though neither of them doubts that John is not at all ready for his interview. Since John's interview is the most salient activity for him at the time, if the above account of *being ready* was correct, the evangelists would not be in disagreement over whether John is ready. The minimal proposition would, once again, fail to be the object of disagreement. Similarly, if the second evangelist insists, saying "No, John is just not ready", and as a result they miss a perfect opportunity to convert John, the first evangelist may hold the second one responsible for what he said. It would be no defense for the second evangelist to claim that what he said was semantically true, because John was clearly not ready for the activity that was most salient to him.

A minimal, invariant proposition is simply not sufficient to explain our communicative practices. We often do not care about the minimal proposition even *within* a given context. It is thus also rarely what we care about in communication *across* contexts. (Years later, John might confront his thesis advisor, demanding to know why he told the interviewing committee that John was ready, when he obviously was not. The thesis advisor's defense that John was ready for something, namely to bolt from the APA, is no more convincing in this new context than it was in the original context.) If Semantic Minimalism were the correct view, we would be no further forward in explaining communication than we would be if Radical Contextualism were true. On both theories, communication depends on what is said, and what is said is an elusive, context-dependent phenomenon.[18]

[18] On the Moderate Contextualist's view, the proposition that is semantically expressed is quite plausibly what we care about in communication, at least in many cases. Certainly, it is easy to see how it is the object of agreement and disagreement, debate and discussion in the scenarios

Semantic Minimalism does not explain how we are able to communicate with each other any better than its alternatives. CL therefore ought not to criticize contextualism on these grounds, since their criticism applies equally to their own theory. Nonetheless, CL are absolutely correct to point out that there is a phenomenon here that needs to be explained. Given that what we care about in communication depends so heavily on contextual features, how is that we are able to understand each other so well? How can we share content across contexts, given how variable the content we care about turns out to be? At this time, we have no satisfying answers to these questions, and we are indebted to Cappelen and Lepore for reminding us that this is so.

REFERENCES

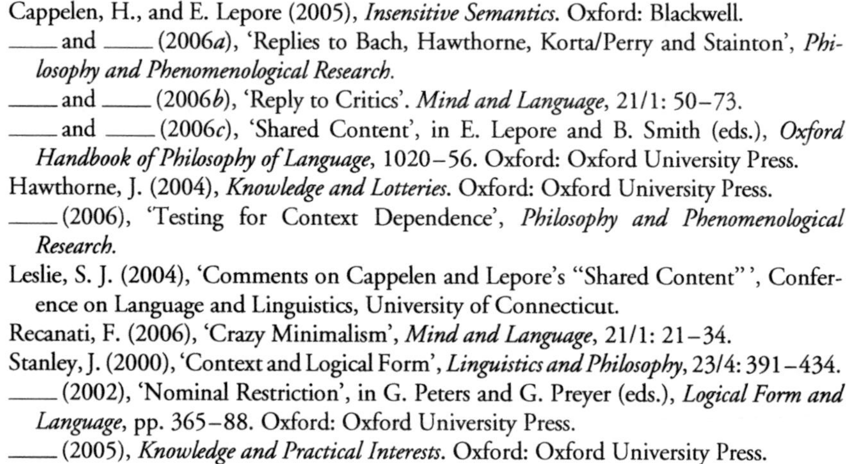

Cappelen, H., and E. Lepore (2005), *Insensitive Semantics*. Oxford: Blackwell.

—— and —— (2006*a*), 'Replies to Bach, Hawthorne, Korta/Perry and Stainton', *Philosophy and Phenomenological Research*.

—— and —— (2006*b*), 'Reply to Critics'. *Mind and Language*, 21/1: 50–73.

—— and —— (2006*c*), 'Shared Content', in E. Lepore and B. Smith (eds.), *Oxford Handbook of Philosophy of Language*, 1020–56. Oxford: Oxford University Press.

Hawthorne, J. (2004), *Knowledge and Lotteries*. Oxford: Oxford University Press.

—— (2006), 'Testing for Context Dependence', *Philosophy and Phenomenological Research*.

Leslie, S. J. (2004), 'Comments on Cappelen and Lepore's "Shared Content"', Conference on Language and Linguistics, University of Connecticut.

Recanati, F. (2006), 'Crazy Minimalism', *Mind and Language*, 21/1: 21–34.

Stanley, J. (2000), 'Context and Logical Form', *Linguistics and Philosophy*, 23/4: 391–434.

—— (2002), 'Nominal Restriction', in G. Peters and G. Preyer (eds.), *Logical Form and Language*, pp. 365–88. Oxford: Oxford University Press.

—— (2005), *Knowledge and Practical Interests*. Oxford: Oxford University Press.

described above. Of course, if Moderate Contextualism is correct, then the proposition that is semantically expressed is, of course, dependent on features of the context. It depends on them in more constrained ways than CL's speech act content does, however. In the main body of this chapter, I sketched an account of how we make use of preambles and the like to help us interpret reports of utterances that were made in different contexts, and how we interpret these reports if we do not know anything about the context of the original utterance. It need not be wholly mysterious how we could communicate across contexts if Moderate Contextualism were true. Still, cross-contextual communication is a remarkable phenomenon, and it is not obvious on any account how it proceeds. I rather suspect that a satisfying account of the phenomenon will belong to psychology, not to semantics.

6

Sense and Insensibility Or Where Minimalism Meets Contextualism

Eros Corazza and Jérôme Dokic

1. THE ESSENCE OF MINIMALISM

As we understand it, semantic minimalism is the view that: (i) an utterance *u* of a (declarative) sentence *S* expresses a proposition *p* whose constituents must all be represented by elements of *S*; (ii) the structure of *p* reflects the logical form of *S*,[1] and (iii) if *S* does not contain indexical expressions, *u* expresses *p* in a context-independent way. This last claim can be illustrated in considering:

(1) Jon is tall

(2) Melons are red

Utterances of (1) and (2) express the propositions *that Jon is tall* and *that melons are red* regardless of the context in which the sentences (1) and (2) are uttered. This amounts to saying that all utterances of (1) and (2) express the very same proposition, i.e. *that Jon is tall* and *that melons are red* respectively.

We shall not distinguish here between propositions and truth conditions; in our terminology, propositions are just truth conditions.[2] Semantic minimalists

[1] A proposition's structure should reflect, for instance, the difference between propositions expressed by sentences like "Jon loves Mary" and "Mary loves Jon". The constituents of the propositions expressed are exactly the same, i.e. Jon, Mary, and the loving relation. Yet the order, and thus the meaning of the sentences, differs. This should be reflected in the structure of the proposition. For the sake and simplicity of our argument, we shall concentrate only on the propositional constituents insofar as the main debate among the various theories we shall discuss turns around the propositional constituents.

[2] Cappelen and Lepore (2005: 3 n. 3) note that minimalism can be spelt out either in terms of propositions or in terms of truth conditions. One issue, which goes beyond the scope of this chapter, is whether talk of constituents and their being represented by elements of a sentence survives eschewing propositions for truth conditions.

claim that propositions are invariant across contexts. If they are right, then truth conditions are also, by definition, invariant across contexts. As we shall see, the crucial question is whether the truth-*values* of propositions can vary within a given possible world. If the answer to this question is positive, then propositions (or truth conditions) determine truth-values only relative to partial situations. For instance, the proposition that Jon is tall may be true relative to one particular situation but false relative to another, even within the same possible world. As will become clear, part of our argument is that the mistake of so-called indexicalism and contextualism is that they unduly transform intuitions about variable truth-values into intuitions about variable truth conditions or propositions.

Minimalists need not deny, though, that some (unambiguous) sentences may express some propositions only relative to a given context. Jane's utterance of:

(3) I am tall

expresses the proposition *that Jane is tall.* If (3) is uttered by Jon, it expresses the proposition *that Jon is tall.* Both Jane and Jon utter the same sentence, yet they express different propositions. The same is true with an utterance of:

(4) This melon is red

When the relevant designated melon is—to give it a name—Plug, it expresses the proposition *that Plug is red*, while if the relevant melon is Plum it expresses the proposition *that Plum is red.* In short, minimalists recognize that some sentences, i.e. those containing indexicals, express a proposition only relative to the context in which the sentence is uttered. When an indexical expression appears in an utterance there is a mandatory process triggered by the linguistic meaning of the indexical expression which requires appeal to some contextual features in order to fix the value of the indexical expression and, therefore, to determine the propositional constituent. This reflects Kaplan's (1977) famous distinction between character and content: the character of an indexical (its linguistic meaning) can be represented by a function taking as argument the context and giving as value the semantic content. If we follow Cappelen and Lepore, the class of indexical expressions is limited to the list mentioned by Kaplan (1977). This list contains only expressions like the pronouns "I", "s/he", "we", . . . , the demonstratives "this", "that", "these", . . . , the adverbs "here", "now", "tomorrow", . . . Roughly, an indexical is an expression whose linguistic meaning directs us to some aspect of context in order to fix the reference. Thus, "I" directs us to the agent of the utterance, while "she" directs us to the relevant female demonstrated by an utterance of "she". If the linguistic meaning of an expression does not direct us to some contextual aspects this expression cannot be classified as an indexical. It is thus context-*in*sensitive and the semantic value of an utterance of this expression will always be the same, regardless of the context in which it occurs. In other words, an expression is context-sensitive inasmuch as its semantic value can vary from context to context. Since the semantic value of an expression like "I", "now", "she", etc. can vary from context to context, these expressions are context-sensitive. On the other hand, on the assumption that the semantic value of expressions like "red", "tall", "ready", does not vary from context to context, these expressions are context-insensitive. The semantic value of "red", for instance, does not vary whether it applies to tomatoes, London buses, or Ian's hair. Tomatoes, London buses, and Ian's hair all have something in common: they are all red (whatever being red turns out to be). In a nutshell, "red" does not pick out a property in one context and another property in another context, i.e. it does not pick out one property when applied to London buses and another when it applies to tomatoes, likewise for "tall" and "ready".[3]

The distinction between indexical expressions—and thus context sensitivity linguistically triggered—and non-indexical ones also shows up in relation to what intuitively counts as understanding of an utterance. One does not understand an utterance containing an indexical expression if one does not identify the referent of the indexical expression, while one can understand an utterance deprived of indexical expression without engaging in a process of identification. Hence, one does not understand an utterance like "I am ready" or "This is red" if one does not identify the referent of "I" and "this". On the other hand, one can understand an utterance of "Aristotle is a philosopher" or "Jane is ready" even if one does not know who Aristotle was or what Jane is ready for. More on this later on.

2. INDEXICALISM AND CONTEXTUALISM

It may be worth mentioning that some people contest the view that the class of indexical expressions is limited to the ones we enumerated. Some go so far

[3] One could argue that, just as there is nothing in the linguistic meaning of "tall" which could orient the hearer to the relevant standard of tallness, there is nothing in the code meaning of "now" or "here" that orients the hearer to the temporal/spatial extent of the time/location referred to. The same with "s/he": nothing in their code meaning orients the hearer to a specific individual. We maintain that there is a difference in the linguistic meaning of "tall" and the linguistic meaning of "now/here". Although the temporal/spatial extent of "now/here" may vary from utterance to utterance their linguistic meaning (or character) operates on a specific time/location to select the relevant extension. Think for instance of "we": nothing in its linguistic meaning tells us how many individuals must enter its extension. Yet its linguistic meaning forces the agent to be part of its semantic value. As for "s/he" their linguistic meaning is incomplete and suggests that the value is also determined by the accompanying demonstration or directing intention (see Kaplan 1977, 1989). On the other hand, nothing in the linguistic meaning of a word like "tall" directs us to a comparative class. All its linguistic meaning suggests is something along "more than the average height" (cf. *The New Shorter Oxford English Dictionary*) without suggesting that a standard of comparison should be part of its extension.

as to claim that proper names are indexicals as well (see, for instance, Burge 1973; Recanati 1993; Voltolini 1995; Pelczar and Rainsbury 1998). Others claim that comparative adjectives such as "rich", "small" (see Stanley 2000; Richard 2004), quantified expressions like "the book", "some students" (see Stanley and Szabo 2000), common nouns like "local", "foreigner", "enemy" (see Partee 1989; Condoravdi and Gawron 1986; Vallée 2003) are context-sensitive expressions as well. A common strategy to represent their context sensitivity is to posit a variable working like a hidden indexical at the level of logical form (see Partee 1989; Condoravdi and Gavron 1986; Stanley 2000; Stanley and Szabo 2000).[4] This view can be labelled *indexicalism* insofar as it explains, to borrow Recanati's terminology, contextual dependence in terms of saturation rather than enrichment. Saturation, unlike (free) enrichment, is a mandatory contextual process. As such, saturation is triggered by an indexical expression working either at the surface level or at the LF level. The case of surface level saturation is furnished by indexical expressions properly called, while the case of saturation operating at the LF level is given by alleged context-sensitive expressions (e.g. "tall", "red", "ready", "all the students", etc.) which do not fall under the traditional category of indexical expressions. The value of each context-sensitive term is thus determined in a similar way to the value of an indexical expression.

The main problem with indexicalism is that it intellectualizes ordinary communication. In an intuitive (albeit, of course, revisable) picture of communication, the hearer understands the speaker's utterance insofar as she grasps the same (or

[4] It may be worth noticing that unlike Cappelen and Lepore (2005: 1 n. 1) we believe that context sensitivity expands to other terms (often called *contextuals*) as well. Among these terms we have: "foreigner", "local", "enemy", "exported", "national", and the like—i.e. terms whose literal meaning suggests that their value also depends on the context in which they are uttered. Someone is an enemy or a foreigner only relative to someone else or some other country: our enemy can be your friend, while one may be a foreigner in France but not in Canada. On the other hand, something can be said to be red, or blue, regardless of the substance/thing to which the term applies. However, whether or not one ultimately includes contextuals in the list of context-sensitive expressions does not affect the contextualist–minimalist debate and, most importantly, does not undermine minimalism. We can propose some criteria for distinguishing contextual terms from non-contextual terms. The former, unlike the latter, for instance, can work anaphorically and can be bound. In "All around England most Arsenal supporters got drunk because after the final a *local* bar was selling cheap alcohol", "local" is bound by, and so its value covaries with, "All around England", while in "Every time Jon visits Paris he meets the *local* jazz guitarists", "local" works like an anaphoric pronoun, suggesting that Jon meets the jazz guitarists living in or around Paris. Similar examples can be constructed with "enemy", "foreigner", and the like, while they cannot be generated with terms like "tall", "red", and the like. In, for instance, "At each farm Jon visited all the tomatoes were red", the value of "red" does not depend on (and does not covary with) the farms Jon visited. This can further be highlighted by the different behaviors of "local" and "red" in "In each market Jon visited, all the tomatoes were red/local". Furthermore, contextuals unlike other terms can have a strict and sloppy reading when appearing in elliptical contexts such as: "Jane saw a local doctor and so did Mary" which can mean that Mary saw a doctor located in Jane's neighborhood (strict reading) or one located in Mary's neighborhood (sloppy reading). On the other hand, a sentence like "Jane ate a red tomato and so did Mary" can have only the strict reading interpretation, i.e. that Mary eats a red tomato.

at least similar) propositions. This is true also of indexical utterances. If Jane, addressing Jon, says:

(5) Today I am happy

Jon understands what Jane says insofar as he comes to know that "I" stands for Jane while "today" stands for the relevant day, say Monday, October 31, 2005 and, therefore, he grasps the proposition *that Jane is happy on Monday, October 31, 2005*. In other words, if one does not know the value of an indexical one does not understand the utterance containing it. To be sure, a competent speaker could interpret the relevant utterance and come to entertain a thought she could express by "The agent of this token was happy when s/he wrote it". This interpretation, based on the knowledge of linguistic rules governing the use of the indexical, cannot be, properly speaking, considered to be an understanding of the relevant utterance. This should not be surprising insofar as indexical expressions can be viewed as terms whose proper function is to exploit contextual aspects in order to anchor language and thought to specific items in our surroundings. In other words, there is what we call an *identification constraint* on the understanding of indexical utterances: in order to understand such utterances, one must identify the semantic values that the indexical expressions have in their context of utterance.[5]

Now the identification constraint does not seem to apply to proper names, at least in the way it applies to *bona-fide* indexical expressions. One need not know who Aristotle is in order to understand an utterance containing "Aristotle". Besides, what does it mean to know who Aristotle is? Does one need to be able to tell him apart from other individuals? Does it mean to possess some information applying only to him?[6]

An analogous point holds for terms like "red" or "tall". If they were to work like indexicals, their extension would vary according to the context in which

[5] Adopting Russell's terminology we could say that one understands the utterance of an indexical insofar as one is acquainted with the value of the indexical. To be acquainted with a relevant day or person, one need not necessarily have to know the name of that person and the relevant date. One can understand your saying "Today I am happy" even if one does not know who you are (simply perceiving you suffices) or which day it is (simply being that day would be enough). See also Korta and Perry (this volume), who emphasize the distinction between being able to express a proposition because one knows the semantic values of the indexicals, and merely being able to give an utterance-bound or reflexive characterization of the proposition because one only has access to the token-reflexive rules associated with the expressions.

[6] For a detailed discussion on the difference between indexicals and proper names and how the latter do not reduce to the former, see Corazza (2004: ch.1). Roughly, proper names and indexicals are different linguistic tools and their differences reflect on some epistemological constraints accompanying their use. Proper names, unlike indexicals, for instance are typically used to refer to objects that are not in the perceptual field of the discussants. One can thus successfully participate in a linguistic interchange even if one is not directly acquainted with the individual referred to by a proper name. It would be more difficult to participate in a discussion involving an indexical, say "that woman in the corner", if one is not acquainted with the relevant woman, i.e. if one is not capable of singling out the relevant woman.

they occur. Thus one would understand an utterance containing "red" or "tall" only insofar as one would identify the exact extension of "red" and "tall" as they appear in the relevant utterance. Now suppose Jon utters:

(6) Jane is too tall

What is the proposition expressed by Jon's utterance? In the indexicalist view, it cannot be the minimal proposition *that Jane is too tall*. It may be the proposition *that Jane is too tall to play with Jon's kids*. Or it may be the proposition *that Jane is too tall to dance with Shorty*, or the proposition *that Jane is too tall to attend Jon's party*, and so on. In each case, the extension of "tall" will probably be different.[7] We can raise two questions here. First, how does the hearer manage to *identify* the non-minimal proposition expressed by Jon's utterance? Second, how does Jon, the speaker, manage to *express* such a proposition to begin with?

The standard indexicalist view is that "tall" in (6) comes with a covert variable, something like "tall relative to standard *x*". In contrast to the case of overt indexicality, there is nothing in the linguistic meaning of the sentence "Jane is too tall" which could orient the hearer to the relevant standard of tallness. Still, the latter is a contextual parameter that she must identify or make explicit in order to understand the utterance. How does such an identification proceed? A common answer is that the hearer must look for the *intentions* of the speaker, by way of reading his mind.

There is no doubt that sophisticated communication demands a lot of mind-reading. However, there are also simple but common situations in which one can understand an utterance such as (6) without making explicit the intentions of the speaker. For instance, the hearer might react to Jon's utterance by just letting Jane play with Peter's kids, who are taller than Jon's. Alternatively, she might encourage Jane to dance with someone taller than Shorty, or to dissuade her from attending Jon's party, and so on. The hearer might do any of these things without engaging in mind-reading or making explicit exactly what standard of tallness is in question in the relevant context. The hearer has correctly understood the speaker (and accepted what he said) even though no specific standard of tallness has come to her mind. If she were asked "In what respect is Jane too tall?", after some reflection she might come up with different and perhaps incompatible answers. The point here is rather intuitive: the relevant standard of tallness

[7] We take the extension of "tall" to be the set of objects to which the predicate "tall" applies in the relevant context. One of the referees pointed out that an indexicalist can take the extension of "tall" to be a constant function from a standard to a function. For instance, the argument of the function may be the standard height of a basketball player and its value the function from objects to truth-values expressed by "tall for a basketball player". It is not clear that this alternative view still deserves to be called "indexicalist", at least with respect to "tall". On any indexicalist view, there has to be some pronoun or covert variable referring to a standard in a given context.

might be in the world rather than in the minds of the speaker and hearer. It might be in the world in the sense that it is determined by the situations of the discussants, including their low-level dispositions to take appropriate action given the context's requirements. The relevant standard of tallness might not be fully represented by either speaker or hearer; it might even be wrongly represented. From the point of view of reacting to the speaker's utterance, mind-reading can be a distraction rather than the key to understanding.

Consider another example. Imagine that Jane is asked to buy some red melons. Jane goes to the market and comes home with the right kind of melons. At no point, though, does it cross Jane's mind whether the redness of the melons concerned the melons' pulp or their skin. (She would probably be surprised should the issue be brought up.) Jane fully understood the order and executed it without having to entertain or grasp the proposition expressed by a sentence like "Melons are red on the inside/outside".

Moreover, it is a mistake to think that the proposition expressed by (6) depends on the intention of the speaker to say something true about Jon's kids, Shorty, or the party. Actually, the speaker might have no such intention in mind. For instance, Jon might just repeat something he has just heard. We might say that in such a case, Jon does not fully understand what he is saying, so that he does not express a complete proposition. Alternatively, one might say that he is expressing a proposition which depends on the intentions of *other* speakers, in a kind of deferential way. We do not find any of these alternatives plausible, at least as a *general* account of linguistic understanding. Minimalism puts forward a much simpler hypothesis. Two people understand each other insofar as they come to entertain or grasp the same minimal proposition, in our example the proposition *that Jane is too tall*. Of course there can be misunderstanding between them in other respects, but it should not come from the hearer's having failed to grasp what the speaker said. As we shall see, though, the proposition shared by speaker and hearer, namely *that Jane is too tall*, is situated, which means that it can have different truth-values in different situations.

In short, contrary to what indexicalists claim, there is generally no identification constraint on the understanding of utterances such as "Jane is too tall" and "Melons are red", relative to standards of tallness or redness. One need introduce neither hidden variables (in the speaker's mind) nor complicated modes of presentation (in the hearer's mind) in order to explain the success of communication.

Another attack on minimalism comes from so-called contextualists.[8] Contextualists differ from indexicalists insofar as they do not posit at the level of logical form variables working like hidden indexicals. Contextualists embrace

[8] The list of the friends of contextualism is almost endless. Among recent versions of contextualism we can mention: Bezuidenhout (2002), Carston (2002), and Recanati (2004). The parents of modern contextualism are: Searle (1978, 1980) Sperber and Wilson (1986), Travis (1985, 1989).

free enrichment.[9] Their main argument rests on the claim that minimalism does not account for the fact that utterances of (6) —Jane is too tall—are not guaranteed to have the same truth-value (in a given world): in some circumstances, utterances of (6) may be true, but in other circumstances, they may be false. If Jane's tallness concerns her being a jockey the utterance may be true, while if it regards Jane being a basketball player it may be false. The contextualist story goes as follows: what an utterance of (6) expresses depends on the context in which it occurs. In the jockey situation it expresses the proposition *that Jane is too tall [for a jockey]* while in the basketball context it expresses the proposition *that Jane is too tall [for a basketball player]*. The bracketed information entering the proposition expressed is contextually supplied. Thus an utterance of (6) is underdetermined and the relevant context furnishes the comparison class with respect to which Jane's tallness is evaluated. It is important to notice that this comparison class ends up in the proposition expressed without being determined by some element appearing in the logical form of the relevant sentence: it ends up in the proposition expressed *via* a process of free enrichment.[10]

We do not claim that all contextualists draw the line between saturation and free enrichment in the same way. A contextualist like Recanati, for instance, would not handle the case of (6) in terms of enrichment. Since, according to him, the contextually supplied information is mandatory, we have rather a case of saturation.[11] Be that as it may, our position differs from both indexicalism and contextualism (whatever extension is given to free enrichment) insofar as we do not commit ourselves to the view that the alleged contextual information enters the proposition expressed.

A similar story can be told about utterances of "Melons are red". The context should determine whether it expresses the proposition *that melons are red [inside]* or *that melons are red [on their surface/skin]*. Following the contextualists, only such enriched propositions can be evaluated as being either true or false (relative to a possible world).

In our view, contextualism faces difficulties similar to indexicalism's. In particular, it saddles understanding with too much cognitive burden. Our point is not merely that speaker and hearer rarely, perhaps never, come to enrich

[9] The chief exponents of free enrichment are the relevance theorists (Sperber and Wilson 1986; Carston 2002). Recanati (2004) and Bach (1994), though in different ways, embrace free enrichment as well.

[10] As we shall see later, we do not deny that the comparison class plays a role when we come to compute the truth-value of the utterance. Unlike the contextualists (and the indexicalists), though, we argue that it does *not* enter as a constituent of the proposition expressed.

[11] Recanati's argument is the following. We have a case of enrichment only if it is possible to have circumstances in which a sentence expresses a complete proposition without appealing to contextual information. That is, if a sentence like "Jane is too tall" can express a full proposition without having to encompass what Jane is too tall for we would have free enrichment when the contextual information concerning what Jane is too tall for is relevant and enters the proposition expressed. Since we cannot imagine a situation in which "Jane is too tall" expresses a complete proposition, we have a case of saturation, i.e. the information what Jane is too tall for is semantically mandatory.

a proposition in the same way and, therefore, rarely entertain the very same proposition. At least some contextualists acknowledge this point, arguing that communication does not rest on two people grasping the very same proposition:

> It seems to us neither paradoxical nor counterintuitive to say that there are thoughts [propositions] that we cannot exactly share, and that communication can be successful without resulting in an exact duplication of thoughts in communicator and audience. (Sperber and Wilson 1986: 193)

Along this line one can argue that two people understand each other insofar as they grasp *similar* propositions. All the potential enriched propositions share the same minimal proposition—in our examples *that Jane is too tall* or *that melons are red.* Contextualists appealing to either free enrichment or saturation seem committed to the view that understanding rests on the grasping of the minimal proposition and some extra contextual aspect coming to enrich it. The latter is likely to vary between the proposition (if any) intended by the speaker and the one (if any) grasped by the audience. Yet for understanding and communication to succeed, the enrichment must be similar enough. How similar it must be, though, remains unspecified. As far as the success of understanding is concerned, minimalism may be a more economical position. The point is that understanding does not depend on there being a unique set of similar, enriched propositions. Perhaps the speaker has no enriched proposition in mind, and in many cases, the hearer can understand the utterance without even trying to identify the relevant extra parameters.

A further argument aiming to undermine minimalism can be summarized as follows. Since minimal propositions do not play any cognitive role, they are dispensable. Carston (2002) and Recanati (2004) go as far as claiming that since we cannot imagine how minimal propositions could play a cognitive role in human psychology, they are not only spurious, they simply do not exist. Following this view, only enriched propositions, the ones the speaker and/or hearer are consciously aware of having expressed, exist and enter the scene.[12] Thus only enriched propositions, i.e. the ones that informed speakers allegedly grasp, have psychological reality and can thus be considered to be what is expressed by the utterance of a given sentence.

Although the criticisms we have formulated against indexicalism and contextualism may not be devastating,[13] we believe that they contribute to undermining these two positions. We also believe that one can propose a version of minimalism

[12] Recanati's availability principle attempts to capture this fact. Recanati claims that the proposition expressed (what is said) corresponds to what a normal speaker/interpreter would say it expresses. Recanati's normal interpreter, though, faces overwhelming difficulties. Actually, since Recanati's normal interpreter, like God, but unlike us, would never make errors, Recanati's contextualist theory turns out to be a non-empirical one (see Davis 2005). In short, since the normal interpreter is the one ultimately determining the proposition expressed and since this interpreter never makes mistakes in interpreting what one says, Recanati's theory cannot be disconfirmed. For this very reason, as Davis aptly points out, it cannot be an empirical theory.

[13] For further criticism of these positions see Cappelen and Lepore (2005: chs. 2–9).

(we could call it *situationalism*[14] or *situated minimalism*) which, along with avoiding the criticisms addressed, on the one hand, against the indexicalist and the contextualist positions and, on the other hand, against the original minimalist position, can incorporate the powerful intuitions underlying such opposing viewpoints as contextualism and minimalism.

3. SITUATING MINIMALISM

As we anticipated, contextualism rests on what we take to be powerful intuitions concerning an utterance's truth-value.[15] For instance, it goes against our intuitions to claim that an utterance of (6) —Jane is too tall—is true/false unrestrictedly. If (6) occurs in the jockey situation it is likely to be true, while if it occurs in the basketball situation it is likely to be false. Similar examples can be furnished with "red", "ready", "strong", "old", etc.[16] In taking on board the contextualist intuitions we, therefore, depart from Cappelen and Lepore's version of minimalism. Yet, we do not think that we are committed to what Cappelen and Lepore characterize as the Mistaken Assumption, i.e.:

> A theory of semantic content is adequate just in case it accounts for all or most of the intuitions speakers have about speech act content, i.e., intuitions about what speakers say, assert, claim, and state by uttering sentences. (Cappelen and Lepore 2005: 53)

Insofar as we distinguish, unlike the contextualists and the indexicalists, between the proposition expressed and the situation according to which it obtains a truth-value, we do not commit ourselves to the view that the semantic content of an utterance (the proposition expressed) must account for all the intuitions that speakers may have concerning a specific utterance. Within our framework these intuitions are captured by the situation in which the proposition expressed is evaluated. In a nutshell, we are minimalists with respect to the proposition expressed and contextualists with respect to the truth-values.

We think that the friends of both contextualism and minimalism fail to appreciate how a given utterance can be said to be true/false in two very distinct ways. That is to say, an utterance *u* of "Jane is too tall", for instance, can be true in two main ways: (i) if it expresses the proposition *that Jane is too tall [for a jockey]* or (ii) if it expresses the proposition *that Jane is too tall* but the latter's truth-value depends on the discourse situation/context/circumstance in which it occurs. While contextualists favoring free enrichment (and, in a different way,

[14] See Corazza (2007).

[15] For a detailed discussion and some scepticism on how speakers' intuitions can shape semantics see Bach (2002).

[16] Contextualists like Searle, Travis, Sperber and Wilson, Recanati, Carston, etc. propose many examples where a change in the context allegedly entails a change in the truth conditions, which in fact we see as a truth-value change.

indexicalists positing a hidden indexical) embrace the first option, we embrace the second one.

If one follows the first path, one can accept the traditional (semantic) view that a proposition is true/false objectively and eternally. It follows that for a proposition to be true/false eternally it must be completed or enriched.[17]

On the other hand, if one follows the second path, a given proposition can change truth-value with a change of the context/circumstance in which it occurs. Truth as an attribute of propositions becomes, *pace* the traditional semantic position, a relativized notion.

Along with the contextualists, minimalists like Cappelen and Lepore hold the view that an utterance expresses a proposition which is true or false regardless of the situation in which it occurs. In short, both minimalists and contextualists embrace the following theorem:

(7) *S* is true iff *p*

where the proposition *that p* gives the truth conditions of the (non-indexical) sentence *S*. (7) can easily be rephrased in terms of utterances:

(8) If *u* is an utterance of *S*, then [*u* is true iff *p*][18]

The difference between contextualists and minimalists concerns the nature of the proposition *p*. While the former assume that *p* is an enriched proposition, the minimalist assumes that, when *S* does not contain indexical expressions, *p* is automatically obtained *via* a disquotational process. If our sentence *S* corresponds to (6)—Jane is too tall—the contextualists would thus represent its truth conditions as follows:

(9) If *u* is an utterance of "Jane is too tall", then [*u* is true iff *Jane is too tall [for a jockey]*]

[17] As Frege puts it (speaking of thoughts where we speak of propositions): "Now is a thought changeable or is it timeless? The thought we express by the Pythagorean Theorem is surely timeless, eternal, unvarying. 'But are there not thoughts which are true today but false in six months' time? The thought, for example, that the tree there is covered with green leaves, will surely be false in six month's time'. No, for it is not the same thought at all. The words 'This tree is covered with green leaves' are not sufficient by themselves to constitute the expression of thought, for the time of utterance is involved as well. Without the time-specification thus given we have not a complete thought, i.e., we have no thought at all. Only a sentence with the time-specification filled out, a sentence complete in every respect, expresses a thought, if it is true, is true not only today or tomorrow but timelessly" (Frege 1918: 53). Since truth-values can shift across possible worlds, the world should be specified as well. It is interesting to note, though, that everybody is a relativist with respect to possible worlds.

[18] This formulation is borrowed from Higginbotham (1988). For a detailed discussion of it see Carston (2002: 50–6). This representation allows us to capture indexicality. Actually, to accommodate indexical expressions our theorem could be rephrased as: (i) If *u* is an utterance of "I am F" and *x* is the agent of *u*, then [*u* is true *iff* *x* is F]; (ii) If *u* is an utterance of "He/she is F", and the agent of *u* refers to *x* with 'he/she', then [*u* is true *iff* *x* is F].

On the other hand, minimalists like Cappelen and Lepore could represent (6)'s truth conditions as follows:

(10) If *u* is an utterance of "Jane is too tall", then [*u* is true iff *Jane is too tall*]

Both representations are unsatisfactory insofar as: (i) a contextualist representation like (9) in appealing to an enriched proposition makes communication more difficult than it should be, from a cognitive point of view, and (ii) a minimalist representation like (10) fails to capture the contextualist intuition that the proposition *that Jane is too tall* can be true when evaluated *vis-à-vis* the jockey situation, while false when evaluated *vis-à-vis* the basketball situation.

As situated minimalists, we agree with Cappelen and Lepore that the truth condition of any utterance of *S* is always the same minimal proposition, for instance *that p*. However, in contrast to the latter, we do not consider theorems such as (7) and (8) to be automatically true. (7) will be guaranteed to be true only if the situation in which it is uttered coincides with the situation in which *S* itself is uttered. Suppose, for instance, that *S* is uttered in a situation in which what is relevant to the truth-value of the utterance is whether or not Jane is too tall to play with Jon's kids (she is). Now theorem (7) will be false if uttered in a different situation in which the proposition *that Jane is too tall* is itself false, perhaps because what is relevant in the latter situation is whether or not Jane is too tall to dance with Shorty (she isn't). Similarly, (8) will be false if there are utterances which are situated in relevantly different ways than the theorem itself. From the point of view of situated minimalism, (11) is a better theorem as far as (6) is concerned:

(11) If *u* is an utterance of "Jane is too tall" and *s* is the situation in which *u* occurs, then [*u* is true *iff* Jane is too tall relative to *s*]

This is because (11) will be true whatever the situation in which it is uttered. It allows for the truth-value of (6) to depend on the situation in which the minimal proposition it expresses (namely *that Jane is too tall*) is evaluated. If the minimal proposition is evaluated *vis-à-vis* the jockey situation (6) is likely to turn out to be true, while if the minimal proposition is evaluated *vis-à-vis* the basketball situation it is likely to be false.[19]

[19] Of course there is a sense in which (11) captures the conditions under which (6) is true. This is not the sense of "truth conditions" that we are working with in this chapter. In our terminology, the truth conditions of an utterance are just the proposition expressed, i.e. what is grasped by the competent speaker/hearer. When Jon says "Jane is too tall", he does not have to identify the situation of his utterance; he is just in it. So (11) should not be taken to imply that the situation *s* gets inside the proposition expressed by "Jane is too tall" in a given context.

In a nutshell, minimalism meets contextualism. That is, like the minimalists and unlike the contextualists, we maintain that the proposition expressed encodes only information triggered by the sentence's literal meaning. Like contextualists and unlike minimalists, we assume that an utterance's truth-value is not context invariant. Our proposal, though, comes with a price: unlike minimalists and contextualists, we reject the view that an utterance's truth-value is absolute. Our position is committed to the view that truth (as an attribute of propositions) is a relative notion, depending on the situation in which the (minimal) proposition is evaluated. This allows us to accommodate the powerful contextualist intuition that it does not make much sense to say that "Jane is too tall" can be true/false regardless of the specific situation in which it occurs and/or with respect to which it is evaluated. In other words, our position does not succumb to the contextualist charge that it does not make sense to evaluate propositions such as *that Naomi Campbell is very rich, that Jon is strong, that Jeff is too old*, etc. with respect to, for instance, the actual world (ignoring standards of evaluation or situations). Naomi Campbell is, no doubt, very rich if compared with the authors of this chapter. Yet she's not that rich if compared to the likes of Roman Abramovich or Bill Gates.

4. EVADING SOME CONTEXTUALIST AND MINIMALIST CHARGES

One of the (many) advantages of the position we are putting forward is that it is not vulnerable to the main criticisms Cappelen and Lepore mount against contextualism. The chief criticism they offer runs as follows: contextualism cannot account for the fact that people can share content across contexts. If, for instance, in context *C* Jon utters:

(12) Melons are red

intending to indicate that melons are red in the inside, and in context *C** Jeff says:

(13) Melons are red

indicating that they are red on their surface, the contextualist is committed to the view that (12) and (13) express different propositions. The contextualist is thus unable to account for the intuition that it is legitimate to claim that both Jon and Jeff said the same thing. Actually, if one hearing (12) and (13) is asked "What did Jon and Jeff say?" a plausible answer would be:

(14) Jon and Jeff both said that melons are red

This implies that there is a level of content that Jon and Jeff share. This similarity of content is captured by the minimal proposition *that melons are red* expressed by both (12) and (13). Since contextualists, and indexicalists, are committed to the view that (12) and (13) express different propositions, say *that melons are red inside* and *that melons are red on the surface* respectively, (14) could never be, contrary to our intuition, an appropriate reply: it would never be true.

Note that the problem cannot be circumvented by claiming that (14) involves a neutral notion of redness which encompasses both Jon's and Jeff's more specific notions. For Jon can say the following:

(15) Melons are red. That's also what Jeff said

which is true, although Jon still intends to say that melons are red in the inside.[20]

Furthermore, if one adopted the contextualist position and argued that terms like "tall" and "red" are context-sensitive, one would be committed to the view that

(16) London buses and tomatoes are red

(17) Jon and Jane are tall

could rarely be true since "red" and "tall", being context-sensitive expressions, do not have the same extension when applying to London buses and tomatoes, and to Jane and Jon respectively.

On the other hand, our position also resists some of the criticism that a contextualist can mount against minimalism. In particular, it is immune to a criticism proposed by Recanati (2004: 92–3). Recanati aims to undermine what may be labeled *unrestricted minimalism*, i.e. the view that a minimal proposition is true/false regardless of the situation in which it occurs. If one, like Cappelen and Lepore, embraces unrestricted minimalism, one may be said to know the truth conditions of a sentence in merely disquotational terms. That is, one would automatically know that:

(18) "Jane is tall" is true iff Jane is tall

(19) "Melons are red" is true iff melons are red

[20] It may be worth mentioning that some indexical utterances also allow elliptical interpretation. Consider Jane saying "I am tired" and Jeff saying "I am tired. That's also what Jane said". Jeff's "That's also what Jane said" can be interpreted either as meaning that Jane said that Jeff is tired or that Jane said that she herself is tired. With (15), though, we do not face this ambiguity. The "That's also what Jeff said" in (15) can mean only that Jeff said that melons are red.

This knowledge of the truth conditions of a sentence merely amounts to a kind of pure disquotational knowledge. This, though, cannot seriously count as knowledge insofar as one would be said to know that:

(20) "Grounglys blot tranglings" is true iff Grounglys blot tranglings

Yet we would not say that one knows, let alone understands, what

(21) Grounglys blot tranglings

means. The mere knowledge of a disquotational theorem of the form " '*S*' is true iff *S*" cannot count as knowledge of what *S* means. Hence, the knowledge of a disquotational theorem like (18)/(19) cannot be taken as a good guide to the knowledge or mastery of a language. Yet we would like to say that knowledge of a sentence's truth conditions should constitute a good guide to what amounts to knowledge of a language. It could be that this argument cannot, *pace* Recanati, be used to undermine the minimalist proposal. For, a minimalist could claim that since a competent speaker does not understand (21) or its constituents s/he does not understand the right-hand side of (20). That is to say, all that a competent speaker of English (i.e. who understands "true", "iff", and the conventions of quotation) can know is that (20) expresses a truth if it expresses anything. Be that as it might be, Recanati's criticism does not apply to our version of minimalism. For one may be said to understand what (21) means only insofar as one is able (at least in principle) to situate it. Since there is no way one can situate (21), there is no way one can be said to understand it.

Our point can be put in the following way. Anyone who has genuine knowledge of (18) and (19) (in the appropriate situation; see our remarks about such theorems in the previous section) can in principle derive new, more complex theorems such as the following:

(22) "Jane is too tall" is true *in s* iff Jane is too tall relative to the standards of *s*

(23) "Melons are red" is true *in s* iff melons count as red in *s*

These theorems make explicit something that was only implicit in (18)/(19), namely the situations relative to which the propositions that Jane is too tall and that melons are red are to be evaluated (*s* can be thought of as specifying a particular situation, or as a variable bound by a universal quantifier). In contrast, one cannot derive from (21) the following:

(24) "Grounglys blot tranglings" is true *in s* iff Grounglys blot tranglings relative to *s*

whose right-hand side clearly does not make sense. Now if (24) does not make sense, (21) is not a genuine theorem either.

As such, of course, (22) and (23) introduce other, more sophisticated propositions, namely the propositions that Jane is too tall relative to the standards of a situation *s* and that melons count as red in a situation *s*. No doubt, a competent speaker knows that "Jane is too tall" can be true in a given situation while false in some other. The same with melons: "Melons are red" is true when speaking about the melons' pulp, while false when speaking about their skin (the melons we know have green skin), and so on and so forth. These more sophisticated propositions—i.e. the propositions which explicitly specify the relevant situation or simply present a bound variable for a situation—may come close to what Perry characterizes as the reflexive truth conditions of an utterance, i.e. the truth conditions generated by the utterance meaning (see Perry 2001). In the case of an indexical utterance *u* like "I am having fun" (said by Jane on October 22, 2005), its reflexive truth conditions correspond to the proposition expressed by "The agent of *u* is/was having fun at the time of *u*". Each competent speaker can grasp these truth conditions.[21] Yet to understand the indexical utterance one needs to grasp, Perry claims, the incremental truth conditions or official content, i.e. the proposition that Jane was having fun on October 22, 2005. We agree with Perry. The understanding of an indexical utterance rests on the grasping of the official content and thus on the identification of the indexical's referent. We do not claim, though, that to understand an utterance like "Jane is too tall" or "Melons are red" one needs to transcend theorems like (22)—i.e. "Jane is too tall" is true ***in s*** iff Jane is too tall relative to the standards of *s*. In other words, we do not commit ourselves with the existence of some incremental truth conditions one needs to grasp in order to understand the utterance. In short, following Perry we distinguish between reflexivity and indexicality, i.e. between what is said using an utterance with an indexical and the identifying conditions at work when reference gets fixed. But we do not commit ourselves with the view that some identifying condition of a given situation must be at work when one utters/understands a sentence like "Melons are red" or "Jane is too tall": "red" and "tall" are not indexicals picking out a given situation. Nor does the utterance as a whole present some hidden indexical selecting the relevant situation.

5. SITUATED MINIMALISM VS. SPEECH ACT PLURALISM

To deal with the kind of worries put forward by the contextualists, Cappelen and Lepore appeal to Speech Act Pluralism.[22] That is the view that:

[21] We could also say that the reflexive truth conditions belong to the sphere of tacit knowledge. The latter are what enable one to master a language.

[22] Cappelen and Lepore recognize that Speech Act Pluralism is not a theory. It merely amounts to a collection of observations, for no systematic theory can be furnished about speech act content.

> [W]hat an utterance says, states, claims, etc. differs from the proposition it semantically expresses. (Cappelen and Lepore 2005: 190)

Roughly, Cappelen and Lepore embrace the views that: (i) the utterance of a given sentence can express, in principle, infinitely many propositions and (ii) the speaker (and the audience) need not be aware of most of the propositions expressed. Furthermore:

> [T]o ascertain what's said, you first have to reconstruct utterances to a point where they express thoughts. There are many ways to achieve this end... No one way is uniquely correct. (Cappelen and Lepore 2005: 192)

Cappelen and Lepore agree with the contextualist appealing to free enrichment that what is said transcends the minimal (semantic) proposition expressed. In other words, the proposition(s) communicated (what is said) differs from the minimal proposition semantically expressed. Among the infinitely many propositions expressed, one is the minimal proposition, but this proposition is not what can explain successful communication. The minimal proposition is the only semantically pertinent proposition, but communication must be explained by appealing to some of the infinitely many propositions pragmatically expressed. Although Speech Act Pluralism differs from contextualism in arguing that many propositions get expressed, it nonetheless comes close to contextualism in committing itself to the view that at least one of the many propositions expressed should capture the speaker's mental content. This proposition looks pretty much like the contextualists' enriched proposition.[23]

Minimalists and contextualists share the same motivation in positing rich mental representations: they want to explain our intuitions about the truth-values of our utterances. When Jon says that Jane is too tall, his utterance is made true, in his situation, by the fact that Jane is too tall to play with his kids. But when Shorty says the same thing, his utterance is false, because in *his* situation what is relevant is whether Jane is or isn't too tall to dance with him (she isn't). In such a case, there is the same minimal proposition, or semantic content, corresponding to the sentence "Jane is too tall", but two truth-values. How is such plurality of truth-values possible within the same world? The minimalist and contextualist answer is that there must be two different *absolute* mental representations, which

[23] It goes without saying that a contextualist and a Speech Act Pluralist could argue that enriched propositions need not be internalized, i.e. that one need not have a mental representation matching the complexity of the enriched proposition. (Note that we are *not* using the notion of mental representation in a way which *implies* the Language of Thought Hypothesis. Perhaps one can mentally represent something without tokening a mental symbol of that thing.) We think that if enriched propositions are not represented, then they do not play, *pace* contextualism and Speech Act Pluralism, an interesting cognitive role. In short, why should one posit enriched propositions or embrace Speech Act Pluralism in order to explain communication if the (enriched) propositions expressed do not get fully represented, one way or the other, by the speaker and her audience? Recanati's availability principle requires that the normal, fully informed, interpreter have a mental representation of the relevant enriched proposition.

one could express by the sentences "Jane is too tall to play with Jon's kids", and "Jane is too tall to dance with Shorty". These representations are absolute in the sense that they are not true or false relative to standards of tallness, since a specific value of tallness is already incorporated in the representations themselves.

The important take-home point is that, like contextualism, Speech Act Pluralism is committed to the view that the cognitive apparatus engaged in communicative interaction is stuffed with rich mental representations. That is, although there may be nothing in a given sentence representing the constituents which end up in the propositions expressed by an utterance, in the speaker's mind there must be appropriate representations of all the relevant propositional constituents ending up in what is said. Within Speech Act Pluralism and the contextualist framework these representations play a central role when people engage in a thought episode and a communicative interchange.

We reckon that both the contextualists who appeal to enriched propositions and minimalists who appeal to Speech Act Pluralism fail to appreciate the insight of Perry's (1986) view that some thoughts can be about something without having to represent that very thing, namely, that we can have, to borrow Perry's happy phrase, "thoughts without representation". The thought one expresses in uttering "It is 3:15 p.m.", for instance, concerns a certain time zone even if one does not entertain a representation of the relevant time zone. Here, we conform to an intuitive notion of representation according to which a subject entertains a representation of an entity (object, property, or whatever) if she grasps a concept (or any non-conceptual mode of presentation) of the entity. Representation is mandatory if the entity is to be inferentially or computationally relevant. In the case in point, no representation of a particular time zone is needed because the subject does not draw any inference hinging on the identity of time zones: all her inferences involving the thought she expresses in uttering "It is 3:15 p.m." take place in the same time zone, typically the one she presently occupies.[24] Yet the subject's thought is anchored to a particular time zone. The important insight is that the gap between the thought and the time zone is not bridged by a representation. In the terminology we introduced before, this thought concerns the relevant time zone because *it is situated in* the relevant time zone.

The same idea expands, we claim, to thoughts expressed by utterances of so-called underdetermined sentences like: "Jane is too old", "Melons are red", "Naomi is rich", "Jeff is ready", etc. The thoughts expressed by utterances of these sentences may concern the fact that Jane is too old *to play with Jon's kids*, that melons are red *inside*, that Naomi is rich *compared to us*, that Jeff is ready *for the exam*, etc. Yet, these thoughts need *not* represent what Jane is too old for,

[24] For further details, see Dokic (2006*a*, 2006*b*). Dokic (2006*b*) suggests that there may be another, more relaxed notion of representation according to which the time zone would be represented, even if it is not inferentially relevant. The distinction Dokic draws between two kinds of representation is largely orthogonal to the present discussion. According to situationalism, there are thoughts without representation even in the relaxed notion of representation.

the location of melons' redness, the comparative class *vis-à-vis* which Naomi's richness is judged, nor what Jeff is ready for. In short, the situation in which one entertains a thought and expresses a minimal proposition need not enter the subject's mind. This can be illustrated by an analogy. When one uses the first person pronoun one automatically refers to oneself. This is guaranteed by the semantics of "I", whose linguistic meaning (or character) operates on the relevant contextual aspect, the agent, and delivers the latter as referent. But one need not entertain a particular representation of oneself when using "I" (although of course one could). The mere fact of using it suffices for the agent to pick up herself as referent and to think about herself. A similar process is at work when one uses so-called underdetermined utterances. The simple fact of entertaining them suffices to have thoughts and express propositions concerning the situations in which they occur. One need not entertain a representation of the relevant situation in order for one's thought and the (minimal) proposition expressed to be situated in that situation. Facts about the speaker such as her location, her identity, the topic of the discourse, perhaps other participants in the linguistic community, etc. suffice to determine the relevant situation in which a thought occurs. This is, at least partly, determined by the fact that the speakers are embodied individuals—that is, by the fact that speakers are necessarily embodied in a given context. This embodiment, though, need not be encapsulated into the speaker's cognitive apparatus. In arguing that the thoughts expressed by so-called underdetermined utterances—like the minimal propositions expressed—are situated, we commit ourselves to the view that lots of our thoughts are anchored to a situation by factors which are not explicitly represented in the speakers' minds.

As far as communication is concerned, two people understand each other insofar as they grasp the same minimal proposition (and thus come to entertain the same minimal thought).[25] This is the case even if the speaker's and hearer's situations are relevantly different. For example, suppose that the minimal proposition (and the thought) expressed by Jane's utterance of "Jeff is ready" concerns the situation in which Jeff is ready for the party while we implicitly take it to concern the situation in which Jeff is ready for the exam. There is an important sense in which we understand Jane's utterance: we correctly take her to announce that Jeff is ready.

In another, non-semantic sense, there is misunderstanding between Jane and us. What is the source of this misunderstanding? We should remember that communication is a dynamic process in which agreement between speaker and hearer should eventually prevail over disagreement. That is, disagreement makes sense only against a background of things commonly agreed by speaker and

[25] As we shall soon see, this is a necessary but not sufficient condition for understanding in the ordinary sense, for if two people are not embodied in the same situation (non-semantic) misunderstanding can occur.

hearer. If we implicitly take Jane to be talking about Jeff's exam, then the risk is that as communication goes on, disagreement will grow to the point of unintelligibility: for instance, we would not understand why Jane wants Jeff to work on his math after the party. If he is ready for the exam, why should he go on studying? Global disagreement is likely to be manifested in an unsuccessful joint activity and/or in our puzzlement about some behavioral output.

Thus, even if, at any given time, the fact that speakers and hearers associate the same minimal propositions with the relevant utterances is a sufficient condition of successful communication, the fact that they share a situation (that they are *co-situated*) is the key to global agreement over time. Indeed, in face-to-face communication we occupy the same relevant context (location, time, possible world) and we share the same situation (we come to our interchange with the background of a set of common beliefs and expectations). Most of the time this simple fact suffices for the dynamic success of our communicative interchanges: we successfully engage in joint attentional activities, our behavioral output conforms to expectations, and so on and so forth. It should be as simple as that.

We are reflective creatures, and when we feel that something has gone wrong in a communicative exchange, we tend to make explicit the situation of the speaker. In doing this, we change our own situation, of course, since we form more sophisticated representations which are themselves situated. For example, we move from the proposition that melons are red to the proposition that they are red inside. The latter situation is no less situated than the former, although the relevant situations are different. The speaker might likewise adopt a reflective stance, and both speaker and hearer can move to a new, common situational ground. A simple question often suffices to trigger the recovery of a shared situation. The moral is that there is nothing like *the* situation of a communicative exchange, which changes over time to maximize agreement.

In a nutshell, the picture we are proposing, *pace* Cappelen and Lepore and *pace* the contextualists appealing to free enrichment, may be characterized as a situationalist and non-intellectualist picture of communication.

Our picture has affinities with versions of utterance-truth or semantic relativism to be found in the recent literature. For instance, Predelli (2005*a*, 2005*b*) suggests that utterance-truth is relative to what he calls "points of evaluation". Predelli argues that from a semantic viewpoint all we have is truth-values at points. Since the establishment of the privileged point is relative, the truth-value of a particular utterance is relative to a specific point of evaluation. Thus, even though all utterances of "Melons are red" express the same fixed semantic content (the minimal proposition that melons are red), the latter can be true relative to some points of evaluation and false relative to others. Since points of evaluation correspond to partial situations rather than whole possible worlds, the latter typically underdetermine the truth-values of utterances occurring within them. Our account differs from Predelli's in that we are more explicit in insisting that thoughts are no less situated than utterances. Predelli (2005*a*: 365) tentatively cites "the speaker's intentions, the topic of conversation, or the expectations of the conversants" as contextual factors relevant to the evaluation of a particular utterance as being true or false. This seems to suggest that these factors are somehow made explicit at the level of thought. As far as we can see, this position can avoid positing rich mental representations in two ways: (i) the relevant contextual factors concurring in the determination of an utterance's truth-value are determined by mental states, such as intentions, but these states do not strictly speaking represent the contextual factors; (ii) the relevant contextual factors are determined by *non-mental* aspects of the situation. Both ways are compatible with situationalism, although of course in each case one must tell a more detailed story on how the relevant contextual factors are determined.

In our view, then, mental representations such as intentions and expectations are themselves situated. For instance, a subject can form the thought that melons are red in a situation in which what counts as being red is the insides of melons. The reflective subject can also think *about* this situation, and explicitly contrast it with other situations (including the situation in which what counts as being red is the skins of melons). Our point is that she can also be unreflective and fail to make explicit the situation relative to which her thought is to be evaluated as true or false. Perhaps the subject has the *disposition* to make her situation explicit, so that there would be a (dispositional) mental state determining the situation of her thought after all, but this disposition is itself explained by the fact that she *is* in a specific situation to begin with, rather than the other way round.

In a similar vein, MacFarlane (this volume) suggests a way of reconciling semantic minimalism with a form of relativism about truth. In MacFarlane's view, a circumstance of evaluation is an ordered pair consisting of a world and what he calls a "counts-as" parameter. So, again, utterances of "Melons are red" always express the same minimal proposition (that melons are red), but may be true relative to some counts-as parameters (according to which what counts as being red is something about the insides of melons) and false relative to other counts-as parameters (according to which what counts as being red is something about the skins of melons).

MacFarlane has recently developed a more radical version of truth-relativism, according to which utterances are true or false relative to contexts of *assessment* (see, for instance, his 2005). Contexts of assessment may be quite external to the situations of speakers and hearers, since they are associated with the *evaluation* of utterances and thoughts, rather than with the contexts in which they are formed and produced. Of course, we agree that an utterance or a thought can be evaluated as true or false relative to any (appropriate) situation we like, even a situation completely external to the subject. For instance, if Jane utters the sentence "It's raining" and thereby grasps the thought that it is raining, the latter can be evaluated as true relative to Jane's situation (because it is raining where Jane is) but false relative to our situation (because we stand in a sunny place).

However, we insist that utterances and thoughts *are* objectively situated quite independently of their semantic evaluation. In other words, there is a fact of the matter as to which situation a particular utterance or thought is anchored on. It follows that there is a *privileged* context of evaluation, namely the situation which rationalizes the subject's actions, inferences, and expectations. Thus, the thought that it is raining should be evaluated with respect to its subject's immediate environment, in part because the success of her action depends on how the weather is there.

MacFarlane (2003) gives the case of future contingents as an illustration of his radical truth-relativism. A subject utters "There will be a sea battle tomorrow", and it is objectively indeterminate whether there will be a sea battle the next day. The truth of the subject's utterance depends on the context of assessment: it is true from the point of view of a future with a sea battle, false from the point of view of a future without a sea battle, and neither true nor false from the present point of view. In this case, the utterance does not seem to be anchored to a unique, objective situation. Perhaps this is so, and there is (objective) situation-relativity as well as truth-relativity. However, two remarks are in order. First, the case of future contingents is quite special (and raises rather complicated issues), and cannot be used to ascertain arbitrary situation-relativity. In most case there are objective situations corresponding to privileged contexts of assessment. Second, the case of future contingents might be described in a different way. It is actually more plausible to say that the subject's utterance *cannot* be evaluated from the present point of view. In fact, its semantic evaluation must wait for the next day. It does not follow that the utterance is not objectively situated. There is no reason to think that the relation of being situated, which relates an utterance to the rest of the world, is itself relative to a particular time. So the utterance is objectively situated, although as a matter of necessity, the subject, however reflective she is, cannot presently know the relevant situation.

6. CONCLUSION

In this chapter, we have put forward the following claims:

- Thoughts are more closely related to minimal propositions than Cappelen and Lepore suggest.
- Objective situations play the role played by the contextualists' enrichment processes and by the open set of propositions expressed by an utterance according to Speech Act Pluralism.
- However, *pace* contextualists and Cappelen and Lepore, situations need not be mentally represented.

- Our position, which we call "situated minimalism" or simply "situationalism", is cognitively more plausible insofar as it does not overburden our (communicative) minds with complex cognitive mechanisms.
- Yet our position captures both the insights of contextualism and of Cappelen and Lepore's minimalism.

In short, propositions can be minimal because they are related to *implicit* situations, i.e. objective situations which (most of the time) fail to be mentally represented. In particular, we just do not need to make explicit at the level of thought the implicit situations of our utterances. Minimal propositions can classify both utterances and thoughts. We stand opposed to two alternative views. Contextualism posits enrichment processes, which are cognitive and representational, in order to specify semantic contents. Speech Act Pluralism posits rich, pragmatically expressed mental representations, in order to compensate for minimal semantic contents. In contrast, we argue that thoughts and utterances have minimal contents but are objectively related to non-cognitive and non-representational situations. This way, our situated minimalism can have the best of both worlds.[26]

REFERENCES

Bach, K. (1994), 'Conversational Implicitures', *Mind and Language*, 9: 124–62.

____(2002), 'Seemingly Semantics Intuition', in J. K. Campbell, M. O'Rourke, and D. Shier: (eds.), *Meaning and Truth: Investigations in Philosophical Semantics* pp. 21–33. New York: Seven Bridges Press.

Bezuidenhout, A. (2002), 'Truth Conditional Pragmatics', *Philosophical Perspectives*, 16: 105–34.

Burge, T. (1973), 'Reference and Proper Names', *Journal of Philosophy*, 70: 425–39.

Cappelen, H. and E. Lepore (2005), *Insensitive Semantics: A Defense of Semantic Minimalism and Speech Act Pluralism.* Oxford: Blackwell.

Carston, R. (2002), *Thoughts and Utterances: The Pragmatics of Explicit Communication.* Oxford: Blackwell.

Condoravdi, C., and M. Gawron. (1986), 'The Context Dependency of Implicit Arguments', in K. Makoto, C. Piñón, and H. de Swart (eds.), *Quantifiers, Deduction and Context*, pp. 1–32. Palo Alto, Calif.: CSLI Publication.

Corazza, E. (2004). *Reflecting the Mind: Indexicality and Quasi-Indexicality.* Oxford: Oxford University Press.

____(2007), 'Contextualism, Minimalism, and Situationalism', *Pragmatics and Cognition*, 15 (1): 115–17.

Davis, S. (2005), 'François Recanati's *Literal Meaning*', MS.

[26] For helpful comments and/or discussions on the subject of this chapter we would like to thank Robyn Carston, Dick Carter, Steven Davis, Julien Dutant, Kepa Korta, David Matheson, Stefano Predelli, François Recanati, Dan Sperber, Richard Vallée, and two anonymous referees for OUP.

Dokic, J. (2006*a*), 'Situated Representations and *Ad Hoc* Concepts', in M. J. Frápolli (ed.), *Saying, Meaning and Referring. Essays on François Recanati's Philosophy of Language*, Palgrave Studies in Pragmatics, Language and Cognition. Houndmills: Palgrave Macmillan.

—— (2006*b*), 'From Linguistic Contextualism to Situated Cognition: The Case of *Ad Hoc* Concepts', *Philosophical Psychology*, 19: 309–28.

Frege, G. (1918), 'Thoughts', in N. Salmon, and S. Soames (eds.), *Propositions and Attitudes* pp. 33–55. Oxford: Oxford University Press, 1988.

Higginbotham, J. (1988), 'Contexts, Models, and Meanings: A Note on the Data of Semantics', in Ruth M. Kempson (ed.), *Mental Representations: The Interface Between Language and Reality*, pp. 29–48. Cambridge: Cambridge University Press.

Kaplan, D. (1977), 'Demonstratives', in J. Almog, J. Perry, and H. Wettstein (eds.), *Themes from Kaplan*, pp. 481–563. Oxford: Oxford University Press, 1989.

—— (1989), 'Afterthoughts', in J. Almog, J. Perry, and H. Wettstein (eds.), *Themes from Kaplan*, pp. 565–614. Oxford: Oxford University Press.

MacFarlane, J. (2003), 'Future Contingents and Relative Truth', *Philosophical Quarterly*, 53: 321–36.

—— (2005), 'Making Sense of Relative Truth', *Proceedings of the Aristotelian Society*, 105: 321–39.

—— (2007), 'Semantic Minimalism and Nonindexical Contextualism', in this volume.

Partee, B. (1989), 'Binding Implicit Variables in Quantified Contexts', *Proceedings of the Chicago Linguistic Society*, xxv, pp. 342–65. Chicago: University of Chicago Press.

Pelczar, M., and J. Rainsbury (1998), 'The Indexical Character of Names', *Synthese*, 114: 293–317.

Perry, J. (1986), 'Thoughts without Representation', *Proceeding of the Aristotelian Society*, 60: 137–52.

—— (2001), *Reference and Reflexivity*. Stanford Calif.: CSLI Publications.

Predelli, S. (2005*a*), 'Painted Leaves, Context, and Semantic Analysis', *Linguistics and Philosophy*, 28: 351–74.

—— (2005*b*), *Contexts: Meaning, Truth, and the Use of Language*. Oxford: Oxford University Press.

Recanati, F. (1993), *Direct Reference: From Language to Thought*. Oxford: Blackwell.

—— (2004), *Literal Meaning*. Cambridge: Cambridge University Press.

Richard, M. (2004), 'Contextualism and Relativism', *Philosophical Studies*, 119: 215–42.

Searle, J. (1978), 'Literal Meaning', *Erkenntnis*, 13: 207–24.

—— (1980), 'The Background of Meaning', in J. Searle, F. Keifer, and M. Bierwisch (eds.), *Speech Act Theory and Pragmatics*, pp. 221–32. Dordrecht: Reidel.

Sperber, D., and D. Wilson (1986), *Relevance: Communication and Cognition*. Oxford: Blackwell.

Stanley, J. (2000), 'Context and Logical Form', *Linguistic and Philosophy*, 23: 391–434.

—— and Z. Szabo (2000), 'On Quantifier Domain Restriction', *Mind and Language*, 15: 219–61.

Travis, C. (1985), 'On What is Strictly Speaking True', *Canadian Journal of Philosophy*, 15: 187–229.

____(1989), *The Uses of Sense: Wittgenstein's Philosophy of Language*. Oxford: Oxford University Press.

Vallée, R. (2003), 'Context-Sensitivity Beyond Indexicality', *Dialogue*, 42: 79–106.

Voltolini, A. (1995). 'Indexinames', in J. Hill, and P. Kotatko (eds.), *Karlovy Vary Studies in Reference and Meaning*, pp. 258–85. Prague: Filosofia-Filosofia Publications.

7

Prudent Semantics Meets Wanton Speech Act Pluralism

Elisabeth Camp

1. SEMANTIC METHODOLOGY

A cautious semanticist will be as minimalist as she can. A minimal theory is lean, clean, and easy to comprehend and implement. Each new parameter we introduce into the theory diminishes these virtues, complicating the lexicon and increasing the theory's computational burden. By these measures of virtue, Cappelen and Lepore's semantic theory verges on the saintly. They maintain that only a highly restricted class of expressions, like "I", "today", "this", "actual", and "local", are context-sensitive; they claim that all other expressions, including "every", "tall", and "good", which are widely believed to be context-sensitive, make the same contribution to every sentence in which they occur.

However, theoretical simplicity comes at a cost. As a matter of empirical fact, distinct utterances of what appear to be the same sentence can communicate dramatically different contents in different contexts. We have to explain somehow how speakers manage to converge on common interpretations of these utterances; and the less of this explanatory work is done by the semantics, the more must be shouldered by the pragmatics. To the extent that one shifts the explanatory burden onto the pragmatics in this way, pragmatics becomes the locus of all the interesting action.

Further, the more one does this, the more indirect the empirical support for one's semantic theory becomes. Our evidence for semantic theorizing must ultimately come from the utterances that ordinary speakers make and the interpretations that ordinary hearers assign to them. However, we never find utterances with meanings sitting around on their own; they are always embedded

Thanks to John Hawthorne and François Recanati for discussion, and to an anonymous reviewer for helpful comments.

within a more complex structure of other speech acts. As Cappelen and Lepore say, "We don't know what it is to have intuitions about truth-values of utterances as such. If we are asked to have intuitions not about what an utterance says, asserts, claims, etc., but just about its truth-value, we are at a loss" (2005: 98).

This fact isn't a problem for a "maximalist", because he maintains that, with few exceptions, the intuitive content of a speaker's primary speech act—what he says, asserts, etc.—just is the semantic content of the uttered sentence. The primary challenge for him is to construct a principled, systematic, and plausibly realizable account of how semantically encoded meaning can produce the dramatically shifting contents we seem to find in different contexts. The minimalist doesn't face this latter challenge, because she rejects the "mistaken assumption" (2005: 53) that the semantics itself should explain ordinary intuitions about the contents of speech acts. Instead, the minimalist faces a different challenge: she must find some other, more indirect way to bring intuitions about speech act content to bear on her semantic theory, on pain of cutting it off from all substantive empirical constraints.

Thus, just like everyone else, Cappelen and Lepore must base their theory on intuitions about speech acts. Specifically, their proposal for isolating semantic content consists of three tests, all of which they admit rely upon intuitions about speech act content:

> These three tests all have the following form: *An expression* e *is context sensitive only if competent speakers have certain intuitions about uses of certain sorts of sentences containing* e. These tests appeal to fundamental features of linguistic communication. (2005: 87–8)

> We use communicated content . . . to 'get at' semantic content. . . . There is of course no other way to proceed. The purpose of the tests is to generate contexts in which semantic content is salient. . . . They are ways to get the audience to notice semantic features of sentences uttered. They create contexts in which our attention is drawn to features of the semantic content expressed by the utterances in question. (2005: 113; cf. also 122, 207)

Given that they employ this familiar methodology, Cappelen and Lepore are not entitled to the blanket claim that

> [I]ntuitions about, and other evidence for, speech act content are . . . not even prima facie evidence that *p* is the proposition semantically expressed by *u*. This is so no matter how refined, reflected, or 'equilibriumized' the intuition in question might be. (2005: 145)

As they say explicitly in the passages cited above, their tests are precisely means for focusing on or refining certain intuitions about speech act content in order to establish something about semantic content.

Because Cappelen and Lepore take the connection between speech act and semantic content to be so tenuous, it's especially important that the intuitions about speech act content that they focus on do accurately reveal semantic content. In §2, I argue that, as they stand, their tests fail to do this, because they suggest that metaphor is semantically context-sensitive. Although some theorists do believe that metaphor is semantic, it is hardly a minimalist view. In §§3 and 4, I'll argue that the culprit is their Massively Permissive version of Speech Act Pluralism (MPSPAP). By ignoring important differences among various indirect reports and speech acts, and in particular differences between *saying* and *claiming*, MPSPAP makes our actual communicative practices seem mysterious and unmotivated. If we draw some salient distinctions among speech acts and reports, however, and restrict the application of Cappelen and Lepore's tests accordingly, then those tests become considerably more reliable.

2. THE TESTS

In this section, I argue that the way Cappelen and Lepore apply their proposed tests makes metaphor appear to be semantically context-sensitive. Many theorists would respond to this by dismissing metaphor, and non-literal speech generally, as an irrelevant distraction. I suspect that Cappelen and Lepore are no exception: they say, for instance, that it's crucial that their arguments against Moderate Contextualism not rely on "irrelevant" factors like non-literality, ambiguity, or vagueness (2005: 42).

However, such a dismissive response would be inappropriate. First, many of the people Cappelen and Lepore would call Radical Contextualists (e.g. Bezuidenhout 2001; Carston 2002; Hills 1997; Recanati 2001) believe that metaphor should at least be included within "what is said", if not within semantic content *per se*. And Josef Stern (2000), who counts as a moderate contextualist if not a minimalist by Cappelen and Lepore's standards, maintains that metaphor is semantically context-sensitive. Given that metaphor is a pervasive linguistic phenomenon whose theoretical status is contested ground, it's incumbent upon the minimalist to have some argument against those views. Further, Cappelen and Lepore themselves appeal to non-literal speech in support of SPAP, as in their example of "the moronic clown" (2005: 196). If non-literal speech can constitute evidence in favor of SPAP, then it should be relevant to discussions of semantic content as well.[1]

My general strategy in this section is as follows. Cappelen and Lepore invariably run their tests on intuitions about the truth of utterances *per se*, or else about the truth of indirect reports of what a speaker *said*. However, they should be equally happy to run their tests on what a speaker *claimed*, since they are committed to the view that 'say', 'claim', 'assert', etc. are all equivalent. And when we apply the tests to metaphorical utterances using 'claim' reports, the tests suggest that

[1] As officially formulated, Cappelen and Lepore's tests merely present necessary conditions on context-sensitivity. Thus, granting that metaphor passes the tests wouldn't force them to conclude that metaphor really is semantically context-sensitive. However, they regularly take the fact that an expression passes the tests to constitute positive evidence for its actually being semantically context-sensitive (cf. e.g. ibid. 88). The same standard should therefore apply to metaphor.

metaphor is semantically context-sensitive. By contrast, the evidence delivered by 'say' reports is considerably weaker. Cappelen and Lepore thus face a choice: either grant that we have evidence for metaphor's being semantically context-sensitive, or acknowledge a significant distinction between saying and claiming. At a minimum, they need to provide some explanation for the shift in intuitions produced by the different illocutionary verbs.

Test 1

> "An Expression is Context Sensitive Only if it Typically Blocks Inter-Contextual Disquotational Indirect Reports": "If the occurrence of an expression *e* in a sentence tends to block disquotational indirect reports (i.e., render such reports false), then you have evidence that *e* is context sensitive" (ibid. 88).

I claim that disquotational 'claim' reports of metaphorical utterances are blocked whenever the utterance and reporting contexts are relevantly different. Here are three examples, designed to mimic Cappelen and Lepore's discussion as closely as possible:

Example 1.1

> C: Alex says, to Bill: "You were right to dump Jane. She's one of those long-stemmed roses. She's overwrought and showy, and her thorns poke you if you try to get too close."
>
> C′: Charlie says, to Bill: "I think I'm in love with Jane. She's soft, fragrant, and always classy. She's a real long-stemmed rose." Bill says: "Alex claims that Jane is a long-stemmed rose, too." Alex rightfully objects that he didn't claim anything like what Charlie did; Bill has misreported him.

The previous evaluation of Bill's indirect report is situated within a real context, C′. Further, reflecting on both contexts from my own current (rather boring) context C″, in which no special assumptions about roses or romance are operative, my intuition is that all three of the following are false:

(1.1.1_c) Alex claimed that Jane is a long-stemmed rose.

(1.1.2_c) Charlie claimed that Jane is a long-stemmed rose.

(1.1.3_c) Alex and Charlie both claimed the same thing: that Jane is a long-stemmed rose.

By Test 1, this should be evidence that metaphor is semantically context-sensitive. By contrast, however, utterances of the following all seem true to me:

(1.1.1$_s$) Alex said that Jane is a long-stemmed rose.
(1.1.2$_s$) Charlie said that Jane is a long-stemmed rose.
(1.1.3$_s$) Alex and Charlie both said that Jane is a long-stemmed rose.

For instance, (1.1.3$_s$) is clearly true if followed by a clause like "but they meant totally different things by it". Admittedly, there are contexts in which (1.1.3$_s$) seems false: for instance, if it's followed with something like "so they agree about Jane". In such contexts, 'say' is being used in a way equivalent to 'claim'. The important point is that there is *a* use of 'say' on which (1.1.1$_s$)–(1.1.3$_s$) are true, and that intuitions about 'say' reports are at least considerably more equivocal than intuitions 'claim' reports.

Example 1.2

C: Jane tells Charlene, "I dumped Bill because he's such a gorilla. I'm looking for someone who can hear people disagree with him without yelling and getting all hot under the collar."

C′: Alice and Charlene are watching *Gorillas in the Mist*, viewing footage of mountain gorillas lazing about and eating leaves. Alice says dreamily, "You know, Bill is such a noble, gentle force of nature, sometimes I think he's a gorilla." Charlene says: "Jane told me that Bill is a gorilla, too. Funny that you ladies agree on so much when you say you hate each other." Charlene has misreported Jane's utterance.

Again, here now in C″, it seems to me that all of the following are false, while the analogous reports involving 'say' are true or equivocal, as above:

(1.2.1$_C$) Jane claims that Bill is a gorilla.
(1.2.2$_C$) Alice claims that Bill is a gorilla.
(1.2.3$_C$) Jane and Alice both claim that Bill is a gorilla.

Example 1.3

C: Cappelen and Lepore have a habit of calling anyone who accepts a semantic referential/attributive ambiguity a moronic clown, in the nicest possible way. When Jerome's new paper comes out, Cappelen tells Lepore, "It turns out that Jerome's a moronic clown too. I'm surprised, given his work on complex demonstratives. Still, his paper has the best arguments I've seen for the view—quite ingenious."

> C′: Meanwhile, James is trying to write a letter of recommendation for Jerome, but he doesn't think Jerome's a good philosopher. Finally, he decides to just be honest. He writes, "You should hire Jerome if you're looking for someone to demonstrate to students how not to do philosophy. He can't construct a valid argument to save his life. Jerome is a moronic clown." Later, Bill is giving Alex a rundown on the latest gossip. Bill says, "Well, I heard that Cappelen claimed that Jerome is a moronic clown. And James claims the same thing, too." Bill is wrong: his reports are inaccurate.

Again, from C″, all three of the following seem clearly false, while the analogous reports involving 'say' are true or equivocal:

(1.3.1$_c$) Cappelen claimed that Jerome is a moronic clown.

(1.3.2$_c$) James claimed that Jerome is a moronic clown.

(1.3.3$_c$) Cappelen and James both claimed that Jerome is a moronic clown.

How might Cappelen and Lepore deal with these cases while holding on to their test? The most obvious option would be to deny that metaphor counts as semantically context-sensitive according to Test 1, by insisting that cross-contextual disquotational 'claim' reports of metaphorical utterances, like (1.1.1$_c$) and (1.1.2$_c$), are *true*. And I think we can find contexts in which such reports do seem true. As Cappelen and Lepore insist, though, it's not enough that there be some such contexts; the reports must be true even in contexts that differ dramatically from the original one. Thus, in particular, both (1.1.1$_c$) and (1.1.2$_c$) should be assessable as true in the same context, and (1.1.2$_c$) should follow automatically from them in that context. This seems highly implausible in its own right.

Further, anyone who does insist that such reports are generally true must decide how to reconcile this with our ordinary assumption that someone who claims *p* thereby commits themselves to obvious consequences of *p*. Can we conclude from the truth of (1.3.1$_c$) that Cappelen is committed to Jerome's being a moron? Can we conclude from the truth of (1.2.1$_c$) that Jane is committed to Bill's being a member of an endangered species? How do such reports function in chains of further reasoning: for instance, how do we assess the truth-value of statements like (1.1.4$_c$)?

(1.1.4$_c$) If what Alex claimed is true, then Jane belongs to a species of flower that is cultivated in greenhouses and is more expensive than carnations.

Anyone who grants that (1.1.4$_c$) is true needs to explain how the consequent can be compatible with other claims that Alex presumably accepts, such as that

Jane is a woman and that women don't grow in greenhouses. Finding such an explanation will be challenging, to say the least. But on the other hand, if we deny that sentences like ($1.1.4_c$) are true, while still retaining the assumption that ($1.1.1_c$) and ($1.2.1_c$) are true, then we will be forced abandon the assumption that knowing that sentences like ($1.1.1_c$) and ($1.2.1_c$) are true tells us anything about what *else* the reported speaker might believe or have committed himself to. Given that nearly any word or phrase can be used metaphorically, and given that nothing in sentences like ($1.1.1_c$) and ($1.1.4_c$) indicates that the original utterances are metaphorical, it seems that we should *never* make claims about conditionals like ($1.1.4_c$) unless we are acquainted with the original context of utterance, because only such direct acquaintance would inform us of the inferential import of a speaker's claim. This seems like an excessively high cost to pay. Instead, it seems clear that we should deny that sentences containing 'claim' that disquote metaphorical utterances are true, and abandon the use of 'claim' reports in general as a test for semantic context sensitivity.

Test 2

> "Context Sensitive Expressions Block Collective Descriptions": "If a verb phrase *v* is context sensitive . . . then on the basis of merely knowing that there are two contexts of utterance in which 'A *v*-s' and 'B *v*-s' are true respectively, we *cannot* automatically infer that there is a context in which '*v*' can be used to describe what A and B have both done . . . it doesn't *follow* that there is a true utterance of 'A and B both *v*'. (ibid. 99)

As formulated here, Test 2 relies on intuitions about utterances of the sentences 'A *v*-s' and 'B *v*-s' from distinct contexts, with the collective description located either in one of those two contexts or in a third. This certainly seems like the right way to run the test. Thus, consider a case involving a paradigmatically context-sensitive expression.

Example 2.1

C: George says, "Jim bought that car". (Pointing at a red Honda Civic)

C′: Charlie says, "Alex bought that car". (Pointing at a blue Lexus)

Supposing that Jim bought the car that George ostended, and that Alex bought the car that Charlie ostended, it doesn't follow that there is a true utterance, in C, C′, or my current context C″, of

(2.1.1) Jim and Alex both bought that car.

Nor can I legitimately pick up on Charlie's utterance in C′ by saying "And Jim did too."[2]

Stern (2000: 69) uses data of precisely this form to argue that metaphor is semantically context-sensitive. He claims that sentences like

(2.1.2) The largest blob of gases in the solar system is the sun, and Juliet *is, too.*

(2.1.3) Juliet is the sun, and Achilles *is, too.*

are "semantically ill-formed". I've argued (Camp 2005) against Stern's interpretation of the data, and specifically against the claim that we need to explain the badness of utterances like (2.1.2) and (2.1.3) semantically. However, Stern is undeniably correct that there is *something* true about appropriate utterances of "The largest blob of gases in the solar system is the sun", "Juliet is the sun", and "Achilles is the sun", and something very wrong with utterances of sentences like (2.1.2) and (2.1.3). This certainly seems like an application of Test 2. If we want to resist the conclusion that metaphor is semantically context-sensitive, we need to think more carefully about just how to apply Test 2.

The official formulation of Test 2 above appeals to the intuition that certain *utterances* are true.[3] If we use this criterion, then the test will support Stern's analysis. Consider the following example.

Example 2.2

C: Jane is an overwrought and showy woman, who only feels comfortable with people of her own socio-economic class, and who takes umbrage at anyone who disagrees with her. After enumerating these facts, Alex says: "Jane is a long-stemmed rose. I'd rather go out with a daisy, you know?"

C′: Kim is a relaxed but sophisticated lady. She has an effortless, impeccably elegant sense of style, a soft and demure way of interacting with others, and she always wears a lovely perfume. After lauding these virtues of Kim's, Charlie says: "I think I'm in love with Kim. She's a real long-stemmed rose. It's rare to meet such a class act."

[2] Cappelen and Lepore claim that for a sentence containing a paradigmatically context-sensitive expression, such as "Frank bought this, and Martha did too", "there are no available interpretations . . . on which Frank and Martha bought different things" (ibid. 101n. 7). Notice, however, that there can be considerable variability in what counts as *the same thing* for a phrase like "that car": say, the same token vehicle (a specific red Honda Civic), or two cars of the same specific type (red Honda Civics), or two cars of a quite general, contextually salient type (the fully loaded edition of a Japanese company's mid-level model). As a result, Frank and Martha might buy different things on some construals of "thing" but not others.

[3] Because Cappelen and Lepore deny that we have intuitions about truth-values of utterances as such, they aren't entitled to run Test 2 this way in any case; this is an independent reason to adopt the modified version I suggest below.

Like Romeo's utterance, Alex's and Charlie's utterances each seem intuitively true in their respective contexts. Further, it would be quite natural for someone who believed that Jane is overwrought and showy to respond to Alex's utterance by saying something like "You're right" or "That's true" (cf. Hills 1997); and it seems plausible that such comments pick up on utterance content—supposing that there is such a thing. However, when the truths of those respective utterances are used as premises to derive collective descriptions, then the conclusion is clearly false, as in (2.2.1):

(2.2.1) Alex's utterance of "Jane is a long-stemmed rose" is true. And Charlie's utterance of "Kim is a long-stemmed rose" is true. Therefore, Jane and Kim are both long-stemmed roses.[4]

Thus, if we frame Test 2 in terms of *utterances*' truth-values, metaphor appears to be semantically context-sensitive. However, when Cappelen and Lepore actually apply Test 2 themselves (2005: 100), they follow a rather different protocol. There, after presenting a true assertion of "Smith weighs 80 kg" in C and a true assertion of "Jones weighs 80kg" in C′, they shift to their own context C″, note that assertions of those very same sentences seem true in that context as well, and then show that we can combine the descriptions in C″. The analogous application to our metaphorical assertions from Example 2.2 gives us (2.2.2):

(2.2.2) Jane is a long-stemmed rose. And Kim is a long-stemmed rose. So Jane and Kim are both long-stemmed roses.

And indeed, I believe the syllogism in (2.2.2) is valid; it's just not sound, because the premises are both false. If that's right, then (2.2.2) doesn't suggest that metaphor passes Test 2.

However, construed in this way, Test 2 gives us little or no evidence about context-sensitivity beyond that already provided by Test 1. Once we've successfully disquoted "weighs 80 kg" from C and from C′ into the single context C″, the possibility of collection shouldn't be surprising. An expression like "today" can't be disquoted to relevantly different contexts; but for those context-pairs for which it can be disquoted, collection then follows automatically.

[4] It's true that we can say things like "Jane and Kim are both long stemmed-roses, albeit in very different senses"; perhaps the collective description in (2.2.1) and (2.2.2) can be heard as elliptical for this. But such a reading precisely *avoids* claiming that the collective description is true in virtue of any common properties that Jane and Kim possess. Thus, it doesn't show that we can "describe what they all have in common by using '*v*' " (2005: 99), as Cappelen and Lepore rightly require. With a gradable adjective like "tall", it's perhaps possible to insist that the Empire State Building, Osama bin Laden, and Billy the third-grader do all share a very general property: being tall. I'm even less of a metaphysician than Cappelen and Lepore, but I don't know what real property or common way of being Jane and Kim could share that would underwrite a substantive reading of "are both long-stemmed roses".

Therefore, insisting on using a disquotational formulation of Test 2 threatens to beg the question against a semantic theorist of metaphor like Stern: in order to apply the test at all, we must restrict our attention to contexts for which collection will go through.[5]

To capture what's true about the original metaphorical utterances in a way that doesn't suggest that metaphor is semantically context-sensitive, we need to appeal to more specific speech acts than Cappelen and Lepore are willing to do. Contrast the following pair of syllogisms:

(2.2.3) What Alex claimed (by uttering "Jane is a long-stemmed rose") is true. And what Charlie claimed (by uttering "Jane is a long-stemmed rose") is true. Therefore, Jane and Kim are both long-stemmed roses.

(2.2.4) What Alex said (by uttering "Jane is a long-stemmed rose") is true. And what Charlie said (by uttering "Jane is a long-stemmed rose" in context C) is true. Therefore, Jane and Kim are both long-stemmed roses.

In (2.2.3), the premises again seem clearly true, and the conclusion false.[6] In this case, however, unlike with (2.1.3) and (2.2.1), we can explain why the conclusion doesn't follow in a way that doesn't support semantic context-sensitivity. By uttering "Jane is a long-stemmed rose", Alex didn't claim that Jane is a long-stemmed rose, but rather that she possesses some set of properties P that happen to be saliently associated with long-stemmed roses in C. And by uttering the same sentence in his context C′, Charlie claimed that Kim possesses some other set of properties Q associated with long-stemmed roses in C′. There's no reason to think that the largely disjoint sets P and Q should be collectible under a common description, in C″ or any other context. I think this explanation is highly plausible. But it entails we shouldn't use 'claim' reports to test for semantic context sensitivity.

By contrast, I hear the premises in (2.2.4) as false. And if that's right, then metaphor doesn't generate a failure to preserve truth through collection, as

5 Further, it's not obvious that cross-contextual disquotation *can't* go through for the premises in (2.2.2). I think we can, albeit with effort, hear the premises as true by importing the relevant assumptions for each sentence from its original context; this would be analogous to an utterance of "Jim bought *that* car and Alex bought *that* one" where the speaker mentally ostends distinct cars from memory. To the extent that we can indeed hear the premises in (2.2.2) this way, then the syllogism's conclusion is once again blocked, in the way that Test 2 requires for semantic context-sensitivity.

6 One could deny, as Davidson (1978) does, that the speakers claimed anything true. But this view flies in the face of ordinary intuitions about metaphorical utterances and their 'claim' reports. In conversation, we do take speakers who have spoken metaphorically to have made speech acts with contents that we can hold them responsible for. Further, hearers can easily deny those claims using the same form of words as the speaker. For instance, within its context of utterance, the most natural way to deny that Jane is overwrought and showy is to utter the negation of the sentence Alex uttered (cf. Hills 1997; Bezuidenhout 2001). An adequate theory of speech acts must explain this.

Test 2 requires: we just have another valid but unsound syllogism. Again, there is undeniably an ordinary use of 'say' on which the premises are true; and in that case we again have a blocked inference, *à la* Test 2. But as I'll argue in §4, there is *an* ordinary use of 'say' on which the premises are false. Thus, if Cappelen and Lepore want a version of Test 2 that doesn't make metaphor appear semantically context-sensitive, they need to employ *this* use of 'say'; neither direct appeal to utterance truth, nor disquotation, nor 'claim' reports, will do.

Test 3

> "Context Sensitive Expressions Pass an Inter-Contextual Disquotational Test": "*e* is context sensitive only if there is a true utterance of an instance of the following schema for Inter-Contextual Disquotation:
>
> (ICD) There are (or can be) false utterances of 'S' even though S.
>
> (Alternatively, run the test in reverse). (Cappelen and Lepore 2005: 105)

As formulated, Test 3 again relies upon intuitions about the truth-values of utterances as such. But because this is not a way of talking that Cappelen and Lepore are entitled to, I'll also run Test 3 on what speakers claim by making their utterances. I reuse context C from 2.2.

(3.1.1) There can be true utterances of "Jane is a long-stemmed rose", even though Jane is not a long-stemmed rose.

(3.1.2) What Alex claimed (by uttering "Jane is a long stemmed rose") is true, even though Jane is not a long-stemmed rose.

(3.1.3) What Alex said (by uttering "Jane is a long stemmed rose") is true, even though Jane is not a long-stemmed rose.

My intuition, insofar as I have intuitions about the truth-values of utterances *per se*, is that (3.1.1) is true. (3.1.2) is, I think, obviously true, assuming that Jane really is overwrought and showy. Finally, I think (3.1.3) is false, or at least equivocal and considerably worse than (3.1.2). At least, then, we find here the same pattern of shifting intuitions depending on the particular verb employed; this again suggests, *pace* Cappelen and Lepore, that 'claim', 'assert', and 'say' are not all equivalent.

3. INDIRECT REPORTS AND ORIGINAL UTTERANCE CENTRISM

Insensitive Semantics is a book about semantic methodology, not about the semantics of specific expressions. Given this, Cappelen and Lepore could simply stick to their guns, and take the discussion of their tests in §2 as *prima-facie* evidence that metaphor is semantically context-sensitive. However, most semantic theorists, and especially minimalists, would be quite surprised if metaphor did turn out to be semantic. I don't believe that it is semantic, and I think that a more general, independently motivated theory of the relation between speech act and semantic contents can explain why it is not. In §4, I'll argue for a distinction between asserting and saying, understood in a specific sense, which supports this view. In order to draw that distinction properly, though, we first need to constrain 'what is asserted' so that it more accurately reflects our broader communicative practices. In this section, then, I ignore the distinction between saying and asserting, and focus on getting a clearer view of saying/asserting/claiming, where "say" is used equivalently to "assert" and "claim".

As Cappelen and Lepore themselves emphasize (2005: 199), indirect reports are just as subject to "speech act pluralism" as any other utterances. Therefore, we must be extremely careful about assuming that an intuition that an indirect report communicates something true is driven by that report's semantic content. Recall, for example, context C of Example 1.2. Suppose that Tom had previously said, "Bill is incapable of delivering criticisms in a respectful and non-hurtful way." Then, in C, someone could felicitously respond to Jane's utterance by saying "Tom says that Bill's a gorilla, too." We wouldn't normally conclude from the acceptability of such a report that Tom himself said or claimed something with the semantic content of "Bill is a gorilla." So at least sometimes, it can be dangerous to follow Cappelen and Lepore's methodology of "tak[ing] our practice of indirect reporting at face value and assum[ing] that the speakers have said [or claimed] what we have the reporters saying that they have said [or claimed]" (ibid. 50).

As Cappelen and Lepore have argued forcefully (1997, 2005), our reporting practices are massively permissive across the board, and not just when it comes to figurative speech. We often accept indirect reports that communicate content which only follows from the uttered sentence's semantic content when that content is combined with quite substantive additional assumptions. Suppose that Cokie, a news reporter, utters (4.1.1):

(4.1.1) Today's nasty weather is likely to depress voter turnout, which will almost certainly favor the incumbent party.

Someone who'd heard (4.1.1) could easily accept the following report if she shared the relevant political assumptions:

(4.1.2) Did you hear that? She's saying/claiming that we're going to let a little rain prevent us from sending those corrupt hooligans back to their suburban McMansions where they belong!

Reports like these undeniably do constitute part of our normal communicative practices. The trouble comes from combining this fact with Cappelen and Lepore's emphatic rejection of Original Utterance Centrism (OUC) (2005: 201). Denying OUC places a report like (4.1.2) on a par with (4.1.1) itself as evidence about what a speaker actually said or claimed. But if Cokie were told about the report in (4.1.2), she would strenuously object to that characterization of what she said; and ordinary hearers who didn't share the specific assumptions operative in the reporting context would think that she was obviously right to do so.

The same thing can happen if we stick to less tendentious reports. Consider the following example:

Example 4.2

> George says to Alex, "I've run into Jim coming out of the Bluebird Diner the last three Monday nights." Alex knows that the Bluebird is rented out to the local chapter of the Democratic Party on Monday nights, so when he sees Bill, he says "George says Jim's been going to the Democratic party meetings at the Bluebird the last few Mondays." Later, when Jerome mentions that the local Democrats' sole project is agitating to raise the city's minimum wage, Bill responds, "Apparently, George says Jim has been going to the weekly Democrats' meetings. Surprising: I always thought he was one of us." When Jerome sees Jim, he says, "The word from George is that you're a big 'living wage' guy." Jim confronts George, saying "How could you reveal my political leanings like that?" George objects that he didn't do or say any such thing; indeed, he didn't even know that the Democrats meet at the Bluebird. George is right to object: he didn't say anything like what Jim said he did.

Each alteration in the successive reports in 4.2 capitalizes on background assumptions that are common and obvious within the specific reporting context. As a result, each successive report would reasonably be accepted as true in its conversational context by a hearer who shared those assumptions and who had heard and accepted the utterance upon which it is immediately based (for instance, by a hearer of Bill's report who had heard Alex's utterance). If relevant features of the reporting context can be "constitutive of" the content of what was originally said, as Cappelen and Lepore maintain (2005: 206), then there should be no need for the hearer to know about George's original utterance. However, through a series of individually acceptable reports, we end up with a highly distorted report. The more links in the chain of 'Telephone', the less substantive the assumptions underwriting each shift in reported content need to be in order to end up with a wildly inaccurate report.

Although our ordinary reporting practices are often quite loose, the ultimate standard for accuracy is clearly fixed by the original context of utterance. In a legal context, for instance, hearsay about what someone said is not admissible as evidence: the court requires direct evidence of the original utterance. More prosaically, anyone on the receiving end of a chain of gossip who wants to figure out what was really said/asserted will find out as much as they can about the original utterance and its surrounding context. This privileging of the original utterance and context reflects the basic purpose of making utterances, which is to commit oneself to certain contents: paradigmatically, to contents that one believes, and wants others to believe. By making a claim, one puts oneself on record as accepting a certain content, and makes oneself liable for either defending its truth or else retracting one's claim (cf. Lewis 1979; Brandom 1983). The purpose of reporting utterances, in turn, is to transmit information about the contents to which speakers have committed themselves across contexts, so that others know what those speakers can safely be assumed to believe, and what they can legitimately be held responsible for.

If assumptions that are operative in dramatically different contexts could be constitutive of the content that I myself said/asserted, then it would be utterly pointless for me to say anything, because the content of what I said/asserted could always shift in ways that were unrecognizable and repugnant to me. Worse, speaking would be extremely dangerous, because I would be potentially liable for all those contents. Speakers can indeed unintentionally commit themselves to contents they're not aware of. But in such cases, the determinative factor is still what a reasonable hearer, located within the original context of utterance and armed with all the assumptions in play in that context, would take the speaker to have committed herself to.

At the very least, then, we need to restrict 'what is said/asserted' to contents that are recoverable by a reasonable hearer of the original utterance. Reports of what is said/asserted that don't meet this standard can still communicate something true, but they are not themselves true.

In fact, however, even this standard is too loose. Although speakers are usually quite open about their communicative intentions, in principle there can always be a significant gap between what a reasonable, charitable hearer would assume the speaker was saying/asserting and the content to which the speaker has strictly speaking committed herself. Genies and oracles, Jesuits in Elizabethan England, insurance companies, and politicians are all infamous for constructing their utterances in surgically precise ways so that they can legitimately deny the validity of what most hearers would assume to be accurate reports of their speech acts. Such utterances are certainly misleading, but we don't ordinarily count them as *false*. For instance, in a legal setting a speaker who knowingly makes such a statement is not liable for perjury if the content assigned on the broader interpretation turns out not to be true.

Condoleeza Rice's statements about US policy on torture offer a particularly blatant example of this. Many reasonable hearers took her statements that "The United States does not transport, and has not transported, detainees from one country to another for the purpose of interrogation using torture", and that the US "will not transport anyone to a country when we believe he will be tortured", to be "unequivocal denunciations" of torture, and the Bush Administration clearly intended the statements to be taken this way. But others noted that rendition for the purpose of interrogation which just happened to end up involving torture, or rendition to a country where the US merely suspected that the detainee might be tortured, are not strictly speaking covered by these statements.[7] As a result, as evidence surfaces of people being tortured during interrogation after US rendition, Rice can legitimately respond that these are not counterexamples to her claim, so long as the relevant officials didn't believe the torture would definitely occur. Rice's original utterances were deplorably misleading; but if those stricter conditions are indeed met (something that is itself far from obvious), then it wasn't strictly speaking false, and hence not a lie.

Cappelen and Lepore deny that our ordinary linguistic practices support any such notion of "what was strictly speaking said/asserted". They claim that the only way to interpret questions about what someone "really", "literally", or "strictly speaking" said is as questions about whether the indirect report would be true considered as a *direct* quotation (2005: 51). But this is false. It's an essential, pervasive part of our ordinary linguistic and legal practices that we do have such a restrictive notion of speech act content, which is distinct both from direct quotation and from the more permissive standards that we more typically employ. Even Clinton had to admit that by uttering "I did not have sexual relations with that woman", he said/asserted that *he* did not have sexual relations with *Monica* (cf. Saul 1999). The assignment of reference to indexicals was never in doubt; the debate came over what conditions of satisfaction were required for them to count as "having had sexual relations", strictly speaking.

A strict interpretation of what someone said/asserted still leaves considerable room for speech act pluralism. In nearly any context, there are substantive, context-specific assumptions in play that even the most casuistic speaker cannot legitimately deny. These assumptions combine with the semantic content of the sentence uttered to produce commitments to multiple propositions that are syntactically and semantically unrelated to the uttered sentence. Thus, we still

[7] See e.g. Richard Bernstein, "Skepticism Seems to Erode Europeans' Faith in Rice", *New York Times* (7 Dec. 2005); see also http://lawofnations.blogspot.com/2005/12/rice-offers-legal-defense-of-rendition.html: "In parsing Secretary Rice's words, look closely at the specific intent or express knowledge that would be required for her statements to be false, and you'll see the role played by lawyers in the drafting of her speech. *The United States does not transport, and has not transported, detainees from one country to another for the purpose of interrogation using torture.* This careful statement is thus true so long as the purpose of an extraordinary rendition was just to interrogate a detainee, with the knowledge that he might be tortured, or was even likely to be tortured. So long as the purpose of the rendition wasn't that he be rendered for "interrogation using torture", Rice is being truthful. Deceptive, obviously, but truthful. . . . Again, this isn't the meaning being attributed to her by favorable commentators."

have a version of SPAP for assertion (and analogous speech acts, like promising).[8] But it is a version of SPAP that makes significantly better sense of our actual conversational practices than Cappelen and Lepore's MPSPAP does. It is also a version that is better suited for semantic theorizing. In fact, I suspect it supports a fairly minimal semantics; but like Cappelen and Lepore, my focus here is on methodology rather than particular cases.

4. WHAT IS SAID AND WHAT IS ASSERTED

The discussion in §3 relied neither on non-literal speech nor on the distinction between saying and asserting; the restrictions on SPAP I advocated there were motivated solely by the need to reconcile our analysis of indirect reports with our broader communicative practices. However, if we want to achieve a fully general understanding of those communicative practices, and in particular if we want to uncover a reliable connection between speech act and semantic content, then we also need to distinguish saying from asserting.

Although Cappelen and Lepore argue for a radical separation between speech act and semantic content, even they don't deny that there are *any* "interesting and informative connections between intuitions about" the two types of content (2005: 57); if they did, as we saw at the outset, then they would cut themselves off from all empirical evidence for their theory. Not only do their tests depend on such a connection; they also say that this connection is essential to explaining why communication isn't miraculous (p. 204). So what is the crucial connection between speech act and semantic content? They claim it is this: a speaker always asserts the semantic content of the sentence she utters, even if that content is typically swamped by a swarm of further propositions:

> The semantic content of a sentence S is the content that all utterances of S share. It is the content that all utterances of S express no matter how different their contexts of utterance. (p. 143)
>
> One of the many propositions asserted by an utterance is the semantic content of that utterance (the proposition semantically expressed). We argued for this in chapters 7–10. (p. 200)

The problem with this claim, however, is that the postulated connection between semantic and asserted content does not always obtain. Intuitively, we want to say, the speaker of a metaphorical utterance doesn't assert or claim her uttered sentence's semantic content. Romeo, for instance, doesn't claim that Juliet is *the sun*, but rather that she is a certain way *S*, which can be described metaphorically as being the sun. If Romeo were really claiming that Juliet is the sun, then he would also be committed to Juliet's being an enormous hot gaseous body. But

[8] For further discussion see Camp 2006*a*.

this is absurd; and Romeo would strenuously deny this commitment, without feeling any pressure to retract his original claim.[9]

What Romeo does do is *say* that Juliet is the sun; and he cannot deny a report that says he said this. What he can and should respond, if he wants to avoid going on record as committed to Juliet's being a hot gaseous body, is that he didn't *mean* (or intend to be taken to mean) what he said—he meant something else instead (Camp 2006*a*). Similarly, two people who utter "That's a fantastic idea" about the same suggestion, where one is sincere and the other sarcastic, do both *say* that the plan is a fantastic idea, but only one means it. The undeniability of such collective 'say' reports, together with the intuitive falsity of the corollary collective 'claim' reports, reflects a theoretical distinction that we need anyway, whatever we call it: the distinction that Austin (1962) described in terms of locutionary and illocutionary speech acts.[10]

Cappelen and Lepore expressly deny the utility of any distinction in this general vicinity. They consistently treat "saying, claiming, asserting etc." as freely interchangeable; and they say repeatedly that the Gricean distinction between what is said and what is implicated "is superficial and of no significance in trying to find semantic content" (2005: 57). The notion of 'what is said' that I'm elucidating is not quite Grice's. On Grice's view, saying is an illocutionary act that requires sincere commitment; otherwise, one merely "makes as if to say". But my locutionary notion, which is close to that employed by others like Bach and Harnish (1979), does much of the work that Grice wanted. In any case, we need some such distinction to explain how non-literal utterances can commit

[9] It's possible that Cappelen and Lepore would simply insist that speakers who speak metaphorically *do* assert the proposition semantically expressed, but that this assertion is charitably ignored in favor of more salient and communicatively relevant propositions. This line of defense is suggested by their claim that "Nothing even prevents an utterance from asserting (saying, claiming, etc.) propositions incompatible with the proposition semantically expressed by that utterance" (2005: 4). By itself, this position is already far from intuitive, especially when it's applied to sarcasm, where the speaker means something like the opposite of what she says. Further, though, Cappelen and Lepore follow this claim with the following: "From this, it further follows that if you want to exploit intuitions about speech act content to fix semantic content, then you have to be extremely careful in so doing. It can be done, and we'll show you how, but it's a subtle and easily corrupted process" (ibid.). What they "show us how" to do is employ the tests discussed in §2. But those tests suggest precisely that we don't ordinarily take speakers of metaphorical utterances to have claimed or asserted the proposition semantically expressed. Further, although non-literal speech makes the case most clearly, the case against treating semantic content as universally asserted content need not rest exclusively on non-literal speech; see e.g. Soames (forthcoming) for evidence from co-referring expressions.

[10] Some theorists deny that two people who utter "That's a fantastic idea" about the same plan, one sincerely and the other sarcastically, or two people who utter "She is the sun" about the same woman, where one means that she is beautiful and the other that she is dangerous, do *say* the same thing. Such theorists then need a further term for what the two people did in common; as I note below, 'utter' will not do, because the sense in which two people 'did the same thing' goes beyond mere quotation to assign values to context-sensitive expressions. I am focusing here on drawing the distinction between locution and illocution, and prescinding from whether and which forms of 'meaning enrichment' should be included within the locutionary act. As I mention below, locutionary 'what is said' is not itself equivalent to semantic content, and so it would not be surprising if it included some enrichment.

their speakers to determinate contents in the manner of assertion without thereby committing them to the semantic content of the uttered sentence.

Given Cappelen and Lepore's skepticism about "what was strictly speaking said", as discussed in §3, we might predict that they will insist here too that the only use of 'say' that's not equivalent to 'assert' is one on which it functions as a device of direct quotation. This claim might seem more plausible here than it did in the context of §3, given that the locutionary notion of 'saying' is so minimal and seems to be largely driven by fairly recondite theoretical concerns. However, it's important to see that 'say' does have an ordinary use denoting a merely locutionary act. We can observe this in the utter naturalness of reports like the following:

(5.1.1) John: "This man here is your department's new quarterback."

(5.1.2) Alex: "When John said that Bill was our new quarterback, I didn't realize he meant it literally: I thought Bill was our new chairman. But now our whole department is practicing the flea-flicker."

(5.2.1) Bill: "She sounds like a real winner. Let's bring her on board right away."

(5.2.2) Alex: "Bill *said* that we should hire Jane immediately. But I think he was being sarcastic—you can never tell with those deadpan Brits. She doesn't seem like his kind of candidate at all."

Because these reports assign values to contextually sensitive terms and permit some substitution of other expressions, they go significantly beyond reporting just the words uttered; they are definitely not direct quotations. But they also explicitly distinguish what was said from what was meant or asserted. Similarly, two speakers A and B, who say "You are my sunshine" to C and D respectively, have uttered, but not said, the same thing: A said that C is A's sunshine, while B said that D is B's sunshine. Neither has claimed that their addressee actually is sunshine; instead, perhaps, A has claimed that C keeps him honest, while B has claimed that D makes him happy when he is sad. To keep track of what is shared and different across utterances like these, then, we need to appeal to all three levels of content: of what is uttered, what is said, and what is asserted.

Even this restricted notion of 'what is said', identified by what can be reported with utterances like (5.1.2) and (5.2.2), still isn't equivalent to semantic content; for instance, it permits substitution of co-extensive expressions with distinct modal profiles. But locutionary 'what is said' is well-equipped to play the role in communication that Cappelen and Lepore assign to semantic content: thus, it is "content the audience can expect the speaker to grasp (and expect the speaker to expect the audience to grasp, etc.) even if she has mistaken or incomplete information" (2005: 184). In particular, it is content that the hearer has access to even if he is mistaken or ignorant about whether the speaker intended to assert the semantic content of her uttered sentence, and that he can use (in conjunction with further assumptions) to determine what she could plausibly have meant. Locutionary content is thus a definite, reliable "starting point" (185) for determining illocutionary (and perlocutionary) content. It is also content that is psychologically real, not least in the sense that hearers appeal to it when asked to justify why they think a speaker could plausibly mean *this* by saying *that.*[11]

5. CONCLUSION

Once we are armed with the distinction between saying and asserting, we can fairly easily revise Cappelen and Lepore's tests so that they no longer suggest that metaphor, and non-literal speech more generally, is semantically context-sensitive. (I leave open the question of whether they are otherwise reliable.) We should formulate the tests using the locution "what the speaker said by uttering S", and check that the reported content meets the standards I sketched in §§3 and 4: it should be acceptable to both the original speaker and to a reasonable hearer of the original utterance who was unsure or mistaken about whether the speaker meant what she said. This is a fairly nuanced standard, to be sure, but it is, I have argued, a standard to which our ordinary communicative practices are indeed sensitive.

In the end, I doubt that shifting from 'what is said/asserted/claimed etc.' to 'what is said' construed restrictively will offer much comfort to the contextualist. Nor does it force us into Speech Act Monism (SPAM). But it does require abandoning the most wanton form of SPAP. On a more temperate view, speakers enact a series of nested speech acts by making any utterance: uttering begets saying, which begets asserting/ordering/promising, which begets indicating/pressuring/warning, and so on; each of these speech acts may itself contain multiple contents. I suggest that this moderate pluralism is both compatible with our ordinary communicative practices and nuanced enough to underwrite a reasonably simple and systematic semantic theory.

Cappelen and Lepore are correct that unrestricted maximalism ultimately collapses into radical relativism. They are also correct that indexicals like "I" and "today" form a clear class of particularly well-behaved context-sensitive terms. But if the minimalist wants to ground her overall semantic theory empirically, then she must draw some distinctions within a pool of fairly messy data that fall between these two extremes. Our reporting practices are one source of such data, but they are not the only source; we also need to examine how speakers and hearers actually use and respond to utterances in conversation. Cappelen and Lepore may not like my way of divvying up the data. But without some

[11] For further discussion of how to identify the relevant content and why it can play this theoretical role, see Camp 2006*a*. For a review of evidence that literal meaning does play a role in the processing of metaphor, see Camp 2006*b*.

such distinctions, we end up with a theory of speech acts that makes communication—that is the process of making and exchanging commitments about how the world is—appear utterly baffling.

REFERENCES

Austin, J. L. (1962), *How to Do Things with Words.* Cambridge, Mass.: Harvard University Press.

Bach, K., and R. M. Harnish (1979), *Linguistic Communication and Speech Acts.* Cambridge, Mass.: MIT Press.

Bezuidenhout, A. (2001), 'Metaphor and What is Said: A Defense of a Direct Expression View of Metaphor', *Midwest Studies in Philosophy*, 25: 156–86.

Brandom, R. (1983), 'Asserting', *Noûs*, 17/4: 637–50.

Camp, E. (2005), 'Josef Stern, Metaphor in Context', *Noûs*, 39/4: 716–32.

____ (2006*a*), 'Metaphor, Contextualism, and What is Said', *Mind and Language*, 21/3: 280–309.

____ (2006*b*), 'Metaphor in the Mind: The Cognition of Metaphor', *Philosophy Compass*, 1/2: 154–70.

Cappelen, H., and E. Lepore (1997), 'On an Alleged Connection between Indirect Speech and the Theory of Meaning', *Mind and Language*, 12/3–4: 278–96.

____ and ____ (2005), *Insensitive Semantics*. Oxford, Blackwell.

Carston, R. (2002), *Thoughts and Utterances: The Pragmatics of Explicit Communication.* Oxford: Blackwell.

Davidson, D. (1978), 'What Metaphors Mean', in S. Sachs (ed.), *On Metaphor*, pp. 41–58. Chicago: University of Chicago Press.

Hills, D. (1997), 'Aptness and Truth in Verbal Metaphor', *Philosophical Topics*, 25/1: 117–53.

Lewis, D. (1979), 'Scorekeeping in a Language Game', *Journal of Philosophical Logic*, 8: 339–59.

Recanati, F. (2001), 'Literal/Nonliteral', *Midwest Studies in Philosophy*, 25: 264–74.

Saul, J. (1999), 'Substitution, Simple Sentences, and Sex Scandals', *Analysis*, 59/2: 106–12.

Soames, S. (forthcoming), 'The Gap between Meaning and Assertion: Why What we Literally Say Often Differs from What our Words Literally Mean', in M. Hackl and R. Thornton (eds.), *Asserting, Meaning, and Implying.*

Stern, J. (2000), *Metaphor in Context.* Cambridge, Mass.: MIT Press.

PART II

ON CRITIQUES OF SEMANTIC MINIMALISM

8

Meanings, Propositions, Context, and Semantical Underdeterminacy

Jay David Atlas

1. MEANING DUALISM AND ITS CRITICISM OF DAVIDSONIAN TRUTH-THEORIES FOR NATURAL LANGUAGE

Many years ago, when the world and we were young, in 1978 in fact, John Searle published in *Erkenntnis* 13: 207–24 (reprinted in Searle 1979: 117–36) a provocative article "Literal Meaning". In the essay Searle considers the sentence 'The cat is on the mat', in circumstances in which the cat and mat are in the prototypical spatial relationship of one being snuggled up to the other, except they are both floating freely in various orientations in outer space, in which there is no gravitational field with respect to which the cat is "above" the mat. Is the cat on the mat? Searle asserts that the notion of a literal meaning of 'The cat is on the mat' depends on assumptions like the existence of a local gravitational field in which 'above' and 'below' have an application. (What this amounts to in the ordinary, earth-bound case is that the assertion of 'The cat is on the mat' is true if and only if the cat is above and touching—in some typical fashion—the mat beneath it. The earth's local gravitational field provides a preferred spatial orientation; freely falling bodies fall "down".) Searle's thesis was that for:

> a large class of unambiguous sentences such as 'The cat is on the mat', the notion of the literal meaning of the sentence only has application relative to a set of background assumptions. The truth conditions of the sentence will vary with variations in these background assumptions; and given the absence or presence of some background assumptions the sentence does not have determinate truth conditions. These variations have nothing to do with indexicality, change of meaning, ambiguity, conversational implication, vagueness or presupposition as these notions are standardly discussed in the philosophical and linguistic literature. . . . [O]ur examples suggest that the assumptions are not specifiable as part of the semantic content of the sentence, or as presuppositions of the applicability of that semantic content . . . (1979: 125–6)

What motivated Searle's conclusion was the lexical properties of the preposition 'on' in English in the sentence 'The cat is on the mat', the consequences of which Searle (1979: 126) diagnosed as the "contextual dependence" of the word 'on'.

At roughly the same time I suggested that in negative sentences like 'The king of France is not bald', the

> English word 'not' creates neither a structurally nor a lexically ambiguous sentence. If on the orthodox view the entry in the lexicon for 'not' is such that 'not' is ambiguous, on the heterodox [Atlas] view the entry for 'not' is such that 'not' is [semantically] non-specific. . . . A reading or semantic representation of a [negative] sentence is not a bearer of truth-value; it is not a proposition or a logical form, though it determines what propositions can be literally meant by the sentence. (Atlas 1977: 322)

There is a similarity between Searle's view and mine, in that we both claimed that the variations of interpretations of the sentence's utterance-meaning in different contexts of utterance did not constitute lexical or scope ambiguities of sense of 'on' or of 'not'. We both claimed that the sentence-type, as contrasted with the sentence-token in a context of utterance, was not to be given a semantic representation that was identical to a proposition or truth-conditions. Where Searle and I differed was whether the notion of the literal meaning of the sentence-type had any application independently of background assumptions. I held that there was a notion of literal meaning of the sentence-type independently of context and that the meaning should not be identified with truth-conditions. Searle, not distinguishing between sentence-types and sentence-tokens in the discussion above, denies my view. In fact he (1979: 125) explicitly denies "that every unambiguous sentence . . . has a literal meaning which is absolutely context free and which determines for every context whether or not an utterance of that sentence in that context is literally true or false".

To the contrary, I held that there was a context-free literal meaning, and that, in a sense of 'determine' best understood as 'constrain', it determined whether an utterance of the sentence in that context is literally true or false.[1] For me, unlike I suppose for Searle and most philosophers at that time, 'The king of France is not bald' was an unambiguous sentence, one without ambiguities of scope, or homonymy of lexical items, for 'not'. In one context an utterance of the sentence would literally express the narrow-scope, predicate negation proposition (or truth-conditions), and in other contexts it would literally express the wide-scope, sentence negation proposition (or truth-conditions). Neither proposition is a literal meaning of the sentence. The sentence-type is not ambiguous between these interpretations or contextual understandings. It is "neutral" between these meanings; it is, technically speaking, *semantically non-specific* between them.[2] The statements made in the assertings of the sentence would, of course, have

[1] See Levinson (2000: 241).

[2] See Zwicky and Sadock 1975; Atlas 1977, 1989, 2005*b*.

a truth-value. Notice that on my view the word 'not' in the sentence plays a role in constraining the literal utterance-meanings, but it does not do so "exhaustively": the literal utterance-meaning is not a disambiguated meaning of the sentence-type, the disambiguation of which depends on selecting one of the meanings of 'not' or one of the scopes of 'not'. The meaning of the sentence-type is non-specific between the choice and exclusion negations, the interpretations that philosophers typically associate with the predicate and sentence negations.

Searle and I both held that indexicality was not the problem; it was not what motivated Searle's notion of the "context dependence" of 'on', and it was not what motivated my notion of the semantical non-specificity, and semantical univocality rather than scope or lexical ambiguity, of 'not'. I did not claim that 'not' contained a hidden indexical term like 'I', 'now', and 'here' or a hidden demonstrative like 'that', 'those', 'this', and 'these', which would fix its reference, the "concept" it referred to, in a context. Nor did Searle make such a claim about 'on'.

I held a view that could be described by this quotation (out of context) from Charles Travis (1996: 451, quoted by Cappelen and Lepore 2005: 6):

> What words mean plays a role in fixing when they would be true; but not an exhaustive one. Meaning leaves room for variation in truth conditions from one speaking to another.

This loose characterization by Travis, one of Cappelen and Lepore's examples of a Radical Contextualist, literally applies to my own view, though my view is not the same as Travis's. Travis (1994: 172, quoted in Cappelen and Lepore 2005: 31) believes that there are some understandings of utterances of the sentence-type 'Ice floats' such that those utterances are true on those understandings, whether or not there are some liquids in which ice-cubes sink. And he thinks that an utterance of 'Ice floats' when dropping an ice-cube into a bowl of a liquid in which it does sink does turn out to be false. From these claims, Travis (1974: 172) concludes that "there is more than one thing to be said in saying 'Ice floats' where those words mean what they do mean in English; more than one thing, that is, each of which is what sometimes would be said in so speaking". It is clear that Travis believes that some assertions of 'Ice floats' are not disconfirmed by the existence of liquids in which an ice-cube would sink. But his explicit qualification is that the assertion must be "rightly understood". In the passage quoted he does not actually give the "rightly understood" interpretation. One could easily imagine him thinking of the sentence on the model of 'Dogs bark' or 'Horses neigh' or 'Dolphins whistle' or 'Humans speak'. Such generic sentences remain true even if there are deaf-mutes or surgically altered dolphins, horses, or dogs.[3] The problem is that an utterance of 'Ice floats' in the case of its being a statement about a liquid in which the ice-cube sinks is false according to Travis. So the utterance cannot be understood as a generic in that context. The aspect of Travis's (1994) view that

[3] See Ziff (1972*a*) and Carlson and Pelletier (1995).

he claims is Wittgensteinian is the claim that the meanings of 'ice' and 'floats' do not, even when combined in a sentence 'Ice floats', determine the understanding of *any* sentence-token in a context—Travis's way of putting the point suggests that the sentence is not ambiguous between generic and "specific" senses; the sentence-token could be interpreted as having the generic understanding or the specific understanding, depending on the context.

Like Wittgenstein, Travis prefers to couch his theory of meaning as a theory of utterance-interpretation only; he does not offer an account of sentence-type meaning at all. Such a view is quite distinct from my own, which was just as non-classical as Travis's, since the sentence-meanings in my theory are not always propositions or truth-conditions or well-defined logical forms either of first-order quantification theory or of Scott-Montague second-order intensional logic. But on my view sentence-types can have context-free semantic content, just not always content that is identical to a truth-condition that is representable by a logical form.

Cappelen and Lepore (2005: 6) characterize Radical Contextualism as positing the condition that "No English sentence S ever semantically expresses a proposition". This is the first of their three conditions that characterize Radical Contextualism. This condition is satisfied by Travis's view and by Wittgenstein's, because they are not trafficking in sentence-types at all. Searle's view, by contrast, is that "Not every English sentence S semantically expresses a proposition", a weaker claim, or alternatively that "For a large class of English sentences, no sentence in the class semantically expresses a proposition."[4]

I held that for some sentence-types, only their utterance-types or utterance-tokens can "express a proposition" or have truth-conditions and take a truth-value. I complicated the picture by distinguishing between sentence-types, sentence-tokens, utterance-types, and utterance-tokens (Atlas 1989, 2005*b*, Levinson 1995). Searle held the view for sentence-tokens. This view is the third of the three views that Cappelen and Lepore (2005: 6) believe characterize "Radical Contextualism". The second of the three conditions is the inescapability of context-dependence of sentence-meanings. That is a view that I reject and that Searle does not explicitly accept. Travis is not in the business of sentence-meanings at all.

So who are the Radical Contextualists if Atlas, Searle, and Travis aren't? Cappelen and Lepore (2005: 5) pin the label on Relevance Theorists, e.g. Sperber and Wilson (1986), Carston (1988, 2002), Recanati (1989, 1993, 2004), neo-Wittgensteinians, and some Sellarsians (unmentioned), Searle and Travis being the neo-Wittgensteinians, I presume. To the extent that Relevance Theorists remain close to the roots of their theoretical assumptions in works like Atlas (1979)—see Kempson (1988: 141 n. 2) and Horn (1989: 433) for historical remarks—to that extent the Relevance Theorists are not Radical

4 There is an excellent criticism of Searle's position in Katz 1981.

Contextualists either. But there are some who do not remain close to those roots. There is at least one (sort of) Radical Contextualist in the lot, namely, Robyn Carston. Cappelen and Lepore (2005: 38) quote a passage from Carston (2002: 29) that does not seem to leave much doubt:

> Underdeterminacy is an essential feature of the relation between linguistic expression and the propositions (thoughts) they are used to express; generally, for any given proposition/thought, there is *no* sentence which *fully* encodes it. . . . Underdeterminacy is *universal* and *no* sentence *ever fully* encodes the thought or proposition it is used to express.

You would not know it from this quotation by Cappelen and Lepore, but this passage is taken from a text in which Carston is presenting competing views. It is only on the next page of Carston's (2002: 30) book that she states that she "is inclined" to take the strong view quoted, though she admits the greater plausibility of the weaker view that "underdeterminacy is widespread" rather than universal!

There is another position of interest to Cappelen and Lepore, which they call 'Moderate Contextualism'. Moderate Contextualists believe that some expressions other than the indexicals and demonstratives, which Cappelen and Lepore call 'the Basic Set of context-sensitive expressions', are context-sensitive. Such a characterization applies to Searle on 'on' and Atlas on 'not', as well as others that we will discuss. Many sentences to which Cappelen and Lepore would assign truth-conditions (or that "semantically express a proposition") do not have context-independent truth-conditions in the view of the Moderate Contextualists. Instead the sentences have "propositional schemas" or "incomplete logical forms" or "semantic templates" etc. in the view of Carston (2002), Sperber and Wilson (1986), Recanati (1993, 2004), Kent Bach (1994*a*), Anne Bezuidenhout (2002), and Taylor (2001).

Cappelen and Lepore (2005: 8–9) believe that there are several strategies to being a Moderate Contextualist. One is being a Surprise Indexicalist, in which context-sensitivity is modeled on the semantics of indexical expressions. For example, David Lewis (1999*a*), DeRose (1999), and Cohen (1999) believe that knowledge attributions are context-sensitive in that evidential standards that may differ from context to context determine whether 'know' is correctly applied in the context.[5] The corresponding semantic claim is that 'know' is a context-sensitive lexical item, like 'I' and 'here'. The second strategy is being a Hidden Indexicalist. Hidden Indexicalists believe that in sentences like 'Fred is tall', the standard of height against which Fred is measured varies from context to context, from midgets to basketball players, so that Fred might be tall for

[5] The examples that provide the intuitive motivation for these views are, in my view, deeply flawed accounts of the linguistic use of 'know' sentences; see Atlas (2005*a*). Philosophers like A. P. Martinich believe in 'criteria of application' for statements—*uses* of a sentence—but not for sentences

a midget and short for a basketball player. Or a more personal standard might obtain, in which a speaker's height is taken as a standard for his assertions; anyone taller than I, I call 'tall'; anyone less tall than I, I call 'not tall'. On such a view, 'tall' is taken to mean 'taller than I', where 'I' is a "hidden indexical" that is not overt in my idiolect's item 'tall'. (I have problems taking 'for a midget' to be the values of an indexical 'for a N'—it's hard to believe that anybody, even a die-hard Contextualist, would say that 'for a N' is a linguistic indexical after a moment's reflection, but that is not to give aid and comfort to Lepore and Cappelen's view that 'tall' is not syncategorematic (Quine 1960: §27)—so I have used a real indexical in this explanation.) The third strategy is the Unarticulated Constituent strategy. The example offered is John Perry (1986) saying that 'It's raining' does not have truth-conditions unless it is treated as expressing 'It's raining at location ℓ', the proposition that is "semantically expressed in an utterance of the sentence" in a context providing a value for a location parameter $^{<}\ell^{>}$ (Cappelen and Lepore 2005: 9).

As a Meaning Dualist, I am a Pragmaticist that is not a Surprising Indexicalist, a Hidden Indexicalist, or an Unarticulated Constituent Contextualist.[6] Though I differ from Searle in the kind of contextualism we espouse, he in *certain* respects, Ruth Kempson (1975, 1988), and, notably enough, Noam Chomsky (1995, 1996) and J. J. Katz (2004) in his last years, are also Meaning Dualists; syntax and the lexicon matters to us. As I argued many years ago (1978*a*), semantical non-specificity presents a major theoretical problem for Davidsonian truth-theories as a theory of sense. The problem is best illustrated by a well-known paper of John McDowell (1976). The problem for McDowell in his Davidsonian days, and a continuing problem for Cappelen and Lepore, was the difficulty created by the semantical non-specificity of negative sentences of the form< The A is not B>. McDowell wrote:

> A theory of truth, serving as a theory of sense for a language, must show how to derive, for each indicative sentence of the language, a theorem of the form 's is true if and only if p', where what replaces 'p' in each case is . . . a sentence giving *the content of propositional acts* which speakers of the language can intelligibly be regarded as performing, or potentially performing, with *utterances* of the sentences designated by what replaces 's'. (1976: 50; my emphasis)

McDowell's (1976) formulation in terms of utterances—following Davidson's example—leads to mischief, as I explained (Atlas 1978*a*). The semantical non-specificity of the negative *sentence*, neutral in meaning between the predicate negation interpretation and the sentence negation interpretation of utterances (Atlas 1989: ch. 4; 2005b: ch. 6), means on McDowell's account that one ought to have as theorems (*a*) <the A is not B> is true if and only the A is not$_{\text{sentential}}$

6 As a Meaning Dualist, I am also a Literalist. I take levels of meaning seriously, in particular literal sentence-type (non-propositional) meaning and pragmatically inferred (propositional) statement-meaning. See Atlas (1989, 2005*b*).

B, and (*b*) <the A is not B> is true if and only if the A is not$_{\text{predicate}}$ B. But such biconditionals cannot be both derivable in an adequate theory; if they were, one could derive <the A is not$_{\text{sentential}}$ B if and only if the A is not$_{\text{predicate}}$ B>, which is absurd. So either McDowell's characterization of a truth-theory of a natural language is incorrect, or it is impossible to accommodate the semantical non-specificity of <the A is not B> in a truth-theory for a natural language, or in Cappelen and Lepore's terms, in a theory that attempts to specify recursively the "propositions semantically expressed" by sentences of a natural language.[7]

The deep irony is that Cappelen and Lepore are no better off than McDowell, since in their paradigm examples of Convention T they (Cappelen and Lepore 2005: 3) write:

(1) Any *utterance* of (1′)

(1′) Rudolf is a reindeer

is true just in case Rudolf is a reindeer, and expresses the proposition *that Rudolf is a reindeer.*

Likewise, they would have to say:

(2) Any *utterance* of S

(S) <the A is not B>

is true just in case the A is not B, and expresses the proposition *that the A is not B.*

Let us take the claim in its two parts: any utterance of <the A is not B> is true if and only if the A is not B. This claim is false; this is just not true of *any* utterance of <the A is not B>. An *utterance* of the sentence might express the sentence (exclusion) negation; it might express the predicate (choice) negation.[8] In neither case is *the utterance* true if and only if the A is not B, where the alleged "truth-condition" on the right-hand side of the biconditional is expressed by a semantically non-specific sentence of the meta-language.[9] Now consider the second part: any utterance of <the A is not B> expresses the proposition *that*

[7] The same argument can be run with other semantically non-specific examples besides the Atlas (1977) 'not' case, e.g. Searle's (1978) 'on' case 'The cat is on the mat', Atlas's (1989: 29–30; 2005: 31–2) 'with' case 'the girl with the flowers', the Bach (1982) 'too' case 'I love you too', the Sperber and Wilson (1986) possessive NP case 'Peter's bat' and similar possessive NP cases in Atlas (2005*b*: 19, 36, 85). I shall return to the possessive NP case below.

[8] The sentence-type expresses neither. See Kempson (1975), Atlas (1975, 1977, 1989, 2004, 2005*b*).

[9] (*a*) The semantically non-specific meta-language sentence is not a translation of the speaker's utterance-meaning designated on the left-hand side of the T-biconditional. (*b*) The semantically non-specific sentence does not have a truth-value or express determinate truth-conditions. (*c*) If (2) were, contrary to fact, correct as an account of a truth-theory, it would again prove the equivalence

the A is not B. Evaluating this claim is problematic, because one would have to know more about Cappelen and Lepore's notion of proposition than they tell us at this early stage of their book. One thing we know about their notion of proposition, though, is that it carries a truth-value. The definite description 'the proposition *that the A is not B*' is not, in the case of a semantically non-specific negative sentence <the A is not B>, a proper description. There is no unique entity described by 'the proposition *that the A is not B*'; there is no such unique proposition, since the unambiguous, semantically non-specific expression-type 'the A is not B' does not express the content either of the exclusion negation or of the choice negation proposition; there is more than one proposition that 'the A is not B' is capable of unambiguously expressing, and the description-predicate '*x* is a proposition *that the A is not B*' will apply equally well, unambiguously and non-uniquely, to the exclusion negation proposition and to the choice negation proposition.

Cappelen and Lepore (2005: 2–3) land in this difficulty since they characterize "the semantic content of a sentence S [as] the proposition that *all* utterances of S express (when we adjust for or keep stable the semantic values of the obvious context-sensitive expressions in S)" (my emphasis), where by context-sensitive expressions they mean the indexicals and demonstratives. They repeat this formulation (ibid. 143) when they write:

> The idea motivating Semantic Minimalism is simple and obvious: The semantic content of a sentence is the content that *all* utterances of S *share*. It is the content that *all* utterances of S *express* no matter how different their contexts of utterance are. It is also the content that can be *grasped and reported* by someone who is *ignorant* about the relevant characteristics *of the context* in which an utterance of S took place. (My emphasis)

The question is whether in the three sentences just quoted they have given three different but co-extensive criteria for what the semantic content of a sentence is. One might argue that the first two sentences give two, non-coextensive characterizations of semantic content. *Shared* content is not the same as *context-independent* content any more than *shared* blue-eyes, i.e. there being blue eyes that, by accident, every boy's girlfriend has (as in *Every boy loves a blue-eyed girl*) is the same as *boy-independent* blue-eyes, there being a blue-eyed girl who is loved by each boy (as in *There is a blue-eyed girl who is loved by every boy*). The third sentence introduces a notion of content that is epistemically context-independent but attributer-dependent and expressed by the complement clauses of indirect discourse sentences <*x* said that *P*>.

The problem is compounded by their claim that *all* utterances must posses the criterial property. Cappelen and Lepore (2005: 54–7) criticize Kaplan (1989), Davidson (1984), McDowell (1987), et al. for their Mistaken Assumption

of the exclusion and choice negation utterance-meanings—a *reductio ad absurdum* of the form of the truth-theory of (2).

that a semantic theory must be anchored in speaker intuitions about "what is said (claimed, stated, asserted)". But Cappelen and Lepore seem to make a parallel mistake in this formulation, that a semantic theory must be anchored in intuitions about "what *all* utterances of a sentence *share* (express, make graspable and reportable)", what in this incautious formulation employing 'express' and 'reportable' I will dub the Least Common Denominator Mistake (or the Lockean Abstraction Mistake). They have a different and better formulation, which I discuss later and which brings Cappelen and Lepore into the framework typical of Searle and Grice. I shall discuss Minimal Propositions again below.

For them the context-sensitive expressions are the grammatically overt ones, the indexicals and demonstratives. Context-sensitivity requires an overt morphosyntactic element in a sentence. "[T]he proposition semantically expressed" by an utterance of the sentence depends contextually on no more than the semantic values of the overt indexicals and demonstratives in the context of utterance. Sentences have semantic contents modulo the values of the indexical and demonstrative parameters.[10] They think that Radical Contextualism is absurd and that if you accept the arguments in support of Moderate Contextualism, the same arguments lead to Radical Contextualism, so that the former position collapses into the latter.[11] Their strategy is to examine the arguments offered by the supporters of Moderate Contextualism and show why those arguments would lead to Radical Contextualism. Cappelen and Lepore see the origin of one type of argument offered by the Contextualists—the Context Shifting Argument, a primary case of which is an allegedly contextually determined shift in the domain of quantification of a quantified Noun Phase—in a view of semantics in which a semantic theory's task is to *assign to each utterance of a sentence a proposition* (or truth-conditions) as its content, where its semantic content is the speech-act content of the utterance. And not only Contextualists make this assumption about semantic theory; so do Kaplan (1989), Davidson (1984), Larson and Ludlow (1993: 334), and McDowell (1987). This assumption about semantic theory is what, more precisely, they call 'the Mistaken Assumption'.[12]

[10] Cappelen and Lepore never talk about the literal meanings of sentences; they always talk about the "semantic content" of a sentence in terms of the "proposition semantically expressed", or the "truth-conditions" of the utterance.

[11] As I have said, the only person I know who comes even close to being a Radical Contextualist is Robyn Carston, and for her it is a bit of a pose—that is not a pejorative: it has the merit of being unboring. So I don't think there are any "official" Radical Contextualists, not that that diminishes the force of Cappelen and Lepore's arguments. They think that Moderate Contextualism is "unstable" and slides by virtue of its arguments down into the abyss (or to use a more scientific metaphor, the potential well) of Radical Contextualism. For me that makes their argument more interesting, since no one is "really" a Radical Contextualist intentionally.

[12] Cappelen and Lepore (2005: 3, 57) tend to think of the semantic content of a sentence as the proposition that *all* utterances of the sentence express (somehow adjusting for the variations in the values of the indexical and demonstrative expressions), or what the utterances "have in common". But whatever the semantic content is, it is obviously not the same as some "lowest

The proper response of Meaning Dualists to Semantic Minimalism is the response I gave to McDowell and Davidson in Atlas (1978*a*). Truth-theories for natural language, whether formulated by McDowell, Davidson, or Cappelen and Lepore, cannot entail true T-sentences for semantically non-specific sentences of a language if the theory takes the forms that McDowell, Davidson, Cappelen and Lepore have required.

2. INCOMPLETENESS ARGUMENTS OF THE MODERATE CONTEXTUALISTS

Cappelen and Lepore (2005: 33–7) review data and arguments from a number of sources the point of which is to support the view that there are sentences that as they stand are "semantically incomplete" in that something—a missing argument (Bach 1997: 228)—must be added to the sentence for it to express a complete and determinate proposition (Bach 1994b). The examples they cite are:

(3) a. It's raining. (Taylor 2001: 53, Perry 1993: 206)
b. Steel isn't strong enough. (Bach 1994*b*: 269)
c. Peter's bat is gray. (Sperber and Wilson 1986: 188)
d. There's no beer left. (Bezuidenhout 2002: 112–13)
e. Fred is ready. (Bach 1997: 228)
f. Jerry has finished. (Bach 1997: 228)
g. John is tall. (Bach 1997: 228)
h. Peter believes that Paderewski the pianist had musical talent. (Bach 1997: 230)

Thus, on the Contextualists' views, to have determinate truth-conditions, these sentences must be understood to express thoughts like the following:

a′. It's raining at Stanford.
b′. Steel isn't strong enough for repelling a uranium-tipped shell.
Steel isn't strong enough to keep the World Trade Towers from collapsing.
c′. The bat that Peter owns is gray.
d′. There's no beer left in the fridge.
There's no non-alcoholic beer left . . .

common denominator" of the various speech-act contents of utterances of the sentence in various contexts. More on this below.

e′. Fred is ready to roll.
Fred is ready for {running, his run}.

f′. Jerry has finished the exam.

g′. John is tall for a Dutchman.

h′. Peter believes that Paderewski the classical pianist playing Mozart had musical talent.

The sentences are conceptually incomplete without being rephrased (expanded). 'It's raining' must be rephrased 'It's raining AT LOCATION'; 'Steel isn't strong enough' must be rephrased 'Steel isn't strong enough {FOR V-*ing*, TO VP}'; 'There's no beer left' must be rephrased 'There's no beer left PREP PHRASE' or 'There's no $_{\text{NP}}$ [. . . beer]$_{\text{NP}}$ left'; 'Fred is ready' must be rephrased 'Fred is ready {TO V, FOR V-*ing*, FOR NP}; 'Jerry has finished' must be rephrased 'Jerry has finished NP'; 'John is tall' must be rephrased 'John is tall FOR AN N'; 'Peter believes that Paderewski the pianist had musical talent' must be rephrased 'Peter believes that Paderewski the ADJ pianist V-*ing* NP had musical talent'; and finally, 'Peter's bat is gray' must be rephrased by 'The bat V-*ed* by Peter is gray'. I do not believe that these examples constitute a natural linguistic kind. It seems obvious that 'It's raining', 'There's no beer left', and 'Jerry has finished' occupy one class, that 'enough', 'tall', and 'ready' occupy another class, that 'Peter's bat is gray' is a separate type, and the belief sentence is yet another.

I wish to discuss the 'Peter's bat is gray' example, since for the purposes of the arguments of this chapter it is more germane. The traditional analysis for the possessive NP is that the difference among 'owning', 'choosing', etc. as interpretations of the possessive amounts to an ambiguity of the NP, as in Chomsky (1972). Then later G. N. Leech (1974, 1990) held that the logical form of the sentence should make an existential claim that there is some relation *R* between Peter and the bat. Kay and Zimmer (1976) and Recanati (1989) took the same view as Leech. Sperber and Wilson (1986: 188) say that the NP is "incomplete" rather than ambiguous, which I thought might be a consequence of what I meant by semantical non-specificity, but I was never absolutely sure whether Wilson would accept this, because of the Gricean principle that had they meant 'semantical non-specificity' they should have said 'non-specific' rather than 'incomplete'. (I never understood what the appropriate Relevance Theoretic analysis of this sentence of Sperber and Wilson's should be.) In the passage in question, Sperber and Wilson (1986: 188) also use 'incomplete' to describe expressions like 'too gray', inviting the completion 'too gray for wearing on an Easter bonnet', and expressions like 'big', inviting the completion 'big for a fruit fly'. For these reasons I put a speech-act theorist like Kent Bach and Sperber and Wilson in one camp as Completeness (conceptual ellipsis) analysts. Though I had never discussed the case in depth, I mentioned my view that the possessive NP was semantically non-specific in Atlas (2005*b*:

85). The following are distinct analyses of a sentence with a possessive (genitive) NP: (*a*) it is ambiguous (Chomsky); (*b*) it is univocal but logically an existential, so expresses a specific but weak proposition (Leech); (*c*) it is semantically non-specific (Atlas); (*d*) it is an "incomplete" proposition, and so conceptually—not syntactically—elliptical (Bach, Sperber and Wilson). Note that analyses (a)—(c) are logical and linguistic analyses. The Completion analysis of (d) is neither. It trades entirely on intuitions about "conceptual content", "propositions", "what is said", "what is said literally", "what is said strictly speaking", et al.

3. WHAT IS SAID

The success of the last analysis relies on the intuitive coherence of the commonsense concept of "what is said". Searle, Travis, Bach, Recanati, Carston, Sperber and Wilson and interested parties have argued fiercely with each other about what is said by 'what is said'. For a discussion of most of the arguments about the application of the concept of "what is said", see Levinson (2000: 165–98, esp. p. 195). To give you some idea of the issues, I shall quote a long passage from Levinson (2000: 194–5), interspersed with commentary, so please be patient:

> Some want to retain Grice's label "what is said" with a narrow application, so that it corresponds to a semantic representation, disambiguated with indexicals resolved, but not necessarily yet expressing any determinate proposition (Bach 1994[*a*]: 144). Others want to expand the notion to cover something much broader, closer to the everyday concept of "what is stated" [*Atlas*: And just what everyday concept is that? The "acceptable" substituends of a sentence S in the complement of *x said that*... in any context you like?]; on this account, any kind of pragmatic resolution or implicatural strengthening up to a level corresponding to a conscious, commonsensical notion of what has been claimed [*Atlas*: Oh, another of those nicely behaved common-sense notions "what has been claimed"!] counts as "what is said" [*Atlas*: Well, now that makes "what is said" a transparently clear notion!] (Recanati 1989). On this account [generalized conversational implicata] belong entirely to the domain of "what is said" (for response, see Horn 1992a, b). Some have tried to isolate out the middle ground between what is given by the semantic representation, perhaps after disambiguation and indexical resolution on the one hand, and full-blown Gricean implicatures on the other hand. Thus Sperber and Wilson (1986) call explicatures the informational enrichments of semantic representations necessary to achieve not only minimal propositions but also ones of sufficient informational content to count as conversational contributions (thus "Fixing your watch will take some time" expresses a proposition, but one too vacuous as it stands to count as the proposition expressed). On this account, [generalized conversational implicata] are explicatures and lie outside the scope of a theory of implicature (which was I think the intention). Carston (1988) has tried to clarify this view, suggesting that the notion "implicature" should be reserved for propositions that are not in any way enrichments of what is said but rather "functionally unrelated" (see Recanati 1989 for

critique). Bach (1994[*a*]) offers the new term 'impliciture' (with an *i*) for the middle ground but he views this in a different way, covering only completions and expansions of the semantic content that are in line with the structure of the sentence (and, as mentioned, pragmatic resolutions of indexicals and ambiguities count for him not as implicatures but as what is said.)

As for the attempts by Relevance Theorists to clarify their notion of "explicature", Levinson (2000: 195–6) mentions six different suggestions by Sperber and Wilson, Carston, and Recanati to explain what an "explicature" is, with Recanati finishing up with the view that, to quote Levinson (2000: 196), "explicatures correspond to a pretheoretical intuition about what a speaker said (Recanati 1993: 246–50)". Thus, we are back where we began, with the so-called common-sense notion of "what is said".[13]

In 1972, when I was a mere child, I found Paul Ziff's (1972*b*) worries about the coherence of the notion of "what is said" impressive and distressing. Ziff concluded his essay as follows:

> The factors that serve to determine what is said, in every sense of that phrase, appear to constitute a hopelessly unmanageable motley. And even if one ignores what is said by implication, the factors serving to determine what is said (in the other senses of the phrase) still appear to be discouragingly disparate and complex. Linguistic, logical, psychological and perceptual factors are all evidently active and interactive. All such factors appear to function as vectors, but what the magnitudes or directions or senses of the different vectors are it is at present impossible to say. There is a cheerless moral to be drawn from all this: One may have a firm grasp of the phonology, morphology, syntax, and semantics of a language, thus a thorough knowledge of the language, and not understand what is said in that language. But who would have thought otherwise? (1972*c*: 38)

Well, it seems, lots of people younger than Ziff in 1972 have since thought otherwise. Whether they were wiser than he is not at all obvious, at least not

[13] Levinson (2000: 196–8) then does yeoman's work in sorting out these suggestions and comparing the Contextualist/Indexicalist approach, initiated by the work of Kaplan (1989) on demonstratives and the Situation Semantics of Barwise and Perry (1983), with the competing Radical Pragmatics paradigm of Atlas and Levinson (1981), Horn (1984), Levinson (2000), and Atlas (2005*b*), which provide an alternative linguistic explanation of the data by appeal to semantical non-specificity and pragmatic Informativeness inferences that narrow or enrich the semantic representations of expression-types in the semantic interpretations of their utterances in context.

To the extent that Cappelen and Lepore succeed in their objections to indexicalist analyses, they are supporting Levinson's critique and providing further reasons why one should take Radical Pragmatics—a form of Meaning Dualism—seriously as a theoretical alternative to Relevance Theory and philosophical Contextualism. To that end, Cappelen and Lepore's ch. 6 "Digressions: Binding and Hidden Indexicals" is a notable criticism of syntactic arguments offered by Stanley (2000) and Stanley and Szabó (2000) to support the indexicality of quantifier domains. Cappelen and Lepore (2005: 79) conclude, "If we are right, the analogy between hidden indexicals referring to contextually salient domains and ordinary overt indexicals breaks down. But if Kaplan is right about the semantics and epistemology of indexicals, it follows that Stanley and Szabó (2000) must be wrong." Cappelen and Lepore (1997, 2002*a*, *b*) have themselves moved in Levinson's Pragmatic direction, as they note (2005: 71).

obvious to me. For Ziffian reasons I cannot find it in my heart to trust the Contextualists' intuitions about the Incompleteness of "what is said" anymore than Cappelen and Lepore (2005: 60 ff) can. Likewise I never found it in my heart to trust Grice's intuitions about a special concept of "what is said", which he intended as an expression of the truth-conditions of the literal meaning of a sentence-token being used to make as flat a statement as disambiguation and the assignment of values to indexicals, demonstratives, and tense markers would permit. As I made clear in Atlas (1979) and (1978*b*), Grice's notion of "what is said" played no privileged role in my theory. Literal senses of sentences did play a role. Inferences from those literal senses and from collateral information in a context of utterance all contributed. The difference between me and the Relevance Theorists in the 1980s was in the nature of the inferential machinery to which we appealed in our theories: mine was a non-monotonic "inference to the best interpretation" (Atlas and Levinson 1981); that of the Relevance Theorists (Sperber and Wilson 1986) was monotonic deductive reasoning. Mine included my and Levinson's (1981) revision of Grice's Maxims; Relevance theorists appealed to their Principle of Relevance: getting the most logical content for the processing dollar. But my attitude to "what is said" meant that I remained silent during the intense debates catalogued by Levinson (2000: 195) and briefly described above. It was not relevant to my theory of utterance-interpretation.

Cappelen and Lepore's last chapter 13, "Speech Act Pluralism", is in effect an extended meditation on the implications of Paul Ziff's (1972*c*) essay "What is Said". In addition, their 8th Speech Act Pluralism Principle (p. 204), "Against Grice: For those engaged in 'semantic vs. pragmatics' talk: sayings and implicatures are both on the pragmatic side of the divide", is just the point made by Levinson (1988, 2000) in his concept of "pragmatic intrusion" into "what is said". The following remark of Cappelen and Lepore (2005: 204) could have been quoted from Levinson: "The very same contextual features that determine the implicatures of an utterance influence what speakers say and assert by that utterance." The same point was made by Jerrold Katz (1972) and Ralph Walker (1975) thirty years ago.

4. MINIMAL PROPOSITIONS AND THE PROBLEM OF OTHER TALKING MINDS

According to Kent Bach (1994*a*, *b*), or a Relevance Theorist like Robyn Carston (1988), sentences like (3b) *Steel isn't strong enough* and (3c) *Peter's bat is gray* (which becomes in Cappelen and Lepore (2005: 61, ex. 3) *Peter's book is gray*), do not, independently of a context, express "complete" propositions; the sentences do not have truth-values. Cappelen and Lepore ask what makes the sentences incomplete. They remark that, apart from "brute intuitions", the Contextualists say only that the sentence does not say for what is the steel strong enough, and that the possessive does not say what the relationship is between Peter and the bat/book, i.e. what does being "his" consist in? As contrasted with this position, Cappelen and Lepore suggest that the sentences express Minimal Propositions, *that steel isn't strong enough* and *that Peter's bat/book is gray*, that are true if and only if: (i) steel isn't strong enough, and (ii) Peter's bat/book is gray.

Cappelen and Lepore (2005: 181) believe that "there is a minimal semantic content or proposition that is semantically expressed by (almost) every utterance of a well-formed English sentence. This proposition is a full-blooded proposition with truth-conditions and a truth-value. This is a substantive disagreement about the metaphysics of content."[14] Second, they claim that the "minimal semantic content has a function in the cognitive life of communicators that no other content can serve". Third, they think minimal semantic content "has a psychological role that no other 'level of content' can fill". Fourth, they think that "theories that do not recognize minimal semantic content are empirically inadequate and internally inconsistent". (They emphasize one further difference, but it is not relevant here.) So if a speaker says, "Steel isn't strong enough", Cappelen and Lepore should and would (I bet) find it compelling that the speaker's utterance can be reported in indirect discourse by the sentence 'Fred said that steel isn't strong enough' without one's feeling that the indirect discourse sentence is elliptical or incomplete. Further, if Fred and Chuck both uttered 'Steel isn't strong enough' on two occasions, one could report by an indirect discourse sentence that Fred and Chuck said that steel isn't strong enough (Cappelen and Lepore 2005: 184–5). Similarly, if a speaker says, "Peter's bat is gray", one may report it by saying that the speaker said that Peter's bat is gray and not merely by saying in direct discourse "The speaker said 'Peter's bat is gray'." The objects of indirect discourse verbs are terms referring to the content of what the speaker said, i.e. for Cappelen and Lepore, to propositions. On their view the proposition that Peter's bat is gray is the proposition semantically expressed by *any* utterance of the sentence 'Peter's bat is gray'. So for Cappelen and Lepore there is a proposition that Peter's bat is gray. It has the property of any respectable proposition; it has truth-conditions; the proposition that Peter's bat is gray is true if and only if Peter's bat is gray. As they (2005: 158) say, "That's it. That's the whole semantic story."

They also assert, importantly for their position, that "the proposition semantically expressed is our minimal defense against confusion, misunderstanding, mistakes and it is that which guarantees communication across contexts of utterance (ibid. 185)." It may not be the speaker's intended utterance-meaning; it may not be the addressee's interpretation of the speaker's utterance. But, as for Grice, it is a public, mutually comprehensible, and inter-subjective semantic entity

[14] These claims about the propositional character of content seem to clash with the earlier claim (ibid. 3 n. 3) that the authors shall remain neutral "on whether semantic content is a proposition".

that speakers, addressees, and audiences can all have easy access to. Cappelen and Lepore (2005: 185–6) notably remark, "Knowledge that this proposition was semantically expressed provides the audience with the *best possible* access to the speaker's mind, given the restricted knowledge they have of that speaker." Knowing what the speaker semantically expressed, the addressee can "infer that there's work to be done in order to figure out exactly what the speaker was trying to communicate". That was also the mechanism for an addressee's thinking that the speaker was trying to conversationally implicate something *à la* Grice from the truth-conditions of Grice's "what was said".

In "Literal Meaning" (Searle 1979: 119–20) John Searle made a point of arguing that the literal meaning of a sentence-token in a context was just the literal meaning of its type. The filling-in of values for referential expressions, e.g. indexicals, demonstratives, and tense markers, in the sentence-token was determined by the senses of the indexicals, demonstratives, and tense markers in the sentence-type. Once filled in, the evaluated item was no longer the same sentence entity; if uttered assertorically by a speaker with the intention that those expressions should take those values, the sentence-token was a statement or assertion whose utterance-meaning happened to coincide with the sentence-token meaning. The sentence type/token distinction is not the same as the sentence-meaning/speaker's utterance-meaning distinction. The notion of sentence-token meaning is close to what Grice wanted for his notion of "what is said". Cappelen and Lepore's notion of minimal proposition is also close to Searle's notion of sentence-token meaning. Searle distinguishes sentence-token meaning from speaker's utterance-meaning, just as Cappelen and Lepore distinguish "semantic content literally expressed by a sentence" from a speaker's "speech-act content".

There has been a lot of agitation by Carston (1988, 2002) and Recanati (2001, 2004) and others about sentence-token meaning not having "psychological reality" and not playing a role in the understanding of utterances. Since for Searle sentence-token meanings are not speaker's utterance-meanings anyway, this claim is a truism for him. For Atlas, as for Chomsky, sentence-type meanings are inputs to the Performance System, where all kinds of contextual information and inferencing result in an interpretation of the utterance. But whether in the Performance System some process of interpretation takes a sentence-type meaning and produces a contextually determined sentence-token meaning as part of utterance-interpretation is a psycholinguistic question that as a philosopher I am not equipped to decide, and I don't think that Carston or Recanati can decide it. Grice and Cappelen and Lepore cannot decide that question either, but they like to think that they can save communication from the *Problem of Other Talking Minds*. Grice's "what is said" and Cappelen and Lepore's Minimal Propositions give everybody knowledge of the speaker's mind, as they put it; at least, it is that part of the speaker's mind in which his knowledge of his idiolect and his expectations about the idiolect of his addressee make him believe that he is publicly committed to a mutually understood content merely by virtue of his saying the sentence.

5. SPEECH ACT PLURALISM

On the other hand Cappelen and Lepore's speech act pluralism implies that there are as many propositions "said" by an utterance as there are contents of acceptable, "intuitively accurate" indirect discourse reports of the utterance of the sentence (p. 197).[15] That's a lot of diverse contents! Then, of all people, Recanati (2004: 92–3) hauls back from this prodigality and proposes that "normal" interpreters know the truth-conditions of utterances and that this knowledge can be elicited in psycholinguistic laboratories by eye-tracking verification experiments. (See work by psycholinguist Michael Tannenhaus and semanticist Martin Hackl and their students Natalie Klein, Lucas Koehler, Jorie Koster-Moeller, and Jason Varvoutis among others.) Then Cappelen and Lepore (2005: 198–9) make a number of sensible and serious methodological points about what kind of utterance-interpretation is the appropriate one in the experiments, how the experimental pictures are interpreted before the matching task with sentences is begun, and how to characterize utterances other than simple assertions. Yet there is a point to Recanati's horror at the prodigality of speech-act propositions expressed. Cappelen and Lepore are willing to bite this bullet, when they write (p. 206):

> We don't think successful communication is easy. On our view, any utterance succeeds in expressing an indefinite number of propositions. One of these, the proposition semantically expressed, is easy to grasp. Others are extremely hard to access and there is no reason to think that any *one* person can ever grasp all that was said by an utterance, not even the speaker. This is how Semantic Minimalism combined with Speech Act Pluralism can account for both the sense in which communication is easy and the sense in which it is impossibly difficult.

Give the admitted freedom and flexibility of paraphrase that is allowable in indirect discourse reports of what someone said, including what Thales of Miletus once (allegedly) said, that everything is made of water, which might be paraphrased as "everything is H_2O", one can be quite sure that Thales would never have understood what he had allegedly said. One could adopt a view by which no one ever understands what he or she says "in its totality", but why bother with totalities? Cappelen and Lepore are not nineteenth-century Hegelians, after all. Their view just seems a Pickwickian position whose consequence is that communication is "impossible". Well, the beginning of a transcendental argument is the premise: communication is possible. The conclusion: there is a limitation on Cappelen and Lepore's speech act pluralism that they have not managed to delineate.

There is no proposition, minimal or otherwise, expressed by the sentence-type/sentence-token meaning (not meaning*s*) of this semantically non-specific

[15] Searle (1979) would deny that utterances, as contrasted with speakers, ever "say" anything.

sentence. If one talks of propositions, one does not get a truth-theory for semantically non-specific sentences like 'Peter's bat is gray'. If Cappelen and Lepore talk of utterances of sentences expressing propositions, do they mean 'proposition expressed by' by 'utterance of', so that an utterance of a sentence expressing a proposition is merely a proposition expressed by a sentence expressing a proposition? Or are they, as I fear, in the grip of their own version of the Davidsonian Mistaken Assumption they accuse Davidson, McDowell, Kaplan, Ludlow, and Larson of making?

6. CONCLUSIONS: MEANING DUALISM AND ITS RELATIONSHIP TO MINIMALISM-PLURALISM

Meaning Dualists like Jay Atlas (1974, 1975, 1977, 1978*a*, 1979), Ruth Kempson (1975, 1988), Noam Chomsky (1995, 1996), and Jerry Katz (2004)[16] are context-dependentialists. For a large class of sentences (especially semantically non-specific ones), their literal meanings express no truth-evaluable contents (propositions), have no logical forms representing them, and have no determinate truth-conditions. They are semantically underdeterminate, not merely semantically underdetermined as in some of the cases discussed by Relevance Theorists (see Atlas 2005*b*). But the literal meaning of the sentence-token, when uttered in contexts where collateral information allows speakers, addressees, and audiences to make inferences to the best interpretation (Atlas and Levinson 1981), constrains the construction of semantically specific speakers' or addressees' or audiences' Utterance Interpretations. To that extent my view now resembles later aspects of Searle, Travis, Bach, Sperber and Wilson, Carston, Recanati, and Bezuidenhout's Relevance Theoretic or contextualist views. Meaning Dualists are not Propositionalists about literal meaning and so are not Minimal Propositionalists like Cappelen and Lepore.

Though they are context-dependentialists, Meaning Dualists are not Indexicalists. They do not believe that indexicals are the only, or even the most theoretically important, model for context-sensitivity any more than they believe that the relationship of a Proper Name to its referent is the only, or even the most theoretically important, model for reference. They do not even think that Proper Names behave like "Proper Names"; some of the complexities were discussed years ago by Tyler Burge (1973) and Paul Ziff (1977). In Atlas (1978*a*) I showed why semantical non-specificity was inconsistent with Indexical Semantics' accounts of meaning, for example, with Montague's, Kaplan's and

[16] Sometimes the following seem to slip over into Meaning Dualism, perhaps without intending to: Stephen Levinson (2000) and Larry Horn (1989), and then, more speculatively: time-slices of Kent Bach (1982, 1987), of Robyn Carston (1988, 2002), of François Recanati (1993), and Corinne Iten (1998, 2005). Maybe even Deirdre Wilson?

Stalnaker's use of the concept "character of a sentence". So in being critical of Indexicalists, Meaning Dualists are like Cappelen and Lepore.

Meaning Dualists are intensionalists. Their views are unlike those of Wittgenstein, Travis, and generally unlike those of speech-act theorists and Relevance theorists whose sole focus is a theory of speaker's utterance-meaning. They, like Chomsky, take seriously the output of the syntax and the lexicon. They agree with John Searle (1978, 1979) when he said that sentence-tokens have the literal meaning of their sentence-types, that speaker's utterance-meaning is not the same as sentence-token meaning. Thus Meaning Dualists reject the Wittgensteinian versions, like John McDowell's, of Donald Davidson's view of a theory of truth for a natural language. Just as Cappelen and Lepore say, those views tend to incorporate the Mistaken Assumption, which is, as Cappelen and Lepore put it, a view of semantics in which a semantic theory's task is to *assign to each utterance of a sentence a proposition* (or truth-conditions) as its content, where its semantic content is *the speech-act content* of the utterance. In this respect, Meaning Dualists are like Grice, who was equally critical of Wittgenstein and Austin's version of the Mistaken Assumption, though unlike Grice they do not believe, as Grice did and Recanati (2004) does, that there is a theoretically interesting notion of "what is said" that is intuitively available to a "normal interpreter", as Recanati puts it. Grice, less satisfied with intuition than Recanati, identifies "what is said" with a notion of the truth-conditions of the literal meaning of a sentence-token that has Cappelen and Lepore's Basic Set of indexical, demonstrative, and tense elements evaluated in the context in which the token is uttered.

There is much to admire in Cappelen and Lepore's criticism of "village contextualism", including Indexicalism. If they had talked of meaningful sentences instead of propositions, they could have avoided some of the difficulties that I have discussed. Their notion of a Minimal Proposition is a notion much more restricted in its applicability than their claim (2005: 181), that "there is a minimal semantic content or proposition that is semantically expressed by (almost) every utterance of a well-formed English sentence", suggests, assuming that the notion of utterance is not vacuously characterized as an expressed proposition.

If they had been less enthusiastic about the use of indirect discourse reports of speech acts to determine the contents of the speech act, they might have constrained their Speech Act Pluralism to something epistemically plausible. Contextual dependency has other forms than Radical and Moderate Contextualism as they understand it. Meaning Dualism, which is a post-Gricean Pragmatics (Atlas 2005*b*), is an alternative. But I cavil. One is grateful for an acute, stimulating, even provocative, imaginative, and vigorously—not to say enthusiastically—argued essay on a central contemporary problem in the philosophy of language.[17]

[17] I am indebted to Kent Bach, Kasia Jaszczolt, AP Martinich, and two anonymous referees. They saved me from several errors, of style, substance, and interpretation. Even more than usual. I am grateful to playwright and poet John Francis Walter.

REFERENCES

Atlas, J. D. (1974), 'Presupposition, Ambiguity, and Generality: A Coda to the Russell–Strawson Debate on Referring', TS, Department of Philosophy, Pomona College, Claremont, Calif.

—— (1975), 'Frege's Polymorphous Concept of Presupposition and its Role in a Theory of Meaning', *Semantikos*, 1: 29–44.

—— (1977), 'Negation, Ambiguity, and Presupposition', *Linguistics and Philosophy*, 1: 321–36.

—— (1978*a*), 'On Presupposing', *Mind*, 87: 396–41.

—— (1978*b*), 'Presupposition and Grice's Pragmatics', Colloquium Lecture, Department of Phonetics and Linguistics, University College, London. May.

—— (1979), 'How Linguistics Matter to Philosophy: Presupposition, Truth, and Meaning', in D. Dinneen and C. K. Oh (eds.), *Syntax and Semantics, 11. Presupposition*, pp. 256–81. New York: Academic Press.

—— (1989), *Philosophy without Ambiguity.* Oxford: Clarendon Press.

—— (2004), 'Presupposition', in L. R. Horn and G. Ward (eds.), *The Handbook of Pragmatics*, pp. 29–52. Oxford: Blackwell.

—— (2005*a*), 'Comments on Jason Stanley's "Against Knowledge Relativism"', at Syntax and Semantics with Attitude: a conference, University of Southern California, Los Angeles, Calif. 16–17 April.

—— (2005*b*), *Logic, Meaning, and Conversation: Semantical Underdeterminacy, Implicature and their Interface.* New York: Oxford University Press.

—— and S. C. Levinson, (1981), '*It*-Clefts, Informativeness, and Logical Form: An Introduction to Radically Radical Pragmatics', in P. Cole (ed.), *Radical Pragmatics*, pp. 1–61. New York: Academic Press.

Bach, K. (1982), 'Semantic Nonspecificity and Mixed Quantifiers', *Linguistics and Philosophy*, 4: 593–605.

—— (1987), *Thought and Reference.* Oxford: Clarendon Press.

—— (1994*a*), 'Conversational Impliciture', *Mind and Language*, 9: 124–62.

—— (1994*b*), 'Semantic Slack: What is Said and More', in S. Tsohatzidis (ed.), *Foundations of Speech Act Theory*, pp. 267–91. London: Routledge.

—— (1997), 'Do Belief Reports Report Beliefs?', *Pacific Philosophical Quarterly*, 78: 215–41.

—— (2005), 'Context Ex Machina', in Z. Szabó (ed.), *Semantics Versus Pragmatics*, pp. 15–44. Oxford: Clarendon Press.

Barwise, J., and J. Perry (1983), *Situations and Attitudes.* Cambridge, Mass.: MIT Press.

Bezuidenhout, A. (2002), 'Truth-Conditional Pragmatics', *Philosophical Perspectives*, 16: 105–34.

Burge, T. (1973), 'Reference and Proper Names', *Journal of Philosophy*, 70: 425–39.

Cappelen, H., and E. Lepore (1997), 'On an Alleged Connection between Indirect Quotation and Semantic Theory', *Mind and Language*, 12: 278–96.

—— and —— (2002*a*), 'Indexicality, Binding, Anaphora and a Priori Truth', *Analysis* (Oct.): 271–81.

—— and —— (2002*b*), 'Insensitive Quantifiers', in J. Campbell, M. O'Rourke, and D. Shier (eds.), *Meaning and Truth: Investigating Philosophical Semantics*, pp. 197–213. New York: Seven Bridges Press.

—— and —— (2005), *Insensitive Semantics: A Defense of Semantic Minimalism and Speech Act Pluralism*. Oxford: Blackwell.

Carlson, G., and F. J. Pelletier, (eds.) (1995), *The Generic Book*. Chicago: University of Chicago Press.

Carston, R. (1988), 'Implicature, Explicature, and Truth-Theoretic Semantics', in R. Kempson (ed.), *Mental Representations: The Interface between Language and Reality*, pp. 155–81. Cambridge: University Press.

—— (2002), *Thoughts and Utterances: The Pragmatics of Explicit Communication*. Oxford: Blackwell.

Chomsky, N. (1972), 'Deep Structure, Semantic Structure, and Surface Interpretation', in Chomsky, *Studies on Semantics in Generative Grammar*, pp. 62–119. The Hague: Mouton.

—— (1995), 'Language and Nature', *Mind*, 104: 1–61.

—— (1996), 'Language and Thought: Some Reflections on Venerable Themes', in Chomsky, *Powers and Prospects: Reflections on Human Nature and the Social Order*, pp. 1–30. Boston: South End Press.

Cohen, S. (1999), 'Contextualism, Skepticism, and the Structure of Reasons', *Philosophical Perspectives*, 13: 57–89.

Davidson, D. (1984), 'On Saying That', in Davidson, *Inquiries into Truth and Interpretation*, pp. 93–108. Oxford: Clarendon Press.

DeRose, K. (1999), 'Contextualism: An Explanation and Defense', in J. Greco and E. Sosa (eds.), *The Blackwell Guide to Epistemology*, pp. 187–205. Oxford: Blackwell.

Horn, L. R. (1984), 'Toward a New Taxonomy for Pragmatic Inference: Q-Based and R-Based Implicature', in D. Schiffrin (ed.), *Georgetown University Round Table on Languages and Linguistics 1984. Meaning, Form, and Use in Context: Linguistic Applications*, pp. 11–42. Washington, DC: Georgetown University Press.

—— (1989), *A Natural History of Negation*, Chicago: University of Chicago Press.

—— (1992*a*), 'Pragmatics, Implicature, and Presupposition', in W. Bright *International Ercyclopedia of Linguistics*, i. 260–6. Oxford: Oxford University Press.

—— (1992*b*), 'The Said and the Unsaid', *SALT II: Proceedings of the Second Conference on Semantics and Lingisistic Theory*, pp. 163–92. Columbus: Ohio State University Linguistics Department.

Iten, C. (1998), 'Because and Although: A Case of Duality?', in V. Rouchota and A. H. Jucker (eds.), *Current Issues in Relevance Theory*, pp. 59–80. Amsterdam: John Benjamins.

—— (2005), *Lingustic Meaning, Truth Conditions, and Relevance: The Case of Concessives*. Houndmills: Palgrave Macmillan.

Kaplan, D. (1989), 'Afterthoughts', in J. Almog, J. Perry, and H. Wettstein (eds.), *Themes from Kaplan*, pp. 565–614. New York: Oxford University Press.

Katz, J. J. (1972), *Semantic Theory*. New York: Harper Row.

—— (1981), 'Literal Meaning and Logical Theory', *Journal of Philosophy*, 78: 203–33.

—— (2004), *Sense, Reference, and Philosophy*. New York: Oxford University Press.

Kay, P., and P. Zimmer (1976), 'On the Semantics of Compounds and Genitives in English', in R. Underhill (ed.), *Sixth California Linguistics Association Proceedings*, pp. 29–35. San Diego: Campanile.

Kempson, R. (1975), *Presupposition and the Delimitation of Semantics*. Cambridge: Cambridge University Press.

—— (1988), 'Grammar and Conversational Principles', in F. J. Newmeyer (ed.), *Linguistics: The Cambridge Survey, ii. Linguistic Theory: Extensions and Implications*, pp. 139–63. Cambridge: Cambridge University Press.

Larson, R., and P. Ludlow (1993), 'Interpreted Logical Forms', *Synthese*, 95: 305–56.

Leech, G. N. (1974), *Semantics*. London: Penguin.

—— (1990), *Semantics*, 2nd ed. London: Penguin.

Levinson, S. C. (1988), 'Generalized Conversational Implicatures and the Semantics/Pragmatics Interface', TS, Department of Linguistics, Stanford University.

—— (1995), 'Three Levels of Meaning', in F. R. Palmer (ed.), *Grammar and Meaning: Essays in Honour of Sir John Lyons*, pp. 90–115. Cambridge: Cambridge University Press.

—— (2000), *Presumptive Meanings: The Theory of Generalized Conversational Implicature*. Cambridge, Mass.: MIT Press.

Lewis D. K. (1999*a*), 'Elusive Knowledge', in Lewis (1999*b*: 418–45).

—— (1999*b*), *Papers in Metaphysics and Epistemology*. Cambridge: Cambridge University Press.

McDowell, J. (1976), 'Truth-Conditions, Bivalence, and Verificationism', in G. Evans and J. McDowell (eds.), *Truth and Meaning*, pp. 42–66. Oxford: Clarendon Press.

—— (1987), 'In Defence of Modesty', in B. M. Taylor (ed.), *Michael Dummett*, pp. 59–80. Dordrecht: Martinus Nijhoff.

Perry, J. (1986), 'Thought without Representation', *Proceedings of the Aristotelian Society*, suppl. vol. 60: 263–83; repr. in Perry (1993: 205–25; 2000: 171–88).

—— (1993), *The Problem of the Essential Indexical and Other Essays*. New York: Oxford University Press.

—— (2000), *The Problem of the Essential Indexical and Other Essays*, expanded edn. Stanford, Calif: CSLI Publications.

Quine, W. V. O. (1960), *Word and Object*. Cambridge, Mass.: MIT Press.

Recanati, F. (1989), 'The Pragmatics of What is Said', *Mind and Language*, 4: 295–329.

—— (1993), *Direct Reference: From Language to Thought*. Oxford: Blackwell.

—— (2001), 'What is Said', *Synthese*, 128: 75–91.

—— (2004), *Literal Meaning*. Cambridge: Cambridge University Press.

Scott, D. S. (1970), 'Advice on Modal Logic', in K. Lambert (ed.), *Philosophical Problems in Logic: Some Recent Developments*, pp. 143–73. Reidel, Dordrecht.

Searle, John (1978), 'Literal Meaning', *Erkenntnis*, 13: 207–24.

—— (1979), *Expression and Meaning*, pp. 117–36. Cambridge: Cambridge University Press.

Sperber, D., and D. Wilson (1986), *Relevance*. Oxford.: Blackwell.

Stanley, J. (2000), 'Context and Logical Form', *Linguistics and Philosophy*, 23: 391–424.
—— and Szabó, Z. (2000), 'On Quantifier Domain Restriction', *Mind and Language*, 15: 219–61.
Taylor, Ken (2001), 'Sex, Breakfast, and Descriptus Interruptus', *Synthese*, 128: 45–61.
Travis, C. (1985), 'On What is Strictly Speaking True', *Canadian Journal of Philosophy*, 15: 187–229.
—— (1994), 'On Being Truth-Valued', in S. L. Tsohatzidis (ed.), *Foundations of Speech Act Theory*, pp. 167–86. London: Routledge.
—— (1996), 'Meaning's Role in Truth', *Mind*, 100: 451–66.
Walker, R. (1975), 'Conversational Implicatures', in S. Blackburn (ed.), *Meaning, Reference, and Necessity*, pp. 133–81. Cambridge: Cambridge University Press.
Ziff, P. (1972*a*), 'Something about Conceptual Schemes', in Ziff (1972*b*: 127–42).
—— (1972*b*), *Understanding Understanding*. Ithaca, NY: Cornell University Press.
—— (1972*c*), 'What is Said', in Ziff (1972*b*: 21–38).
—— (1977), 'About Proper Names', *Mind*, 86: 319–32.
Zwicky, A., and J. Sadock (1975), 'Ambiguity Tests and How to Fail Them', in J. P. Kimball (ed.), *Syntax and Semantics 4*, pp. 1–35. New York: Academic Press.

9

Semantic Minimalism and Nonindexical Contextualism

John MacFarlane

1. INTRODUCTION

My niece is four and a half feet tall—significantly taller than the average 7 year old. With this in mind, I might say "Chiara is tall", and, it seems, I would be speaking truly. Yet it also seems that if her basketball coach were to say "Chiara is tall" while discussing who should play which position on the team, he would not be speaking truly. What can we conclude about the *meaning* of "tall"?

Moderate Contextualists conclude that the sentence must be context-sensitive, in a way that goes beyond the context sensitivity of "Chiara" and "is" (which we may presume are being used in reference to the same girl and time). They reason as follows. If I am speaking truly and the coach is speaking falsely, we must be saying different things. Since we are using the same sentence, and using it "literally", this sentence must be context-sensitive. Used at my context, it expresses the proposition that Chiara has significantly greater height than the average 7 year old; used at the coach's context, it expresses the proposition that she has significantly greater height than the average member of team he coaches.

Cappelen and Lepore (2005) reject this reasoning, but only at the last step. They agree that different things are said in the two contexts I have described, but they deny that anything interesting follows from this about the *meaning* of "Chiara is tall". They can do this because they are *Speech Act Pluralists*: they hold that indefinitely many different things can be said in a single utterance. So, although I have said that Chiara is tall for a 7 year old, and the coach has said that she is tall for a member of the basketball team, that is consistent with there *also* being something that we have *both* said—namely, that she is (just plain) tall. It is this that Cappelen and Lepore take to be the invariant semantic content of the sentence we have used. Thus they can concede to the Moderate

Contextualist that different things have been said in the two contexts, while resisting the conclusion that the sentence used is context-sensitive.

This deployment of Speech Act Pluralism helps deflect one argument against the view that there is a single proposition that is semantically expressed by *every* use of "Chiara is tall" (fixing the girl and the time). But it does nothing to make it plausible that there *is* such a proposition. Indeed, most contextualists, including some who accept Speech Act Pluralism, take it to be obvious that there *cannot* be any such proposition, on the grounds that there is no such thing as being just plain tall (as opposed to tall for a 7 year old, or tall for a team member, or tall compared to a skyscraper, or . . .). That there is in fact such a proposition—a bona fide, truth-evaluable proposition, not a "proposition radical" or anything schematic—is the central tenet of what Cappelen and Lepore call *Semantic Minimalism*. It is this, chiefly, that distinguishes them from the philosophers they call *Radical Contextualists*. If it should turn out that there is no such "minimal" or (borrowing a phrase from Ken Taylor) "modificationally neutral" proposition, then Cappelen and Lepore will have no choice but to embrace the Radical Contextualists' conclusion that there is no hope for systematic theorizing about the propositions expressed by sentences in contexts.[1] After all, they accept all of the Radicals' arguments against the Moderates.

Our first order of business, then, should be asking what might be thought to be problematic about such propositions—since Moderate and Radical Contextualists are united in rejecting them—and considering whether Cappelen and Lepore have said enough to dispel these worries. I am going to argue that, although Cappelen and Lepore misidentify the real source of resistance to minimal propositions, and so do not address it, this worry *can* be addressed. However, the strategy I will describe for making sense of Semantic Minimalism is not one that Cappelen and Lepore can take on board without cost. For my way of "making sense" of Cappelen and Lepore's view can, with a slight shift of perspective, be regarded as a way of making sense of Radical Contextualism, a position they regard as incompatible with their own (and indeed as hopeless).[2]

2. THE INTENSION PROBLEM

Let's call the proposition putatively expressed in every context of use by the sentence "Chiara is tall" (fixing girl and time) *the proposition that Chiara is (just*

[1] Note that this is not at all the same as the claim that systematic semantics is impossible. What Radical Contextualists reject is only a certain conception of what semantics must accomplish.

[2] Because my concern here is with the coherence of Semantic Minimalism, I will not address the arguments Cappelen and Lepore muster in favor of that doctrine (most of them arguments *against* the contextualist alternative).

plain) tall (at time *t*—I will henceforth omit this qualification). According to Cappelen and Lepore, "[t]his proposition is not a 'skeleton'; it is not fragmentary; it's a full-blooded proposition with truth conditions and a truth value" (2005: 181). What they mean, presumably, is that it has a truth value at every circumstance of evaluation (since propositions may, in general, have different truth values at different circumstances of evaluation).

I believe that most philosophers' worries about minimal propositions are rooted in puzzlement over the question this claim naturally provokes: at *which* circumstances of evaluation is the proposition that Chiara is (just plain) tall true? Here I'm using the technical term "circumstance of evaluation" the way David Kaplan taught us to use it in *Demonstratives* (1989). A circumstance of evaluation includes all the parameters to which propositional truth must be relativized for semantic purposes. Though Kaplan himself included times in his circumstances of evaluation (and contemplated other parameters as well), the current orthodoxy is that circumstances of evaluation are just possible worlds.[3] In this setting, our question becomes: at which possible worlds is the minimal proposition that Chiara is (just plain) tall true? I'll call this the *intension problem* for minimal propositions (using the term "intension" for a function from possible worlds to truth values for propositions, or to extensions for properties and relations).

It's easy to feel pressure to make this intension very, very weak. After all, being tall for a 7 year old does seem to be a *way* of being tall. So it is natural to think that the proposition that Chiara is (just plain) tall must be true at every world at which the proposition that Chiara is tall for a 7 year old is true. Similar reasoning will move us inexorably towards the conclusion that, no matter what reference class *F* we pick, the proposition that Chiara is (just plain) tall is weaker than the proposition that she is tall for an *F*. After all, even being tall compared to an ant is a way of being tall. We are left with the surprising conclusion that the minimal proposition that Chiara is (just plain) tall is true at every world at which Chiara has any degree of height at all.

That's odd enough. It gets even odder when we run the same argument with "short" and conclude that the proposition that Chiara is (just plain) short is true at every possible world in which she is not absolutely gigantic. It follows that at all but a few very odd worlds, Chiara has both the property of being (just plain) tall *and* the property of being (just plain) short. And that does not sit well with our feeling that *being tall* and *being short* are incompatible properties.

[3] Kaplan included times because he thought the tenses were best understood as propositional operators, which need a parameter to shift (1989: 502–3). This view of tenses is now rejected by most semanticists, so there is no longer a compelling reason to include a time parameter in circumstances of evaluation (see King 2003). But everything I say in this chapter about the orthodox framework could be said (with minimal modifications) about a Kaplan-style framework as well.

Cappelen and Lepore do not themselves embrace this view about the intension of *tall.* They do not reject it either. They present it as one of several possible views one might adopt about the metaphysics of tallness (2005: 171):

- A thing is tall if there is some comparison class with respect to which it is tall.
- A thing is tall if it is tall with respect to its *privileged* comparison class.
- A thing is tall (at time *t*) if it is tall with respect to the comparison class that is appropriate to its situation (at *t*).
- A thing is tall if it is taller than the average of all objects with height.

All of these views are problematic; indeed, Cappelen and Lepore point out many of the problems themselves. But they don't think that solving these problems, or deciding between these options, is part of their job as semanticists. Their charge is language, not the metaphysics of properties. Having argued to their satisfaction that "tall" is not context-sensitive, they are content to leave it to the metaphysicians to sort out just what an object has to be like in order to have the property that "tall" invariantly expresses.

This response is fine, as far as it goes. Semanticists should not be required to be metaphysicians (or physicists or biologists or ethicists). They need not give informative answers to questions about the intensions of properties.[4] However, in taking resistance to minimal propositions to be grounded in a misguided demand for an informative *specification* of their intensions, Cappelen and Lepore have missed what is most troubling about their doctrine. Semantic Minimalism is problematic not because it does not *provide* an answer to questions about the intensions of its minimal properties and propositions, but because it requires that there *be* answers to such questions.

Suppose that you are examining some ants on the sidewalk. Most of the ants are tiny, but one is significantly bigger than the rest. "That's a big one", you say. After a while, the ants begin to disappear though a barely perceptible crack in the concrete. When the last ant, the bigger one, squeezes through, you say, "Boy, that ant is small." At this point a Semantic Minimalist appears and begins to question you in a most annoying way:

> "Wait a second. You just said that that ant was big. Now you say it's small. I didn't notice it changing size. So which is it, big or small?"
>
> "Well, it's big for an ant, but small compared to most of the other things we can see."
>
> "Fine, but I'm not asking about these properties; I'm asking about plain old bigness and smallness. You said (among many other things) that the ant

[4] It is not difficult for the Semantic Minimalist to give *uninformative* answers: for example, "a thing has the property of being tall (in some world *w*) just in case it is tall in *w*".

> was (just plain) big, and then that it was (just plain) small. Do you suppose it could have had both properties, bigness and smallness?"
>
> "No . . ."
>
> "So which is it, then? Or don't you know?"

The question seems completely inappropriate. But why should it, if the Semantic Minimalist is right that there is a property of being (just plain) big which is always expressed by "big", and a property of being (just plain) small which is always expressed by "small"? Why shouldn't we be able to entertain questions about which things have these properties? It is not enough to point out that semanticists need not answer metaphysical questions. For even the answer "I have no idea" seems out of place here.[5]

It might be suggested that we reject such questions because we aren't *aware* of the minimal propositions that are semantically expressed by our sentences, but only of the more determinate contents of our speech acts. But such a line would be incompatible with what Cappelen and Lepore say about the cognitive role of the minimal content. They say that "the proposition semantically expressed is that content the audience can expect the speaker to grasp (and expect the speaker to expect the audience to grasp, etc.) even if she has such mistaken or incomplete information" about the context (2005: 184–5). Explaining how a speaker could use the (presumably quite weak) proposition that A is red in order to make a much more determinate claim about A's color, they say: "The audience can assume that the speaker knew that this [the proposition semantically expressed] was trivial and was not interested in conveying such trivialities with his utterance and can, therefore, infer that there's work to be done in order to figure out exactly what the speaker was trying to communicate" (pp. 185–6). All of this assumes that both speaker and audience are aware of the proposition semantically expressed. (Indeed, the second claim assumes some mutual knowledge about the *intension* of this proposition.) If Cappelen and Lepore were to abandon this assumption, they would open themselves up to the objection that their minimal propositions play no real cognitive role in communication.

Alternatively, the Minimalist might say that the reason speakers find the question in our dialogue inappropriate is that they have mistaken views about the semantics of terms like "big" and "small". They implicitly take these words to be context-sensitive, when in fact they invariantly express the properties of being (just plain) big and (just plain) small.

It should be obvious, however, that this response would completely undermine the positive case for Semantic Minimalism. For the contextualist can use exactly

[5] It should be clear that the problem does not stem from the *vagueness* of "big" and "small". It would not help the Semantic Minimalist here if we allowed the intensions of bigness and smallness to be functions from possible worlds to fuzzy extensions (mappings of objects to degrees of truth) or partial functions from possible worlds to extensions.

the same trick—attributing confusion or error about the semantics of these terms to ordinary speakers—to dismiss the evidence Cappelen and Lepore have mustered that terms like "red", "tall", and "know" do not behave like context-sensitive expressions. For example, Cappelen and Lepore make much of the fact that we report others who utter the sentence "Chiara is tall" as having said that Chiara is tall, without much regard to differences in our contexts. The practice of making such "intercontextual disquotational indirect reports" only makes sense, they say, if "tall" semantically expresses the same property in every context. But the contextualist can accept this conditional and conclude that the practice *doesn't* make sense—that it embodies a fundamental mistake people implicitly make about the semantics of their own terms, a mistake that the contextualist hopes to correct. (This is, in fact, a common line for contextualists to take, although they sometimes also question the uniformity or the relevance of the data about intercontextual indirect reports: see DeRose, forthcoming.) Cappelen and Lepore need to say something to block this kind of move. Whatever they say, it will presumably also block *them* from appealing to massive speaker error or confusion in explaining our rejection of the question in the dialogue above as somehow absurd or inappropriate.

To recap. The intension problem is the problem of saying just what a world must be like if the proposition that Chiara is (just plain) tall is to be true at that world. Cappelen and Lepore rightly put this aside as a metaphysical question, not a semantic one. But they fail to see that there is a semantic problem lurking in the immediate vicinity. If Semantic Minimalism is true, then the intension problem should have a solution (even if the solution is not known to us). But we do not treat it as having a solution at all. We reject as inappropriate questions that ought to have perfectly definite answers if there is such a property as being (just plain) tall and that property has an intension.

3. MINIMAL PROPOSITIONS WITHOUT INTENSIONS?

In view of this problem, it is worth asking whether a Semantic Minimalist can coherently deny that minimal propositions, like the proposition that Chiara is (just plain) tall, have intensions.

In orthodox frameworks of the kind favored by most Moderate Contextualists, this option is not open. For propositions have truth values relative to circumstances of evaluation. If circumstances of evaluation are just possible worlds, then propositions have truth values relative to worlds: in other words, they have intensions. So if there is a proposition that is semantically expressed by "Chiara is tall" at every context of use, it must have an intension. At this point, contextualists conclude *modo tollente* that there is no such proposition, while Cappelen and Lepore conclude *modo ponente* that, since there *is* such a proposition, it must have an intension.

We can go beyond these two alternatives by thinking a bit differently about circumstances of evaluation. Possible worlds will presumably be one component of our circumstances of evaluation (otherwise, what will our modal operators shift?), but nothing stops us from introducing other components as well. (Indeed, semanticists have for various reasons suggested adding times, "standards of precision", and other parameters.) So let's think of a circumstance of evaluation as an ordered pair consisting of a world and a "counts-as" parameter, which we can model as a function from properties to intensions (functions from worlds to extensions). The "counts-as" parameter is so called because it fixes what things have to be like in order to *count as* having the property of tallness (or any other property) at a circumstance of evaluation.[6]

As before, we say that propositions have truth values at circumstances of evaluation. But now our circumstances are not just worlds, so it no longer follows that propositions have truth values at worlds. This is why it is not appropriate to ask about the truth value of the proposition that Chiara is (just plain) tall at a possible world (including the actual world). For there will in general be *many* circumstances of evaluation that have a given world as their world parameter but differ in their "counts-as" parameter. Our proposition will be true at some of these circumstances and false at others. So it does not have an intension (a function from possible worlds to truth values).[7] This should be a welcome result for the Semantic Minimalist, who no longer has to say that there is a (context-invariant) answer to the question: does Chiara have the property of being (just plain) tall, in the actual world, or not?

Following Kaplan, we say that an occurrence of a sentence is true just in case the proposition expressed is true at the circumstance of the context.[8] Which circumstance of evaluation is the "circumstance of the context" in this framework? The world parameter of the circumstance of the context is, of course, just the world of the context. But the counts-as parameter will be determined in complex ways by other features of the context, including the topic of conversation and the speaker's intentions. In a context C1 where I'm talking about 7-year-olds, the counts-as function might assign to the property of being (just plain)

[6] Note that the function assigns an intension to *every* property, not just "minimal" properties. This is important because, as Cappelen and Lepore point out (2005: 172–5), the same kinds of arguments that may lead one to doubt that the property of *being tall* has an intension can also be run for the property of *being tall for a giraffe*.

[7] Of course it has an "intension" in a broader sense: a function from *circumstances of evaluation* to truth values.

[8] "If c is a context, then an occurrence of ϕ in c is true iff the content expressed by ϕ in this context is true when evaluated with respect to the circumstance of the context" (Kaplan 1989: 522). Semanticists sometimes ascribe truth to *utterances* rather than to occurrences of sentences in contexts, but as Kaplan notes, the notion of an utterance is proper to pragmatics, not semantics. It is especially odd to find Speech Act Pluralists like Cappelen and Lepore ascribing truth and falsity to utterances (e.g. in their "intercontextual disquotational test", 2005: 105), since on their view an utterance can express indefinitely many propositions, which (one assumes) need not all have the same truth value at the circumstance of the context.

tall the same intension it assigns to the property of being tall-for-a-7-year-old. In a context C2 where I'm talking about members of the basketball team, the counts-as function might assign to the property of being tall the same intension it assigns to the property of being tall-for-a-team-member. Thus the circumstance of C1 can differ from the circumstance of C2 even if the two contexts are situated in the same world (say, the actual world). And as a result, an occurrence of "Chiara is tall" in C1 can differ in truth value from an occurrence of "Chiara is tall" in C2, even if the same proposition is expressed by both.

We can now say precisely what goes wrong in the story about the ants (above). The problem is *not* that there is no such proposition as the proposition that the ant is (just plain) big. The present view concedes that there is such a proposition, and that this proposition is perfectly suitable, in general, for use in questions and answers. In general, we look to contextual factors to determine a counts-as parameter that (together with the world of utterance) can settle a truth value for the proposition in context. In the ant story, however, the context fails to determine a single counts-as parameter, because the questioner has deliberately made salient two incompatible counts-as parameters: the one that was in play when the ant was first described as big and the one that was in play when it was later described as small. The question "which is it, big or small?" presupposes that the context determines sufficiently what counts as having the properties of bigness and smallness. But the questioner in this case has ensured that this presupposition cannot be met. That is why we (rightly) reject the question and find *every* answer (even "I don't know") to be inappropriate.

As far as I can see, the view I have just described is consistent with Semantic Minimalism, as Cappelen and Lepore describe it. It allows that "Chiara is tall" expresses the same proposition at every context of use (fixing girl and time). This proposition is not a "schema", but "a full-blooded proposition with truth conditions and a truth value", that is, a truth value at each circumstance of evaluation. Granted, the proposition does not have a truth value at each *possible world,* but that is just what we should expect in a framework where there is more to circumstances of evaluation than just worlds.[9]

On this picture, the sentence "Chiara is tall" is not context-sensitive in the sense that it expresses different propositions at different contexts. But it *is* context-sensitive in the sense that the truth of an occurrence of it depends on features of the context—not just the world of the context, but the speaker's intentions, the conversational common ground, and other such things.[10] Accordingly,

9 "Temporalists" who take circumstances of evaluation to be world/time pairs do not think that propositions have truth values relative to worlds, either.

10 Interestingly, Cappelen and Lepore give two distinct definitions of "context-sensitive", corresponding roughly to these two senses (2005: 146). According to the first, "To say that *e* is context sensitive is to say that its contribution to the proposition expressed by utterances of sentences containing *e* varies from context to context." According to the second, "To say that *e* is context sensitive is to say that its contribution to the truth conditions of utterances *u* of a sentence S

this brand of Semantic Minimalism might also be described as a kind of contextualism: what I have elsewhere called *Nonindexical Contextualism*.[11] This way of describing it brings out how close it is to Radical Contextualism. *Too* close, Cappelen and Lepore may feel! However, it is immune to their best arguments against Radical Contextualism, so if they are going to reject it, they need fresh reasons.

4. CONTEXT SHIFTING ARGUMENTS RECONSIDERED

An advantage of the framework I have just sketched is that it offers a different (and perhaps deeper) diagnosis than Cappelen and Lepore's of what goes wrong in Moderate Contextualists' uses of Context Shifting Arguments (CSAs). Unlike Cappelen and Lepore's diagnosis, this one does not require Speech Act Pluralism, though it is consistent with it.

Let's consider again the general form of a Context Shifting Argument. We describe two occurrences of the same sentence, S, one in context C1, the other in context C2. We then observe that intuitively the former is true, while the latter is false. Assuming these intuitions are accurate, we can conclude the following:

(1) At C1, S expresses a proposition that is true at the circumstance of C1.

(2) At C2, S expresses a proposition that is false at the circumstance of C2.

We *cannot* conclude, however, that the proposition S expresses at C1 is different from the proposition S expresses at C2. For if the circumstance of C1 is different

containing *e* (in some way or other) references various aspects of the context of *u*." In the framework I have described, these two definitions are not equivalent.

[11] See my "Nonindexical Contextualism" (forthcoming). See also MacFarlane 2005*a*, *b*, where I describe nonindexical contextualist views in order to distinguish them from views I regard as genuinely "relativist". I take it that the account developed by Predelli 2005, to which I am much indebted, is also a form of nonindexical contextualism. Instead of countenancing an extra parameter of circumstances of evaluation, as I do here, Predelli conceives of points of evaluation as something like state descriptions (which fix the extension of every property and relation expressible in the language). There are state descriptions according to which Chiara falls into the extension of both "four and a half feet tall" and "tall", and others according to which she falls into the extension of the former but not the latter. Which state description is "the circumstance of the context" will depend not just on the world of the context, but on other features of context as well. I think that the differences between these two versions of nonindexical contextualism are largely notational. I prefer to "factor out" my circumstances of evaluation into a world component and a catch-all counts-as parameter, because it is convenient to have a separate "world" parameter of circumstances for modal operators to shift. If we let them shift state descriptions wholesale, then "That could have been red" could come out true just because what counts as red might have been different, even if the color of the object demonstrated could not have been different—surely an undesirable result. But this is not a fatal objection to Predelli's approach: as Kenny Easwaran has pointed out to me, Predelli could allow his modal operators to shift state descriptions "retail", the way quantifiers shift assignments.

from the circumstance of C2, our two occurrences of S can diverge in truth value even while expressing the same proposition.

Nothing about the general point I am making here depends on circumstances of evaluations being anything other than just worlds. Suppose S is the sentence "Bush won the US Presidential election in 2000", and suppose that the world of C1 is different from the world of C2. Then an occurrence of S in C1 could diverge in truth value from an occurrence of S in C2, not because different propositions are expressed, but simply because the circumstances of the two contexts are different. (Say, Bush won in the world of C1, but lost in the world of C2.)

Thus, a CSA establishes that the propositions expressed are different only given an additional premise:

(3) The circumstance of C1 = the circumstance of C2.

Normally users of CSAs do not even mention (or perhaps see the need for) this premise, because in orthodox frameworks it is relatively easy to secure. In these frameworks, a circumstance of evaluation is just a possible world, so (3) amounts to

(4) The world of C1 = the world of C2.

So the user of a CSA has only to describe contexts that take place at the same world and differ only in other ways—in the topic of conversation, for example—and the CSA *will* establish that what is said at C1 is different from what is said at C2.

Cappelen and Lepore seem to accept all of this reasoning. They accept that the CSAs used by contextualists show that something different is said at the two contexts described. Their point is that this does not show that the proposition *semantically expressed* is different, because (given Speech Act Pluralism) the proposition semantically expressed is only one of many things said.

If we adopt the framework described in the last section, however, we can reject the contextualists' reasoning in a more fundamental way. For in this framework it is no longer true that a circumstance of evaluation is just a world. This makes it much more difficult to construct a CSA for which (3) holds. It is no longer sufficient to ensure that C1 and C2 are situated at the same world; we must also make sure that these contexts determine the same counts-as function. This is relatively easy to do when we are making up CSAs to demonstrate the indexicality of "I", "here", or "now", but difficult or impossible when we are making up CSAs to demonstrate the indexicality of "knows", "tall", and other such terms. That is why CSAs work in the former cases but not in the latter.

5. CONCLUSION

I have offered up this version of Nonindexical Contextualism as a way of making sense of Semantic Minimalism. If Cappelen and Lepore accept my exegesis, then they can block Context Shifting Arguments in a different way than they do in *Insensitive Semantics*, and without invoking Speech Act Pluralism. If they do not accept it, then they must find another way to explain why speakers reject questions that should admit of answers (if only "I don't know") if minimal propositions have determinate intensions.

In closing, a Hegelian thought. In a recent paper, Stefano Predelli (2005) has offered up his own version of Nonindexical Contextualism as a way of making sense of Radical Contextualism. It is striking, I think, that a plausible interpretation of Semantic Minimalism and a plausible interpretation of Radical Contextualism should come out looking very similar! This suggests that, far from being fundamentally opposed, the two positions are just the two one-sided ways of grasping the truth about context sensitivity that are available when one supposes that propositions have truth values at possible worlds. *Thesis:* Semantic Minimalism. *Antithesis:* Radical Contextualism. *Synthesis:* Nonindexical Contextualism.

REFERENCES

Cappelen, H., and E. Lepore (2005), *Insensitive Semantics: A Defense of Semantic Minimalism and Speech Act Pluralism.* Oxford: Blackwell.

DeRose, K. (forthcoming), " 'Bamboozled by our own Words": Semantic Blindness and Some Objections to Contextualism', *Philosophy and Phenomenological Research.*

Kaplan, D. (1989), 'Demonstratives', in J. Almog, J. Perry, and H. Wettstein (eds.), *Themes from Kaplan*, pp. 481–564. New York: Oxford University Press.

King, J. (2003), 'Tense, Modality, and Semantic Values', in *Philosophical Perspectives*, 17, *Language and Philosophical Linguistics*, pp. 195–245.

MacFarlane, John (2005*a*), 'Making Sense of Relative Truth', *Proceedings of the Aristotelian Society*, 105: 321–39.

—— (2005*b*), 'The Assessment Sensitivity of Knowledge Attributions', *Oxford Studies in Epistemology*, 1, ed. T. Szabo-Gendler and J. Hawthorne, pp. 197–233.

—— (forthcoming), 'Nonindexical Contextualism', *Synthese.*

Predelli, S. (2005), 'Painted Leaves, Context, and Semantic Analysis', *Linguistics and Philosophy*, 28: 351–74.

10

Minimal (Disagreement about) Semantics

Lenny Clapp

1. INTRODUCTION

The semantic minimalist maintains that for every grammatical sentence the semantic values of the words it contains (perhaps relative to a context) and the logical form of the sentence determine a unique proposition that is the *semantic content* of the *sentence* (perhaps relative a context). The truth conditional pragmatist denies that *sentences*, even relative to a context, encode such semantic contents.[1] My purpose here is to argue that on this point of contention Semantic Minimalism faces a daunting challenge, one that its advocates have thus far failed to meet. The challenge, which I will call the *naturalistic challenge*, is this. Suppose it is a fact that a sentence S (perhaps taken relative to a context) encodes proposition P as its *semantic* content. What *fixes*, or *grounds*, this fact? In other words, of the uncountably many propositions or sets of truth conditions there are, what makes it the case that P, as opposed to P*, is *the* semantic content of S? I think that it is agreed on all sides that *if* it is a fact that P is the semantic content of S (perhaps relative to context), then this fact must be grounded in natural psychological and/or sociological facts concerning the abilities and practices of competent speakers and interpreters. If the alleged facts concerning semantic content are not somehow grounded in such natural facts, then semantics would not fit into Chomsky's cognitive paradigm in linguistics, nor even into the broader project of "naturalizing epistemology". This is a consequence that I believe all parties would like to avoid.[2] Indeed, though no

[1] Representatives of Semantic Minimalism include Soames (2002), Borg (2004), and Cappelen and Lepore (2005*b*), and representatives of Truth Conditional Pragmatics include Carston (2002), Recanati (2004), and Neale (2004).

[2] Passages such as the following suggest that the semantic minimalists I consider here think that facts concerning the semantic contents of sentences are, in various ways, grounded in facts concerning the linguistic abilities and practices of competent speakers: "let me borrow from the framework made familiar by Chomsky, Fodor, and others. I assume a broadly modular picture

semantic minimalist has *explicitly* addressed the naturalistic challenge, semantic minimalists have apparently been motivated to provide an account of semantic content which illustrates how such facts are grounded in facts concerning the ability and behavior of competent language users.

In what follows I will first explain in general terms the dispute between Truth Conditional Pragmatics and Semantic Minimalism, and then I will consider three potential responses to the naturalistic challenge: The first response to the challenge is provided by Borg (2004); the second by Soames (2002); and the third by Cappelen and Lepore (2005*a*, *b*, *c*). I will argue that none of these responses is adequate. The tentative conclusion is then that even if Semantic Minimalism were correct in maintaining that associated with every grammatical sentence S (perhaps relativized to a context) there is a unique proposition that is the semantic content of S, such facts would fall outside the explanatory domain of empirically oriented semantics that is concerned to explain the abilities and practices of competent language users. I will conclude with some remarks concerning the consequences of this conclusion for the debate between Semantic Minimalism and Truth Conditional Pragmatics.

2. SEMANTIC MINIMALISM AND TRUTH CONDITIONAL PRAGMATICS

Both Semantic Minimalism (SM) and Truth Conditional Pragmatics (TCP) have developed as responses to counterexamples against traditional Frege and/or Davidson inspired semantic theories which utilize what I call the "assign and combine model". According to this model, what is said by an uttered sentence is determined compositionally by the relevant syntactic structure of the sentence, and the semantic values of the words in the sentence (some of which can be determined only relative to contexts). Thus, according to this model, what competent interpreters do when they come to understand what is expressed by an utterance is, first, determine the logical form of the utterance and what words occur in it. Then, relying on their lexical knowledge, they assign semantic values to these words; at this stage interpreters appeal to context to assign semantic

of the mind, containing discrete bodies of information and encapsulated processes acting on that information, dealing with such subjects as vision, hearing . . . and of course language. The language faculty, as I conceive of it, is comprised of at least three sub-domains: orthography and vocalized speech recognition, syntax, and semantics. The semantic information the faculty contains is of quite limited form; say just that required for generating the truth-conditions of complex linguistic items on the basis of their parts and their mode of composition. It is this quite constrained item (the 'minimal proposition' . . .) which feeds out of the language faculty" (Borg 2002: 23). " . . . semantic claims about the expressions of a language are . . . social claims about the conventions and commonalities found in a linguistic community" (Soames 2002: 71). "The proposition semantically expressed is that content the speaker can expect the audience to grasp (and expect the audience to expect the speaker to expect them to grasp)" (Cappelen and Lepore 2005*a*: 214).

values to indexicals and demonstratives. Finally, they apply their knowledge of the compositional semantic theory for their language to the logical form and the semantic values of the words, and thereby arrive at the truth conditions of, or equivalently what is said by, the utterance.[3] A semantic theory according to this model consists of a finite number of rules stating how semantic values of lexical items are combined, in accordance with the logical form, to determine truth conditions; a semantic theory thus expresses a function *from* the logical form of a sentence and the semantic values of words in the sentence *to* the truth conditions of the sentence.

Since semantic theories that utilize this "assign and combine" model express a function *from* (i) logical forms and (ii) the semantic values of words (relative to contexts), *to* truth conditions, they are subject to counterexamples of the following form. Suppose that according to such a semantic theory sentences S and S′ (perhaps identical) have (i) the same logical form, and (ii) there are contexts C and C′ such that the semantic values of the words in S relative to C are the same as those of S′ relative to C′, *but* the truth conditions of S in C are not the same as the truth conditions of S′ in C′.[4] Such a pair of sentences and contexts would constitute a counterexample against an assign and combine theory because it would demonstrate that, contrary to the theory, the truth conditions of sentences relative to contexts are not a *function* of the "formal" properties and features described in conditions (i) and (ii). For example, consider two utterances of 'Osama Bin Laden is tall'. Since there are no context-sensitive words in the sentence, conditions (i) and (ii) are satisfied for any pair of contexts. (I will ignore tense throughout this chapter.) But now consider the intuitive truth conditions of utterances of this sentence in the following contexts. In context C one is attempting to identify the ten largest organisms that have ever lived. In such a context an utterance of 'Osama Bin Laden is tall' would intuitively express something *false*. In context C′ one is discussing the sizes of terrorist leaders. In such contexts an utterance of the sentence would intuitively express something *true*. Hence 'Osama Bin Laden is tall' constitutes at least an apparent counterexample against the assign and combine model.

The debate between the proponents of TCP and SM concerns what the appropriate response is to such apparent counterexamples. Advocates of TCP maintain that such examples demonstrate that the assign and combine model is inadequate for natural language. They maintain that such counterexamples demonstrate that the "formal" semantic properties and features described in

[3] The semantic minimalist need not be committed to the strong claim that this three-step process accurately describes the cognitive processing competent speakers actually perform. They can retreat to a weaker and vaguer claim to the effect that this three-step process is a sort of rational reconstruction that accurately models the sort of processing interpreters perform.

[4] What Cappelen and Lepore (2005*b*) call "Context Shifting Arguments" are alleged counterexamples in which S is identical to S′. And what they call "incompleteness arguments" are a special sort of context shifting argument.

conditions (i) and (ii) are insufficient to determine truth conditions, and that other information and inferences, *pragmatic* information and inferences, are required. According to TCP, interpreting an utterance is a two-step process. The first step is identical to the process described by the assign and combine model except that according to TCP the output of this purely semantic processing is not propositional; it is not truth conditions, nor "what is said". In the words of Neale, the result of this purely semantic decoding of a sentence X is merely "a *blueprint* for . . . what someone will be taken to be saying when using X to say something" (2004: 85). The second step consists of pragmatic processes that utilize the blueprint produced in the first step, and information provided by the context of utterance, to produce fully propositional, truth-conditional, content. According to TCP then, propositions, or truth conditions, are not semantically encoded; only *blueprints for* truth-conditional content are semantically encoded.[5]

The advocates of SM, however, maintain that the alleged counterexamples against the assign and combine model do not undermine the model.[6] They maintain that advocates of TCP mistakenly take such alleged counterexamples to undermine the model because TCP does not distinguish between two sorts of propositional content: *speech act content*, and *semantic content*. According to SM there are two sorts of facts concerning truth conditions: facts concerning the truth conditions of speech acts and facts concerning the truth conditions of sentences (relativized to contexts). Moreover, SM maintains that the *semantic content* of a *sentence* S (relative to a context) and *the speech act content* of an utterance (in, or relative to, the same context) are typically radically different. In the following passage Cappelen and Lepore express this radical divergence:

speakers use sentences to make claims, assertions, suggestions, requests, . . . statements, raise hypotheses, inquiries, etc., the contents of which can be (and typically are)

[5] An anonymous referee has suggested that this "blueprint" model does not apply to Recanati. Recanati claims that "it is possible for an utterance to receive a non-literal interpretation *without the literal interpretation of that utterance being ever computed*" (2004: 29). The worry is that this is incompatible with the idea that an interpreter must compute the blueprint corresponding to an utterance *before* engaging in pragmatic reasoning to determine what is intuitively said by the utterance. But there is no incompatibility here. What Recanati calls "the literal interpretation" is a development of the mere linguistic meaning of an utterance, and thus—to translate Recanati's terms into mine—a "literal interpretation" is a pragmatic development of a blueprint. For example, with regard to Nunberg's example involving an utterance of 'The ham sandwich has left', Recanati suggests that the "proposition literally expressed [is] the absurd proposition that the ham sandwich itself has left without paying" (2004: 29). The absurd literal proposition is about a particular ham sandwich, and thus is a *development of* the mere linguistic meaning of the sentence.

[6] Semantic Minimalism is one of three influential responses to alleged counterexamples on behalf of the assign and combine model. The other two are what I have elsewhere (Clapp forthcoming) referred to as "Kaplan's Strategy" and "Grice's Strategy". (Lepore 2004 refers to these as "semantic proposals" and "pragmatic proposals", respectively.) As I agree with SM that Kaplan's and Grice's strategies are not adequate for defending the assign and combine model from counterexamples, I will not criticize them here.

radically different from the semantic contents of . . . these utterances. The speech act content . . . depends upon a potentially indefinite range of facts about the speaker, his audience, their shared context . . . *These facts have no bearing on the semantic content of the utterance.* (2005c: 211; my italics)

Borg also draws a sharp distinction between our intuitive judgments of speech act content and the semantic content of sentences. Borg identifies "what is said" with speech act content, and she uses the "notions of [*oratio obliqua*] and judgments of what is said interchangeably" (2002: 8 n. 1). She declares that

there is *no* semantically privileged notion of 'what is said', and thus no considerations concerning *oratio obliqua* should constrain or otherwise affect our semantic theorizing. (2002: 7)

Indeed, SM maintains not only that speech act content is radically different from semantic content, but moreover SM maintains that competent speakers have intuitive access only to speech act content. Soames, for example, writes,

we ought to give up the assumption that individual speakers have internalized semantic theories that provide them with the means of identifying the propositions semantically expressed by sentences and distinguishing them from other propositions the sentence may be used to assert or convey. Having done this, we have no reason to expect that whenever two sentences semantically express the same proposition [or two utterances of the same sentence express the same proposition] competent speakers who understand the sentences will recognize that they express the same proposition . . . (2002: 71–2)

By positing a layer of semantic content that is not only radically different from what is intuitively said by utterances but also hidden from our intuitive judgments, SM is able to insulate the assign and combine model from apparent counterexamples. For any apparent counterexample involving S in C and S′ in C′, SM will maintain that the intuitive judgment that S in C expresses different truth conditions than does S′ in C′ concerns only speech act content, and not semantic content. Because semantic content is not accessible to our intuitive judgments, the apparent counterexamples provide no reason for thinking that the semantic content of S in C and S′ in C′ are distinct. And thus there is no counterexample against the assign and combine model because the model applies only to semantic content, and not to speech act content.

There can be little doubt that *if there is* in addition to intuitively accessible speech act content a layer of more theoretic semantic content that is tailor-made for the assign and combine model, then SM succeeds in insulating the assign and combine model from apparent counterexamples. But once one discerns the underlying theoretical motivations of SM, the significance and relevance of the naturalistic challenge becomes evident.[7] For this additional layer of truth

[7] An anonymous referee has suggested that the underlying theoretical motivation for SM is not merely to preserve the assign and combine model, but moreover to account for linguistic

conditions seems to be an *ad hoc* posit, the only purpose of which is to preserve the assign and combine model at some level of abstraction. What reason, independent of the assign and combine model, can be provided for thinking there is such a layer of truth-conditional content? Indeed, if the semantic content of S (relative to contexts) is, as the advocates of SM insist, radically different from the intuitive content competent speakers express and communicate to each other using S, then how *could* this alleged fact be fixed by, or grounded in, the psychological processes and/or social practices of competent speakers and interpreters? And if such natural facts do not fix the fact that P, as opposed to some other proposition P*, is the semantic content of S (relative to a context), then what role could such content play in theorizing about how competent speakers are able to express their thoughts and communicate using language?

3. WHY BORG FAILS TO MEET THE NATURALISTIC CHALLENGE

Borg maintains that our tacit purely linguistic knowledge is encapsulated in a module which realizes a Davidson-style semantic theory. According to Borg,

> there is a discrete language faculty, containing specialized bodies of knowledge and operations on that knowledge, dealing with phonetics, orthographics, syntax, and semantics. ... It would ... fall within the purview of the language faculty to calculate the mental representation of the truth-condition of the natural language sentence 'The cat is on the mat', where what is constructed is a language of thought sentence which exhibits connections to the external world just to the extent that the language of thought expressions out of which it is constructed exhibit such relations (to put it crudely, since CAT hooks up to cats, and MAT hooks up to mats, the truth-conditions for the natural language sentence 'the cat is on the mat' turns on how things stand with some cat and some mat). (Borg, 2004: 84)

It might seem that the sort of cognitivist Davidsonian view Borg is advancing is well-suited to provide a response to the naturalistic challenge. The challenge, put in terms of Borg's example sentence, is this: "Suppose that the proposition semantically encoded by 'The cat is on the mat' is P, and not P*. What makes it the case that P, as opposed to P*, is the semantic content encoded by the sentence?" Borg can respond that P rather than P* is the semantic content because the semantic component of the language faculty, which is an encapsulated mental

communication. (See e.g. "the seven virtues of SM" described by Cappelen and Lepore 2005*b*: 151–4.) But I think this suggestion confuses the issue: All parties in the debate—both advocates of SM and advocates of TCP—want to account for linguistic communication. Moreover, it is generally agreed that *if* the assign and combine model applied to our linguistic abilities, then many aspects of linguistic communication would be accounted for. The debate concerns whether or not the assign and combine model *really does* apply to our linguistic abilities; for the sorts of counterexamples offered by the advocates of TCP provide cogent reasons for thinking it does not.

module, "calculates" mental representations that she would represent something like this:

(1) 'The cat is on the mat' IS TRUE *IFF* THE CAT IS ON THE MAT.

The capitalized items represent expressions in the language of thought. And Borg maintains that the content of an expression in the language of thought is "determined by its connection to a certain object, or a certain property, in the world". So, the language faculty of a competent interpreter will take a sentence as input, and calculate a biconditional such as (1) which represents the truth conditions encoded by the sentence in virtue of the way the language of thought expressions "hook up" to the world. As Borg puts it, "word–world relations [are] (somewhat derivatively) . . . a proper part of the language faculty" (2004: 85). Hence in response to the naturalistic challenge Borg can respond that 'The cat is on the mat' encodes P, as opposed to P*, because of the way the semantic component of the language faculty functions. So on Borg's view the semantic facts are fixed by psychological facts concerning competent interpreters, though according to Borg the facts that do the fixing concern the unconscious processes of the semantic component of the language faculty, which are not in any way "constrained or affected" by intuitive judgments of speech act content.

Borg's example sentence, 'The cat is on the mat', and what she says about the semantic content of this sentence, reveals that the response to the naturalistic challenge sketched above is not adequate. Borg says that the semantic content of 'The cat is on the mat' is something to the effect that "some cat" is on "some mat". Consider two such propositions:

(P) {*w*: in *w*, at particular time *t*, the cat Fatty is sitting squarely in the middle of a doormat in front of #10 Downing Street}

(P*) {*w*: in *w*, at particular time *t*, the cat Fluffy is sitting squarely in the middle of a doormat in front of the White House}

Unless the language faculty fixes one of these propositions as *the* semantic content of 'The cat is on the mat', Borg's response fails to respond to the naturalistic challenge. If 'The cat is on the mat' semantically encodes the proposition that some particular cat is on some particular mat, then—if it is to adequately respond to the naturalistic challenge—the language faculty must determine *which* particular cat, Fatty or Fluffy, or Fuzzy, or . . . is on *which* particular mat. But, as Borg's loose gesture in the direction of "some cat" and "some mat" betrays, the language faculty, simply by translating English into mentalese, will fail to do this.

Clearly then Borg should deny that 'The cat is on the mat' has as its semantic content a singular proposition involving some particular cat and some particular mat. Rather, she should follow Lepore (2004) and maintain that sentences containing definite descriptions semantically encode propositions corresponding to Russellian expansions of those descriptions. On this view then the language component would "calculate" something like this biconditional:

(1a) 'The cat is on the mat' IS TRUE IFF (∃ !x)(∃ !y)[CATx & MATy & ON(<x,y>)]

This particular sentence of mentalese is now, and has always been, obviously false, since there are many cats and many mats. And thus whenever a speaker utters 'The cat is on the mat' she will be uttering a sentence which encodes an obviously false proposition. This result of course conflicts with our intuitive judgments concerning the truth conditions of such utterances, but this conflict should not deter Borg from adopting a Russellian analysis. For on her view our intuitive judgments concerning the truth conditions of utterances must not "affect our semantic theorizing" (2002: 7). Because Borg insulates her semantic theory from the intuitive semantic judgments of competent interpreters, there can be no "conflict" between her semantic theory and such intuitive judgments.

But putting the matter this starkly underscores the significance of the naturalistic challenge for Borg's version of SM. If the facts about semantic content are so radically different from, and are not in any way affected by, the intuitive semantic judgments of competent interpreters, then what fixes these facts? What makes it the case that P, and not P*, is the semantic content of 'The cat is on the mat'? Borg's response is that the language faculty links 'The cat is on the mat' to 'THE CAT IS ON THE MAT' and this sentence of mentalese hooks up to P, and not P*. But this response only relocates the problem. For what, if not the intuitive judgments of competent language users, makes it the case that THE CAT IS ON THE MAT hooks up to P, and not P*? Above I noted that if Borg's response is to succeed, each sentence in the language of thought, for example, 'THE CAT IS ON THE MAT', must "hook up" with a *unique* proposition, and thus Borg cannot allow that 'THE CAT' hooks up with different cats on different occasions.[8] So it seems that the language of thought correlates of definite descriptions must have a Russellian semantics (or some other sort of contextually invariant semantics). But merely invoking a Russellian analysis of definite descriptions is not going to solve the fundamental problem. Set aside the

[8] An anonymous referee suggested that Borg could allow that 'the cat'—and its mentalese correlate—refers to different cats on different occasions by positing a "demonstrative element" within the phrase. But to posit such "hidden indexicals" in response to counterexamples is to embrace what Borg calls "contextualism" (2004: 44–8) and Borg considers contextualism to be a version of TCP. So positing such hidden indexicals is antithetical to Borg's project. In Clapp (forthcoming), I call the strategy of undermining counterexamples by positing hidden indexicals "Kaplan's strategy".

questions concerning definite descriptions, and consider the other expressions in the language of thought. For example, what exactly is the contextually invariant semantic value (or extension) of 'ON' and what makes it the case that *that*, rather than some other extension, is *the* extension?

Consider a world w^* in which there is only one cat, Fluffy, and only one mat, m, and, for reasons that do not concern us, in w^* (at the relevant time) Fluffy is hovering one inch over m, though Fluffy's tail periodically brushes m.[9] Now suppose, for reductio, that the language faculty for competent speakers links, via Davidsonian calculations, the natural language sentence 'The cat is on the mat' with 'THE CAT IS ON THE MAT' and that this sentence in the language of thought hooks up to one and only one proposition P. Now either the semantic content of 'The cat is on the mat' is true in w*, or not. That is, either $w^* \in P$, or $w^* \notin P$. Thus, if it is facts concerning the semantic module of the language faculty that make it the case that P is the semantic content of 'The cat is on the mat' then there must be something about this semantic module which determines whether or not $w^* \in P$. But, according to Borg, all that semantic modules do is produce instances of representations such as (1) and (1a), and the calculation of such representations will not suffice to determine whether or not $w^* \in P$. Thus such calculations in the language faculty will not suffice to determine a proposition that can serve as *the* semantic content of 'The cat is on the mat'. The initial challenge was, "What, if not the judgments and practices of competent speakers, makes it the case that P is the semantic content of 'The cat is on the mat'?" And Borg's response was, "The language faculty links 'The cat is on the mat' to 'THE CAT IS ON THE MAT' and the unique content of this sentence of mentalese is P. That's what makes it the case that P is the semantic content of 'The cat is on the mat'." But now it is apparent that Borg's response merely relocates the problem. For what, if not the judgments and practices of competent speakers, makes it the case that the content of 'THE CAT IS ON THE MAT' is P, rather than P*?[10]

That Borg's appeal to a Davidsonian language of thought model fails to address the naturalistic challenge is disguised as a result of Borg's conflation of, and equivocation between, two importantly different notions of *truth conditions*.[11]

9 This example is inspired by similar situations described in Searle (1978).

10 I am not, at this point, claiming that there is no answer to this question. I am claiming that Borg's appeal to a language module which calculates T-theorems merely replaces the original question concerning the semantic content of natural language sentences with the corresponding question for the corresponding sentences of mentalese. That is, Borg's view merely replaces the question "Why is P, and not P*, the semantic content of 'The cat is on the mat'?" with "Why is P, and not P*, the semantic content of THE CAT IS ON THE MAT?" To meet the naturalistic challenge Borg must now answer this latter question.

11 This conflation of two notions of truth-conditions is also noted by Recanati: "The central idea of truth-conditional semantics (as opposed to mere 'translational semantics') is the idea that, via truth, we connect worlds and the world. If we know the truth-conditions of a sentence, we know which state of affairs must hold for the sentence to be true. T-sentences display knowledge of

Sometimes Borg uses 'truth conditions' in such a way that *truth conditions* are *representations*, specifically T-theorems such as (1) and (1a). But other times Borg uses the term to refer to *truth makers*, entities relative to which representations are evaluated for truth or falsity (e.g. possible worlds, situations, facts, etc.). Borg does not appreciate the inadequacy described above because she infers *from* the plausible premise that the language faculty produces some sort of T-theorem-like representations *to* the conclusion, which is not at all plausible, that the language faculty all by itself fixes the *truth-maker* truth conditions encoded by sentences. This equivocation is apparent in the following passage in which Borg summarizes her view with regard to an utterance of the indexical sentence 'That is mine':

> to grasp the literal content of an utterance of 'that is mine' one need only entertain a thought of the form: *α belongs to β*. We have already noted that to find out more precisely what belongs to whom, one needs to look beyond the information which is linguistically encoded, yet this does not entail that the language faculty alone is incapable of yielding complete [truth-maker] truth-conditions (or 'fully saturated propositions', if one prefers proposition talk). For the [T-theorem] truth-conditions of such token sentences can be generated entirely within the language faculty; for instance, . . . the proper [T-theorem] truth-condition for a token of 'that is mine' is simply:
>
> (2) If t is a token of 'that is mine' uttered by β, and the token of 'that' therein refers to α then t is true iff α is β's. (p. 206)

The advocate of TCP is willing to grant to Borg that every competent speaker of English has a modular language faculty, and even that their understanding of utterances of 'That is mine' is partially explained by the fact that this faculty produces instances of (something like) (2). Indeed, it seems to me that the advocate of TCP must grant that the cognitivist Davidsonian model is very plausible with regard to our competence with regard to *linguistic meaning*, i.e. with regard to what Neale would call *blueprints*. Since TCP does maintain that *sentences* encode such blueprints, the advocate of TCP can agree with Borg that, in a sense, sentences encode *T-theorem* truth conditions. But the advocate of TCP denies that such blueprints themselves determine propositional content, or *truth-maker* truth conditions. For according to TCP *truth-maker* truth conditions are determined only after a blueprint is developed via pragmatic processes which depend upon contextually variant sorts of information. So, in equivocating between the two sorts of truth conditions, Borg is conflating the two aspects of meaning—now using that term in the most general sense—that TCP is concerned to distinguish, namely meaning qua blueprints and meaning qua propositional content.

truth-conditions in that sense only if the right-hand-side of the bi-conditional is used, that is, only if the necessary and sufficient condition which it states is transparent to the utterer of the T-sentence. If I say 'Oscar cuts the sun is true iff Oscar cuts the sun', without knowing what it is to 'cut the sun,' then the T-sentence I utter no more counts as displaying knowledge of truth conditions than if I use it without knowing who Oscar is" (2005: 185).

4. WHY SOAMES FAILS TO MEET THE NATURALISTIC CHALLENGE

Soames (2002) offers a different sort of potential response to the naturalistic challenge. Soames, like Borg, also attempts to ground facts concerning the semantic content of sentences in facts concerning what competent speakers and interpreters do. But whereas Borg appeals to putative facts concerning the cognitive processing which account for an individual's semantic competence, Soames appeals to sociological facts concerning the linguistic judgments and behavior of a linguistic community:

> semantic claims about the expressions of a language are not claims about the individual psychologies, or states of mind, of language users; rather they are social claims about the conventions and commonalities found in a linguistic community. (Soames 2002: 71)

The relevant conventions and commonalities fix the "competency conditions" for using S (assuming S has no indexical features). The competency conditions for S consist of "information grasp of which explains speaker's ability to understand it, and be able to use it competently" (2002: 56). Since what counts as *understanding* and/or *competent use* of S can be determined only by a community of language users, the competency conditions for S are fixed by sociological facts.

Moreover, the competency conditions associated with S fix the semantic content of S. According to Soames, "the information (proposition) [S] semantically encodes . . . is invariant from context of utterance to context of utterance" (2002: 55). This is simply to say that if we are to assign to each (non-ambiguous, non-context-sensitive) sentence *type* a unique proposition as its semantic content, then semantic content cannot vary from utterance to utterance, as does speech act content. Thus, "the constant information semantically encoded by a sentence must be carefully distinguished from the varying information it is used to convey [and/or or assert] in different contexts" (ibid.). But what determines the core semantic content from all the other information that is conveyed and/or asserted by an utterance of S? The core semantic content is, according to Soames, the minimal core of information that is determined by the competency conditions associated with S as opposed to information which is grasped by interpreters in virtue of special features of the contexts in which S is uttered.

Soames is especially concerned with the semantics of proper names, and his view is best illustrated in terms of one of his examples involving proper names.[12] Consider an utterance by Soames of

(3) Carl Hempel lived on Lake Lane in Princeton

[12] Soames is of course aware that proper names are often not uniquely referring; e.g. many streets may be named 'Lake Lane'. As it is not directly relevant to my concerns, I will ignore this complication throughout the chapter.

to a graduate student in the philosophy department at Princeton University. In such a context of utterance both the speaker and the interpreter have mutual knowledge of each other's expertise in analytic philosophy. Given this special mutual knowledge, Soames's utterance of (3) conveys, and probably even asserts, to the student *that Prof. Carl Hempel, the great philosopher of science, lived on Lake Lane in Princeton.* But this relatively rich proposition is not the semantic content of sentence (3) because this proposition is not determined solely by the competency conditions associated with (3). For instance, Soames explains, "one doesn't have to know that Carl Hempel was a philosopher at all in order to understand and be a competent user of the name ['Carl Hempel']" (2002: 64). What then is the core semantic content expressed by (3)? According to Soames it is the singular, or Russellian, proposition consisting of Carl Hempel—under no description whatsoever—and the property of having lived on Lake Lane in Princeton. It is "the conditions governing what it is to be a competent user of an arbitrary proper name n" (p. 65) that determine this singular proposition to be the semantic content of (3).

So according to Soames it is the competency conditions associated with S, as established by a community of language users, that determine what the semantic content of S is. This view concerning what metaphysically determines the semantic content of a sentence S implies a sort of epistemological procedure for discerning what the semantic content of a given sentence S is: "If S is a sentence that doesn't contain indexicals or other context-sensitive elements, then the semantic content of S (i.e. the proposition it semantically expresses) should consist of information that a competent speaker who assertively utters S asserts and intends to convey *in any context* in which S is used nonmetaphorically (without irony, sarcasm, and so on) with its normal literal meaning" (Soames 2002: 57; my emphasis). Since the semantic content of S is fixed by the competency conditions associated with S, and the competency conditions do not vary across normal contexts, the semantic content of S cannot vary across normal contexts, where a *normal* context is, roughly, a context in which S is used *literally.* So to discern the semantic content of S, it will suffice to find the proposition that is conveyed and/or asserted by *every* literal utterance of S.[13] To put the idea somewhat metaphorically, let each literal utterance of S determine a set of asserted or otherwise conveyed propositions. To discern the semantic content of S, take the *intersection* of *all* these sets; the semantic content of S is

[13] The restriction to *literal* utterances, or as Soames says 'normal' utterances, is intended to rule out sarcastic, metaphoric, and other non-literal utterances. Such non-literal utterances must be excluded on pain of every sentence expressing no semantic content at all. Suppose that the one proposition that all non-sarcastic utterances of e.g. 'John is nice' convey is the proposition that John is nice (ignoring tense). But a sarcastic utterance of the sentence will not convey the proposition that John is nice, but rather that John is not nice. Thus, if the sarcastic utterance is taken into account, there is no proposition conveyed by every utterance, and thus the sentence has no semantic content at all. Hence the need to exclude sarcastic and other non-literal utterances from the intersection procedure.

the proposition that is a member of every such set. In what follows I will refer to this general procedure for discerning the semantic content of S as the *intersection procedure.*

As presented thus far there is a glitch in the intersection procedure for discerning semantic content. For it is plausible that whenever a proposition P is conveyed, so are some of its obvious entailments. If this is right, then the intersection procedure will never yield a unique proposition, since every proposition obviously entails some distinct proposition. For example, suppose, as is plausible, that every literal utterance of 'Dogs bark' conveys the proposition *that dogs bark. That dogs bark* obviously entails the proposition *that either dogs bark or pigs fly*. And therefore the intersection procedure does not distinguish between *that dogs bark* and the disjunctions this proposition obviously entails as being *the* semantic content of 'Dogs bark'. Because obvious entailments of conveyed propositions are also conveyed, the intersection procedure will never yield unique propositions as semantic contents. It is relatively clear, however, what the intuitively correct results should be, and thus Soames proposes to solve this problem by invoking the following intuitive idea: the fact that *that dogs bark* is conveyed by an utterance of 'Dogs bark' *explains* the fact that the disjunction is conveyed, but not vice versa. As Soames puts it, "there is an explanatory priority here" (2002: 61). Thus, in order to avoid the problematic result that the intersection procedure does not yield *unique* propositions, Soames appeals to this intuitive idea of explanatory priority. The amended intersection procedure is then expressed in the following principle (ibid. 62):

> SC1. A proposition p is semantically expressed by a sentence s *only if* p [is a member of the intersection] and there is no other proposition q such that the fact that q [is a member of the intersection] explains why p [is a member of the intersection].

The real problem with the intersection procedure, however, is not that it will result in *too many* candidates to serve as the semantic content of S, but rather that it will not yield *any* candidates; sometimes, often, the intersection procedure will yield the empty set. What this means is that for many sentences S the sorts of facts that Soames says fix the semantic content of S fail to fix the semantic content of S; i.e. Soames's response to the naturalistic challenge is inadequate. Soames himself has acknowledged this shortcoming with the intersection procedure, and in response he has, correctly in my view, rejected SM in favor of TCP.[14] One

[14] In the following passage Soames rejects his earlier view that sentences encode propositions, or truth conditions, and endorses the view of TCP that sentences encode only something like blueprints for asserted propositional content: "the semantic content of a sentence in a context is often not something asserted by an utterance of the sentence in that context. Instead, its function is to constrain the candidates for assertion in certain ways, while allowing speakers and hearers a degree of freedom to operate within these constraints" (2005: 357).

of the examples that Soames (2005) provides to motivate this rejection of his former view again involves identity and proper names. First, let us apply the intersection procedure to the identity sentence

(4) Carl Hempel is Peter Hempel.

According to Soames, the intersection procedure applied to (4) will yield the result that its semantic content is simply the singular proposition relating the referent, Hempel, to himself via the identity relation; the semantic content cannot contain any descriptive information because there is no descriptive information, no mode of presentation, that is conveyed by *every* literal utterance of (4). The only proposition (with explanatory priority) conveyed by *every* literal utterance of (2) is the singular one. Since semantic content is compositional—recall that the real motivation for positing semantic content is to preserve a layer of truth-conditional content that preserves the assign and combine model—it follows that a knowledge ascription such as

(5) Mary knows that Peter Hempel is Carl Hempel.

has as its semantic content the singular proposition that relates Mary, the referent, to the singular proposition encoded by (4) via the *knowledge* relation. Now suppose that Mary, a graduate student in philosophy at Princeton, knows that Carl Hempel is a great philosopher of science, and she has just been introduced to Peter Hempel, but she does not know that Peter Hempel is Carl Hempel. Scott understands Mary's failure to identify Peter and Carl, and he intends to convey this to his audience with a literal utterance of the negation of (5):

(Neg-5) Mary does *not* know that Peter Hempel is Carl Hempel.

Again because semantic content must obey compositionality, the semantic content of (Neg-5) must be the singular proposition which denies that the *knowledge* relation holds between Mary and the singular proposition semantically encoded by (4). The problem is that this negated proposition is *obviously* false, but competent speakers do *not* interpret Scott as conveying obviously false information with his literal utterance of (Neg-5). As Soames puts it, "no ordinary conversational participant—not even those fully apprised of Peter Hempel's identity—would dream of accusing the speaker of falsely asserting that Mary doesn't know of the pair consisting of Mr Hempel and Mr Hempel that the former is the latter" (2005: 374). The upshot is that *no* proposition is conveyed by *every* literal utterance of (Neg-5). For, as Soames argues, no one proposition containing descriptive information is conveyed by *every* literal utterance of (Neg-5), and Scott's utterance of (Neg-5) does not convey the singular proposition with no descriptive content. So the intersection contains no propositions containing descriptions of Mr Hempel, nor does the intersection contain the singular proposition containing only Mr Hempel. There is thus *no* proposition conveyed by *every* literal utterance of (Neg-5); the intersection procedure yields the empty set. Hence, the intersection procedure yields the result that (Neg-5) has no semantic content—*or at least the result that its semantic content is not truth-conditional.*

One might think that the problem arises only because of Soames's acceptance of the principle of semantic innocence, according to which the semantic content of a sentence remains constant regardless of whether the sentence appears on its own or as a clause in a larger sentence. But the problem arises regardless of one's allegiance to semantic innocence. Consider

(Neg-4) Carl Hempel is not Peter Hempel.

As Soames argues, the semantic content of (Neg-4) cannot contain any descriptive information, since the descriptive information conveyed by utterances of (Neg-4) varies from utterance to utterance. So the only plausible candidate that could serve as the semantic content of (Neg-4) is the necessarily, and obviously, false singular proposition denying that Mr Hempel is related to himself via the identity relation. But this necessarily false singular proposition cannot be the semantic content of (Neg-4) either. For consider the graduate student Mary; though she is a bit confused about Mr Hempel, she is certainly a competent user of both 'Peter Hempel' and 'Carl Hempel', and thus she is a competent user of (Neg-4). But if she were to sincerely and literally utter (Neg-4) she would not convey the necessarily and obviously false singular proposition that Mr Hempel is not self-identical. So again the intersection procedure yields the empty set—there is no proposition that can serve as the semantic content of (Neg-4).

The two examples above involve proper names, and thus one might think that it is Soames's direct reference account of the semantic content of proper names that is the source of the problems for the intersection procedure. But, first, this response gets matters backwards: the direct reference account of proper names is a *consequence* of the intersection procedure; Soames uses the intersection procedure to argue against description theories and thereby support Kripke's direct reference theory. Second, there are many obviously problematic sentences that do not contain proper names. Consider

(6) The woman cannot continue.[15]

Some of the problems result from the definite description. Clearly competent speakers can and do use (6) to convey information about different women, so the

[15] A similar sentence is discussed by Carston (2002) and Borg (2004).

only hope for the semantic minimalist is to endorse a Russellian semantics for definite descriptions; if Soames were to endorse some sort of referential treatment, the intersection procedure would yield no one proposition as being *the* semantic content. But a Russellian treatment of the definite description will result in the intersection procedure again yielding the empty set. For it is implausible to suppose that any competent speaker will *ever* use (6) to convey, among other things, that there is one and only one woman in existence. But Soames (2002) must endorse an even stronger claim, namely, that competent speakers *always* use (6) to convey this obviously false proposition. But this strong claim is clearly false. Since not every literal utterance of (6) by a competent speaker conveys, among other things, that there is one and only one woman in existence, it again follows that the intersection procedure yields the empty set. The result of the intersection procedure is that no proposition is the semantic content of (6).

The verb phrase of (6), with its elided direct object, is problematic for similar reasons. Competent speakers use literal utterances of (6) to say of various specific women that they cannot continue doing various specific activities: studying, working, running, breathing, etc. But of course the activity about which something is being said varies from utterance to utterance, and thus no one specific activity can feature in the semantic content of (6). In a move analogous to the appeal to Russell's existential analysis of the definite description, Soames (2002) might claim that the elided direct object is replaced by an existential quantifier (perhaps one that is somehow both singular and plural). So the semantic content of (6) would then be something along the lines of, *that the woman cannot continue doing something(s).* (I am here ignoring the problems with the definite description, as well as tense.) But this analogous response fails for analogous reasons. It is extremely implausible that competent speakers *ever* use (6) to convey the obviously (and perhaps *necessarily*) false proposition *that the woman cannot continue doing something(s).* But, again, Soames (2002) needs to endorse an even stronger claim: namely, that competent speakers, when speaking literally, *always* use (6) to convey this obviously (and necessarily) false proposition. But this strong claim is, again, clearly false.[16]

[16] If the elided direct object is to be replaced by an existential quantifier, then there is a possible scope ambiguity between the negation and this "hidden" quantifier. The two resulting potential propositions can be represented as follows:

(i) Not Some X (Mary can continue X)
(ii) Some X Not (Mary can continue X)

(For the sake of simplicity I have replaced the definite description with 'Mary'.) I have argued, in essence, that (i) cannot serve as the semantic content of 'Mary cannot continue' because it is obviously and necessary false, and thus it is clearly not conveyed by every utterance of the sentence. Proposition (ii) cannot serve as the semantic content of 'Mary cannot continue' for somewhat different reasons, for (ii) is obviously and necessarily true and there is no reason to suppose that such an obviously true proposition could not serve as the common semantic core. The reason that

Consideration of sentences such as (6) ought to cause one to wonder if the intersection procedure *ever* yields a unique result. Is there *any* sentence S and proposition P such that it is even relatively plausible that every literal utterance of S conveys P?[17] It is somewhat ironic that the examples Soames (2002) provides to support the thesis that "the phenomenon of asserting more than the semantic content of the sentence one utters is all but ubiquitous" (2002: 77) seem to do more to support the thesis that the intersection procedure often fails to yield a proposition. Consider Soames's "Coffee, Please" example:

A man goes into a coffee shop and sits at the counter. The waitress asks him what he wants. He says, "I would like coffee, please." The sentence uttered is unspecific in several respects—its semantic content does not indicate whether the coffee is to be in the form of beans, grounds, or liquid, nor does it indicate whether the amount in question is a drop, a cup, a gallon, a sack, or a barrel. (2002: 78)

Given that the sentence 'I would like coffee' could be used to assert that one has any one of the wide diversity of desires Soames gestures toward, and many others as well, how plausible is the claim that there is some unique proposition that is conveyed by *every* literal utterance of 'I would like coffee'? Or, to account for the indexical "I", our question really needs to be, "How plausible is it that for every class of utterances of 'I would like coffee' where the referent of "I" is held fixed, there is some proposition such that every utterance in the class conveys this proposition?" Again taking our cue from Russell's existential analysis of definite descriptions, if there were such a proposition it would have to be a very abstract sort of existential proposition concerning a desire regarding some entity or event that bears some sort of relation to coffee, in some form or other. For only such an abstract existential generalization could be conveyed by both, for example, Hillary Clinton's utterance of 'I want coffee' used to indicate her preference concerning the color of a formal gown she is buying, and also by her utterance of the sentence to instruct her staff that the caterers should serve coffee, and not tea, at a fundraising breakfast for her constituents. Could such an abstract existentially generalized proposition serve as the semantic content of 'I would like coffee' (or 'Hillary Clinton would like coffee')? I am skeptical

(ii) cannot serve as the semantic content is that this claim would violate the explanatory priority constraint built into the intersection procedure. Suppose that Scott utters (6) and thereby conveys, say, that Emma cannot continue endorsing semantic minimalism. *Because* this proposition has as one of its obvious entailments the existential generalization of the direct object position, namely (ii), by uttering (4) Soames also asserts proposition (ii). That is, the general proposition (ii) is conveyed only because the more specific proposition is conveyed, and thus (ii) has a lower explanatory priority, and cannot serve as the semantic content of (6).

[17] The obvious place to look for such pairs would be in abstract and technical areas of language use, such as advanced science and mathematics. Bach (1994) defends the intermediate view that *some* commonplace sentences semantically encode unique propositions, while other commonplace (non-indexical) sentences do not encode propositions. Here I am not concerned with this intermediate sort of view; here I am concerned to argue only that *not every* (non-indexical) grammatical sentence semantically encodes a unique proposition.

that any such existentially generalized proposition could be formulated, but the point is moot. For even *if* there were some very abstract existentially generalized proposition such that *every* possible literal utterance of 'I would like coffee' (by Hillary Clinton) conveyed this proposition, it is clear that no such proposition would, for every such utterance, have *explanatory priority*.

Recall that in order to avoid the result of the intersection procedure yielding *too many* candidate propositions to serve as *the* semantic content of a sentence, the procedure was amended so that only propositions with *explanatory priority* were candidates for semantic content. Now consider Hillary's utterance of 'I would like coffee' used to assert proposition

(A) *that Hillary Clinton wants the caterers to serve the liquid made from coffee in the usual way at the fundraising breakfast.*

If Hillary's utterance succeeded in asserting this proposition, then it is at least plausible that it would also assert all of the obvious entailments of (A), including all of the obvious existential generalizations of (A); some of these existential generalizations might be thought to be asserted by *all* of Hillary's literal utterances of 'I would like coffee'. One such existential generalization is

(B) *that Hillary Clinton wants some event E to take place were E bears some relation R to some form F of coffee.*

Suppose that both (A) and (B) are conveyed, indeed asserted, by one of Hillary's utterances of 'I would like coffee'. Which proposition has explanatory priority? Does the fact that (A) is asserted explain the fact that (B) is asserted, or does the fact that (B) is asserted explain the fact that (A) is asserted? Clearly the former is the case. It is (A) that Hillary intends to assert, and that she does assert this relatively specific information is what explains how she also manages to assert the existential generalization (B) (granting for the sake of argument that (B) is asserted). The general point is that even if one could find some existentially generalized proposition that all possible literal utterances of 'I would like coffee' by Hillary Clinton asserted, such an abstract proposition could not serve as the semantic content of 'I would like coffee' (relativized to Hillary Clinton) because it would not be *explanatorily prior* to all of the more specific propositions Hillary asserted.[18]

[18] A point of clarification: I do *not* deny that every competent speaker must associate very general information of the sort represented by (B) with utterances of 'Hillary Clinton would like coffee'. I agree that information of roughly the sort (B) represents must be included in the linguistic meaning, the ***blueprint***, encoded by 'Hillary Clinton would like coffee'. I *do* deny that this very general sort of information is always *asserted, conveyed*, or otherwise *communicated* by literal utterances of 'Hillary Clinton would like coffee'. Moreover, *if* this very general information is asserted, or otherwise communicated, by some utterance of 'Hillary Clinton would like coffee', then it is communicated

Perhaps then the advocate of SM should not appeal to existential generalization to articulate what the semantic content of 'I would like coffee' (relativized to Hillary Clinton) is. Perhaps he should just say that the semantic content of 'I would like coffee' (relativized to Hillary Clinton) is simply

(C) *that Hillary Clinton would like coffee*

and that's that. But we must be careful here not to confuse the two notions of truth conditions. Nobody denies that every utterance of the following T-theorem is true:

(7) 'I would like coffee', relativized to Hillary Clinton, is true iff Hillary Clinton would like coffee.

The naturalistic challenge for SM is, what conditions, what possible worlds, satisfy, or make true, 'I would like coffee' (relativized to Hillary Clinton) and moreover what determines that just those situations, as opposed to others, are the ones that make true the sentence? For example, is the sentence (relativized to Hillary Clinton) made true by situations in which Hillary wants Bill to spill hot coffee, as opposed to warm milk, on himself? And what determines whether or not situations of this kind satisfy the sentence (relativized to Hillary Clinton)? Simply being told that the sentence (relativized to Hillary Clinton) encodes the proposition *that Hillary Clinton wants coffee* does nothing to answer these questions.

At this point the semantic minimalist may start to wonder if I am demanding too much. Perhaps the appropriate response to the naturalistic challenge is not to attempt to ground (alleged) facts about the semantic content of sentences in the cognitive processing of competent speakers, nor in the judgments and behavior in communities of competent language users. Perhaps the appropriate response is to pass the buck: If the challenge is metaphysical, then perhaps it should be left to the metaphysicians. This is the response endorsed by Cappelen and Lepore.

5. WHY CAPPELEN AND LEPORE FAIL TO MEET THE NATURALISTIC CHALLENGE

Recall the naturalistic challenge. Suppose SM is correct, and every sentence S has as its semantic content some proposition P (perhaps relative to contexts), where the semantic content of S is typically "radically different" (Cappelen and Lepore. 2005*a*: 211) from the speech act contents interpreters intuitively judge

only in virtue of being entailed by some more specific proposition that is also communicated by the utterance, in which case the more specific proposition has higher explanatory priority.

utterances of S to assert. What then fixes or determines the purely semantic fact that P, rather than P*, is the semantic content of S? Cappelen and Lepore do not, to my knowledge, address precisely this objection, though it is, I suggest, what is really behind the two objections against SM they do consider.[19] The first, which they call the "metaphysical objection", calls into question the existence of propositions which might serve as the semantic contents of certain sentences. For example, a critic advancing the metaphysical objection denies that there is a unique proposition that is the semantic content of 'Osama Bin Laden is tall'. The second objection considered by Cappelen and Lepore, which they call "the psychological objection", is that even if there were such a proposition, it would "play no role whatsoever in the mental life of communicators" (2005*b*: 182). My purpose in this section is thus to analyze the responses Cappelen and Lepore provide to these objections and discern whether or not these responses suggest a way for SM to meet the naturalistic challenge.

The objector raising the metaphysical objection doubts, for example, that the sentence 'Osama Bin Laden is tall' encodes a proposition, or expresses truth conditions. Cappelen and Lepore present this objector as posing the question "what is it to satisfy the semantic truth conditions of '[Osama Bin Laden] is tall?' " (2005*a*: 205, ignoring tense). And here is Cappelen and Lepore's reply:

> Our quick, and we think completely satisfactory, reply is given by . . . [(8p)]:
>
> (8p) 'Osama Bin Laden is tall' semantically expresses the proposition *that Osama Bin Laden is tall.*

At this point we are very much in danger of again making the mistake, illustrated in the above passage from Borg, of conflating the truth-maker sense of 'truth conditions' and the T-theorem sense of 'truth conditions'. To answer the question, which concerns *truth-maker* truth conditions, they must do more than *mention* (8p); they have to make an *assertion* by *using* (8p), and thereby specify—with the use of the right-hand side of the biconditional—the proposition P that is, allegedly, the semantic content of 'Osama Bin Laden is tall'. It is not clear that they have even attempted to make such an assertion, but let us suppose they had. What would follow?

[19] That this is so is suggested by the fact that neither objection on its own really makes much sense. The critic advancing the psychological objection apparently grants that sentences do encode propositions, but denies that such propositions play any role in the mental life of communicators. This is a strange position. If S encodes P, and Mary understands, or interprets, or utters, S, then is P not "playing some role" in Mary's mental life? In what other way could a *proposition* "play a role" in Mary's mental life? The critic advancing the metaphysical objection, on the other hand, grants that sufficiently precise sentences encode propositions, but maintains that some insufficiently precise sentences, e.g. 'Osama Bin Laden is tall', fail to encode (complete) propositions. As Cappelen and Lepore point out, this critic occupies an unstable position (and one reminiscent of logical atomism at that). The task of "precisifying" 'Osama bin Laden is tall' would lead to a regress of not yet precise enough sentences: 'Osam Bin Laden is tall'; 'Osama bin Laden is tall *for a man*'; 'Osama Bin Laden is tall for a man *born in Asia*'; 'Osama Bin Laden is tall for a man born in Asia, and *not born prematurely*', etc.

First, note that, according to Cappelen and Lepore, the content we interpreters intuitively judge this assertion to have is probably "radically different" than the semantic content the sentence encodes. This is because, again, the speech act content we interpret utterances as asserting "depends on a potentially indefinite range of facts about [Cappelen and Lepore], and [we interpreters] and [our shared context] . . . These facts have no bearing on the semantic content of the [sentence uttered]" (2005*a*: 211). Given the sharp distinction that SM *must* draw between intuitive speech act content and encoded semantic content, and the difficulty of distinguishing them,[20] Cappelen and Lepore's confidence that they have succeeded in helping us discern the proposition encoded by 'Osama Bin Laden is tall' is misplaced. If intuitive speech act contents are as different from semantic contents as Cappelen and Lepore suggest, then it seems that simply uttering a sentence will never suffice to specify the semantic content of a sentence.

But these worries are somewhat tangential to the naturalistic challenge, which grants to Cappelen and Lepore both that 'Osama Bin Laden is tall' encodes a unique proposition P, and even that they can somehow communicate to us what this proposition is. The naturalistic challenge in this case amounts to the following question. Suppose 'Osama Bin Laden is tall' encodes P. What fixes this alleged semantic fact? Why does the sentence encode P, as opposed to some other proposition P*? Consider, for example, a possible world w^* in which Osama Bin Laden is 5′11″. Is w^* in the semantic content of 'Osama Bin Laden is tall' or not, and what determines this? Even ignoring the difficulty Cappelen and Lepore face in communicating to us the semantic content of 'Osama Bin Laden is tall', the appeal to (8p) does nothing to address the naturalistic challenge.

Thankfully for my purposes, however, Cappelen and Lepore do not stop with their quick appeal to (8p), for they imagine their objectors responding to their quick appeal to (8p) as follows:

> I can't take this theory seriously unless you tell me more about what the right-hand side of [that] bi-conditional mean[s] (or require[s], or demand[s] or . . .). (2005*a*: 205).

Now for the reasons stated above, the imaginary objector who wants to know what proposition is the semantic content of 'Osama Bin Laden is tall' is right to demand more information, for an assertion of (8p) is too polluted with speech act content to specify for interpreters whatever the unique proposition encoded by

[20] Cappelen and Lepore assert that "if you want to use intuitions about speech act content to fix semantic content, you must be extremely careful. It can be done, but it's a subtle and easily corrupted process" (2005*a*: 199). They seem to think that the way it can be done, if one is careful enough, is by applying three "tests" for finding out whether or not an expression is context-sensitive. But, even granting that these tests are adequate tests for real context-sensitivity, it is obvious that they will not suffice for the task at hand. According to SM there are relatively few real context-sensitive expressions. So consider a sentence S that contains no such expressions. (I continue to ignore tense.) How are tests for context-sensitive expressions going to help us determine what the semantic content of S is?

the sentence is. But that objector is not me; I am willing to grant to Cappelen and Lepore that some proposition P is the semantic content of the sentence. What I demand to know is why P, and not P*, is the semantic content. Fortunately what Cappelen and Lepore say in response the imaginary objector also at least addresses the naturalistic challenge. Here's what Cappelen and Lepore say:

> If you think there is such a thing as tallness [and Cappelen and Lepore are confident that you do], then let that be the semantic value of 'tall' in 'Osama Bin Laden is tall' and in answer to the question as to what it takes for that sentence to be true we say that it is whatever it takes for Osama bin Laden to have that property. (2005*a*: 208)

Now Cappelen and Lepore confess that they are not accomplished metaphysicians, and thus they have only some crude guesses as to what it takes for something to instantiate tallness. And thus they confess that they really do not know what it takes for the sentence to be true; i.e. since they do not know what it takes for Osama to instantiate tallness, they do not know if world w^* (a world in which Osama Bin Laden is 5′11″) is a member of the truth conditions of 'Osama Bin Laden is tall'. But, they do not think this is an embarrassment for SM, for the objector's view that they "qua semanticists, are required to respond to this challenge" is "absurd" (2005*a*: 206).

So Cappelen and Lepore's response to their imaginary objector who demands to know the truth conditions of 'Osama Bin Laden is tall' is this. Of the many potential truth conditions—worlds in which Osama is 5′10″, 5′11″, 6′, etc.—they do not know which are the semantic truth conditions of the sentence, because these conditions are determined by certain deep and hoary metaphysical facts concerning the real nature of tallness, and they, being mere semanticists, do not know what these facts are. Note, however, that in excusing themselves from responding to their imaginary objector in this way Cappellen and Lepore actually address the naturalistic challenge head-on: According to Cappelen and Lepore, if P is the semantic content of 'Osama Bin Laden is tall' then what determines this fact is not anything to do with how speakers use this sentence to communicate; rather what determines this fact are deep and as of yet unknown metaphysical facts concerning Osama and tallness. So, generalizing now, according to this response to the naturalistic challenge what makes it the case that P, as opposed to P*, is the semantic content of S is unknown facts concerning the individuals and properties referred to by the words in S. Does this appeal to as of yet unknown metaphysical facts concerning the real natures of properties and individuals constitute an adequate response to the naturalistic challenge?

I suggest that it does not, or at least it does not if one thinks that the explanatory domain of semantics pertains to empirical questions about how competent language users communicate by using language and does not concern questions about, for example, the real nature of tallness. If you are interested in explaining how competent language users are able to communicate by uttering 'Osama bin Laden is tall', and the alleged semantic content of this sentence is determined not by the communicative abilities and practices of competent speakers but instead by metaphysical facts concerning the real nature of Osama and tallness, then you will have no interest in semantic content. I am thus agreeing with Cappelen and Lepore about the sorts of issues semanticists should concern themselves. They are correct that is absurd to require semanticists to address metaphysical questions concerning, for example, the real nature of tallness. (It might even be absurd to expect anyone to answer such questions.) But if it is such metaphysical facts that determine that P is the semantic content of S, it follows that it is absurd to require semanticists to address questions concerning semantic content. If knowing whether or not proposition P is the semantic content of 'Osama Bin Laden is tall' requires one to address issues concerning the real nature of tallness, then questions concerning semantic content should be addressed not by semanticists, but by metaphysicians (if at all).

One might respond on behalf of Cappelen and Lepore that I am incorrectly assuming that the metaphysical issues concerning, for example, the real nature of tallness are wholly distinct from issues concerning the abilities and practices of competent speakers. If the fact that P is the semantic content of 'Osama Bin Laden is tall' is in part determined by metaphysical facts concerning the real nature of tallness, but these metaphysical facts are themselves determined by the abilities and practices of competent speakers, then it would not be absurd to require semanticists to address issues concerning semantic content. I have two points in response to this suggestion. First, Cappellen and Lepore would not endorse this suggestion, since they maintain that it is absurd to require semanticists to address metaphysical issues; clearly then they take such metaphysical issues to be independent of issues concerning the abilities and practices of competent speakers. Second, I find the suggestion plausible. It may be no longer be popular, but it seems to me that seemingly deep questions about the natures of properties and individuals collapse into questions concerning our linguistic abilities and practices. I find this familiar idea plausible because I cannot take seriously the possibility of some hard-working metaphysician discovering that, contrary to the beliefs and practices of competent speakers, giraffes are *really* not tall. But invoking this familiar idea at this point in the dialectic only serves to reintroduce the naturalistic challenge: if the facts concerning semantic content are determined by metaphysical facts, yet these metaphysical facts are in turn determined by facts concerning the abilities and practices of competent speakers, then semantic content is, in the end, determined by facts concerning the abilities and practices of competent speakers. So, semantic content is relevant to semantic theorizing after all. But, again, how *could* facts concerning semantic content be fixed by the abilities and practices of competent speakers, given SM's claim that the speech act contents communicated by speakers "can be (and typically are) radically different from the semantic contents of... utterances" (2005*a*: 211)?

How do Cappelen and Lepore respond to the psychological objection? Recall the objection: even if there were a unique proposition encoded by, for example,

'Osama Bin Laden is tall', it would "play no role whatsoever in the mental life of communicators" (2005*b*: 182). How do Cappelen and Lepore respond to this objection, and does their response provide SM with a way to meet the naturalistic challenge? Cappelen and Lepore suggest that the semantic content encoded by a sentence plays the following role in the cognitive life of communicators: "minimal semantic content is a 'shared fallback content' and . . . this content serves to guard against confusion and misunderstandings" (2005*a*: 215). Cappelen and Lepore remind us of all the ways a speaker and interpreter can fail to have a "shared context": they can have distinct beliefs about what the other believes and knows, about their perceptual environment(s), about the content of the preceding discourse, etc. All such divergences lead to communicative breakdowns of various sorts. Cappelen and Lepore suggest that "the proposition semantically expressed is our minimal defense against confusion/misunderstanding/indifference, and it is that which guarantees communication across context of utterance" (2005*a*: 214). But *why* can minimal semantic content, yet not speech act content, play this role in our cognitive lives? The reason, according to Cappelen and Lepore, is that semantic content, unlike speech act content, does not depend upon such variable and potentially confused features of context: "the proposition semantically expressed is that content the speaker can expect the audience to grasp (and expect the audience to expect the speaker to expect them to grasp) even if they have mistaken or incomplete communication-relevant information" (2005*a*: 214).

This explanation of why semantic content, as opposed to speech act content, can serve as this minimal defense against confusion suggests a response to the naturalistic challenge. If P is the semantic content of sentence S, then what makes it the case that P, as opposed to P*, is the semantic content of S is this: *all* competent speakers *s* can expect *all* competent interpreters *i* to grasp (and *s* can expect *i* to expect *s* to expect *i* to grasp) P upon witnessing a literal utterance of S, yet *s* cannot have this expectation for P*. In other words, the proposal for meeting the naturalistic challenge that can be extracted from Cappelen and Lepore's response to the psychological objection is that if P is the semantic content of S, then what makes this the case is that the *competency conditions* for using S fix P, as opposed to some other proposition P*, as the proposition encoded by S.[21] But this is the very proposal suggested by Soames (2002), which was shown to be inadequate in the previous section of this chapter (and also in Soames 2005). The problem, in short, is that if P were determined to be the semantic content of S by the *competency conditions* associated with S, then the result of applying what I earlier called the *intersection procedure* to S would

[21] If Cappelen and Lepore endorse this strategy of response to the naturalistic challenge they cannot merely *stipulate* that there is a proposition (the semantic content of S) that is conveyed by every utterance S. Such a stipulation would get the order of explanation wrong. According to the intersection procedure, if P is the semantic content of S then it is so *in virtue of the fact* that P is the unique proposition conveyed by every utterances of S.

yield one, and only one, proposition; i.e. one, and only one, proposition would be conveyed by *every* (literal) utterance of S. But, as was demonstrated in the previous section, for many sentences S the intersection procedure does not yield any truth evaluable content; it yields no *proposition.*[22] Note, however, that this conclusion does *not* entail that there is no common core of *linguistic meaning* associated with every grammatical sentence. Cappelen and Lepore are correct at least to the extent that communication would be impossible if every sentence did not encode *some sort of blueprint for constructing communicated content.* It is, I suggest, this non-truth-conditional linguistic meaning that serves as our "minimal defense against confusion" and as the "starting point" for linguistic communication (2005*a*: 214–15).

6. CONCLUSION

The tentative conclusion is that either sentences (perhaps relativized to contexts) do not encode truth-conditional semantic content, or they do but such encoded content falls outside the explanatory domain of empirically oriented semantics that is concerned to explain the abilities and practices of competent language users. The conclusion is tentative because I have here considered only three potential responses to the naturalistic challenge; I cannot claim to have considered all the possible responses available to SM.

Let us suppose, however, that the tentative conclusion is correct, and moreover let us further suppose that the advocates of SM have no interest in positing a layer of pure semantic content that exists wholly independent of the abilities and practices of competent language users. Let us suppose, in short, that TCP is endorsed instead of SM. To what extent must the advocates of SM revise their general approach to semantic theory? The answer is, "very little". For TCP and SM agree that there is a minimal linguistic meaning associated with every grammatical utterance. They agree, moreover, that though this minimal linguistic meaning is distinct from asserted or otherwise conveyed truth-conditional content, it is nonetheless the common core, the "starting point", without which communication would be impossible. Moreover, they agree that though *speech act content* depends upon all sorts of contextually specific factors concerning both speakers and interpreters,[23] the linguistic meaning associated with an utterance remains fixed across contexts. The only way in which the advocate of SM is required to revise his position is this: he will have to concede

[22] Elugardo (this volume) demonstrates with a number of interesting examples that, in effect, for many sorts of grammatical utterances the intersection procedure yields no proposition, and thus semantic content cannot play the role of "minimal fallback content".

[23] That is, SM and TCP are in agreement concerning what Cappelen and Lepore refer to as "Speech Act Pluralism". See Cappelen and Lepore 2005*b*: ch. 13.

that the compositionally determined minimal core of linguistic meaning does not all by itself determine truth-conditional content, but rather a sort of blueprint for constructing truth-conditional content in particular contexts.[24]

Given the cogency of the arguments advocates of SM have proffered to distinguish the sort of meaning that is encoded in *sentences* from the sort of meaning that is intuitively conveyed by *utterances*, it is difficult to discern what could motivate principled resistance to this revision. This suggests that the appearance of significant schism between analytic philosophers of language and semantic theorists who advocate SM and those who advocate some form of TCP is for the most part an illusion, resulting from the fact that the focus of the semantic minimalists' theorizing is the context-invariant linguistic meanings competent speakers associate with sentence types, whereas the focus of truth-conditional pragmatists'-theorizing concerns the processes competent interpreters utilize to infer *from* an utterance of sentence with a certain invariant linguistic meaning *to* a context specific speech act content.

REFERENCES

Bach, K. (1994), 'Conversational Impliciture', *Mind and Language*, 9: 124–62.

____ (1987), *Thought and Reference*. Oxford: Clarendon Press.

Bezuidenhout, A. (2002), 'Truth Conditional Pragmatics', in *Philosophical Perspectives, 16, Language and Mind*, ed. J. Tomberlin.

Borg, E. (2002), 'The Semantic Significance of What is Said', *Protosociology*, 17, *Semantics and Reported Speech*.

____ (2004), *Minimal Semantics*. Oxford: Oxford University Press.

Cappelen, H., and E. Lepore (2005*a*), 'A Tall Tale: In Defense of Semantic Minimalism and Speech Act Pluralism', in G. Preyer and G. Peters (eds.), *Contextualism and Philosophy*. Oxford: Oxford University Press.

____ and ____ (2005*b*), *Insensitive Semantics: A Defense of Semantic Minimalism and Speech Act Pluralism*. Oxford: Blackwell Publishing.

____ and ____ (2005*c*), 'Radical and Moderate Pragmatics: Does Meaning Determine Truth Conditions?' in Z. Gendler Szabó (ed.), *Semantics versus Pragmatics*. Oxford: Oxford University Press.

Carston, R. (2002), *Thoughts and Utterances: The Pragmatics of Explicit Communication*. Oxford: Blackwell Publishing.

Clapp, L. (forthcoming), 'In Defense of Context Shifting Arguments', in Robert Stainton and Chris Viger (eds.), *Compositionality, Context and Semantic Values. Studies in Linguistics and Philosophy*. Dordrecht: Springer.

[24] A very similar proposal for amending SM is made by MacFarlane (this volume). MacFarlane suggests that SM deny that a proposition (i.e. the semantic content encoded by a sentence) is equivalent to an intension (i.e. a function from possible worlds to truth values); rather on MacFarlane's proposal a *proposition* will yield an intension only relative to a "counts-as" function. Such functions are determined by features of contexts of utterance and interpretation including "the speaker's intentions, the conversational common ground, and other such things". Thus what MacFarlane calls a *proposition* is roughly equivalent to what I have called, following Neale, a *blueprint*.

King, J., and J. Stanley (2005), 'Semantics, Pragmatics, and the Role of Semantic Content', in Z. Gendler Szabó (ed.), *Semantics versus Pragmatics.* Oxford: Oxford University Press.

Lepore, E. (2004), 'An Abuse of Context in Semantics: The Case of Incomplete Definite Descriptions', in Anne Bezuidenhout and Marga Reimer (eds.), *Descriptions and Beyond: An Interdisciplinary Collection of Essays on Definite and Indefinite Descriptions and Other Related Phenomena.* Oxford: Oxford University Press.

Neale, S. (2004), 'This, That, and the Other', in Anne Bezuidenhout and Marga Reimer (eds.), *Descriptions and Beyond: An Interdisciplinary Collection of Essays on Definite and Indefinite Descriptions and Other Related Phenomena.* Oxford: Oxford University Press.

Pietroski, P. (2005), 'Meaning Before Truth', in G. Preyer and G. Peters (eds.), *Contextualism and Philosophy.* Oxford: Oxford University Press.

Recanati, F. (2004), *Literal Meaning.* Cambridge: Cambridge University Press.

——(2005), 'Literalism and Contextualism: Some Varieties', in G. Preyer and G. Peters (eds.), *Contextualism and Philosophy.* Oxford: Oxford University Press.

Reimer, M (2002), 'Do Adjectives Conform to Compositionality', in *Philosophical Perspectives, 16, Language and Mind,* ed. James Tomberlin.

Searle, J. (1978), 'Literal Meaning', *Erkenntnis,* 13: 207–24.

——(1980), 'The Background of Meaning', in J. Searle, F. Kiefer, and M. Bierwisch (eds.), *Speech Act Theory and Pragmatics.* Dordrecht: Reidel.

Soames, S. (1989), 'Direct Reference, Propositional Attitudes, and Semantic Content', *Philosophical Topics,* 15: 47–87.

——(2002), *Beyond Rigidity: The Unfinished Semantic Agenda of Naming and Necessity.* Oxford: Oxford University Press.

——(2005), 'Naming and Asserting', in Z. Gendler Szabó (ed.), *Semantics Versus Pragmatics.* Oxford: Oxford University Press.

Sperber, D., and D. Wilson (1986). *Relevance.* Oxford: Oxford University Press.

Stanley, J., and Z. Szabo (2000), 'On Quantifier Domain Restriction', *Mind and Language,* 15: 219–61.

Travis, C. (2000), *Unshadowed Thought: Representation in Thought and Language.* Cambridge, Mass.: Harvard University Press.

11

Minimal Propositions, Cognitive Safety Mechanisms, and Psychological Reality

Reinaldo Elugardo

PART ONE

1. Minimal Propositions

Cappelen and Lepore's Semantic Minimalism is based on the familiar idea that natural language is semantically compositional: the meaning of every sentence of a natural language *L* is compositionally fixed solely by the meanings of its syntactic constituents, and its syntactic structure (2005: 144–5).[1] The meaning assigned to a sentence of *L* is the output of a finite, recursively definable, computational procedure defined over a finite stock of semantic primitives. The procedure is a bottom–up, semantically interpretative, process extending from a sentence's lexical parts, through its phrasal parts, and onto its clausal parts, which includes the sentence itself. [2] Cappelen and Lepore add something else to this familiar picture: the semantic content of a non-indexical sentence is a complete,

[1] All page references to *Insensitive Semantics* (henceforth, *IS*) will be made in the text. Throughout *IS*, Cappelen and Lepore speak of an expression's "semantic value" (relative to an interpretation of the language) rather than its meaning. Nothing of importance turns on this as far as this chapter is concerned. By "semantic value", they mean the extension of an expression, which could be an object, an ordered n-tuple of objects, a function, a truth-value, etc., depending on the expression's semantic type.

[2] Semantic compositionality doesn't require that primitive syntactic constituents have only one semantic value or even a precise extension. The mapping of (possibly imprecise) semantic inputs at the lexical level into (possibly imprecise) semantic outputs at the sentential level can be many-to-many—that would just be a case of semantic ambiguity (assuming that the sentence in question has one single syntactic analysis). On the other hand, if one also holds that the semantic content of a sentence must always be some single, truth-evaluable, non-vague proposition (again, assuming that the sentence has only one syntactic analysis), then lexical ambiguity and vagueness will have to be resolved at the level of primitive syntactic constituents. But that requirement comes from the belief that every meaningful sentence must express a complete, truth-evaluable, proposition, and not from the grammatical properties of language *per se*.

truth-evaluable, proposition that has no semantically unarticulated constituent: every constituent of the proposition expressed corresponds to some formal bit in the sentence's syntax (*IS* 3–4).[3] Call these propositions, "minimal propositions".

So far, this picture of natural language semantics is shared by others with whom Cappelen and Lepore disagree, most notably, Stanley (2000) and Stanley and Szabó (2000). The difference is that Cappelen and Lepore deny what the others hold, namely, that many linguistic expressions are implicitly context-sensitive.[4] In particular, they deny that common nouns, adjectives, and verbs have hidden, unvoiced, indexicals or variable-slots in their form. By Cappelen and Lepore's lights, natural languages like English have only a few context-sensitive expressions and those are just the "obvious" ones, such as indexicals, bare demonstratives, temporal adverbs, and spatial locatives. They comprise what Cappelen and Lepore call "the Basic Set of Context Sensitive Expressions" (*IS* 1–2).[5]

To sum up: on Cappelen and Lepore's view, the semantic content of a sentence, relative to a context (and interpretation of the language), is the minimal proposition that it expresses given its semantic compositional structure and the meanings of its component parts.[6] Utterances in turn are said to inherit their

[3] Semantic Minimalists need not hold that propositions are structured entities. For instance, they could hold that propositions are sets of possible worlds. I use the notion of 'propositions-as-structured-wholes' in this section for expository reasons and because some Minimalists do hold that view, e.g. Borg 2005 and Salmon 2005. For their part, Cappelen and Lepore are neutral about the metaphysics of propositions. In a recent reply to Bach (forthcoming), Cappelen and Lepore (forthcoming) claim that they are not committed to the view that the semantic content of every meaningful sentence is a proposition or truth conditions. They say as much in a footnote at *IS* 3. However, it's hard to see how their arguments against Moderate and Radical Contextualism can succeed since those arguments presuppose that the semantic content of a non-indexical sentence really is a complete proposition. By the same token, Radical Contextualists can grant, without inconsistency, that if a sentence has semantic content, then its semantic content isn't a proposition, not even an incomplete one. Talk about "the semantic content of a sentence" is just another way, and a misleading way at that, of talking about the use of a sentence in public discourse, and there isn't anything proposition-like about linguistic use. I doubt, however, that Cappelen and Lepore would find that construal of "semantic content" acceptable, despite their professed neutrality on the matter.

[4] By "context sensitivity", Cappelen and Lepore mean the property of an (unambiguous) expression's shifting in extension from context to context without a corresponding shift in intension.

[5] What makes Cappelen and Lepore's Semantic Minimalism *minimalist*, as they use their label, is that they restrict 'context-sensitivity' only to what is triggered by members of the Basic Set. Emma Borg, who is sympathetic to Cappelen and Lepore's general program, argues that their 'context-sensitivity-by-enumeration-of-the-Basic-Set' approach is not a fruitful way of characterizing the minimalist position in semantics and does not help clarify the real dispute between Minimalists and Contextualists. She offers an alternative approach in her chapter for this volume.

[6] The qualifier, 'relative to a context', is needed to handle sentences that contain explicit indexicals, demonstratives, temporal and spatial adverbs, and grammatically marked tensed expressions. This view of semantic content begs the question against those, like Kent Bach and Scott Soames, who hold that the semantic contents of some index-free sentences are propositional matrices, and not because the sentences contain some explicit or implicit context-sensitive element but because their semantically significant parts, plus their syntactic structure, don't add up to anything that is a

semantic contents from the uttered sentences (taking into account any explicit, sub-sentential, context-sensitive elements). And so, the semantic content of an utterance is, relative to a context, always a minimal proposition. The question of whether this view is tenable will be taken up in the next two sections.

2. The "Incredulous Stare" Objection

Consider sentences [1]–[3]:

[1] Dumbo is big

[2] There is beer in the refrigerator

[3] Every philosopher wears glasses

According to Cappelen and Lepore, an utterance of [1] semantically expresses the minimal proposition that Dumbo is (plain) big. For any utterance of [1] to be true, it matters not whether Dumbo is big for a baby elephant, big for a mammal, or big for a circus animal. The predicate, 'is big', doesn't implicitly contain a free variable that takes, for each context of use, a different contextually salient comparison class as its semantic value. It is instead a complete predicate that expresses the property of being big and its extension is the set of all and only (plain old) big things. Thus, all that matters for any utterance of [1] to be true is that Dumbo be (plain old) big. An utterance of [2], regardless of the context, expresses the minimal proposition that there is beer in the refrigerator. Whether the utterance is true doesn't depend on whether the speaker is referring to a contextually salient refrigerator; and, even if he is, it doesn't matter whether the refrigerator in question contains a bottle of beer (as opposed to a droplet of beer on the inside panel). Rather, the truth of any utterance of [2] depends only on whether there is exactly one refrigerator in existence and, if there is, whether it contains some (non-zero) quantity of beer. An utterance of [3], irrespective of the context, expresses the proposition that every philosopher wears glasses. It has the truth-value it has regardless of whether the speaker is referring to a certain group of philosophers; and, even if he is, his utterance is true (or false) independently of whether everyone in the said group wears bifocals, sunglasses, etc. Its truth depends only on whether every philosopher, whomever and wherever, wears glasses (regardless of the type of glasses). If that condition is met, then every utterance of [3] is true; if not, then every utterance of [3] is false.

proposition or that has truth-conditions. See Bach 1994, 2001, 2005; Soames 2005. Cappelen and Lepore reject the standard arguments for incomplete propositions on the grounds that they depend on unreliable, verificationist, semantic intuitions about context-sensitivity and because the arguments are "unstable" (*IS* 59–68). Kent Bach replies (forthcoming) that the arguments for incomplete propositions are not arguments for context-sensitivity and don't rely on any such notion. Resolving this particular dispute is beyond the scope of the chapter. For pro-arguments for semantic incompleteness, see Searle 1978, 1980; Travis 1985.

Now many will dismiss the above claims as being utterly implausible. Here's an "intuition pump" to back up this reaction. Suppose I uttered [1] to you in a context in which it is clear to both of us that I am referring to a certain baby elephant named 'Dumbo'. I then ask, 'Okay, tell me, did I say something true? Or did I say something false?'. You probably will reply, 'Well, that depends. Do you mean whether Dumbo is big for an elephant, or whether he is big for a mammal, or what?' I reply, 'Neither. I am simply asking whether Dumbo is big. Either he is or he isn't. Which is it?' Most likely, you will stare at me incredulously, and protest that my question makes no sense. 'It assumes', you'll argue, 'that there is a correct answer quite apart from any standard one might use for counting things as big.' I reply that whether there is a standard for counting things as big is irrelevant: 'I am not asking whether there is a way of deciding or a way of telling whether Dumbo is big. I am asking instead whether Dumbo is big. Period. If he is big, then every utterance of 'Dumbo is big' is true regardless of the context, provided that the speaker is referring to our Dumbo. But if Dumbo isn't big, then every utterance of that same sentence is false regardless of the context, provided that the speaker is referring to Dumbo by 'Dumbo'. I just want you to tell me which is it. Is he big or is he not big? Answer now!' At this point, you will stare at me incredulously once again. And so would most competent speakers of English. The same "intuition pump" can be used for [2] and [3] and for many other sentences.

Cappelen and Lepore attempt to deflect the "Incredulous Stare" objection by distinguishing *what a sentence says* (in the language), which is the proposition that the sentence semantically expresses in the language, from *what is said* by the speaker (*IS* 150). The latter—the 'what is said' by a speaker in the act of uttering a sentence—is the content of an *illocutionary* speech-act, and it may be something that the speaker asserted or conversationally implied.[7] By contrast, what a non-indexical sentence says is its semantic content, which is the minimal proposition that any utterance of the sentence encodes irrespective of the context of use. What a sentence says can also be the content of a *locutionary* act of uttering the sentence.[8] With this distinction in place, Cappelen and Lepore's

[7] I will follow Cappelen and Lepore in using 'speech-act content' to refer to the propositional content of an illocutionary speech-act, i.e. any proposition that the speaker asserts, implicitly conveys, or otherwise implicates by her utterance (*IS* 204). Bear in mind that, according to them, no context-insensitive sentence semantically expresses an incomplete proposition. If no incomplete proposition is expressed by a context-insensitive sentence, then there are no pragmatically enriched propositions either (beyond what is grammatically required, e.g. saturation of indexical slots). But others strongly disagree. I propose, then, that we take 'speech-act content' to also include what Bach, Robyn Carston, and others call "pragmatically enriched propositions", "completed propositions", "propositional expansions", etc.. These are not all the same thing but they are all said to be the outputs of some optional, top–down, pragmatic process. I will also follow Cappelen and Lepore in using 'semantic content' to refer just to the minimal content of a locutionary speech-act.

[8] Cappelen and Lepore can use this distinction to save their Minimalism and, at the same time, concede a major criticism raised in Carston 2002, 2004; Recanati 2004; Sperber and Wilson 1986, Soames 2005. The criticism is that minimal propositions cannot be the semantic contents

reply to the aforementioned objection is that a speaker can assert any or all of the things (and more) mentioned above about Dumbo, for example, that Dumbo is small for an elephant but big for most animals kept in the zoo[9]—it's just that, given Semantic Minimalism, none of those things is semantically encoded in her utterance. The same applies in the case of sentences [2] and [3].

Cappelen and Lepore's distinction between what a sentence says and what a speaker says is important. Ignoring it can lead to some unnecessary confusion about what an indirect speech-report is a report of—the content of an illocutionary act? the content of a locutionary act?—given that 'to say' can be used to cover both types of a linguistic acts when it takes a clausal complement as its object. However, their distinction also forms the backdrop to a more important objection to Semantic Minimalism.

3. The Psychological Objection

As previously noted, Cappelen and Lepore sharply distinguish what a sentence says from what a speaker says. It is therefore unsurprising to find them saying things like the following:

> Our semantic content (the proposition semantically expressed) *is not identical* to what the speaker said. *It cannot, and is not meant to, play the roles that what the speaker said can play. It is not meant to serve functions (cognitive or otherwise) that the speech act content can serve.* (*IS* 181, cf. 150; italics added)

of linguistic utterances and, at the same time, the contents of illocutionary speech-acts. The reason often given is that semantics cannot deliver a pragmatic-free, context-independent, notion of what is asserted in an utterance of an indexical-free sentence. On my reading of *IS*, Cappelen and Lepore can and should concede all that since they distinguish the proposition that an *utterance* semantically expresses from the proposition that *the speaker* asserts, states, or conveys—only the latter can be (for Cappelen and Lepore) the thing said ("what is said"), which in turn is never (for them) *just* the semantic content of the utterance (*IS* 200). On the other hand, in *IS* 150 and 181, which I quote below, they maintain that the thing said or asserted is never the semantic content of the utterance, and they also appear to be saying in these passages that an utterance's minimal semantic content is not even a part of what is said or asserted. One wonders, though, how we could produce true, inter-contextual, disquotational speech-reports about what the *speaker* said in an utterance of the component clause used in our report if the report is only about what was semantically expressed in the reported *utterance*.

[9] This is, in effect, Cappelen and Lepore's 'Speech-Act Pluralism' according to which speakers perform, in a single utterance, multiple speech-acts that differ in content (*IS* 199–206). The determinants of what a speaker said are pragmatic, highly variable, and context-dependent. What a speaker said depends on the speaker's communicative intentions and on what the speaker and hearer mutually know, believe, or assume about each other and about their shared context. It will also depend on the psychological states of other speakers who are not participants in the original context of utterance, e.g. speech-reporters (*IS* 201). No algorithm can fix in advance the contents of what a speaker said (*IS* 197–9). Different propositions can thus be equally good candidates of the things said depending on how the aforementioned factors are weighted and sorted. Therefore, there can be no uniquely correct answer to the question about what a speaker said since indefinitely many propositions can be asserted in a single utterance. The same holds in the case of indirect speech-reports: there can be no uniquely correct answer to the question about what is said in an indirect speech report about the reported utterance.

The same theme occurs in this passage:

We should point out that even though much about our view is Gricean in perspective, our way of classifying contents (i.e., to contrast the proposition semantically expressed by an utterance u of a sentence S with the speech act content of u) distinguishes us (at least terminologically) from Grice. For Grice, there's an important distinction between what a speaker says with an utterance and what she conversationally implicates with that utterance. He thinks of the former more or less along the lines of what we have been calling the proposition semantically expressed. *It is important for us* (a) *not to identify the proposition semantically expressed with the proposition asserted* (*or said*), and (b) *for that reason not to reserve the label 'what is said' for the proposition semantically expressed.* (*IS* 180, cf. 150; italics added)

Thus, for Cappelen and Lepore, *what is said* and *what a speaker said* come to the same thing: they are assertions, which in turn are distinct from the minimal semantic content of an utterance. Utterance content is (for Cappelen and Lepore) the minimal proposition expressed. No one therefore ever asserts a minimal proposition, strictly speaking. Given the two passages above, it follows that no minimal proposition can serve the role of an assertion. When we factor in Speech-Act Pluralism, we get the result that, among all the many things that a speaker asserts or states in a single utterance, not one is the minimal proposition semantically expressed by the speaker's utterance.

Now it is very tempting to conclude, on the basis of these passages and on what has just been said, that minimal propositions play no substantive role in linguistic communication.[10] Robyn Carston and François Recanati are two critics who defend that viewpoint. In the passage that follows, Recanati denies that minimal propositions are the things that sentences say (since "the rules of language" cannot determine, on their own, any such proposition as the semantic content of a sentence); but he agrees with Cappelen and Lepore that minimal propositions aren't speech-act contents and concludes that they serve no role in linguistic communication:

the minimal proposition which the Syncretic View posits as the semantic content of the utterance, and which results from saturation alone, is not 'what the sentence says'. . . It is not autonomously determined by the rules of the language independent of speaker's meaning. At the same time, the minimal proposition does not correspond to an aspect of what the speaker asserts and cannot be abstracted from it. . . The minimal proposition is a hybrid which goes beyond what is determined by the rules of the language yet has

[10] For purposes of discussion, let us stipulate that a proposition is psychologically real in linguistic communication only if the hearer must identify or represent it in the process of recovering speaker meaning or it is the thing that the hearer infers in working out the speaker's communicated message and implicatures. Despite its vagueness, this definition will do since some critics of Semantic Minimalism have something like it in mind when they deny the psychological reality of minimal propositions.

no psychological reality and need not be entertained or represented at any point in the process of understanding the utterance... (Recanati 2004: 64)

The unstated premise in Recanati's argument is that a proposition has a cognitive role in linguistic communication only if it is the semantic content of a sentence or it is the speech-act content of some illocutionary act (assuming those exhaust all the possibilities). Carston also argues that minimal propositions are psychologically unreal, but she thinks that another role that propositions can play in communication is that of a premise "in the derivation of implicatures", a role she thinks that no minimal proposition plays because they are often "uninformative, irrelevant, and sometimes truistic or patently false":

It is the enriched propositions that are communicated as explicatures and which function as premises in the derivation of implicatures; the uninformative, irrelevant, and sometimes truistic or patently false minimal propositions appear to play no role in the process of utterance understanding, which is geared to the recovery of just those propositional forms which the speaker intends to communicate. (Carston 2004: 8)

The following example, taken from Carston 2004, captures Carston's and Recanati's concerns.

Tom and Sue

Sue: How is Mary feeling after her first year at university?

Tom: She didn't get enough units and can't continue.

Being intelligent and linguistically competent, Sue interprets Tom's utterance as implicitly meaning [4] and takes him to be conversationally implicating [5]:

[4] Mary did not pass enough *university course* units *to qualify for admission to second year study* and, *as a result*, Mary cannot continue *with university study*.

[5] Mary is not feeling very happy.

Given their shared assumptions and background knowledge, Tom expected Sue to understand him as asserting [4] and as implying [5]. For her part, Sue arrived at [4] by assigning Mary as the referent of 'she' and by freely enriching Tom's utterance with some general background information she has about universities, course credits, and university admission standards—in particular, her knowledge that one's failure to pass a certain number of university course units can be a causal factor in one's disqualification from further university study.

Now according to Semantic Minimalists, [6] rather than [4] is the minimal content of Tom's utterance, assuming that the semantic meaning of 'and' is simply that of logical conjunction—the "causal consequence" meaning that Tom conveyed with his use of 'and' is screened off:

[6] Mary did not get enough units and Mary cannot continue.

However, Sue didn't recover [6]—she did not take Tom to be saying anything that is truth-conditionally equivalent to [7], such as [6]:

[7] Mary cannot continue and Mary did not get enough credits.

Thus, the minimal content of Tom's utterance is not the proposition that Sue cognitively grasped. Nor did [6] serve as a premise in her derivation of Tom's implicature. She would have to have added [6] to a large set of rather extraneous assumptions and beliefs in order to derive [5]—assumptions and beliefs that bear no obvious inferential links to a claim about Mary's current state of mind. By contrast, the enriched proposition [4], in conjunction with beliefs about Mary's valuations, her desires, and her plans, makes the derivation of [5] more "cost-efficient", cognitively speaking.

Cappelen and Lepore can grant many of these points. They admit that there is "a sharp distinction between how we think about what utterances say and what the real content of those utterances is" (*IS* 98). Given that [6] is "the real content" of Tom's utterance and bears little connection to Sue's question about Mary's current state of mind, [6] is not the salient proposition that Tom communicated to Sue, as Cappelen and Lepore will agree (*IS* 180–1).[11] It is simply not "how we think about" the content of utterances. Still, they will say, it doesn't follow that no minimal proposition is psychologically real. Just the opposite is true: "One of the many propositions asserted by an utterance is the semantic content of that utterance (the proposition semantically expressed)" (*IS* 200). How that squares with the two passages that we began this section with remains to be seen. Suffice it to say that, on Cappelen and Lepore's view, *part* of what Tom asserted in his response to Sue's question is [6], even though she didn't hear him as asserting [6] and even though he really didn't assert [6]—he asserted [4] instead (among other things).

[11] Contextualists offer different reasons for denying the minimal proposition (allegedly) expressed in [6] is what Tom's utterance semantically expressed. Relevance Theorists would rule out [6] because it isn't the most "optimally relevant" interpretation of Tom's utterance—it's not worth the cognitive effort (*vis-à-vis* generating lots of new and informative cognitive states with the least amount of cognitive cost) to interpret him as meaning [6]; see Carston 2002; Sperber and Wilson 1986. Recanati would rule out [6] because hearers are not consciously aware of it as being the proposition that Tom stated or asserted in his response to Sue's query. In other words, [6] fails Recanati's Availability Principle (2004). Cappelen and Lepore criticize the Relevance Theorist's view (*IS* 176–86) and Recanati's view (*IS* 186–9 and 196–9).

In the next section, I will take up Cappelen and Lepore's reasons for thinking that minimal propositions are always part of what is asserted. But, for now, let's conclude with their summary of the Psychological Objection:

> What communicators actually care about in a discourse exchange is the speech act content and only the speech act content. What they care about is what the speaker said, asserted, claimed, stated, suggested, asked, etc. If the semantic content is, so to speak, always hidden, if it never surfaces, than what purposes does it serve? Isn't it just an idle wheel? This objection might seem particularly worrisome given what we ourselves said about the propositions semantically expressed . . . they are peculiar, to say the least. (*IS* 176–7)

Ockham's Razor kicks in at this point: we should reject Semantic Minimalism because it posits "peculiar" entities that play "no role in the actual process of communication" and, at best, resides in "semantic heaven" (Recanati 2004: 96).

Cappelen and Lepore dismiss the Psychological Objection on the grounds that linguistic communication *without* minimal propositions is *impossible*. It's time that we turn to their defense of this rather strong claim, a claim that will be examined in Part Two.

4. The Psychological Reality Thesis

Cappelen and Lepore defend three theses that make up what I will call "The Psychological Reality Thesis":

(i) "any coherent account of linguistic communication" must recognize minimal propositions as having a cognitive role in communication (*IS* 144)

(ii) "this minimal semantic content is an essential part of all communicative interactions. The minimal semantic content has a function in the cognitive life of communicators that no other content can serve." (*IS* 181)

(iii) "minimal semantic content has a psychological role that no other 'level of content' can fill" (*IS* 181)[12]

(i) and (ii) entail that an adequate empirical theory of linguistic communication *must* posit minimal propositions. By the same token, minimal propositions are "not meant to serve functions (cognitive or otherwise) that the speech act content can serve"—they serve an entirely different role in linguistic communication (*IS* 181). They serve instead as cognitive safety mechanisms in situations in which speakers/hearers are mistaken, misinformed, ignorant of, or lack communication-relevant information about the context of utterance (*IS* 183,

[12] One might reasonably think that (iii) actually says nothing more than what (ii) already says. I take 'psychological role' in (iii) to be encompassing more than just the kind of cognitive role that (ii) says is "an essential part of all communicative interactions". (iii) is compatible with the claim that minimal propositions serve other non-communicative psychological roles that no other "level of content" can serve. I consider a few possibilities at the end of this chapter.

185). Despite partial or even massive ignorance, speakers can agree on what was said (in the locutionary sense of 'to say'). They can even correctly report, in one context, what a speaker said in another context to another audience.[13] The best explanation of this phenomenon, say Cappelen and Lepore, is that participants in a conversation can grasp the context-invariant minimal propositions of another speaker's utterances. Hearers can fall back on these meanings when they are ignorant of or mistaken about certain features of the context. Communication across different contexts would surely be impossible if there were no "fall-back" propositions.

Here is an example of the kind of thing that Cappelen and Lepore have in mind:

Cheney and Rumsfeld

> Secretary of Defense Rumsfeld is in his office reviewing the latest casualty reports from Iraq. He has lost track of time and has forgotten that he has an important briefing with President Bush and Vice-President Cheney at the White House. The meeting was scheduled for 3.00 p.m.—it is now 3.30 p.m. Cheney suddenly walks into Rumsfeld's office and utters [8] with some consternation:
>
> [8] The President is waiting!
>
> Surprised by Cheney's unexpected visit, Rumsfeld responds with [9], mistakenly thinking that Cheney meant that Bush is ready to meet them for dinner:
>
> [9] I'll just be a minute—by the way, which room in the White House did the President say we will be dining in?

Suppose that [8] contains no covert context-sensitive element in its logical form (see *IS* 69–83). Also, suppose that no utterance of [8] expresses a proposition that has unarticulated constituents. We shall assume that, in this example, 'the President' refers to George W. Bush and that 'is waiting' is unambiguous and expresses *readiness*. Then, Cheney's utterance encodes the minimal proposition, *George W. Bush is waiting*, and is true just in case George W. Bush is waiting.

The minimal proposition that Cheney's utterance semantically encodes is a "starting point" for discourse understanding: it serves to pare down what Cheney was talking about (*IS* 185). Knowledge that Cheney's utterance simply means *George W. Bush is waiting also* provides Rumsfeld "with the *best possible* access

[13] Actually, that won't be the case if the uttered sentence contains an indexical or a demonstrative the contextual referents of which are unknown to reporters in other contexts. (See Montminy 2006.) Some Minimalists are aware of this problem and have tried to address it. See Borg 2005.

to" Cheney's mind, given "the restricted knowledge" that he has of Cheney in their shared context (*IS* 185). For instance, Rumsfeld knows that Cheney was talking *about George W. Bush* (and not about anyone else), and he knows that Cheney was *saying of* Bush that he is *waiting* (as opposed to running, eating, etc.). So, even though Cheney didn't assert that George W. Bush is waiting, it is part of what he asserted. Cheney presumably expected Rumsfeld to take him as saying at least that much. So, even though Rumsfeld has some false beliefs about their shared context, he can make use of what he knows about the content of Cheney's remark to figure out what Cheney meant. Serving as a "starting point" is a cognitive function in linguistic communication if anything is.

In light of these sorts of considerations, Cappelen and Lepore conclude that the following is true only of minimal propositions:

[F1] "The proposition semantically expressed is that content the speaker can expect the audience to grasp (and expect the audience to expect the speaker to expect them to grasp) even if they have mistaken or incomplete communication-relevant information." (*IS* 184)

[F2] "The proposition semantically expressed is that content the audience can expect the speaker to grasp, etc. even if she has such mistaken or incomplete information." (*IS* 184–5)

[F3] "The proposition semantically expressed is that content which can be grasped and expressed by someone who isn't even a participant in the context of utterance." (*IS* 185)

[F4] "The proposition semantically expressed is that content which speakers and audiences know can be transmitted through indirect quotation or reproduction (in the form of tapes, video, recordings, etc.) to those who find themselves in contexts radically different from the original context of utterance." (*IS* 185).

Minimal propositions are, then, psychologically real entities that do some important explanatory work if Cappelen and Lepore are right. However, as I will try to show, [F1]–[F4] are not true of minimal propositions in all cases. If they are not, then the debate about the cognitive role of minimal propositions in linguistic communication remains unresolved.

PART TWO

1. A Critique of the Psychological Reality Thesis

The general structure of my argument is this. First, I will describe cases in which a speaker and/or addressee has some mistaken assumption, misinformation, or little information about the original context of utterance. Then, I will argue that in some of these cases the content that the speaker/addressee *could expect* the other to grasp, despite these epistemic limitations, is speech-act content and not a minimal proposition. In the other cases, the minimal proposition that is expressed isn't one that the speaker/addressee could expect the other to grasp without attributing irrationality or incompetence to the person. If I can show both things, then minimal propositions don't always serve the cognitive role that Cappelen and Lepore assign to them; in some cases, only speech-act contents play the role in question. The cases that I will be describing involve intra-sentential reference-shifts, conversational snippets, solecism, and sub-sentential speech-acts. This may seem like overkill, but it is important to see that all four cases are ubiquitous and, thus, pose a genuine problem for Cappelen and Lepore's view.

2. Intra-Sentential Reference-Shift: The Case Against Theses [F1] and [F2]

Consider sentence [10] (from Nunberg 1979):

> [10] Yeats did not enjoy hearing Maude read *him* aloud.

[10] is ambiguous since the pronominal can be interpreted as having an indexical occurrence or an anaphoric occurrence. Let's consider a case in which the pronominal is being used as an indexical. Two mutual acquaintances of William Butler Yeats are discussing Yeats's disdain for Ezra Pound, who just happens to be standing nearby. One speaker informs the other that Yeats encountered another mutual friend, Maude, reading some of Pound's poems aloud at a local recital. In recounting the story, the speaker utters [10] and points to Pound when she utters 'him'. Given the lexical content of 'him' and the context in which [10] is uttered, the speaker referred to Pound. Relative to that context, the minimal proposition expressed is therefore the weird proposition that Yeats did not enjoy hearing Maude read (in the sense of reading a poem) Ezra Pound (the man) aloud.

Our speaker asserted no such thing since she did not intend to say something that entails the rather strange false claim that Maude read Pound (the man, not his writings). Nor could she expect her friend to take her as asserting anything of the sort unless she thinks her friend is incompetent. In which case, [F1] is dubious: the minimal content of an utterance isn't always the thing that a speaker can expect her audience to grasp as the thing said or as part of what is asserted. Nor, in our example, could the speaker's friend expect her to grasp that strange proposition unless the friend has some doubts about the speaker's rationality. In which case, [F2] is also suspect. Instead our speaker asserted, and her addressee took her to be asserting, among other things, that Yeats did not enjoy hearing Maude read Pound's *poems* aloud. That is not, however, the minimal semantic content of the utterance since 'poems' is not derivable from the meanings of the constituents of [10] and its structure—it is instead a speech-act content of the speaker's illocutionary act of assertion.

We can run the same argument in the case where the pronominal in [10] is interpreted as being anaphorically linked to 'Yeats'. Imagine a case similar to the one described above, except that this time Maude is reading Yeats' poems aloud and the conversational topic is Yeats's modesty and his shyness. By hypothesis, 'him' in [10] is co-indexed with its referential antecedent and thus subject to a *C*-command rule. Semantically, 'him' in [10] is strictly co-referential with 'Yeats', if the standard "rule-by-rule" picture of compositionality that Cappelen and Lepore assume applies. Thus, Yeats is the semantic value of 'him' in [10] since he is the semantic value of 'Yeats'. On this interpretation, the sentence semantically expresses the bizarre proposition that William Butler Yeats did not enjoy hearing Maude read William Butler Yeats (the man) aloud.

Once again, our speaker asserted no such thing, given that she is competent, intelligent, and cooperative. Nor, as I argued earlier, could she expect her friend to interpret her utterance in that way even if the friend were utterly in the dark about the referent of 'Yeats'. Thus, [F1] is false. Conversely, no intelligent person who lacks information about the original context of utterance could expect a speaker of [10] to be trying to convey this absurd proposition unless he thought the speaker was punning on 'read' or was really incoherent, neither of which is the case. Thus, [F2] fails in this instance too.

Now Cappelen and Lepore could make two replies. The first is that [10] expresses no context-independent minimal proposition if 'him' is functioning as an indexical. If [10] doesn't express a minimal proposition, then the example fails. The second is that, if 'him' is anaphoric on 'Yeats', then [10] really expresses two distinct propositions assuming that 'read' is understood univocally. In that case, the speaker would be asserting only one of them and not the bizarre proposition. If that is how it should go, then my second example also fails because [F1] and [F2] would then still hold.

The first reply can be granted without too much damage. After all, once a semantic value is contextually assigned to the indexical pronoun, then the speaker's utterance of [10] does express an absurd minimal proposition. My argument should still go through if that is the only proposition that is semantically expressed. But it might not be, which takes us to the second reply.

If [10] is really semantically ambiguous, then 'Yeats' must be more than just a Millian marker—it would also have to encode some additional lexical material, such as 'writer/poet'.[14] Now Cappelen and Lepore take no position in their book

[14] This may not be true since you could get the same ambiguous readings using 'He did not enjoy hearing Maude read him aloud' or 'That man did not enjoy hearing Maude read him aloud', if you tell the story about Yeats, Pound, and Maude right. It is not part of the lexical meaning of

on whether proper names have connotation. So, for the sake of argument, I will assume that they can adopt this view. Assume, then, that [10] really is ambiguous between its most natural reading and the strict but bizarre reading mentioned above. To arrive at the intended interpretation given the standing conventional meaning of 'read', we assign the *poet* sense of 'Yeats' to the pronominal. Then, on that sense-assignment, the predicate, '*x* read him (= Yeats) aloud', expresses the property of being an individual who read some of Yeats's poems aloud. The semantic value of 'him' in [10] will then be different from the semantic value of its antecedent, 'Yeats', as desired—it refers parasitically or deferentially to Yeats's poems rather than to Yeats himself.

Notice, though, that the semantic value of 'him', on this second reading, is determined in part by the semantic value of the complex expression, "Maude read him (= Yeats) aloud", of which it is a constituent. The natural intuitive meaning of [10] isn't fixed by a bottom–up, compositional, process.[15] But, according to Cappelen and Lepore, minimal propositions are the semantic outputs of a bottom–up compositional analysis on sentences. Consequently, the intuitively natural reading of [10] is not a minimal proposition. The "semantic ambiguity" gambit won't help block the negative implications of the Yeats example—and of intra-sentential, polysemous, reference-shifts in general—for Cappelen and Lepore's view.

3. Conversational Snippets: The Case Against Thesis [F3]

Thesis [F3] says that speakers who are not participants in the original context of utterance can express the proposition that is semantically expressed in an utterance made in that context, even in situations of ignorance, and that the proposition will always be a minimal proposition. I shall argue that [F3] isn't true in all cases primarily because conversations are often patchworks of snippets, pauses, and ungrammatical short-cuts. Here is one such case.

Bernie, Harry, and Joe

> It is July, 1947. Two friends, Bernie and Harry, are having a few beers at their favorite local sports tavern in Brooklyn, New York. Harry notices that Bernie is reading the sports pages of the *New York Daily News*. The following conversation then ensues:
>
> *H*: How did—what's-his-face?—do yesterday against the Giants at Ebbets?

'he' in English, nor is it a semantic constraint on the extension of 'that man', that their contextually determined referents be a writer or a poet. The same might be true in the case of a proper name like 'Yeats'.

15 By that I mean that the semantic value assigned to the terminal node of a daughter branch of a semantic tree for [10] is determined, in part, by the semantic value assigned to its mother branch and other branches, rather than the converse.

> *B*: Who?
>
> *H*: You know who!
>
> *B*: Well, [Turns to the page containing the baseball box scores from the day before] hmmm, . . . two doubles, a homerun, and a walk in five at bats, 4 rbi's, two stolen bases, no errors.
>
> *H*: He done good!
>
> Joe the bartender, who was eavesdropping, knows what Bernie said in response to Harry's question. For, he had attended the game in question and thus was able to deduce the player's name, based on the information that Bernie relayed and on memory: it was Jackie Robinson, the famous baseball player for the Brooklyn Dodgers.

Given the relevant background information, and the conversational exchange between Harry and Bernie, Joe was able to identify Robinson as Harry's intended referent of 'he' and the dummy singular term, 'what's-his-face'. And even though he wasn't a participant in the speech-exchange, Joe was able to correctly infer that Bernie also recognized who Harry meant. He correctly understood Bernie to have said that Jackie Robinson got two doubles, a homerun, etc. And yet, there is no minimal proposition on the basis of which Joe was able to arrive at this speech-act content. Keep in mind that Joe initially had no information about who Harry meant by his utterance of 'what's-his-face'.

Bernie, Harry, and Joe is a case, then, in which a non-minimal propositional content satisfies condition [F3] but no minimal proposition did because none was semantically encoded in Bernie's last utterance. He instead produced a string of quantificational noun phrases none of which semantically expressed a proposition. The string wasn't elliptical for a previously uttered sentence that expressed a proposition. Bernie was transmitting, in serial form, information from a baseball boxscore and, in doing so, he was answering Harry's question, but he wasn't uttering a sentence, making a statement, or expressing a proposition by his last utterance.

If we have ellipsis here, then the deleted material (italicized below) would be something like [11]:

> [11] *What's-his-face got* two doubles, a homerun, a walk in five at bats, *had* 4 rbi's, and *committed* no errors.

On some theories of syntactic ellipsis, the italicized linguistic material would have to have been explicitly available at some earlier part of the discourse and implicitly contained, but not pronounced, in the uttered string of quantificational noun phrases. However, the appropriate inflected forms of the verbs 'to get', 'to have', and 'to commit', were not explicitly tokened prior to Bernie's utterance. This then doesn't look like a case of syntactic ellipsis, at least not on certain theories anyway, and it certainly doesn't seem to be like VP-ellipsis, sluicing, etc.[16] Still, Joe was able to work out the communicated proposition that Jackie Robinson got two doubles, a homerun, etc., without having to start with a minimal proposition. There could be, then, cases in which no minimal proposition is cognitively accessible (because none was expressed) to an epistemically disadvantaged agent but who still manages to recover a communicated speech-act content.

4. Solecism and Context Constructions: The Case Against Thesis [F4] (and [F1] Again)

Cappelen and Lepore contend that people in epistemically impoverished situations cannot understand what a speaker said by an utterance unless they grasp, or can be expected to grasp, the minimal semantic content of the utterance. If the sentence uttered contains no indexical or other context-sensitive expressions, then grasping the minimal semantic content is a matter of understanding the meaning of the sentence uttered. However, as I shall argue, even in bad situations, people can understand an utterance even though they couldn't have understood—and thus, couldn't be expected to have understood—the uttered sentence simply because it is semantically anomalous or incoherent.

In a famous study Wason and Reich (1979) report that a sign posted on the wall of a London hospital casualty department read as follows:

[12] No head injury is too trivial to ignore

People generally took [12] to mean:

[13] However trivial a head injury might appear, it should not be ignored.

Strictly speaking, [12] doesn't mean [13] but means [14], which conflicts with [13]:

[14] However trivial a head injury might be, it should be ignored.

16 On other theories of syntactic ellipsis, ellipses don't contain ordinary, unpronounced, linguistic material that is grammatically elided at some level of syntactic representation. Rather, they are maximal INFL projections that already contain empty categories in their syntactic form and which get contextually filled in with items from the appropriate lexical categories. It is debatable whether Bernie's last utterance meets the last part of this description of a syntactic ellipsis since there is no evidence that there is some available lexical item that context supplies and which yields something like [11]. For a detailed survey and discussion of syntactic theories of ellipsis, see Merchant 2001; Stainton 2006.

For years, the hospital staff and patients interpreted [12] to mean [13] (as the original sign-makers had probably intended) rather than [14] but never discovered their error—they erred in interpreting the quantifier scope of 'no head injury'. Most likely, they related the words in [13] "to the *situation* being depicted, where the actions demanded are clear, and so interpret the message as a reminder of what should be done", namely, treat head injuries (Sanford 2002: 191). The hospital staff members and patients created, in effect, a plausible but mistaken interpretation of [12] without first fully determining its semantic meaning. If that is what actually happened, then we have a case in which "pragmatics, in the form of situation-specific knowledge, overrides full local semantic interpretation" (Sanford 2002: 191). More importantly, short of attributing irrationality to the hospital attendants, they *couldn't be expected* to grasp [14] as the literal meaning of [12] given that they interpret the latter as meaning [13]. [F1] is therefore false in this case as well, assuming that the proposition semantically expressed in [12] is a minimal proposition.

Turning our attention to [F4], notice that it implies that the literal content of an utterance can be known to be *transmitted* to others by indirect quotation even if they don't know that the speaker in question was being ironic or sarcastic at the time. By "known to be transmitted", Cappelen and Lepore mean that a participant in a speech-exchange knows that an indirect quotation of a fellow participant's utterance conveys the literal content of that utterance (adjusting for deictic elements). The question, as mentioned earlier, is whether an indirect quotation reports the content of an illocutionary speech-act or the semantic content of a locutionary speech-act. Cappelen and Lepore can't mean the latter in their formulation of [F4] since they deny that the content of an indirect quotation and the literal semantic content of the reported utterance can be strictly correlated one-to-one (Cappelen and Lepore 1997, 1998). For example, suppose that Lepore utters, 'All the students in my logic class failed the final exam', in a conversation with Cappelen. Cappelen then later reports to a student who is in Lepore's logic class, 'Professor Lepore said that you failed the final logic examination'. Intuitively speaking, Cappelen's indirect speech report is true, but the complement clause he used in reporting what Lepore said is not semantically equivalent to the sentence that Lepore actually used. Thus, an indirect quotation can be true in one context even though it semantically fails to convey the literal content of the reported utterance made in another context. So, if the correlation is that loose, then one can't know in advance that the literal content of an utterance is conveyed by an indirect quotation. In that case, [F4] is false.

On the other hand, if an indirect quotation reports the content of an illocutionary speech-act, then [F4] fails again but for a different reason: linguistic creativity. Clark and Gerrig (1983) and Clark (1997) present just such a case. It is an extract from a newspaper column on roommates, written by Erma Bombeck, the famous satirist:

[15] Stereos are a dime a dozen

On its own, [15] makes perfectly good sense given the idiomatic expression "a dime a dozen":

[16] Stereo systems are very common.

Imagine, however, that you and I don't know the particulars of Bombeck's context of utterance (= that particular newspaper column in which she used [15]). I just know that she used [15] in one of her columns. Suppose that I report to you what Bombeck said (in the illocutionary sense of 'to say') by indirectly quoting her with [17]:

[17] Bombeck said that stereos are a dime a dozen.

Readers of that particular column would know that I would be mistaken in reporting, with [17], that Bombeck said [16] or that she asserted what [15] literally means non-idiomatically. Bombeck did not say (in the illocutionary sense of 'to say'), by her use of [15] in her column, that stereos are (literally) a dime a dozen although she did token those words. Nor did she say by her utterance of [15] that stereos are very common. In order to arrive at Bombeck's meaning, namely [18], one would have to know that she was using 'stereo' as a metonym for *roommates who own stereo systems*, which is what Bombeck expected her readers to do when they read [15]:

[18] Roommates who own stereo systems are very common.

The moral here is that indirect speech-reports that ascribe the minimal proposition expressed can fail to transmit what the speaker actually said (in the illocutionary sense of 'to say') in contexts in which the speaker is using language creatively and expects his audience to recognize that he is. Hence, [F4] is false in certain cases if the semantically expressed proposition is a minimal proposition.

5. Sub-Sentential Speech-Acts: The Case Against the Joint Sufficiency of [F1]–[F4]

The last case that I will present is admittedly controversial since it involves the notion of a sub-sentential speech-act.[17]

[17] Some philosophers hold that such cases are either not genuine speech-acts or not genuinely sub-sentential but elliptical (Stanley 2000). But see Elugardo and Stainton (2004) and Stainton (2005) for a reply.

Mario and Sal

> Mario is having dinner with his friend, Sal, and pours him a glass of white wine. He notices that Sal is trying to read the wine bottle label. Mario raises the bottle, points to it, and utters:
>
> [19] from France.
>
> Later that evening, at a local grocery store, Sal tells Gina about his dinner with Mario. When she asks where the bottle of wine that Mario served him was imported from, Sal replies:
>
> [20] Mario said that the bottle of wine was imported from France.
>
> The next day, Gina reports to her husband, Tony:
>
> [21] Mario said that the bottle of wine he served Sal at dinner yesterday was a French import.

In uttering [19], Mario asserted of the bottle of wine that it is from France. One reason for thinking that he did perform a genuine speech-act is that, if contrary to fact, the bottle of wine had been from Spain, Mario would then have been mistaken in what he said about the bottle of wine. If Mario knew that it was from Spain but uttered [19] anyway, he can be rightly accused of having told a lie, which is evidence that he asserted something. Furthermore, Sal can easily infer from what Mario said by his utterance of [19] that there is at least one thing that is from France. He couldn't make that inference unless Mario said something that could be used as a premise in an argument, which is further evidence that Mario asserted a proposition. Given the contexts in which they are used, [20] and [21] are thus true indirect speech reports of what Mario said.

Now what Mario uttered was a prepositional phrase, not a sentence, not even an ellipsis (Stainton 1995). He didn't utter an elliptical sentence since no prior linguistic material was available for syntactic deletion, given that he began the conversation by uttering [19]. Furthermore, the context didn't make salient a particular English expression that is a candidate for syntactic deletion.

Prepositional phrases don't semantically express propositions—at best, they express functions from objects to relations involving those objects (Elugardo and Stainton 2001). Consequently, Mario's utterance didn't semantically encode a minimal proposition. But then, the proposition that he expected Sal to grasp couldn't be the semantic content of his utterance since no such proposition was semantically expressed—the semantic content expressed is instead a function. The proposition that Mario expected or could have expected Sal to grasp is one that Mario communicated by uttering [19] and by making the wine bottle perceptually salient in the original context (Elugardo and Stainton 2003). What plays the cognitive role implicitly defined in [F1]–[F4] in this example is a speech-act content and not any minimal proposition. Notice, also, that since Mario's utterance is discourse-initial, the proposition he asserted serves as "starting point" for Sal: Sal knew that Mario was referring to his wine bottle, even though he did not use a linguistic device to refer to it, and that Mario was saying of it that it was from France. Speech-act contents can sometimes serve as cognitive-safety mechanisms.

6. A Brief Recap

I've presented four examples that collectively provide *prima-facie* strong counter evidence to Cappelen and Lepore's claim that minimal propositions serve as cognitive safety mechanisms. All four exhibit at least one of the following two patterns. Pattern 1: no minimal proposition is semantically expressed but speakers and hearers figure out what was said despite that; in which case, neither could reasonably be expected to grasp any minimal proposition since none was expressed. Pattern 2: a minimal proposition is semantically expressed but it fails to play some or all of the roles that Cappelen and Lepore described, even in situations of ignorance and misinformation. Communicated speech-act contents play those roles instead. Let's turn now to some objections.

7. Objections and Replies

Objection 1

My examples are based on the mistaken assumption that grasping a minimal proposition is always a necessary first step for recovering speech-act content. The Psychological Reality Thesis implies no such thing.

Reply to 1

This objection in effect concedes my point. Suppose that grasping a minimal proposition is unnecessary for recovering, in situations of ignorance and misinformation, what a speaker said. If hearers can recover the speech-act content anyway in those cases, as expected by the speaker or the hearer (or both), then that shows that minimal propositions aren't essential for fulfilling those roles in linguistic communication. They are cognitively idle, at least in those sorts of cases.

Objection 2

Cappelen and Lepore never claimed that every time things go awry, speakers and interpreters invoke minimal propositions to fall back on—their claim is only that minimal propositions are invoked sometimes and that sometimes they are the only contents that will do the trick. Thus, they can grant that sometimes minimal propositions won't do as cognitive safety mechanisms and that speech-act contents can serve as well or even better than minimal propositions in some instances. What hasn't been shown, and what probably can't be shown, is that minimal propositions *never* do the work that Cappelen and Lepore say they do.

Reply to 2

I grant the very last point, but if my arguments work, then minimal propositions are *never* the *only* things that will serve as "fall-back" interpretations in epistemically impoverished contexts. That contradicts the conjunction of the Psychological Reality Thesis and [F1]–[F4].

Rejoinder

Perhaps, though, as Objection 2 suggests, Cappelen and Lepore could give up their strong claim that minimal propositions are essential in linguistic communication but still preserve the heart of their view by insisting that minimal propositions serve an important cognitive role in some communicative exchanges.

Reply

True, but as the Emma Bombeck example shows, without having additional information about the original context of utterance and the speaker's communicative intentions, one is in no position to grasp what the speaker said based solely on an indirect, disquotational, speech-report. Information about whether the speaker was speaking ironically, sarcastically, etc., is also required. Knowledge of the minimal proposition expressed won't be enough to ensure that one has grasped even a part of what the speaker in another context asserted.

Objection 3

Even if minimal propositions never serve as cognitive safety mechanisms, and even if speech-act contents can sometimes serve that role in those situations, minimal propositions may serve other psychological roles, ones that only they can have. Here are two:

(a) Minimal propositions are the outputs of a semantic compositional process that speakers and hearers implicitly know in virtue of being semantically competent in their language.

(b) Minimal propositions are the denotations of complement clauses in indirect speech-reports made in situations of ignorance or misinformation about the context of utterance.

First Reply

I grant (*a*) since it is close to being a definitional truth. Still, minimal propositions are not the only things that can be the final outputs of a semantic compositional analysis of a novel utterance. Consider a slight variation on *Mario and Sal.* Mario utters, 'from France and I bought it on wholesale', as he points to his bottle of wine. His utterance is novel under the circumstances. Presumably, Sal understood what Mario said in that context. He did so, in part, by computing the coordinating phrase that Mario uttered. Hence, Sal did some linguistic processing: he determined the semantic value of the entire phrase by assigning the proper semantic values to its constituents given its form. (Notice that Sal didn't interpret 'it', in Mario's utterance, as being co-indexed with 'France'; rather, he interpreted it as an indexical whose semantic value is the demonstrated wine bottle.) The output is a proposition, all right. But it's not a minimal proposition since it has an unarticulated constituent, namely, Mario's bottle of wine.

Second Reply

Proposal (*b*), which says that only minimal propositions are the denotations of complement clauses used in indirect speech-reports, won't work because speech-act contents can also be the denotations of such clauses too when used in situations of ignorance or misinformation. To use a famous example from Donnellan (1966), imagine that Jones uttered, 'Smith's murderer is insane', referring to Brown, a famous serial murderer. Jones doesn't know who Brown is and is mistaken in thinking that Smith was murdered. I can still report truthfully what Jones said by his utterance with 'Jones said that Brown is insane' to someone who knows Jones, knows of Brown, but who is ignorant of Jones's mistaken belief about Smith and who doesn't know that Jones is ignorant of Brown's identity. In the reporting context, the that-clause I used refers to a speech-act content and not to the minimal proposition expressed by Jones's utterance since, by hypothesis, the minimal proposition expressed is a general proposition rather than a singular proposition about Brown. This is yet another case where speech-act contents are cognitively no different from minimal propositions—both can be designated by the that-clause of an indirect speech report. What is needed to defeat the Psychological Objection is an account of the cognitive role(s) that *only* minimal propositions have and that are also required in linguistic communication.

I've argued in this chapter that Cappelen and Lepore have not shown that minimal propositions, and only minimal propositions, always play the kind of cognitive role they attribute to them. They are right to point out that speech-participants often have incomplete communication-relevant information or mistaken beliefs about the shared context or about the original context. However, in both cases, grasping the minimal propositions expressed won't always help in figuring out the speaker's communicative intentions. The reason is that, in some cases, participants don't expect speakers to be communicating the literal meanings of their utterances. So, the Psychological Objection still stands.

CONCLUSION

I will close with a brief comment. Conceding the Psychological Objection isn't necessarily such a bad thing for Cappelen and Lepore—they would just have to give up the Psychological Reality Thesis. Giving up the Psychological Reality Thesis is consistent with, and in the spirit of, another view they defend in other published writings, namely, the view that semantics should not be methodologically constrained by pragmatics, in particular by considerations about the psychology of linguistic communication or by considerations about the psychological roles of our indirect speech reporting practice (Cappelen and Lepore 1997, 1998, cf. *IS*, ch. 4).

In fact, they really have no choice but to give up the Psychological Reality Thesis.[18] First, let's assume along with Cappelen and Lepore that, at the very least, an adequate semantics for a language L must assign a minimal proposition P as the semantic content of a context-insensitive sentence S of L if and only if every literal utterance of S in L expresses P.[19] What does it mean to say that a literal utterance of S in L expresses P? If it is just another way of saying that P is the minimal content of S, regardless of our best judgments about what is said, then the aforementioned adequacy constraint on semantics is vacuous if Semantic Minimalism is true. But then, minimal propositions aren't entities that *must* serve some essential and distinctive role in communication that no enriched proposition could serve. We don't have to view them as such if we abide by Cappelen and Lepore's methodological dictum. We thus have no reason to accept the Psychological Reality Thesis, and the goal of rebutting the Psychological Objection becomes completely unmotivated. So, granting the Psychological Objection isn't a concession—but it certainly widens the gap between pragmatics and semantics considerably.[20]

On the other hand, suppose that what it means to say that a literal utterance of S expresses P is that P is always one of the many things that any competent speaker would be asserting by her utterance of S, as Cappelen and Lepore sometimes claim in *IS*. In that case, the aforementioned adequacy condition

[18] I am indebted to Lenny Clapp for the line of argument developed in this paragraph and in the next, and for pressing me on some of the points made in this section.

[19] One who agrees with Cappelen and Lepore that no free pragmatic processes intrude in the combinatorial semantic interpretation of sentences can reject this general constraint on semantics. Kent Bach, who identifies himself as a "Radical Semantic Minimalist", rejects it on the grounds that, because some context-insensitive sentences are semantically incomplete, not every grammatically well-formed, indexical free, declarative sentence must semantically express a complete proposition (Bach forthcoming).

[20] Emma Borg is a Semantic Minimalist who embraces the idea that the gap between semantics and pragmatics is very wide and that nothing having to do with speaker's intentions should be allowed to contaminate our semantic theorizing, which is completely "bottom–up". See Borg, this volume.

on semantics is non-vacuous. For, what makes *P* the minimal semantic content of *S* is certain psychological facts about how speakers and hearers use *S* to communicate information. Seen in this light, it would make sense for Cappelen and Lepore to defend the Psychological Reality Thesis and to try to rebut the Psychological Objection, but at the cost of giving up Semantic Minimalism. After all, the minimal proposition, *Steel is strong enough* (full-stop), is never one of the many things that competent speakers are trying to convey or assert by their utterances of 'Steel is strong enough'. It can't then be the semantic content of the sentence. Cappelen and Lepore would also have to give up their methodological dictum that semantics should be unconstrained by pragmatics.

We've reached the proverbial fork in the road: either concede the Psychological Objection but hold on to Semantic Minimalism, thereby widening the gap between semantics and pragmatics even more so, or give up Semantic Minimalism and Cappelen and Lepore's methodological dictum. Since they want to hold on to Semantic Minimalism and reject the idea of a pragmatically enriched truth-conditional semantics, it is clear what they should choose.[21]

REFERENCES

Bach, K. (1994), 'Conversational Impliciture', *Mind and Language*, 9: 124–62.

—— (2001), 'You Don't Say?', *Synthese*, 128: 15–44.

—— (2005), 'Context ex Machina', in Z. Szabó (ed.), *Semantics versus Pragmatics*, 15–44. Oxford: Oxford University Press.

—— (forthcoming), 'The Excluded Middle: Semantic Minimalism without Minimal Propositions', *Philosophy and Phenomenological Research*.

Borg, E. (2005), *Minimal Semantics*. Oxford: Clarendon Press.

Cappelen, H., and E. Lepore (1997), 'On an Alleged Connection between Indirect Quotation and Semantic Theory', *Mind and Language*, 12: 278–96.

—— and —— (1998), 'Reply to Richard and Reimer', *Mind and Language* 13: 618–21.

—— and —— (2005), *Insensitive Semantics*. Oxford: Blackwell.

—— and —— (forthcoming), typescript 'Reply to Bach', *Philosophy and Phenomenological Research*.

Carston, R. (2002), *Thoughts and Utterances*. Oxford: Blackwell.

—— (2004), 'Relevance Theory and the Saying/Implicating Distinction', in L. Horn and G. Ward (eds.), *Handbook of Pragmatics*, pp. 633–57. Oxford: Oxford University Press.

Clark, H. H. (1997), 'Dogmas of Understanding', *Discourse Processes*, 23: 567–98.

—— and R. J. Gerrig (1983), 'Understanding Old Words with New Meanings', *Journal of Verbal Learning and Verbal Behavior*, 22: 591–608.

[21] I am indebted to Kent Bach, Emma Borg, Lenny Clapp, Shannon Finnegan, Martin Montminy, Jeff Pelletier, and Rob Stainton for their helpful comments. An earlier version was presented at a book symposium on *Insensitive Semantics*, which was held at the 2005 Canadian Philosophical Association Meeting, in London, Ontario. Herman Cappelen was the commentator and delivered an excellent set of comments for which I am very grateful. I would also like to thank the two OUP referees for their very helpful comments and suggestions.

Donnellan, K. (1966), 'Reference and Definite Descriptions', *Philosophical Review*, 77: 281–304.

Elugardo, R., and R. J. Stainton (2001), 'Logical Form and the Vernacular', *Mind and Language*, 16: 393–424.

—— and —— (2003), 'Grasping Objects and Contents', in A. Barber (ed.), *Epistemology of Language*, pp. 257–302. Oxford: Oxford University Press.

—— and —— (2004), 'Shorthand, Syntactic Ellipses, and the Pragmatic Determinants of What is Said', *Mind and Language*, 4: 442–71.

Grice, H. P. (1967), 'Logic and Conversation', in P. Cole and J. Morgan (eds.), *Syntax and Semantics*, iii. 41–8. New York: New York Academic Press.

Merchant, J. (2001), *The Syntax of Silence*. Oxford: Oxford University Press.

Montminy, M. (2006), 'Semantic Content, Truth Conditions and Context', *Linguistics and Philosophy*, 29: 1–26.

Nunberg, G. (1979), 'The Non-Uniqueness of Semantic Solutions: Polysemy', *Linguistics and Philosophy*, 3: 143–84.

Recanati, F. (2004), *Literal Meaning*. Cambridge: Cambridge University Press.

Salmon, N. (2005), 'Two Conceptions of Semantics', in Z. Szabó (ed.), *Semantics versus Pragmatics*, pp. 317–28. Oxford: Oxford University Press.

Sanford, A. J. (2002), 'Context, Attention and Depth of Processing during Interpretation', *Mind and Language*, 17: 188–206.

Searle, J. (1978), 'Literal Meaning', *Erkenntnis*, 13: 207–24.

—— (1980), 'The Background of Meaning', in J. Searle, F. Kiefer, and M. Bierwisch (eds.), *Speech Act Theory and Pragmatics*, pp. 221–32. Dordrecht: Reidel.

Soames, S. (2005), 'Naming and Asserting', in Z. Szabó (ed.), *Semantics versus Pragmatics*, pp. 356–82. Oxford: Oxford University Press.

Sperber, D., and D. Wilson (1986), *Relevance*. Oxford: Blackwell.

Stainton, R. J. (1995), 'Non-Sentential Assertions and Semantic Ellipsis', *Linguistics and Philosophy*, 18: 281–96.

—— (2005), 'In Defense of Non-Sentential Assertion', in Z. Szabó (ed.), *Semantics versus Pragmatics*, pp. 384–457. Oxford: Oxford University Press.

—— (2006), *Words and Thoughts*. Oxford: Oxford University Press.

Stanley, J. (2000), 'Context and Logical Form', *Linguistics and Philosophy*, 18: 101–39.

—— and Z. Szabo (2000), 'On Quantifier Domain Restriction', *Mind and Language*, 15: 219-61.

Travis, C. (1985), *The Uses of Sense*. Oxford: Oxford University Press.

Wason, P., and S. S. Reich (1979), 'A Verbal Illusion', *Quarterly Journal of Experimental Psychology*, 31: 591–7.

12

Minimalism and Modularity

Philip Robbins

Semantic minimalism is an austere and sober doctrine. At its core are two claims. First, semantic interpretation is licensed and driven by syntax at every step. There are no unarticulated constituents of propositional content. Second, features of the context of utterance guide the interpretation of only a small class of expressions, namely, those with overtly indexical features. Pragmatic processes, which draw on this contextual information, play only a modest part in semantic interpretation. Advocates of the headier doctrine of contextualism deny both of these claims (Recanati 2004).

Within minimalism there are more and less stringent construals of the claim about context-sensitivity. On one construal, only 'objective' ('narrow', 'non-perspectival') features of the context—such as the agent, time, and location of utterance—are factored into the interpretation of context-sensitive expressions (Borg 2004*b*). Contextual features that count as 'subjective' ('wide', 'perspectival'), such as the speaker's referential intentions, are semantically irrelevant. I'll call this *strong minimalism.* (Recanati 2005 calls it *conventionalism.*) A more liberal notion of context-sensitivity allows for the addition of subjective features to the mix (Cappelen and Lepore 2005).[1] I'll call this *weak minimalism.*

The distinction between strong and weak minimalism is important. A hallmark of the minimalist program, and part of what makes it appealing, is the way it neatly divides semantics from pragmatics, a division that depends on sharply restricting the role of pragmatic processing in truth-conditional interpretation. Contextualists, by contrast, insist that the determination of truth-conditions is pragmatic through and through (Recanati 2004). One worry about weak minimalism, then, is that by granting the semantic relevance of a larger assortment of contextual features, it gives away too much to the contextualist. A related, more

[1] As Cappelen and Lepore put it: "We don't (need to) assume that the semantic value [of context-sensitive expressions] is fixed by purely 'objective' features of the context of utterance" (2005: 148). They go on to say that they don't know of any theorist who assumes otherwise. But Borg is clearly in the contrarian camp: "Though 'objective' features of the context of utterance, like who is speaking, when they are speaking and where they are located, are admissible, richer features, which require access to the speaker's mental state, are not similarly admissible" within a theory of semantic interpretation (Borg 2004*b*: 30).

important worry is that by admitting the relevance of these further features, weak minimalists—like their contextualist opponents—implicitly commit themselves to a view of the architecture of the language faculty that is at odds with the empirical record. This commitment exposes weak minimalism to a potentially deadly weapon in the anti-contextualist arsenal: the argument from modularity (Borg 2004*b*). For those of us who prefer minimalism to contextualism but prefer their minimalism in a less strict form, this argument presents a serious problem. The main goal of this chapter is to solve this problem. First I'll explain the argument from modularity (§1). Then I'll explain why the argument misfires, focusing on the relation between semantics and 'mindreading', with special attention to how evidence from clinical psychology bears on that issue (§§2–3). I'll close with some more general remarks about minimalism and contextualism (§4).

1. THE ARGUMENT FROM MODULARITY

In philosophy, as elsewhere, sometimes the best defense is a good offense. A case in point is Borg's (2004*b*) defense of minimalism, in which she argues as follows:

(P1) The semantics component of the language faculty is modular.[2]
(P2) Contextualism is inconsistent with the modularity of semantics.
Hence, contextualism is false.

According to Borg, friends of minimalism have nothing to fear from this line of attack, because their view *is* consistent with the modularity of semantics. But while this is plausibly true of Borg's (strong) version of minimalism, it does not seem to be true of the weak version. The result is a parallel argument against the view of Cappelen and Lepore (2005):

(P1) The semantics component of the language faculty is modular.
(P2*) Weak minimalism is inconsistent with the modularity of semantics.
Hence, weak minimalism is false.

In short, if the argument from modularity works, it doesn't just work against contextualism. It also works against a well-known brand of minimalism.

To see why, consider first the claim that semantics is modular. The term 'modularity' (and its cognates) is central to modern psychology, but it is far from

[2] Modularity is not an absolute property, but a relative (i.e. gradable) one: it admits of degrees. Hence, when theorists use the term 'modular', they usually mean modular "to some interesting extent" (Fodor 1983: 37). In what follows, the notion of modularity should be understood in this qualified sense.

univocal. Indeed, it has come to mean a dizzying variety of things (Segal 1996; Samuels 2000). For present purposes, the most relevant kind of modularity is the classical kind, first articulated by Fodor (1983). A Fodorian module is a special-purpose information-processing device that operates more or less autonomously with respect to the system in which it is embedded. To be more precise, Fodorian modules are distinguished by a set of nine features, the most important of which is 'informational encapsulation'. A mechanism is informationally encapsulated just in case its operations have access to only a proprietary subset of the information contained by the system as a whole. For this reason modular processes are said to be 'local', in the sense that they can draw on little or no exogenous information.

Uncontroversial examples of Fodorian modularity are thin on the ground. But it is widely believed that mechanisms of defeasible inference—mechanisms of the sort engaged by commonsense and scientific reasoning—are *not* modular. The hallmark of defeasible inference is non-monotonicity, meaning that conclusions drawn on this basis may be withdrawn on receipt of new information, even if the initial information is retained. For example, consider a case of abduction, or inference to the best explanation. Suppose the fuel gauge in your car reads 'E' (for 'empty'), and you conclude on this basis that the fuel tank is empty. Were you to discover that the fuel gauge is broken, or that there is a short in the electrical system, you would (or should) retract this conclusion.[3] Defeasible inference is a global process, rather than a local one: it is sensitive to most, if not all, of the information at the system's disposal.[4] If semantics is modular, then, truth-conditional interpretation cannot involve defeasible inference to any significant extent. Strong minimalism is safe on this score, since on this view interpretation is largely a matter of deduction via compositional rules, and deductive inference is indefeasible. According to contextualism, however, truth-conditional interpretation relies heavily on pragmatic processes, and pragmatic processes rely heavily on defeasible inference (Recanati 2002). Hence, contextualism runs afoul of the (alleged) modularity of semantics.

It's a short step from this claim (P2) to the analogous claim about weak minimalism (P2*). According to weak minimalism, assigning truth-conditions to utterances of sentences that contain overtly indexical expressions may involve thinking about the speaker's referential intentions. For instance, in order to interpret an utterance of the sentence

(1) That is one cute baby!

[3] Deductive inference, by contrast, is monotonic. Suppose the fuel gauge in your car reads 'E', and you conclude that your car has a fuel gauge. No matter what new information comes along, your conclusion is here to stay, and rightly so.

[4] This helps to explain the intractability of the 'frame problem' in AI. Solving the frame problem means giving a computational account of defeasible inference, and global processes tend to elude capture in a computational net (Fodor 2000).

one has to know the intended referent of the bare demonstrative 'that'. But thinking about a speaker's intentions to refer, like thinking about their mental states (beliefs, desires, intentions, and the like) more generally, seems to be a global process, not a local one. Borg illustrates this point with a non-linguistic example:

> [I]magine that you see Sally filling a glass of water from the tap. Then you might reason as follows: "The best explanation for this action is that Sally is thirsty and wants a drink; therefore Sally is thirsty and wants a drink." Clearly this is a non-demonstrative [i.e. defeasible] piece of reasoning and it is susceptible to the influence of an open-ended range of contextual factors. For instance, say that you know that Sally has just come in with Sourav and that Sourav is wearing running gear and looks out of breath, then the best explanation for Sally's action might be that Sourav is thirsty and Sally is getting a drink for him. Or imagine that Sally has just glanced at her potted plant, then the best explanation might be that she wants to water her plant. So a range of contextual factors can matter in determining an intentional attribution and there is no determinate boundary at the outset on which facts could turn out to be relevant (and this is just to note that the process looks distinctly unencapsulated). (2004*b*: 78–9)

Since strong minimalists deny that intentional attribution (or any other sort of 'subjective' feature detection) is relevant to semantic interpretation, their view is plausibly consistent with locality. Assuming Borg is right, weak minimalists are in a different boat. On her view, if semantics is modular, their brand of minimalism is untenable (Borg 2004*a*).

In order to rescue weak minimalism from this predicament, one has to do at least one of two things. Either one has to undermine the case for thinking that semantics is modular, or one has to undermine the case for thinking that modularity can't be squared with weak minimalism. In the next two sections I'll explore each of these options in turn.

2. IS SEMANTICS MODULAR?

In order to show that a cognitive process is modular, one needs to show that the process has most of the features characteristic of a modular process. Of these features, informational encapsulation is only the most central. Modular processes are also supposed to be domain-specific, fast, mandatory, inaccessible to consciousness, neurally localizable, and functionally dissociable, *inter alia* (Fodor 1983). The more of these features semantic interpretation can be shown to have, the more plausible it will seem that the semantic component of the language faculty is a module. But two features are clearly non-negotiable: informational encapsulation and functional dissociability. If either of these features is absent, so is modularity. Hence, in what follows, I'll restrict the discussion of semantic modularity to these two features.

The issue here is plainly an empirical one. But settling it is not a straightforward matter. For there is no way to tell whether a given piece of empirical evidence supports (or conflicts with, or is neutral with respect to) the hypothesis that a cognitive process has some paradigmatically modular feature without making some initial assumptions about what that process consists in. And what those assumptions should be is precisely what's at issue in the larger debate. Thus, it won't do to argue that semantics has the dual earmarks of modularity by presenting evidence that semantic processing *as characterized by strong minimalism* has the dual earmarks of modularity. Rather, one has to produce evidence that semantic processing characterized in a sufficiently neutral manner—at a minimum, in a manner consistent with both strong and weak minimalism—has those two features. As we'll see, this is not easy to do.

2.1. Informational Encapsulation

At first glance it might seem obvious that truth-conditional interpretation is an encapsulated process. This is how Borg sees it:

> Clearly information encapsulation holds good for literal semantic intepretation. I will see or hear a sentence as meaning what it in fact does mean regardless of other things I believe or, in general, what I hope a given speaker is going to say . . . Though I do not expect there to be an alligator in the corridor of my philosophy department, still a cry of "There's an alligator in the corridor!" means that there is an alligator in the corridor and, though I may have my doubts about the veracity of this report, it can lead me, cautiously, to investigate the matter. Yet, if semantic understanding were susceptible to expectations or to my general view of the world and my current situation, it is hard to see how this could happen. (Borg 2004*b*: 90)

Borg's confidence on this score, however, seems misplaced. The actual situation is much less clear-cut. To see why, it's important to bear in mind that, according to minimalism, an essential part of the job description of the semantic mechanism is the assignment of truth-conditions, or propositional content, to utterances (Borg 2004*b*; Cappelen and Lepore 2005).[5] And in many, many cases—arguably the vast majority of cases—it seems difficult, if not impossible, to assign truth-conditions to an utterance without drawing on background information about the context of utterance. Borg's own example is a case in point. Under ordinary circumstances, assigning truth-conditions to an utterance of

(2) There's an alligator in the corridor!

[5] This view of the scope of semantics is widespread in philosophy of language these days, though it is far from universal (exceptions include Pietroski 2003). See Horisk 2005 for helpful discussion of the issue.

seems to require knowing *which* corridor the speaker is referring to. This is not the kind of knowledge that the language faculty can come up with on its own. Hence, if the process of interpreting utterances of sentences like (2) requires knowing the truth-conditions of those utterances, it seems unlikely that this process is encapsulated.

Examples of this sort can be freely multiplied. Consider the following:

(3) I'm going to the bank.

(4) That [*pointing to a picture in a fashion magazine*] is Stella's dress.

(5) Bill loves computer puzzles.

In (3), in addition to determining the identity of the speaker (to fix the referent of 'I'), one needs to determine whether the speaker's destination is a financial institution or a topographical feature (riverbank, snowbank, etc.). In (4), one needs to determine the intended referent of the demonstrative, as well as the intended referent of the genitive construction (a dress designed by Stella? owned by her? worn by her at the Oscars?). In (5), one needs to interpret the proper name (which Bill?), as well as the compound noun (a puzzle game played on a computer? a puzzle about computer malfunction?). In all of these cases, the requisite information is extralinguistic, and in most of them, accessing it involves thinking about the speaker's intentions. If the interpretation process were encapsulated, information of this sort would appear to be off-limits.[6]

In short, it's far from obvious that truth-conditional interpretation *is* an encapsulated process. However, contrary to what the preceding remarks might suggest, it's also far from obvious that it *isn't*. For, as Borg (2004*b*) shows, it is possible to interpret utterances of sentences containing context-sensitive expressions on a purely formal basis, simply by cueing off the syntax and ignoring background information about speaker's intentions and the like. It's just that the resulting interpretations look rather different than what one might naïvely expect. For example, to interpret the bare demonstrative in (4), one has only to introduce a singular concept of the referent. Doing so does not require knowing how to pick out the referent via perception, memory, or on any other epistemically substantial basis. Nor does it require access to the speaker's referential intention. All it requires is that the hearer interpret the demonstrative as a genuinely referential (i.e. non-descriptive) expression (Borg 2004*b*: 186 ff.).

Of course, this particular strategy won't work for all the examples above, which cover a broad range of linguistic phenomena (not just demonstratives but definite descriptions, genitives, compound nouns, ambiguity, etc.). Indeed, it may not even pan out for (4), the case it fits best. But that isn't the point.

[6] As we'll see later, however, this restriction on the flow of information to a module may be merely apparent. See §3 for discussion.

The point is that, though there's no good evidence that semantic interpretation is *not* encapsulated, there's also no good evidence that it *is*. As things stand, the issue of semantic encapsulation—and to that extent, the issue of semantic modularity—is up for grabs.

2.2. Functional Dissociability

On the list of leading indicators of modularity, the property of functional dissociability ranks near the top, alongside encapsulation. To show that semantics has this property, one needs to furnish evidence of cases in which semantic competence is selectively impaired or preserved relative to other cognitive capacities, linguistic or otherwise. Of special interest here are cases of normal semantics with deficits in 'mindreading' (Baron-Cohen 1995), since the existence of such cases would support the strong minimalist's claim that the capacity for literal speech interpretation does not require the capacity to discern speakers' intentions. Of related interest are cases of normal semantics alongside deficits in commonsense reasoning or other capacities grounded on defeasible inference.[7] Borg (2004*b*) points to several clinical disorders that seem to fit the bill, including Asperger syndrome, schizophrenia, and Williams syndrome. She suggests that patients with these disorders have normal syntax and normal semantics despite deficits in mindreading and linguistic pragmatics (Asperger syndrome and schizophrenia) or severe mental retardation (Williams syndrome). Borg quotes several passages from the clinical literature, but her discussion is brief and sketchy. A closer look at the clinical picture reveals serious flaws in her argument for the dissociation hypothesis. Let's consider each of the three disorders in turn, starting with Asperger syndrome.

Asperger syndrome (AS) is a pervasive neurodevelopmental disorder marked by problems with social interaction and communication, together with restricted, repetitive, and stereotyped patterns of behavior, interests, and activities. As far as language skills go, individuals with AS typically acquire more or less normal syntax, semantics, and phonology on a more or less normal schedule, but they tend to have great difficulty carrying on a normal conversation (Frith and Happé 1994). Some of this difficulty stems from the fact that they tend to interpret speech in an overly literal way. For example, one child with AS, when told to "stick your coat over there", asked in earnest for some glue; another responded to the indirect request "Can you pass the salt?" as if it were a question about

[7] Strictly speaking, in order to show that capacity X is functionally dissociable from capacity Y, one needs to show that X and Y are doubly dissociable, that is, dissociable in both directions (Shallice 1988). For this purpose, one needs to show two things: first, that X can be intact while Y is impaired; second, that X can be impaired while Y is intact. Evidence from studies of patients with severe agrammatic aphasia suggests that mindreading and commonsense reasoning are both dissociable from semantics (Varley and Siegal 2000). In what follows, I will focus on the dissociation hypothesis with the opposite polarity.

their motor ability (Frith 2003). Accordingly, individuals with AS are puzzled by irony, sarcasm, slang, metaphor, and other forms of figurative speech.

There is no question that pragmatics is impaired in AS. Semantics in AS, by contrast, appears to be relatively spared, though there is considerable evidence that individuals with AS egocentrically reverse pronouns (e.g. using 'you' to refer to oneself) and demonstratives (using 'this' instead of 'that', and 'here' instead of 'there') (Frith 2003).[8] But this is not enough to show that semantics is functionally dissociable *in the relevant sense*. What's needed, in addition, is evidence that AS individuals have core deficits in mindreading or commonsense reasoning. But not only is there no such evidence, there is evidence to the contrary.

First, AS individuals acquire the lexicon much as normals do. According to an influential theory of lexical acquisition, this capacity relies heavily on core mindreading skills, such as the ability to discern speakers' referential intentions (Bloom 2000). Second, AS individuals perform like normals on a range of standard mindreading tests, including first-order and second-order false-belief tasks (Bowler 1992).[9] To be sure, mindreading in AS is not wholly intact. For example, AS individuals' performance on certain advanced mindreading tasks, such as the faux pas detection test (Baron-Cohen et al. 1999) and the 'strange stories' test (Jolliffe and Baron-Cohen 1999), tends to be below par. But successful performance on these particular tasks requires highly sophisticated mindreading, that is, mindreading skill at a level that is plausibly beyond what literal speech interpretation might require. It's an open possibility, then, that individuals with AS have enough of an ability to discern speakers' intentions to understand literal speech, but not enough of this ability to understand irony, sarcasm, conversational faux pas, and the like. Third, AS individuals have normal or high IQ. Fourth, and finally, these individuals perform at least as well as normals on tests of causal-mechanical reasoning, a type of reasoning that draws heavily on the capacity for defeasible inference (Baron-Cohen et al. 1999, 2001).

Similarly, and for much the same reasons, the clinical profile of schizophrenia does not support the idea that semantics is functionally dissociable from pragmatics in the relevant sense (that is, dissociable from mindreading and commonsense reasoning). Schizophrenia is a complex disorder, with three distinct subtypes (paranoid, catatonic, hebephrenic). Depending on the subtype, patients may

[8] There is also evidence that high-functioning autistics are abnormally prone to errors in the literal semantic comprehension of complex sentences (Just *et al.* 2004). This is noteworthy because AS is widely viewed by clinicians as a close relative of high-functioning autism (Baron-Cohen 2003).

[9] The classic example of a false-belief task is the Sally–Anne task (Wimmer and Perner 1983). Here, subjects observe a puppet show featuring two characters, Sally and Anne. After Sally puts her marble into a basket and leaves, Anne takes the marble from the basket and puts it into a box. The subject is then asked where Sally thinks her marble is (belief attribution) or where Sally will look for her marble (behavioral prediction). This is a 'first-order' false-belief task, since it involves thinking about someone else's (mistaken) belief about the world. In 'second-order' false-belief tasks, subjects are asked to read and answer questions about stories in which one character has a mistaken belief about another character's mental state.

exhibit a heterogeneous array of symptoms, including delusions, hallucinations, flat affect, asociality, anhedonia (inability to feel pleasure), abulia (poverty of will), alogia (poverty of speech), disorganized speech, and bizarre behavior. It has also recently been shown that schizophrenics have difficulty understanding stories involving irony, metaphor, and other forms of nonliteral language (Langdon et al. 2002), as well as difficulty understanding hints and jokes (Corcoran 2000; Polimeni and Reiss 2006). However, there is no evidence that schizophrenics are impaired on performance of first-order false-belief tasks, and many schizophrenics (namely, those with passivity symptoms) perform normally on second-order false-belief tasks as well (Corcoran 2000). More generally, there is no evidence that core mindreading is defective in schizophrenia. Likewise, there is no evidence that commonsense reasoning is defective in these patients. To top it off, there is considerable evidence of defective semantic processing in schizophrenia, at least at the lexical level (Rossell and David 2006). All in all, then, the clinical picture of schizophrenia lends no substance to the claim that semantics is dissociable from pragmatics (again, in the operative sense).

Finally we turn to the case of Williams syndrome. This is a remarkable condition, in that affected individuals display a high degree of language function in tandem with a broad spectrum of severe cognitive deficits (Karmiloff-Smith et al. 1995; Bellugi *et al.* 2000). Though some individuals with Williams syndrome (WS) are of normal overall intelligence, the overwhelming majority are severely retarded, with IQ typically in the 40–60 range. They perform poorly on standard tests of visuospatial cognition, hand–eye coordination, numerical cognition, and simple problem solving. As far as getting by in the real world, they're helpless: they can't tie their shoelaces, find their way to the grocery store, add two numbers together, retrieve things from a cupboard, tell left from right, judge distances, or even negotiate stairs. But they are also talkative and sociable, often to a fault. Individuals with WS are prone to bouts of empty chatter, and they are naturally inclined to hug total strangers. The global picture of WS, Borg (2004*b*) suggests, is of intact language—including intact semantics—accompanied by defective central cognition.

Once again, however, the facts of the case don't support the dissociation claim. For not only is semantics more or less intact in WS, so is pragmatics. For example, individuals with WS appear to have little or no difficulty understanding stories involving sarcasm and metaphor (Karmiloff-Smith et al. 1995). Moreover, there is good evidence that these individuals are proficient at reading off a person's mental states from their facial expressions, posture, gait, and gestures. This suggests that at least a fundamental component of mindreading—the 'social-perceptual', as opposed to the 'social-cognitive', component—is intact in WS (Tager-Flusberg and Sullivan 2000).[10] In sum, the case of Williams syndrome does not count as a case of semantic dissociation.

10 More on the distinction between these aspects of mindreading below, in §3.2.

3. MODULARITY, MINDREADING, AND MINIMALISM

In this section I want to switch gears and examine the second premise of the argument from modularity (P2*). This is the claim that weak minimalism is inconsistent with semantic modularity. In particular, I will argue that, for all we know, this claim may be false.

3.1. Two Kinds of Involvement

To get the ball rolling, here is a reconstruction of Borg's (2004*b*) argument for the inconsistency thesis (P2*):

(IC1) The operations of modular mechanisms involve only local, not global, processes.

(IC2) Defeasible inference is a global process.

(IC3) According to weak minimalism, literal semantic interpretation involves mindreading.

(IC4) Mindreading involves defeasible inference.

Hence, if semantics is modular, then weak minimalism is false.

The argument appears to be valid, but only the second premise (IC2) seems secure. The remaining three premises call for closer scrutiny.

Each of the premises in question contains the term 'involve'. So before trying to assess their truth-value, we need to get clear about what this term means. Like most terms in natural language, the term 'involve' is equivocal. For present purposes we can distinguish two senses, one weak and the other strong:

(*Weak Inv*) Given a pair of processes P and P^*, P *weakly involves* P^* just in case P causally depends on P^*.

(*Strong Inv*) Given a pair of processes P and P^*, P *strongly involves* P^* just in case P is at least partially constituted by P^*.

Thus, involvement in the weak sense is a type of causal dependence, whereas involvement in the strong sense is a type of constitution relation.[11] The first question to ask, then, concerns the first premise of the argument (IC1). In which of these two senses is it fair to say that the operations of Fodorian modules do not involve global processes, like defeasible inference?

[11] For more on the distinction between causal dependence and constitution, and its philosophical significance, see Block 2005.

The most plausible answer, I think, is: only in the strong sense, not the weak. The reason is that causal dependence is cheap. Even the best candidates for modularity causally depend upon paradigmatically global processes. For example, mid-level vision is causally influenced by visual imagination, and speech production is causally influenced by belief fixation (Carruthers 2002). If we understand involvement in the weak sense, it will turn out that *no* cognitive process is modular—an unacceptable result, especially for proponents of the argument from modularity. Constitution, by contrast, is relatively expensive. So if we understand involvement in the strong sense, the story of modularity has a happier ending. No one suggests that mid-level vision is constituted by visual imagination, or that speech production is constituted by belief fixation. But this means that, for the argument for inconsistency to go through, the third and fourth premises (IC3 and IC4) also have to be read as claims about constitution, as opposed to mere causal dependence. This is where the trouble starts.

Consider the first of these two premises (IC3): the claim that, if weak minimalism is true, semantic interpretation involves mindreading. As before, on the weak reading, this claim is hard to resist. But the same cannot be said of the strong reading. Nothing in the weak minimalist picture requires that literal interpretation is actively constituted by mindreading. What the picture requires is only that mindreading mechanisms causally influence semantic processing, for example, by supplying information about speakers' intentions that bears on speech interpretation. It's important to note here that strong minimalism allows for mindreading to causally influence literal interpretation, for example, in ambiguity resolution (Borg 2004*b*: 140 ff.).[12] Since there's no metaphysical difference between this account of the role of mindreading in semantics and the account of that role given by weak minimalism, there's no reason to think that mindreading is constitutively involved in one case but not the other. In short, given that the argument requires the strong reading of IC3, this premise can be rejected.

And the trouble doesn't stop there. There is a parallel worry about the second premise of the pair (IC4): the claim that mindreading involves defeasible inference. As before, the requisite kind of involvement is constitution, not merely causal dependence. And as before, the claim is suspect. This may come as a surprise to readers, so it is worth taking the time to discuss a bit.

3.2. From Mindreading to Bodyreading

The claim I want to defend in this section is this: mindreading mechanisms, at least of the type that might figure in literal speech interpretation, are based primarily on social *perception*, not social *inference*. That is why mindreading

[12] This further justifies the claim that IC3 and IC4 must be read as claims about constitution. Otherwise the same form of argument could be used to infer that strong minimalism is inconsistent with modularity as well.

does not involve defeasible inference in the strong, constitutive sense required by the argument from inconsistency. To put the point another way: even if semantic interpretation were partly constituted by some sort of mindreading, it wouldn't follow that semantics isn't modular, since (*a*) the relevant mindreading mechanisms could be modular, and (*b*) there's nothing in the modularity story that rules out process-constitutive (or process-dependent) information flow between modules.

This is a bold claim, however, and it calls for some defense. The reason for the boldness is that we are accustomed to thinking of mindreading as a capacity for rather high flights of cognition. In both theory-theory and simulation theory, the two leading accounts of mindreading, the focus tends to be on mindreading understood as the capacity to attribute propositional attitudes—that is, beliefs, desires, and other fairly rarified mental states—a capacity that is tapped by false-belief tasks and their ilk. According to both accounts of this capacity, it is constituted largely by inference: in the case of theory-theory, inference mediated by a folk 'theory' of psychology; in the case of simulation theory, inference carried out in the course of imaginative self-projection into another person's perspective (Stich and Nichols 1993). Given this emphasis in the literature, there is a tendency to overlook the possibility that much, if not most, everyday mindreading is of a humbler sort.[13] It involves the attribution of emotions, current intentions, and other fairly low-level mental states, and it is constituted by perceptual processing of information about a person's facial expressions, posture, gait, gestures, vocal inflection, and the like.

As noted earlier (in §2.2), this is what Tager-Flusberg and Sullivan (2000) call the social-perceptual component of mindreading, as distinct from the social-cognitive component.[14] Gallagher (2001) calls it 'bodyreading', a term that emphasizes the way behavioral cues drive rapid, on-line judgments about a person's mental state. To assess competence at this type of mindreading, subjects are given simple perceptual tasks to perform. Examples include tests of the ability to judge a person's emotional state from their facial expression; the 'reading the mind in the eyes' test, which involves judging a person's mental state from a photograph of the eye region alone; the 'which one is thinking?' test, which involves deciding whether or not a person is thinking based on their direction of gaze; and the 'social attribution' task, which tests the ability to interpret visually ambiguous stimuli in mentalistic terms, using a version of the classic Heider-Simmel cartoon of moving geometric shapes (Baron-Cohen 1995; Klin et al. 2000). These social-perceptual tasks make different information-processing demands on the subject than social-cognitive tasks such as the Sally–Anne

[13] If, indeed, much mindreading goes on at all—a point that is not beyond controversy (see e.g. Gallagher 2001; Bermúdez 2003; Zahavi 2006). In what follows, I'll set aside this (still more) radical possibility.

[14] Goldman (2006) distinguishes between 'low-level' and 'high-level' mindreading, along similar lines.

task. Preliminary evidence from functional neuroimaging studies suggests that perceptual and cognitive mindreading activate different regions of the social brain, namely, medial temporal cortex plus amygdala versus medial prefrontal cortex (Tager-Flusberg and Sullivan 2000). Of the two strands of mindreading, it is widely believed that the perceptual strand is developmentally prior.

Now, suppose that weak minimalism is correct, and that literal speech interpretation has something to do with discerning speakers' referential intentions, a kind of mindreading. Why might one think that this kind of mindreading is chiefly of the low-level, perception-driven variety? The reason is simple. As noted earlier, individuals with Williams syndrome have more or less normal language, including normal semantics and pragmatics, despite performing poorly on tasks that involve high-level, inference-driven mindreading, such as false-belief tasks (Tager-Flusberg and Sullivan 2000).[15] These same individuals perform normally on tests of perceptual mindreading. So if the mindreading faculty contributes to semantic processing, as weak minimalism proposes, then it cannot be the cognitive component that is doing the work. It must be the perceptual component.[16]

A further point in favor of this idea is as follows. Individuals with WS have more or less normal pragmatics (including the ability to understand irony, sarcasm, and other forms of nonliteral speech), and it is generally agreed that pragmatics requires mindreading. Individuals with Asperger syndrome have pragmatic deficits, and they do well at cognitive tasks, like understanding false-belief narratives, and poorly at perceptual tasks, like 'reading the mind in the eyes' (Baron-Cohen et al. 1997). This suggests that it is low-level mindreading that plays the lead role in high-level (i.e. non-literal) speech comprehension. But if low-level mindreading normally suffices for high-level speech comprehension, it seems likely that it normally suffices for low-level (i.e. literal) speech comprehension as well. In the case of AS individuals with normal semantics, then, sophisticated mindreading plays a compensatory role—doing the work that is normally done by mindreading of a lower order.

3.3. Inconsistency Resisted

If what I've said in this section is on the right track, the argument purporting to show that semantic modularity rules out weak minimalism (i.e. P2*, the second

15 The evidential situation is actually more complicated. Karmiloff-Smith et al. (1995) argue that high-level mindreading is largely preserved in these individuals, based on studies of their performance on standard false-belief tasks. For critical discussion of those studies, see Tager-Flusberg and Sullivan 2000.

16 Relatedly, Smith et al. (1996) argue that early lexical acquisition may be driven in large part by relatively low-level perceptual processing, the work of a "dumb attentional mechanism". Their developmental hypothesis, and the empirical findings that support it, dovetail nicely with the hypothesis on offer here.

premise of the argument from modularity) does not go through. I suggested two reasons for this. First, weak minimalists are not committed to the claim that semantic processing is constituted by mindreading, only to the claim that the former causally depends on the latter. Second, it's an open possibility that mindreading for language is constituted chiefly by perception, rather than by inference; hence, it's an open possibility that mindreading for language is a local process, rather than a global one. If either of these claims is correct (and I believe both are), the argument fails, and we are left without a reason to endorse P2*. This is bad news for friends of the argument from modularity.

At this point, strong minimalists have a range of options. First, they could fashion a new, sturdier argument for P2*. This is an open possibility, though without some indication of what such an argument would look like, it is hard to assess its prospects. Second, they could try to salvage the present argument for P2*, in one of two ways. One way would be to argue that, according to weak minimalism, literal interpretation only weakly involves mindreading, and mindreading only weakly involves defeasible inference. The trouble with this strategy is that it invites a *tu quoque* reply. After all, strong minimalists also allow for mindreading to causally influence the interpretation process (namely, in resolving ambiguity). By parity of reasoning, then, modularity should preclude weak and strong minimalism alike.

Another way to defend the argument for P2* would be to grant that, according to weak minimalism, literal interpretation strongly involves mindreading, and to argue that mindreading for semantics strongly involves defeasible inference. The trouble with this second strategy is twofold. First, it doesn't seem that mindreading is involved in the weak minimalist account of interpretation in a metaphysically different way than it is in the strong minimalist account. And if there is no metaphysical difference here, the *tu quoque* charge applies again. Second, it's not clear why mindreading for semantics has to be a constitutively inferential capacity, as opposed to a perceptual one. An argument to this effect is needed, and furnishing one is a nontrivial task—especially given the evidence from Williams syndrome, in which only the inferential component of mindreading is impaired but both semantics and pragmatics are preserved.

All in all, it seems that defenders of P2*—and *a fortiori*, defenders of the argument from modularity—have an uphill battle to fight.

4. BEYOND MINIMALISM

In this chapter I've been concerned mostly with a dispute within the minimalism camp. I've argued that strong minimalists (who deny that extralinguistic capacities like mindreading have anything to do with literal speech interpretation) are wrong in thinking that weak minimalists (who adopt a more liberal view of semantic processing in relation to other capacities) are undone by facts about the architecture of the language faculty. Moreover, they're wrong in two respects. First, they're wrong in thinking that there's a good reason to think that the semantic mechanism is a module, in Fodor's strong sense. Second, they're wrong in thinking that there's a good reason to think that, if semantics were modular, then weak minimalism would be false. In short, the argument from modularity, which purports to refute weak minimalism, does not work.

So much, then, for *that* version of the argument from modularity. Recall (from §1) that the original version of the argument targeted, not a faction within the minimalist camp, but a different camp altogether: the contextualists. That argument ran as follows:

(P1) The semantics component of the language faculty is modular.

(P2) Contextualism is inconsistent with the modularity of semantics.

Hence, contextualism is false.

I argued that, if this form of argument works, it also works against weak minimalism. Likewise, if it doesn't work against weak minimalism, it won't work against contextualism either. It seems that settling the dispute between minimalists and contextualists will have to wait for another day.

The argument from modularity, however, has implications that go well beyond this dispute. In particular, the argument raises a host of questions about the relation between linguistic capacities, like literal and non-literal speech interpretation, and non-linguistic capacities, like mindreading and commonsense reasoning, as well as questions concerning the architecture of those capacities. As a preliminary exploration of such issues, the discussion in this chapter has only scratched the surface. There may be gold in these hills.[17]

REFERENCES

Baron-Cohen, S. (1995), *Mindblindness*. Cambridge, Mass.: MIT Press.

____ (2003), *The Essential Difference*. New York: Basic Books.

____ T. Jolliffe, and S. Wheelwright (1997), 'Is there a "Language of the Eyes"? Evidence from Normal Adults, and Adults with Autism or Asperger Syndrome', *Visual Cognition*, 4: 311–31.

____ M. O'Riordan, V. Stone, R. Jones, and K. Plaisted (1999), 'Recognition of Faux Pas by Normally Developing Children and Children with Asperger Syndrome or High-Functioning Autism', *Journal of Autism and Developmental Disorders*, 29: 407–18.

____ S. Wheelwright, V. Scahill, A. Spong, and J. Lawson (2001), 'Are Intuitive Physics and Intuitive Psychology Independent? A Test with Children with Asperger Syndrome', *Journal of Developmental and Learning Disorders*, 5: 47–78.

[17] Thanks to José Bermúdez, Sara Bernal, Emma Borg, Claire Horisk, Shaun Nichols, Sally Parker Ryan, and Sven Rosenkranz for helpful comments and sage advice.

Baron-Cohen, S., S. Wheelwright, V. Stone, and M. Rutherford (1999), 'A Mathematician, a Physicist, and a Computer Scientist with Asperger Syndrome: Performance on Folk Psychology and Folk Physics Tests', *Neurocase*, 5: 475–83.

Bellugi, U., L. Lichtenberg, W. Jones, Z. Lai, and M. St George (2000), 'The Neurocognitive Profile of Williams Syndrome: A Complex Pattern of Strengths and Weaknesses', *Journal of Cognitive Neuroscience*, 12 (suppl): 7–29.

Bermúdez, J. L. (2003), 'The Domain of Folk Psychology', in A. O'Hear (ed.), *Minds and Persons*, pp. 25–48. Cambridge: Cambridge University Press.

Block, N. (2005), 'Review of *Action in Perception*', *Journal of Philosophy*, 102: 259–72.

Bloom, P. (2000), *How Children Learn the Meanings of Words*. Cambridge, Mass: MIT Press.

Borg, E. (2004*a*), 'Formal Semantics and Intentional States', *Analysis*, 64: 215–23.

—— (2004*b*), *Minimal Semantics*. Oxford: Oxford University Press.

Bowler, D. M. (1992), 'Theory of Mind in Asperger's Syndrome', *Journal of Child Psychology and Psychiatry*, 33: 877–93.

Cappelen, H., and E. Lepore (2005), *Insensitive Semantics*. Oxford: Blackwell.

Carruthers, P. (2002), 'The Cognitive Functions of Language', *Behavioral and Brain Sciences*, 25: 657–74.

Corcoran, R. (2000), 'Theory of Mind in Other Clinical Conditions: Is a Selective "Theory of Mind" Deficit Exclusive to Autism?', in S. Baron-Cohen, H. Tager-Flusberg, and D. J. Cohen (eds.), *Understanding Other Minds*, pp. 391–421, 2nd edn. Oxford: Oxford University Press.

Fodor, J. (1983), *The Modularity of Mind*. Cambridge, Mass.: MIT Press.

—— (2000), *The Mind Doesn't Work That Way*. Cambridge, Mass.: MIT Press.

Frith, U. (2003), *Autism*, 2nd edn. Oxford: Blackwell.

—— and F. Happé (1994), 'Language and Communication in Autistic Disorders', *Philosophical Transactions of the Royal Society of London B*, 346: 97–104.

Gallagher, S. (2001), 'The Practice of Mind: Theory, Simulation, or Primary Interaction?', *Journal of Consciousness Studies*, 8: 83–108.

Goldman, A. (2006), *Simulating Minds*. Oxford: Oxford University Press.

Horisk, C. (2005), 'The Surprise Argument for Truth-Conditional Semantics', *Protosociology*, 21: 20–40.

Jolliffe, T., and S. Baron-Cohen (1999), 'The Strange Stories Test: A Replication with High-Functioning Adults with Autism or Asperger Syndrome', *Journal of Autism and Developmental Disorders*, 29: 395–404.

Just, M. A., V. L. Cherkassky, T. A. Keller, and N. J. Minshew (2004), 'Cortical Activation and Synchronization during Sentence Comprehension in High-Functioning Autism: Evidence of Underconnectivity', *Brain*, 127: 1811–21.

Karmiloff-Smith, A., E. Klima, U. Bellugi, J. Grant, and S. Baron-Cohen (1995), 'Is there a Social Module? Language, Face-Processing, and Theory of Mind in Individuals with Williams Syndrome', *Journal of Cognitive Neuroscience*, 7: 196–208.

Klin, A., R. Schultz, and D. J. Cohen (2000), 'Theory of Mind in Action: Developmental Perspectives on Social Neuroscience', in S. Baron-Cohen, H. Tager-Flusberg, and D. J. Cohen (eds.), *Understanding Other Minds*, pp. 391–421, 2nd edn. Oxford: Oxford University Press.

Langdon, R., M. Davies, and M. Coltheart (2002), 'Understanding Minds and Understanding Communicated Meanings in Schizophrenia', *Mind and Language*, 17: 68–104.

Pietroski, P. (2003), 'The Character of Natural Language Semantics', in A. Barber (ed.), *Epistemology of Language*, pp. 217–56. Oxford: Oxford University Press.

Polimeni, J., and J. P. Reiss (2006), 'Humor Perception Deficits in Schizophrenia', *Schizophrenia Research*, 141: 229–32.

Recanati, F. (2002), 'Does Linguistic Communication Rest on Inference?', *Mind and Language*, 17: 105–26.

____ (2004), *Literal Meaning*. Cambridge: Cambridge University Press.

____ (2005), 'Literalism and Contextualism: Some Varieties', in G. Preyer and G. Peter (eds.), *Contextualism in Philosophy*, pp. 171–96. Oxford: Oxford University Press.

Rossell, S. L., and A. S. David (2006), 'Are Semantic Deficits in Schizophrenia Due to Problems with Access or Storage?', *Schizophrenia Research*, 82: 121–34.

Samuels, R. (2000), 'Massively Modular Minds: Evolutionary Psychology and Cognitive Architecture', in P. Carruthers and A. Chamberlain (eds.), *Evolution and the Human Mind*, pp. 13–46. Cambridge: Cambridge University Press.

Segal, G. (1996), 'The Modularity of Theory of Mind,' in P. Carruthers and P. K. Smith (eds.), *Theories of Theories of Mind*, pp. 141–57. Cambridge: Cambridge University Press.

Shallice, T. (1988), *From Neuropsychology to Mental Structure*. Cambridge: Cambridge University Press.

Smith, L. B., S. S. Jones, and B. Landau (1996), 'Naming in Young Children: A Dumb Attentional Mechanism?', *Cognition*, 60: 143–71.

Stich, S., and S. Nichols (1993), 'Folk Psychology: Simulation or Tacit Theory?', *Philosophical Issues*, 3: 225–70.

Tager-Flusberg, H., and K. Sullivan (2000), 'A Componential Theory of Mind: Evidence from Williams Syndrome', *Cognition*, 76: 59–89.

Varley, R., and M. Siegal (2000), 'Evidence for Cognition without Grammar from Causal Reasoning and "Theory of Mind" in an Agrammatic Aphasic Patient', *Current Biology*, 10: 723–26.

Wimmer, H., and J. Perner (1983), 'Beliefs about Beliefs: Representation and the Constraining Function of Wrong Beliefs in Young Children's Understanding of Deception', *Cognition*, 13: 103–28.

Zahavi, D. (2006), *Self and Subjectivity*. Cambridge, Mass.: MIT Press.

13

Minimalism, Psychological Reality, Meaning, and Use

Henry Jackman

1. MINIMALISM AND CONTEXTUALISM

There are familiar aspects of our linguistic practice that point towards the conclusion that many, if not most, terms in our language are semantically context-sensitive. For instance, in some contexts (discussing professional basketball players) we deny that someone is "tall" if they are under, say, 6′7″, while in others (discussing 2nd grade students) we claim that someone is "tall" if they are over 5′1″. What counts as "tall" in some contexts does not in others, and many have argued that the semantics for "tall" should reflect this (call these "context shifting arguments"). Further, some argue that, even with the meaning of "John" fixed, in absence of a surrounding context, sentences like "John is tall" or "John is ready" can seem to have no determinate meaning at all, that is to say, we have no idea just *what* is being said by such sentences in the absence of any completing context (call these "incompleteness arguments").[1]

By contrast, Herman Cappelen and Ernie Lepore (hereafter CL) present a general argument that they take to show that such commonly offered reasons in favor of the context sensitivity of terms like "tall" can't be good. This argument distinguishes 'moderate' contextualism (which takes only *some* expressions—like "tall", "flat", "know"—to be context-sensitive), from "radical" contextualism (which takes *every* expression to be context-sensitive). The argument runs roughly as follows:

(1) Moderate contextualism entails radical contextualism.

(2) Radical contextualism is incoherent.

[1] For versions of such arguments for contextualism, see, for instance, Bezuidenhout 1997; Carston 2002; Recanati 2001, 2004; Searle 1978.

therefore,

(3) Moderate contextualism is false.

therefore,

(4) Minimalism is true.

CL try to establish premise (1) by arguing that the sorts of context shifting and incompleteness arguments that support moderate contextualism can also (with a little imagination) be used to support radical contextualism, so that if they provide us with any reason to be a moderate contextualist, they provide us with reasons to be a radical one.[2] Premise (2) is, in turn, defended on the grounds that the truth of radical contextualism makes communication impossible, since no two people are ever in exactly the same context.[3] Further, if radical contextualism were true, it would be impossible to even *state* the view, so the explicit endorsement of it is incoherent.[4] The resulting position, "Semantic Minimalism", holds that there are virtually *no* semantically context-sensitive expressions in English once you get past the standard list of indexicals and demonstratives such as "I", "you", "this", and "that".

Aside from the bare claim that the view is manifestly implausible (and the proverbial incredulous stare), there are three main reasons for thinking that minimalism can't be true.[5]

The Processing Objection

The sorts of invariant contents that CL postulate violate what Recanati refers to as an "availability constraint" on what is said. Namely: "What is said must be intuitively accessible to the conversational participants."[6] The sorts of invariant contents that CL postulate are not accessible in such a fashion. Indeed, what is accessible often only seems to be the more context-sensitive contents, and CL themselves are unable to specify non-homophonically what the invariant contents of our utterances are supposed to be. Consequently, such contents do not seem like candidates for generating the context-sensitive sayings and implicatures that we grasp in conversation. Minimal contents do not seem suitable to play any role in the psychological processing relevant for language understanding and thus lack "psychological reality".

[2] See CL 2005: ch. 3.

[3] Ibid., ch. 8. The arguments here are structurally very much like those presented against holism in Fodor and Lepore 1992. For reservations about arguments of this form, see Jackman 1999, 2003.

[4] See CL 2005: ch. 9.

[5] One could also argue against Minimalism by attempting to diffuse CL's arguments against contextualism. However, I will not be concerned with such arguments that minimalism *needn't* be true, only with the ones purporting to show that it *can't*.

[6] Recanati 2004: 20. (He adds the qualification "Unless something goes wrong and they do not count as 'normal interpreters' ", but that will not be relevant here.)

The Learning Objection

CL are able to fit semantic minimalism with our intuitions about what is said in various contexts by combining it with what they call "Speech Act Pluralism" (hereafter SAP), which they characterize as follows:

> No one thing is said... by any utterance: rather, indefinitely many propositions are said... What is said (asserted, claimed, etc.) depends on a wide range of facts other than the proposition semantically expressed. It depends on a potentially indefinite number of features of the context of utterance and of the context of those who report on (or think about) what was said by an utterance. (CL 2005: 4)

According to SAP, the semantic content of a sentence is only one of the many things said on any occasion of its utterance, so intuitions about what was said on any given occasion are to some extent distanced from what the semantic content of the sentence uttered must be.

However, given that what is consciously accessible remains varied and context-sensitive, SAP may seem to leave CL's purportedly invariant contents unlearnable. Since the most salient thing said is usually not the minimal content, it might seem that, even if there were some invariant content that each of us associated with any given word, there would be no way to be sure that each of us attached the *same* invariant contents to the words in our languages. If I always minimally meant something like "appears red under some condition or other" by "red",[7] while my parents always minimally meant, say, "appears red under *normal* conditions", there would be no way for me to learn that I was mistaken, since in any given context, we might still use our words in exactly the same way.

SAP allows the people who 'minimally' mean very different things to still manage to say the same thing with the same words in any given contexts, and thus make it difficult to see how communication requires that groups of speakers converge on the same minimal contents. As long as their differing minimal contents lead both speaker and hearer to non-minimal contents that were shared, communication would continue to go smoothly.

The Supervenience Objection

Semantic minimalism also seems to be in tension with the idea that what we mean by our terms is a function of how we use them. Our usage shows a high degree of context sensitivity, and unless one could show that there is a stable pattern behind this usage, it might seem as if semantic minimalism is incompatible with any sort of 'naturalism' about meaning. If, as the contextualist argues, there is no non-pleonastic property that all of the things that we call, say, "red" share, then

[7] CL 2005: 160.

it is hard to see how our use of the term could determine an invariant meaning that is constant through all of our applications of the term.

Such objections are familiar, and many find them to be, in some form or another, persuasive. However, the prospects for meeting these three objections are not as bleak as most opponents of minimalism suggest, provided that one understands minimalism in the context of a certain sort of externalism about mental and semantic content.

2. SEMANTIC EXTERNALISM

Semantic externalism takes the contents of one's thoughts and utterances not to be determined by one's 'narrow' psychological states. That is to say, externalism allows that the truth conditions of what we say and think are at least partially determined by factors that do not play a role in either conscious or unconscious processing. These include, but are not limited to, the history of our terms' usage, how they are used in our society, and the actual make-up of our environment. To take the two best known examples of this, the externalist allows that (*a*) two people who are internally identical could mean different things by "water" if the actual substance they applied it to in their respective environments had a different underlying microstructure (while their typical phenomenal properties were the same),[8] or (*b*) two people who are internally identical could mean different things by "arthritis" if the term was used differently in their respective environments (even if they were unaware of these differences).[9]

The literature on semantic externalism highlights a tension within our unreflective notion of psychological states. Psychological states were taken to both be states with a *processing role* in that they were realized in the head and were the subject of empirical psychology, and states with a *cognitive role* in that they were true or false and the subject of more 'normative' disciplines like epistemology. The externalist suggested that if there were states of these two types, they could not be easily identified. Hence Putnam's original claims that "meaning ain't in the head", and that what we meant by our terms was independent of our 'psychological states' (Putnam 1975). Of course, this use of 'psychological' is somewhat tendentious, and some have insisted that 'psychological' states are 'wide' as well (Burge 1979, 1986). Consequently, I'll be here using "cognitive" for this wider sense and reserve "processing" for the narrow states.

Communication can be understood in both a 'practical' and a 'normative' way. The 'practical' way requires only that it produce successful coordination of the behaviors of the participants involved. The 'normative' way requires that the hearer actually grasp a thought with the content that the speaker was

[8] Putnam 1975. [9] Burge 1979.

expressing. Externalism was traditionally motivated at least in part by a desire to explain our apparent ability to communicate in this more 'normative' fashion across both social and historical contexts (whether it be a botanist's ability to understand our comparatively uninformed discourse about Boston Ivy, or our ability to understand, say, Aristotle's writings about gold). For the externalist, meaning and content are more 'invariant' than they might otherwise seem, and ensuring this invariance requires accepting the idea that the truth conditions of our thoughts and utterances can often be quite different than we might (non-homophonically) specify them as being.[10] Crucially, it cannot be required for two people to grasp the same content, that their narrow psychological states have some shared non-relational property (like a shared high-level description or image). Shared narrow contents are neither necessary nor sufficient for communication in this more normative sense.

Semantic Externalism has a more 'normative' conception of the relation between use and meaning, and the contents associated with this more normative framework should be thought of as distinct from whatever is needed to give a causal explanation of linguistic processing. Unfortunately, while these two stories are distinct, they are often run together in the literature in this area. On the one hand, there is a tendency to look at a plausible empirical story about language processing and treat it as if it translates directly to what we should think the more 'normative' contents of our cognitive states should be. This running together of the two types of story produces a familiar form of 'psychologism' about cognitive content. Some varieties of contextualism may, to a certain extent, be guilty of this. On the other hand, it is equally unjustified to take constraints that are placed on our accounts of cognitive content, and treat them as applying to an empirical account of language processing as well. To do so would to be guilty of, for want of a better word, a type of 'philosophism' about psychological processing. For instance, our intuitive idea of cognitive content is plausibly one in which, among other things, we produce utterances that are true or false and communicate by sharing thoughts with the same content. However, it is far from clear that such requirements transfer directly, or at all, to our account of psychological processing. In particular, it is far from clear that any story of language processing needs to find a place for such invariant and shared contents.

Both psychologism and philosophism involve taking a monistic view towards content and communication, treating the psychological and philosophical story

[10] Indeed, Putnam's original presentation of semantic externalism seems to have emerged from his desire to defend the idea that the meaning of terms remained invariant through changes in our scientific theories. Also, one should note that the commitment to invariance characteristic of externalism is a *defeasible* one, and that in some cases we do treat the meanings of our terms as having changed over time or as varying between two people in a single community. It will eventually be suggested that the invariance associated with minimalism should be understood as defeasible in this way.

as if they should be the same, or at least isomorphic to each other. It will be argued below that minimalism is much more plausible once this sort of monism is rejected.

3. MINIMALISM AND PROCESSING

The 'processing objection' has much less bite if the sorts of contents that the minimalists are talking about are understood as *externalist* contents, since such contents were never plausibly part of a simple processing story. Anyone offering the 'processing objection' against minimalism also needs to show that the relevant sense of 'psychological processing' is not one that rules out contents conceived in the more traditional externalist way as well.[11]

For instance, Recanati argues that the non-contextualist position is incompatible with truth conditional semantics, given that we can't non-disquotationally specify the truth conditions for sentences like "John cut the sun".[12] While one might want something more than mere disquotation, an endorsement of semantic externalism requires that our ability to specify the truth conditions of our utterances may not be as extensive as may have originally been assumed. Someone who has a very thin, and largely mistaken, conception of what airfoils are, can still be treated as meaning *airfoil* by "airfoil" in virtue of deferring to experts who have mastered the term. Consequently, we need to ask (1) how 'psychologically real' such externalist contents are, and (2) what, if any, reason we could have for doubting that invariant contents aren't at least this psychologically real as well. It would be unfair to use stronger requirements of psychological reality when evaluating the minimalist's talk about content than one does with the externalist's.[13]

Invariant contents may have no "psychological role" if by that we mean a certain kind of *processing* role, but if by "psychological role" we mean *cognitive* role, then they certainly do.[14] Further, it is precisely such non-processing

[11] Unless, of course, the contextualist plans to reject standard varieties of externalism as well.

[12] Recanati 2004: 92–3.

[13] This is not to deny that there may be conceptions of psychological reality that the externalist contents could meet while the minimal ones could not (after all, for many—but by no means all—externalist contents, the correct application conditions are *actually* known at least by the *experts*). However, even if such conceptions of psychological reality could be found, they are not strong enough to underwrite the processing objection.

[14] Recanati makes the following remark about minimal propositions: "Let the semanticist use it if he or she wants to, provided he or she agrees that . . . the minimal proposition has no psychological reality. It does not correspond to any stage in the process of understanding the utterance, and need not be entertained or represented at any point in that process" (2001: 89). CL object to this remark since they take the *cognitive* role of minimal contents to show that they have "psychological reality", while Recanati takes their lack of *processing* role to show that they don't. With the exception of his use of "psychological reality", I think that the minimalist can accept Recanati's claim here, which really could be viewed as the suggestion that the minimalist can keep invariant propositions for the

related cognitive roles that CL stress when they discuss the importance of invariant contents.[15] CL explicitly endorse the more 'Fregean' conception of communication as requiring shared thoughts,[16] and they defend the claim that invariant contents have the cognitive role of ensuring communication by allowing us to grasp thoughts with the same content as our interlocutors in spite of our different contexts.

If invariant contents are meant to play this sort of cognitive rather than processing role, then CL's *laissez-faire* "that's just a problem for the metaphysicians" attitude towards just what these invariant contents are can seem more understandable.[17] It would be comparable to the claim that it is up to the scientists to discover just what we mean by "gold" or to the judges to determine just what we mean by "culpable negligence". If the invariant contents played a causal role in processing, then it might seem as if the semanticist *should* be able to say what they were, but if the invariant contents play no processing role, then there is no reason to think that finding these contents shouldn't be more properly a problem for the metaphysicians, judges, scientists, and other investigators of the world that our words are ultimately about. Like any externalist, the minimalist will insist that the contents of our words can only be specified by investigating what they are about, not through any sort of *a priori* conceptual analysis.

Unfortunately, the fact that invariant contents need not play any role in psychological processing is often obscured by CL's presentation of their own position. Indeed, while I've been at some pains to distinguish the cognitive from the processing role that minimal contents could be candidates to play, CL freely admit that "If there's a difference between having a cognitive function and corresponding to a stage in processing or having psychological reality, we don't know what that difference consists in."[18] Having a cognitive function and corresponding to a stage in processing are, as suggested above, two different ways of having psychological reality, and just because invariant contents are psychologically real in the first sense (and most of CL's reasons for thinking that invariant contents are psychologically real relate to this first sense), it does not follow that they will be psychologically real in the second.

Their choice of terminology does not help matters either. The term "minimalism" has a familiar use from Recanati (a minimalist view is one that minimizes the distance between sentence meaning and what is said),[19] but while CL are minimalists in Recanati's sense, so are many of the "moderate contextualists" (e.g. Stanley 2000) that CL take their minimalist view to be *opposed* to. The

cognitive role, provided that they don't take them to have a processing role. Indeed, given that the roles are different, it would seem possible to be a minimalist about cognitive content and adopt the most extreme form of contextualism (what Recanati refers to as "Meaning eliminativism" (2004: 146–51)) for one's processing story.

[15] CL 2005: 184–5. [16] Ibid. 153. [17] Ibid., ch. 11.
[18] Ibid. 186. [19] Recanati 2004: 7.

most obvious sense in which CL's views could be called "minimalist" seems to be that, in comparison to most semantic theories, it *minimizes the number* of context-sensitive expressions in our semantics.[20] However, there is nothing in the view that suggests that the *type* of content that is invariant should be in any way 'minimal'. Unfortunately, CL's references to the invariant semantic contents as "minimal semantic contents" can lead one to misread the role of invariant contents in a way that would make their position appear vulnerable to the processing objection.

After all, given the many different ways that a term like "tall" is used, what all of these uses would have in common might seem to be very thin, general, or 'minimal', and thus calling invariant semantic content "minimal" would suggest that one wanted something thin enough to be processed by everyone who used the term.[21] Consider CL's discussion of dancing:

> Some people dance by stepping, some crawl around the floor (like Martha Graham), some have music, some don't have music, some jump in the air, some wave their arms, some hold on to other people, some are alone, some slide on ice, some fly in the air, etc. What do all these activities have in common in virtue of which they are all dancing? (CL 2005: 161)

While this can seem like a straightforward metaphysical question, the implicit assumption that there *is* something which all these activities have in common can make it sound as if there is something in our heads that leads us to call all of these activities "dancing". However, if invariant content bears a normative relation to use, there is no reason to think that *all* of the activities mentioned above need have *anything* in common, since it could very well turn out that some things which we called "dancing" were not, in fact, instances of dancing at all. Contextualism keeps semantic values close to actual usage, and there is no reason to think that the minimalist can, or should, do this.[22] The more normative/externalist conception of content allows that everyone who uses a term means the same thing by it because they all committed to the same satisfaction conditions for the use of that term, even if there is no shared 'minimal' non-relational thing that is being processed in all of their heads.

20 "The most salient feature of Semantic Minimalism is that it recognizes few context sensitive expressions" (CL 2005: 2). Their division of the field as a choice between radical contextualism, moderate contextualism and minimalism also encourages this interpretation.

21 Compare recent 'minimalist' accounts of truth (Horwich 1990; Wright 2001), which take the 'minimal' concept of truth to be one that we can all agree on (the disagreements relating to whether the concept extends beyond the minimal one). Minimal contents might be (mis)understood as a generalized version of this.

22 Further, this reduces the problem posed by those accounts that suggest that the application of our terms are prototype driven and thus that there may not be any objective property in common among all the items to which a single term is applied (see, for instance, Lakoff 1987). The minimalist could admit that actual use is generated by a prototype while insisting that the invariant content that is abstracted from the use so generated need not reflect the prototype's structural features.

Because of this, we should be careful when considering claims like: "The proposition semantically expressed is our minimal defense against confusion/misunderstanding and it is what guarantees communication across contexts of utterance."[23] At one level this claim is true. Invariant contents ensure communication across contexts. Nevertheless, it is less clear how well they defend against confusion and misunderstanding. They ensure communication, in that they ensure that people in different contexts will be talking about the same things, but they do not in the sense of ensuring that there is some minimal core of one's concept that will be found in each person's conception. That is to say, it ensures communication in a normative rather than practical sense. However, confusion and misunderstanding often result when people have radically different *conceptions* of what they are talking about, and externalist (and minimalist) content only ensures that people are talking about the same things, not that they conceive of them in the same way. Indeed, even with shared invariant contents in place, speech act pluralism will allow for lots of miscommunication, because even if there is a minimal content that is shared, the main thing the speaker is trying to get across typically won't be the minimal content.

Further, one should not think of the invariant contents as the starting points from which speakers can be expected to derive the other propositions expressed in a context. Speech act pluralism allows that its semantic content is just one of many contents expressed by an utterance in a particular context, but it would be a mistake to see the 'minimal' content as the more 'basic' content from which the other contents can be generated. It seems misleading of CL to argue:

> How does it help an audience to know that this minimal proposition was expressed?. . .Our response is simple: it is a starting point. Suppose, for the sake of argument, that the proposition *A is red* is trivially true [i.e. it is true if A is red on some surface or other under some condition or other] . . . The audience knows that the speaker is talking about A and its redness, not, for example, about oysters, France or Relevance Theory. There's a lot of stuff to talk about in the universe. The proposition semantically expressed pares it down considerably. Knowledge that this proposition was semantically expressed provides the audience with the *best possible* access to the speaker's mind, given the restricted knowledge that they have of the speaker. It is trivial that A is red on some surface or other under some condition or other. The audience can assume that the speaker knew that this was trivial and was not interested in conveying such trivialities with his utterance and can, therefore, infer that there is work to be done in order to figure out exactly what the speaker was trying to communicate. (Ibid. 185–6)

If invariant content bears a normative relation to use, we shouldn't expect it to play this role. There is no reason to think that the invariant content need be

[23] CL 2005: 185. See also: "the proposition semantically expressed is that content the audience can expect the speaker to grasp (and expect the speaker to expect the audience to grasp, etc.) even if she has . . . mistaken or incomplete information [about the context]", or "The minimal semantic content is a "shared fallback content" and . . . this content serves to guard against confusion and misunderstanding" (ibid. 184–5, 185).

psychologically available in a fashion that would allow the speaker or hearer to draw inferences about the point of an utterance using it.

4. MINIMALISM AND LANGUAGE LEARNING

It should also be clear that, if the minimalist is a semantic externalist, the "learning" objection lacks bite. For the externalist, speakers are not "conceptually autonomous" in the sense of having, on their own, complete command of the conditions of application for the terms in their language, since the meaning of their terms extends beyond both their discriminatory capacities and the descriptions available to them.[24] This will have considerable consequences for what externalists should take language learning to require.

The idea that speakers are conceptually autonomous can lead one to think that two speakers share a language only if the two languages they independently speak are of exactly the same *type*. Learning a language thus involves acquiring autonomous mastery of a language that is type identical to the target language. However, the externalist should understand neither sharing a language nor learning a language the way that the model of the autonomous speaker suggests. In particular, Putnam's "division of linguistic labor" metaphor suggests that I can be understood as sharing a language with other members of my community because we look to each other for help when deciding how our terms are correctly applied. Two autonomous speakers, even if they spoke in *exactly* the same way, would not, in this sense, *share* a language at all. Non-autonomous speakers are understood as speaking the same language not in virtue of speaking two type identical languages, but rather in virtue of both taking part in a single (*token* identical) linguistic practice.[25]

Further, this conception of what it is for two people to speak the same language brings with it a correspondingly different sense of what it is to *learn* a particular language. Learning a language involves being initiated into a particular linguistic practice, and it need not involve achieving anything like complete mastery of the practice in question. Just as I can mean *arthritis* by "arthritis" even if I haven't mastered every aspect of the doctor's usage, my learning to mean by "red" what my parents meant by it does not require that we use the term in precisely the same way.

Since the contents involved have a type of cognitive rather than processing reality, skepticism about whether my parents and I mean the same thing by

24 Indeed, speakers' discriminatory capacities often appear to underdetermine or even misidentify what they are talking about. A typical example of underdetermination is Putnam's use of "beech" and "elm" (Putnam 1975: 226), while the best known discussion of misidentification is Burge's discussion of Bert's belief that he has arthritis in his thigh (Burge 1979).

25 This line of thought is developed in considerably more detail in Jackman 1998*a*.

"red" seems unmotivated. Such worries would make sense if we thought of the minimal content as some unconscious representations from which our actual use was generated. Such representations would be ontologically independent, and so the question of whether they were tokens of the same type would be a legitimate one. However, if the invariant contents of our terms are not independent of each other in this way, then endorsing minimalism should not lead to skepticism about whether I mean by "red" what my parents do by it

5. MINIMALISM AND SUPERVENIENCE

The superveniance objection is perhaps the most serious problem for the minimalist position, and ultimately may be what lies behind most people's reservations about the view.

Even if one accepts CL's arguments that moderate contextualism leads to radical contextualism and that radical contextualism is incoherent, there remains a question of what such arguments manage to establish. In particular, such arguments would seem to leave the minimalist in a position familiar from the literature on vagueness. Epistemicists like Timothy Williamson and Roy Sorensen present what can seem like fairly compelling arguments to the effect that all of our terms *must* have precise extensions.[26] In spite of this, many philosophers refuse to take epistemicism seriously because they are convinced that the extensions of our terms just *can't* be as precise as the epistemicist requires. Our terms can only be as precise as our usage and environment make them, and nothing in what determines meaning seems like it could, for most terms in the language, produce the purportedly required level of precision.[27]

In much the same way, the minimalist argues that we are committed to the meanings of our words having certain properties (in this case context-invariance rather than precision) that intuitively our use of language does not seem up to producing. If CL are right, we may be committed to the existence of context-invariant contents, but it doesn't follow from this commitment that there actually *are* such contents. Just as the epistemicist should back up the claim that we are committed to meanings being precise with a story about how there could be such things, the minimalist owes us a story about how our seemingly context-sensitive practice of word usage could produce context-invariant meanings.[28]

[26] Since admitting that any of our terms have semantically borderline cases can seem to quickly commit us to explicit contradictions (see Williamson 1994; Sorensen 2001).

[27] For a dissenting view of this last claim, see Williamson 1994; Jackman 2004.

[28] Of the two, the minimalist may be better off in that it might seem more plausible to think that shared context-invariant meanings could supervene upon our usage than perfectly precise ones. On the other hand, the epistemicist may be in a stronger position given that our commitment to classical logic will seem to many to be stronger than our commitment to, say, the truth of collective ascriptions.

Simply being an externalist doesn't remove these problems, since some explanation of how our utterances get their cognitive content is still owed. Nevertheless, since externalism presupposes a more 'normative' relation between meaning and use, the problem can seem less insuperable than it might have otherwise. For the externalist, meanings are the types of things for which our commitments about them contribute to what they are,[29] and if we are committed to the meanings of our terms being invariant, then that can help make it the case that they are.

While the idea that meaning is determined by use might point towards contextualism, given how context-sensitive the use of our terms often is, CL rightly point out that important parts of our usage actually suggest that our words have invariant contents. These aspects of our usage include the following:

Intercontextual Indirect Belief Reports

Paradigmatically context-sensitive expressions do not allow for intercontextual indirect belief reports. For instance, if John said "I'm hot today", Peter cannot truly say the next day that "John said that I'm hot today", rather he would need to say "John said that *he* was hot *yesterday*". Purportedly context-sensitive expressions like, say, "tall", do not seem to display this behavior. If John claims that he is tall in one context, we can truly claim "John said that he was tall" in another. (See CL 2005: 88–99.)

Reports under Ignorance

Sometimes a person reporting on an utterance might be ignorant of the relevant contextual features of the original context of utterance. That ignorance, however, needn't influence (what we take to be) the truth value of the indirect report. (Ibid. 93.)

Reports Based on Mistaken Assumptions

Sometimes the reporter has false beliefs about the original context of utterance. Such false beliefs need not influence (what we take to be) the truth value of the disquotational indirect report. (Ibid.)

Collective Ascriptions

If John said "Peter is tall", and Mary said "Peter is tall", then we can say that "John and Mary both said that Peter was tall" even if John and

[29] For a more extended discussion of this see Jackman 1996, 1998*a*, 2003.

Mary are in different contexts not only from us, but also from each other. We cannot, in a similar way, say that "John and Mary both said that it was hot today" if they each said "it is hot today" on different days. (Ibid. 99–104.)

These aspects of our usage are important, and often overlooked, but they are *defeasible* and one can't tell a priori that any adequate semantic theory for our language must endorse these aspects of our linguistic practice over others. The fact that our practice embodies a commitment to invariance doesn't entail that it is a necessary criterion of adequacy for any semantic theory. Our commitment to invariance is just one (heavy) commitment among others, and it may have to be given up if it is incompatible with too many of the rest. The question becomes, then, which is more deeply entrenched, those aspects of our usage that point towards contextualism or those that point towards invariantism?

We see a similar tension in the literature on semantic individualism. Given that each individual uses a their words differently, the idea that meaning is a function of use might seem to point towards an individualistic semantics according to which, say, someone who used "arthritis" in the way we did but also applied it to pains in his thigh would mean something different by "arthritis" than we do. However, other aspects of our usage (interpersonal indirect belief reports, collective ascriptions, deference) point towards such a speaker still meaning what we do by "arthritis". In the "arthritis" cases most argue that those aspects of usage that support socially shared meanings trump those that support more individualistic meanings.[30] However, the question of whether or not meaning should be equated with social or individual usage cannot be settled for an entire language at once. In some cases the standard meanings are *not* ascribed to the idiosyncratic speaker (whose usage may differ too radically from the standard, or who may simply be unwilling to defer to the standard usage of a particular term).[31] In much the same way, the question of whether meanings are invariant or contextually sensitive may have to be settled on a word-by-word basis, and for each particular word the question will ultimately be an empirical/metaphysical one.[32]

Minimalism involves the very strong claim that for *every* word outside of CL's basic set, those aspects of our usage favoring invariance will trump those favoring contextualism. The radical contextualist is committed to the equally strong claim that such invariance-favoring considerations will *never* trump the contextualist ones. The moderate contextualist, by contrast, can take the view that for some words the considerations favoring invariantism will be more central, while for others, the contextualist considerations may win out.

[30] Burge 1979 being, of course, the classic expression of this view. There are, of course, some dissenters (such as Bilgrami 1992; Davidson 1987, 1994).

[31] For a discussion of this, see Jackman 1998*b*.

[32] Consequently, it may be surprising which expressions turn out ultimately to be semantically context-sensitive (*pace* CL 2005: 112).

CL claim that moderate contextualism collapses into radical contextualism because the standard arguments for moderate contextualism (context shifting, incompleteness) can be extended with a little imagination to all terms in the language. This may be true if moderate contextualism is motivated solely by such arguments, but the sort of argument for moderate contextualism considered here is different. A term might be taken to have a contextually sensitive semantics because there is no acceptable way of systematizing our usage of it that preserves the intuition that meaning is invariant. The fact that this might be true of a term like, say, "ready" would give us no reason to think that it need to be true for terms like "flat" or "every". All three terms might be subject to context shifting and incompleteness arguments, but it is arguably only the first that does not seem to have a single leading candidate for what its invariant meaning should be.

How plausible an invariant semantics is for any given term may ultimately depend upon the strength of the candidates for its proposed invariant meaning. Given that I've suggested both that the questions of whether our words have invariant or context-sensitive semantic contents should be settled on a piecemeal rather than wholesale basis, and that this question need not be resolvable in a purely a priori fashion, I won't commit myself here to how I think most of our vocabulary will ultimately play out. Nevertheless, I will note that the case for invariantism certainly seems stronger for some words than for others.

For instance, certain words (quantifiers like "every" or connectives like "and") have clear leading candidates for what their invariant meaning would be (unrestricted quantification, logical conjunction). Of course, such candidates may be out of line with much of our everyday usage, and people might be unwilling to give up the literal truth of everyday claims like "there is no beer left" in order to preserve the idea that they could truthfully report claims made using such words from other contexts. Nevertheless, this is not a problem if, like CL, we endorse Speech Act Pluralism. SAP gives one a considerable degree of flexibility in determining the function between use and meaning, by allowing one to say, for instance, that when someone utters "there is no beer left", they have still *said* (not just implicated) something true. The minimal semantic content of the utterance (there is no beer left in the universe) may still be something false, but that is only one of the many things said in the context, and the most salient of these may be that there is no beer left in the fridge. Consequently, the intuition that we have said something true doesn't count against proposed semantic analyses that make the sentence false. SAP allows one's metaphysics/semantics to be comparatively revisionary because it allows that everyday utterances that don't fit the proposed semantic analysis can still be used to make true claims.

'Absolute' terms like "flat" might also lend themselves to this sort of analysis. With such terms there are clear leading candidates for what the term should mean, and such candidates can serve as the norm against which the other uses are understood. SAP makes it less worrisome that most of our usage fails to live up to these norms, and the invariantist account is also more plausible when we remember that the other speech acts (the true claim you may communicate by "the table is flat") are not generated by some sort of conscious or unconscious inference from the invariant one.

However, things are less clear with terms like "ready" or "tall" where there seems to be no non-arbitrary way to settle on a candidate for what the invariant meaning should be. It is these cases, where there seem to be *many* equally good candidates for what the invariant meaning should be, that may lie behind many people's doubts about minimalism.[33] A commitment to invariance might give us reason to settle on a single meaning for such terms, but there is no reason to think that anything in our usage or the world has already settled on one.[34] The degree of freedom one gets from a normative conception of the relation between use and meaning allows one to equate meaning with a leading candidate even if that candidate is out of line with much of our actual usage. However, if there are *multiple* equally good candidates, this freedom doesn't give one the ability to *arbitrarily* select one of the candidates and say that that is what everyone has always meant.

If there is no leading candidate for what a word's invariant meaning could be, there would still seem to be two alternatives to becoming a contextualist about the term in question. The first of these would involve adopting some sort of supervaluational account for expressions that don't have clear leading candidates for their meanings.[35] The other would be to adopt some sort of error theory about the semantic values of the relevant terms.[36]

Neither of these options will be explored here, but I hope to have shown that many of the prima-facie problems for semantic minimalism are, if not

[33] This seems to be the basic worry behind MacFarlane (this volume): "Semantic Minimalism is problematic not because it does not *provide* an answer to questions about the intensions of its minimal properties and propositions, but because it requires that there *be* answers to such questions." We assume that claims like "I don't want to know whether John is tall for a basketball player or tall for a 6 year old, I just want to know whether he is just plain *tall*" don't seem to make sense because it seems as if nothing in our use of "tall" would have determined a particular extension for (just plain) "tall" rather than the more specific claims.

[34] The similarity with vagueness is, once again, evident here. A commitment to bivalence may give us reason to precisify a term that has multiple equally good candidate interpretations, without giving us any reason to think that our usage has already done so. As with epistemicism, minimalism would be more plausible in these cases if our metaphysics of properties was comparatively 'sparse' (see Heck 2003; Lewis 1983), but such strong metaphysical commitments don't seem otherwise well motivated. As should be clear from Jackman 2004, I'm inclined to deal with this by suggesting that the epistemicist should allow subsequent precisification to be retroactively read back into current contents, and one could argue that a committed minimalist should do this as well, particularly when it comes to dealing with the 'open texture' of language.

[35] Such as that found in Field 1973 or Wilson 1982.

[36] See Cappelen 2005: 6–7. This second response has some appeal for moral terms like "fair", where the pull of invariance is extremely strong. (We might be more willing to say that there was no such thing as fairness than we would be willing to say that what *is* fair just varies from context to context (*pace* Unger 1995).) It seems, however, that for most terms our commitment to invariance is a defeasible one, and if no invariant meaning could be found for "tall", we would be more willing to give up on some collective ascriptions than we would be willing to give up on the idea that anything is 'really' tall.

eliminated, at least reduced considerably when the view is understood from within an externalist framework. It is not clear how eager Cappelen and Lepore would be to embrace such a framework for their view, but I hope to have given some reasons for thinking that they should. [37]

REFERENCES

Bezuidenhout, A. (1997), 'Pragmatics, Semantic Underdetermination and the Referential/Attributive Distinction', *Mind*, 106/423: 375–409.

Bilgrami, A. (1992), *Belief and Meaning*. Cambridge: Blackwell.

Burge, T. (1979), 'Individualism and the Mental', in P. E. French, T. A. Uehling, and H. K. Wettstein (eds.), *Midwest Studies in Philosophy, iv. Studies in Metaphysics*, pp. 73–121. Minneapolis: University of Minnesota Press.

____ (1986), 'Individualism and Psychology', *Philosophical Review*, 95: 3–45.

Cappelen, H. (2005), 'Reply to MacFarlane', paper presented at the 2005 Pacific Division Meeting of the American Philosophical Association.

____ and E. Lepore (2005), *Insensitive Semantics*. Cambridge: Blackwell.

Carston, R. (2002), *Thoughts and Utterances: The Pragmatics of Explicit Communication*. Oxford: Blackwell.

Davidson, D. (1987), 'Knowing one's own Mind', reprinted in P. Ludlow and N. Martin (eds.), *Externalism and Self-Knowledge*, pp. 87–110. Stanford, Calif.: CLSI Publications, 1998.

____ (1994), 'The Social Aspect of Language', in B. McGuinness and G. Oliveri (eds.), *The Philosophy of Michael Dummett*, pp. 1–16. Dordrecht: Kluwer.

Field, H. (1973), 'Theory Change and the Indeterminacy of Reference', *Journal of Philosophy*, 70 (Aug.): 462–81.

Fodor, J., and E. Lepore (1992), *Holism: A Shopper's Guide*. Cambridge: Blackwell.

Heck, R. (2003), 'Semantic Conceptions of Vagueness', in J. Beall (ed.), *Liars and Heaps*, pp. 106–27. Oxford: Oxford University Press.

Horwich, P. (1990), *Truth*. Oxford: Blackwell,

Jackman, H. (1996), '*Semantic Norms and Temporal Externalism*', Ph.D thesis, University of Pittsburgh.

____ (1998*a*), 'Convention and Language', *Synthese*, 117/3: 295–312.

____ (1998*b*), 'Individualism and Interpretation', *Southwest Philosophy Review*, 14/1: 31–8.

____ (1999), 'Moderate Holism and the Instability Thesis', *American Philosophical Quarterly*, 36/4: 361–9.

____ (2003), 'Charity, Self-Interpretation, and Belief', *Journal of Philosophical Research*, 28: 145–70.

____ (2004), 'Temporal Externalism and Epistemic Theories of Vagueness', *Philosophical Studies*, 117/1–2: 79–94.

Lakoff, G. (1987), *Women, Fire and Dangerous Things*. Chicago: University of Chicago Press.

[37] I'd like to thank Herman Cappelen, Ernie Lepore, and members of the 2005 Lisbon seminar on *Meaning and Communication* and two readers from OUP for comments on earlier versions of this chapter.

Lewis, D. (1983), 'New Work for a Theory of Universals', *Australasian Journal of Philosophy*, 61/4: 343–77.

Putnam, H. (1975), 'The Meaning of "Meaning" ', reprinted in his *Mind, Language and Reality*, pp. 215–71. New York: Cambridge University Press.

Quine, W. V. O. (1960), *Word and Object*. Cambridge, Mass.: MIT.

—— (1987), 'Indeterminacy of Translation Again', *Journal of Philosophy*, 84/1: 5–10.

Recanati, F. (2001), 'What is Said', *Synthese*, 128: 75–91.

—— (2004), *Literal Meaning*. Cambridge: Cambridge University Press.

Searle, J. (1978), 'Literal Meaning', *Erkenntnis*, 13: 207–24.

—— (1987), 'Indeterminacy, Empiricism, and the First Person', *Journal of Philosophy* 84/3: 123–46.

Sorensen, R. (2001), *Vagueness and Contradiction*. New York: Oxford University Press.

Stanley, J. (2000), 'Context and Logical Form', *Linguistics and Philosophy*, 23: 391–434.

Unger, P. (1995), 'Contextual Analysis in Ethics', *Philosophy and Phenomenological Research*, 55: 1–26.

Williamson, T. (1994), *Vagueness*. London: Routledge.

Wilson, M. (1982), 'Predicate Meets Property', *Philosophical Review*, 91/4: 549–89

Wright, C. (2001), 'Minimalism, Deflationism, Pragmatism, Pluralism', in M. Lynch (ed.), *The Nature of Truth*, pp. 751–87. Cambridge, Mass.: MIT Press.

BACK TO SEMANTIC MINIMALISM

14

Minimalism versus Contextualism in Semantics

Emma Borg

I think it is fair to say that not so long ago in philosophy of language formal semantic theories occupied the central ground: not everyone pursued a formal approach to theories of meaning, but lots of people did.[1] These days, the natural descendant of the formal approach, known as minimalism, has been consigned to the margins: not everyone rejects minimalism, but lots of people do. Minimalism is rejected in favour of contextualism: roughly, the idea that pragmatic effects are endemic throughout truth-evaluable semantic content. In *Insensitive Semantics* (henceforth *IS*) Herman Cappelen and Ernie Lepore (henceforth CL) try to redress this balance by presenting a robust defence of minimalism. I agree with lots of what they write: I too would like to defend minimalism against the contextualist hoard and I think, as do CL, that the way to do it is to reject things like the contextualist's context-shifting arguments. Furthermore, I think the reasons for rejection are, broadly speaking, the reasons CL give. So, it might seem that there is little for me to say in this chapter. Unfortunately, however, even though advocates of minimalism are thin on the ground and even though I believe we ought to present a united front to the opposition, I do have some concerns about the way in which CL frame the debate.[2] So, in this chapter I'm going to suggest that CL fail to locate the core of the debate between the two semantic programmes and that, as a result, the kind of minimalism they end up advocating concedes too much to the contextualist camp. However, despite the negative aims of this chapter, it should be remembered that, overall, I believe CL are on the right side in semantics.

The structure of the chapter is as follows. First, I'll introduce the players in the debate a little further, outlining the minimalist and contextualist positions

[1] Of course, exactly what constitutes a formal approach to semantics is something which is itself open to question, but it's not a question I'll address here.

[2] CL recognize that the way they present the debate is somewhat idiosyncratic but argue that it helps to present things as they do because it makes explicit the shared assumptions in the area (*IS* 11–14). The present chapter can be seen as raising a worry for this latter claim.

and sketching the contextualist arguments against minimalism. Then, in § 2, I'll explore the nature of contextualism in more detail, looking in particular at CL's use of the terms 'radical contextualism' and 'moderate contextualism' and seeing who falls under which label. I will argue that the definitions they give for their own terms fails to capture the true divide in the contextualist camp and suggest an alternative reading which partitions the figures in the way that they want. Then, in § 3, I'll turn to the nature of minimalism and consider a number of properties which could be taken to be constitutive of the minimalist approach. I will suggest that it is one of these properties, formalism, which is essential but that, given this feature, the kind of minimalism CL ultimately advocate turns out not to be minimal enough.

1. THE DEBATE BETWEEN MINIMALISM AND CONTEXTUALISM

As noted above, contextualists want to claim that pragmatic effects are endemic throughout the literal truth-evaluable content expressed by sentences. Depending on the way in which we understand various technical terms, we might say that the contextualist is committed to rich pragmatic effects throughout what is said by a sentence, or throughout the proposition expressed, or throughout semantic content. In what follows, I'll use this last terminology, taking contextualists to claim that pragmatics infects semantic content in a substantial way.[3] Contextualism is the natural descendant of speech act theories of meaning, a school of thought embracing the later Wittgenstein, Austin, Sellars, and many others. Exactly who counts as a contextualist in the current arena is a question I will return to below, but we might think of Travis, Searle, Recanati, and the relevance theorists (Sperber and Wilson, Carston, and many others) as the seminal figures here. The natural enemy of the contextualist, then, is the minimalist. According to minimalists there are minimal propositions (or minimal truth conditions, or minimal-whatever-else-a-semantic-theory-might-run-on) which are the result of little or no pragmatic processing and which are available to provide the literal meaning of sentences. These minimal propositions are not equivalent to what people uttering sentences normally communicate, but that, the minimalist

[3] There is disagreement about the way in which the term 'semantics' is deployed in this area. Sperber and Wilson, for instance, use 'linguistic semantics' to talk just about that portion of meaning which is recoverable from lexical and compositional knowledge alone, allowing that this item may well be sub-propositional. Bach also uses the term 'semantics' in a similar way. However, I will use the term to refer to the proposition which gives the literal or truth-conditional content of the sentence as uttered on a given occasion. On this understanding, if it turns out that lexical and combinatorial knowledge fails to determine such a proposition (with this being delivered only once rich contextual effects have been taken into account) then it will turn out that pragmatics infects semantics. Nothing hangs on this terminological point, so feel free to recast what follows in terms of 'propositions expressed' or 'literal meaning' or whatever you'd prefer.

claims, is no objection to minimal propositions as providers of semantic content. Minimalists are the descendants of those who advocated formal approaches to meaning, a school of thought with a long history, embracing theorists like Frege, the early Wittgenstein, and Carnap. Exactly who counts as a minimalist is a question I will return to in § 3.

Contextualists run a number of arguments against the minimalist view that pragmatic effects play only a very limited role in semantic content, as follows:

1.1. Context Shifting

Imagine that Jill is 5 years old and five feet tall. Intuitively, relative to a context of utterance in which 5-year-olds are being discussed, the proposition literally expressed by an utterance of 'Jill is tall' is true since Jill is tall for a 5-year-old. However, relative to a context in which basketball players are being discussed the proposition expressed is false, since Jill is not tall for a basketball player. A change in truth value for the proposition literally expressed by the utterance of a sentence, without any change in the relevant facts (i.e. Jill does not grow or shrink between contexts), entails that the sentence is in some way context-sensitive. It expresses different propositions in different contexts of utterance. Thus, although the sentence 'Jill is tall' doesn't (obviously) contain any of the usual suspects for context sensitivity (such as an indexical or a demonstrative), it seems that the sentence is context-sensitive anyway.[4]

1.2. Incompleteness

Some sentences on their own fail to express complete propositions so there is no 'minimal proposition' for these sentences to express. For instance, there is no proposition expressed by the sentences 'Steel isn't strong enough' or 'Jill is ready'. We only reach the level of a proposition once we find out from a context of utterance what steel isn't strong enough for or what Jill is ready to do. Thus although these sentences don't (obviously) contain any of the usual suspects for context sensitivity, it seems they are context-sensitive anyway.

1.3. Inappropriateness

Some sentences express complete propositions without contextual enrichment, but these propositions are not the ones speakers express by uttering those sentences. For instance, we could specify a minimal proposition, free from contextual enrichment, for sentences like 'There is nothing to eat', or 'Mending the bridge will take some time', or 'Jack has had breakfast', but what speakers who produce these sentences actually assert are enriched propositions such as

[4] For ease of presentation, I will ignore the issue of tense here and below.

There is nothing to eat in the house, Mending the bridge will take a significant amount of time, and *Jack has had breakfast today*. Thus although the sentences don't (obviously) contain any of the usual suspects for context sensitivity, it seems that they are context-sensitive anyway.

1.4. Indeterminacy

One might argue that, at the level of thought, content is indeterminate unless one specifies a context of thinking. If this is right, then there could be no source for the determinacy of linguistic content outside a context of use. This line of argument against the kind of determinate linguistic content supposed by the minimalist seems to be endorsed by Charles Travis.[5]

In *IS*, CL concentrate on arguments (i) and (ii). In fact, they claim that these are the only arguments adduced in favour of contextualism in the literature (*IS* 9–10). However, while (i) and (ii) are the main arguments given in favour of the contextualist view, it does seem that at least some advocates of contextualism also appeal to arguments like (iii) and (iv). With this in mind, let's turn now to consider the nature of contextualism in a little more detail.

2. VERSIONS OF CONTEXTUALISM

In their initial description of the opponents of minimalism, CL draw a fundamental divide between what they call 'radical' and 'moderate' contextualists:

- *Radical contextualists* claim that *every* expression of a natural language is context-sensitive. (*IS* 5–6)
- *Moderate contextualists* claim that *some* expressions of a natural language, which are not obviously context-sensitive, are in fact context-sensitive. (*IS* 7)

For CL, radical contextualists include Travis, Searle, Recanati, and the relevance theorists, while moderate contextualists include those who argue for the context sensitivity of quantified phrases (e.g. Stanley and Szabo), belief statements (e.g. Richard and Perry) and epistemic claims (e.g. DeRose). CL then have two main aims: first they aim to show that moderate contextualism is doomed to collapse into radical contextualism. Second, they aim to show that radical contextualism is fatally flawed.

However, as far as I can see, few (if any) of the theorists CL classify as radical contextualists actually fit the definition they give for this position. The problem is that many of these theorists run inappropriateness arguments against minimalism (given as (iii) in the previous section). For instance, in Robyn Carston's 2002 defence of relevance theory she explicitly distinguishes between

[5] See Travis 1997.

incompleteness arguments against minimalism (where appeals to pragmatic processes are necessary to yield a complete proposition since the linguistic content of a sentence alone fails to do so) and cases where appeals to pragmatic processes are necessary to yield the proposition expressed even though the sentence itself is capable of yielding a proposition without such contextual input. Thus she writes:

> There is a second set of cases for which a pragmatic process is required to arrive at the proposition intended by the speaker, even though the representation recovered without this process is fully propositional and could, therefore, be argued to constitute what is said by the utterance.[6]

The examples she gives for this second class include 'Something has happened' and 'I haven't eaten lunch'. In each case the suggestion is that the sentence itself, prior to pragmatic processing, can yield a complete proposition, though not the one the speaker intended to convey. Furthermore, Carston is not alone in utilizing this form of argument; for instance, it is also explicitly appealed to in Recanati 2004: 23.

Now minimalists, including CL, will obviously seek to reject the claim that these cases support contextualism and they will do so by driving a wedge between semantic content and speech act content. However, the point at issue here is whether someone like Carston is even *entitled* to run the argument that she does. For endorsing an inappropriateness argument entails the denial of the claim that every expression of a natural language is context-sensitive (since some sentences are assumed to deliver complete propositions prior to pragmatic input). Thus an inappropriateness argument should not be available to any radical contextualist. Two thoughts suggest themselves here: perhaps CL were simply wrong to class relevance theorists as radical contextualists, rather they should be seen as lying on the moderate side of the divide, claiming that most but not all expressions are context-sensitive. However, this way of carving things up seems somewhat odd, since relevance theory is usually taken as an archetypal instance of the strongest variety of contextualism. On the other hand, then, perhaps CL should not have characterized radical and moderate contextualists in the way they did. Perhaps the real division does come between theorists like Sperber and Wilson, Carston, Recanati, and Travis on the one side and moderate contextualists (theorists like Stanley and Szabo) on the other, but not for the reason that CL give.[7] It is this latter possibility that I want to explore now.

As noted, CL divide radical and moderate contextualists in terms of the number or range of expressions they treat as context-sensitive (all expressions being context-sensitive makes you a radical contextualist, less than all a moderate

[6] Carston 2002: 26.

[7] Certainly, as CL note, theorists like Stanley and Szabo have taken themselves to be opposed to theorists like Sperber and Wilson, so this might suggest any dividing line should, at least initially, cleave between such theorists.

one). I've suggested that under this definition not everyone they call a radical contextualist really is one. However there is another respect in which CL's characterization of their opponents seems debatable, for it seems that the kind of contextualist they really have in their sights is one who wants to extend the basic set of context-sensitive terms to include a number of other expressions (perhaps ranging to include all expressions). That is to say, it is someone who argues that, for instance, 'red' and 'man' and 'knows' are *just like* 'I' and 'now' and 'tomorrow', for all such expressions provide syntactic triggers via which features of the context of utterance come to contribute to semantic content. Perhaps the clearest example of a theorist in this mould is the advocate of a 'surprise indexical' or a 'hidden indexical' approach for some class of terms.[8] So for instance we find Stanley and Szabo arguing that every common noun in fact cohabits at the syntactic level with a hidden indexical.[9] On this kind of view it is clear what makes a term like 'man' context-sensitive: it is the presence in the term's basic syntactic structure of a genuinely indexical element, an element whose function precisely is to take one from a context of utterance to a content. Given this sort of contextualism, CL seem right to object both that ordinary speakers don't put 'man' on their list of context-sensitive terms and that such expressions fail their three tests for genuine context sensitivity.[10]

However it seems that not all contextualists are proposing a hidden indexical view when they reject the minimalist dictum that contextual inputs to literal content should be maximally constrained. Rather it seems that what they are proposing is that there are forms of context sensitivity *not* capturable on the model of the context sensitivity of the members of the Basic Set. For instance, Travis apparently rejects the idea that the context sensitivity he is concerned with should be treated as simply on a par with that exhibited by indexicals and demonstratives:

There are several respects in which the present phenomena are *unlike* central cases where the parameters approach seems promising. One difference is this. In the central cases, such as 'I' and 'now', pointing to given parameters seems to be part of the terms meaning what they do.... By contrast, it is not part of what 'green' means, so far as we can tell, that

[8] CL (*IS* 8–9) give three strategies employed by their moderate contextualists. The 'Surprise Indexical' and the 'Hidden Indexical' moves involve treating the expression in question as genuinely on a par with members of the Basic Set (the incontrovertibly context-sensitive expressions; see *IS* 2 and § 3.ii below), either because it is an indexical in its own right (the surprise move) or because it contains hidden indexical elements. I'll concentrate on the hidden indexical view in what follows, but the points carry over directly to the surprise indexical view. The third strategy which CL give—the unarticulated constituent move—seems prima facie very different. On this view, certain sentences are held to be context-sensitive but this is not due to any pronounced or unpronounced element in the sentence. The thrust of the argument to follow is that it is a mistake to treat this kind of free pragmatic enrichment as being equivalent to an expansion of the members of the Basic Set.

[9] Stanley and Szabo 2000. Their position in this paper is actually somewhat more complicated, positing two such hidden indexicals for each noun (and Stanley 2005*a* has since somewhat revised the position), but the details of their account are not essential here.

[10] *IS* ch. 7.

speakings of it speak of, or refer to, such-and-such parameters. If its contribution, on a speaking, to what is said *is* a function of some parameters—say, implausibly, the speaker's intentions—saying so is not part of what 'green' means. The parameter approach does not *automatically* suggest itself as it did with 'I'.[11]

More explicitly, Carston 2002 identifies what she calls the 'Isomorphism Principle', one formation of which she cites from Fodor and Lepore 1991: 333: if a sentence S expresses the proposition P, then syntactic constituents of S express the constituents of P. Discussing various examples which look prima facie problematic for the principle, she writes that the approach she supports 'allows that pragmatic processes can supply constituents to what is said [i.e. to the proposition expressed] without any linguistic pointer, in which case the Isomorphism Principle does not hold'.[12] So, it would seem that relevance theory (at least as Carston envisages it) is not simply a variant of the hidden indexical view.[13]

What these quotes highlight, I think, is that many contextualists do not think of all context sensitivity as on a par with that displayed by members of the Basic Set. Rather they hold that there are some contextual effects which cannot be traced to any element in the grammatical form of a sentence. Although CL do recognize the contextualist move to incorporate instances of pragmatic intrusion without syntactic trigger, or what we might call top–down pragmatic effects, in their initial characterization of contextualism (*IS* 9), they treat it entirely on a par with a move to expand the Basic Set. Yet they give no argument to support this equivalence.[14] Furthermore, it is not clear that there can be any way of expanding the Basic Set to include an additional grammatical item to accommodate the effects we are interested in, since ex hypothesi these effects are not grammatically triggered. Thus the idea that we can make do with a single model of how context affects content, based on the behaviour of words like 'I' and 'that', seems problematic.

[11] Travis 1997: 93. [12] Carston 2002: 23

[13] See also Recanati 2002: 316. Passages such as this one also shed doubt on CL's classification of Recanati as one of their radical contextualists. In the passage he offers a definition of unarticulated constituents as elements provided by the context which are not required by anything in the syntax of the sentence. However, if, as CL suppose, Recanati held all expressions to be context-sensitive, it would seem that all pragmatic effects would turn out to be mandatory (i.e. syntactically required), hence, on this interpretation, his category of optional unarticulated constituents would seem doomed to be empty.

[14] Perhaps this is too strong, for one could imagine CL responding that they do have an argument to support their equivalence claim, namely the fact that sentences which don't contain overt context-sensitive items fail their tests for genuine context sensitivity (see *IS*, ch. 7) and thus must be non-context-sensitive, however we understand context sensitivity. The tests for genuine context sensitivity turn on how speakers can be reported, e.g. if you uttered S in a previous context, can I now use exactly the same sentence in this context to report you? If so, the suggestion is, S is not context-sensitive. There are two points to note here: first, there might be scope for maintaining a difference between the way that members of the Basic Set interact with reporting and the way in which elements introduced only by the context of utterance interact with reporting (a point noted by Bezuidenhout 2006). Secondly, there may be questions to be raised about the accuracy of the tests CL rely on here; see Gross 2006.

It seems to me, then, that the key question to ask in classifying theorists here is not 'how many expressions do you think are context-sensitive?' but 'what do you think are the mechanisms of context sensitivity?' Specifically, we should ask whether a theorist allows the context of utterance to act on semantic content *even when such action is not demanded by the syntax of the sentence.*[15] Thus we might borrow CL's terminology to mark this rather different distinction. From this perspective, we might think of moderate contextualists as those who think all context sensitivity mirrors that to be found amongst members of the Basic Set. Since they deny the Basic Set assumption we might not count such theorists as minimalists, though they share the minimalist's key intuition that there is an exclusively syntactic route to semantic content. Radical contextualists on the other hand, deny this last assumption. For them there can be free pragmatic enrichment, not all contextual effects are triggered by elements in the syntax of a sentence. Notice that, although this is certainly not the way in which CL define their own terms, the mapping of theorists to positions does now seem to match the one they give, since, on the current definition, relevance theorists and Recanati do count as radical contextualists. However, we should also note that redefining things in this way would undermine one of the key arguments of *IS*: the idea that moderate contextualism is doomed to collapse into radical contextualism. With the positions understood as making claims about the *range* of context-sensitive expressions this prediction of collapse seems potentially plausible, but with the positions understood as making claims about the *mechanisms* of context sensitivity it seems wrong.

To summarize: an initial, apparently quite minor point concerns CL's terminology. Any contextualist who runs an 'inappropriateness' line of argument against minimalism cannot be a radical contextualist in CL's terms. So it seems to me that they are mistaken to count (at least some) relevance theorists and Recanati in this camp. However, on closer inspection, I think this minor point reveals a rather more substantial worry. CL seem to treat all forms of contextualism as advocating some kind of extension of the Basic Set; however there is reason to think that the most strident contextualists have a stronger claim than this in mind. For they suggest not merely that there are more context-sensitive terms than the minimalist admits, but that the model of context sensitivity she offers, in terms of the behaviour of the members of the Basic Set, is inadequate to cope with the vast range of contextual effects on semantic content. Sometimes context gets into the picture without any syntactic trigger—if this is right then it is not merely a question of adding a word or two to the Basic Set but of proffering an entirely different picture of the relationship between semantics and pragmatics. This is a point I'll return to below, but now let us turn to consider the nature of the opposing minimalist school of thought.

[15] King and Stanley 2005 also take this point to be crucial, marking a distinction between what they term 'weak' and 'strong' contextual effects. See also Borg 2004*b*.

3. THE DEFINING FEATURES OF MINIMALISM

In this section I would like to canvass four features which we might take as definitive of the minimalist approach to semantics. Some are explicitly endorsed by CL, others are not, but I hope that by exploring this range of features we can see where the argument with contextualism really lies.

3.1. Propositionalism

One feature we might envisage minimalism endorsing is 'propositionalism'. The term is introduced by Kent Bach in his paper 'The Excluded Middle' where he defines it as 'the conservative dogma that every indexical free declarative sentence expresses a proposition'. Now, prima facie, the question of whether or not sentence content makes it to the propositional level (or is truth-conditional) might not seem to be of much interest or importance. However on closer inspection this matter seems to go right back to the fundamental schism in philosophy of language between those who think that sentences (relativized to contexts of utterance) possess genuine, truth-evaluable content in their own right (and who go on to endorse some kind of formal approach to semantics) and those who think that it is only at the level of the utterance that it makes sense to talk about real meaning or to ask for truth-evaluable content (and who thus advocate a speech act approach to semantics). Contextualists follow the latter school of thought and argue that in a wide range of cases there are good reasons for thinking that no proposition is expressed prior to rich contextual input. The minimalist follows the former school of thought and rejects the contextualists' arguments, claiming instead that there are no good reasons to deny propositionality to the contents expressed by (indexical free) sentences, independent of any contextual input.[16]

One point we should note at this juncture, however, is that Kent Bach in the same paper in which he introduces the term 'propositionalism' also denies that it is an essential feature of a minimalist programme. More specifically, he argues for a position he terms 'radical minimalism' which 'in rejecting Propositionalism . . . is more radical, indeed, more minimalist than [CL's] version of Semantic Minimalism. It does not imagine that sentences that intuitively seem

16 In conversation, Herman Cappelen stressed that this is all *IS* is committed to—the claim that contextualist arguments against propositionalism are flawed. CL thus wish to remain agnostic on the truth of propositionalism (though since they are happy to allow that sentences like 'Jill is ready' express propositions, it is not immediately obvious what an example of a well-formed sentence which fails to express a proposition could look like for them). The minimalism advocated in Borg 2004*a* thus goes further than CL: it holds as a default assumption that all well-formed sentences express propositions and argues that, since contextualist arguments are flawed, propositionalism should be retained.

not to express propositions at least express "minimal propositions". Radical Semantic Minimalism, or simply Radicalism, says that the sentences in question are semantically incomplete—their semantic contents are not propositions but merely "propositional radicals".'[17] Thus, according to Bach at least, it is clearly not definitive of minimalism that it embrace propositionalism. According to Bach, there is a clear division to be drawn between sentences which are incomplete (i.e. fail to express propositions) and those which are not. In the former case, these sentences should not be viewed as context-sensitive—there is no element in the sentence which appeals to the context of utterance—rather they are simply incomplete, expressing propositional radicals not propositions. Since he claims incomplete sentences are not context-sensitive (unless they also contain members of the Basic Set), Bach argues that this is a form of minimalism, not contextualism.

However, although I don't have the space to pursue this point fully, it seems to me that Bach's radical minimalism risks a potential slide into contextualism.[18] For instance, relevance theorists are explicit in claiming that linguistic semantics (the theory dealing with word meaning and rules of composition) fails (at least in many cases) to deliver a proposition:

> What are the meanings of sentences? Sentence meanings are sets of semantic representations, as many semantic representations as there are ways in which the sentence is ambiguous. Semantic representations are incomplete logical forms, i.e. at best fragmentary representations of thoughts.[19]

This is not, for them, to say that linguistic semantics is improper or impossible, but simply to note that it deals (in at least some cases) with sub-propositional items. If we want propositional content, according to Sperber and Wilson, then in many cases we need to concentrate on speech acts, just as Bach's radical minimalism contends.[20] Furthermore, it would seem that the fundamental distinction Bach draws in other work between impliciture and implicature (where the former diverges from semantic content only by making *explicit* material *implicit* in the utterance, rather than giving further pragmatically conveyed propositions in the sense of Gricean implicatures) might fit well within something like the relevance theoretic framework. For they too are keen to draw a distinction between a pragmatically enhanced proposition which makes *explicit*

[17] Bach forthcoming.

[18] The similarities between Bach's position and that of certain contextualists is discussed at greater length in Carston 2005; the point is also made by Jason Stanley in his 2005*b* review of Recanati's *Literal Meaning*.

[19] Sperber and Wilson 1986: 193. We might note that this passage lends some credence to CL's categorization of Sperber and Wilson as their kind of radical contextualist.

[20] One point of difference between Bach and Sperber and Wilson concerns the number of sentences treated as semantically incomplete, with Bach claiming incompleteness for far fewer sentences. However, as CL object in *IS*, it is not clear what criterion, other than brute intuition, can be in play to determine this limited set of incomplete sentences.

material which is *implicit* in the utterance (their notion of an explicature) and a pragmatically enhanced proposition which spells out further things the speaker might convey by her utterance (implicatures). Thus, although Bach disagrees with any classification of his position as contextualist, still it seems that there are some reasons to view his position alongside that of theorists like Sperber and Wilson. Given these similarities between Bach's radical minimalism (with its rejection of propositionalism) and at least some contextualist approaches, it seems to me that there remains a good reason to treat propositionalism as a defining feature of minimalism.[21]

As an aside here, we might ask why a minimalist should adhere to propositionalism in the first place—is there any reason beyond the negative one that she thinks the contextualist arguments against propositionalism are flawed? Well, one first point to notice is how powerful this negative reason might be thought to be. Since we don't possess an independent, objective account of exactly what propositions there are in the world, or how to individuate or otherwise characterize these propositions, it seems that the onus of proof lies with the contextualist in showing that the representational content possessed by sentences *cannot* count as propositional. If she lacks good arguments to this end, and given that ordinary speakers are happy to treat many sentences as expressing propositional content (or as being truth-evaluable—witness the ubiquity of truth-evaluation tests in linguistics), it might well seem that there is simply no reason for the minimalist to refrain from assigning propositional status to all such contents. An additional motivation, however, is suggested by CL who contend that minimal propositions are required since they play a unique role in communication. As we will see below (§ 3.iii), I think there are problems with this view. Instead, I would suggest that propositionalism might acquire additional motivation from other areas. For instance, to assess an argument as deductively valid it seems required that the premises and conclusion of the argument all express complete, truth-evaluable propositions. Yet, if this is right, then it obviously entails that sentences are capable of doing more than expressing mere propositional fragments. Of course, an opponent of propositionalism might reject this point, claiming that it is only arguments under a given interpretation (i.e. with a context supplied) which can be assessed for validity, thus that sentences alone are not required to express complete propositions. To explore this point fully, however, would take us too far afield; thus all I want to claim here is that there are areas, outside the direct concerns of communication, to which the minimalist might think to look to motivate her acceptance of propositionalism.

So, since this chapter is concerned with an elucidation of minimalism rather than a defence of it, let's leave the motivation for propositionalism to one side for now, noting only that the assumption that indexical-free declarative sentences

[21] Other parties to the debate seem to agree with this; for instance Recanati (2003: 90) uses a denial of propositionalism in his initial definition of contextualism.

do express complete propositions without pragmatic enrichment may well be thought to be a defining property of minimalism as against contextualism. Yet since CL don't explicitly sign up to propositionalism there are obviously further defining features of minimalism which are important to them, so let's turn to these now.

3.2. The Basic Set Assumption

As CL note, ordinary speakers have strong intuitions about which are the context-sensitive expressions in their language. If you point out to an English speaker that 'I' has the rather odd property of depending for at least part of its meaning on the context in which it is uttered and then ask our subject to list other words 'like "I" in this respect' you can expect to be given terms like 'this' and 'that' and 'today', not expressions like 'man' and 'red' and 'thirteen'. Minimalists seek to preserve this intuition by admitting only the obviously context-sensitive expressions as genuine syntactic triggers for contextual input (CL thus claim that the class of context-sensitive terms is exhausted by those Kaplan listed plus or minus a bit).[22] I think CL are right to treat the Basic Set assumption as a defining feature of minimalism, but we should be clear about exactly what this assumption commits us to. Specifically, we need to hold apart surprise and hidden indexical views of the kind sketched in § 2, which flout the Basic Set assumption, and hidden argument place views, which do not.

Hidden indexical views are versions of hidden argument place views, but one clearly could advocate hidden argument places where these places are filled by existentially quantified variables rather than by indexicals. CL recognize that it is only the former view which is actually incompatible with their version of minimalism, however they still reject the hidden argument approach (*IS* 97). They don't discuss their reasons for this rejection in any detail, so it is hard to know why they dislike hidden argument place views so much. Yet I would suggest that, in certain cases at least, such an approach provides a more credible version of minimalism than the one to which CL are committed.[23] For such a view can preserve something like a law of non-contradiction—the idea that a sentence and its negation cannot both be true in the same situation. For instance, consider the sentence 'Jill is ready': according to CL this expresses the minimal proposition that *Jill is ready* and presumably the sentence expresses something true in any situation in which Jill is ready. On the other hand, the sentence 'Jill is not ready' expresses the minimal proposition that *Jill is not ready* and this

[22] *IS* 2

[23] The hidden argument view, with respect to certain terms, is endorsed in Borg 2004*a*: 230. The claim that it provides a more appealing version of minimalism has been queried, in conversation, by Tim Williamson. He suggested that since, in general, minimalism is not designed to answer to our intuitions about truth-conditions, it is unclear that complicating one's syntax at this point actually brings one more explanatory power than the simpler CL account.

presumably expresses something true in any situation in which Jill is not ready. However, it seems that there are many situations in which both sentences will then be true together (for instance, where Jill is ready to go to the party but not ready to take the exam). Yet since, for CL, the second sentence is just the negation of the first, this looks problematic.[24]

This is a worry which the hidden argument place version of minimalism can avoid. If the underlying form of 'Jill is ready' is taken to be of the more complex form [∃x Rjx] (where 'R' stands for the relationship of being ready) then it is clear how 'Jill is ready' and 'Jill is not ready' can both be true at the same time, given a narrow scope reading of the negation in the second sentence.[25] Furthermore, I would suggest that this form of minimalism does not turn on suspect intuitions about changes in truth value across contexts (i.e. the 'context shifting arguments' outlined in § 1). Instead it rests on a concern for non-contradiction and on empirical evidence about the correct lexical entry for our expressions (which will include any available syntactic evidence). So, although CL reject both hidden indexical and hidden argument place moves, I think minimalism may be a more credible theory if it is allowed to appeal to existentially marked argument places, at least where syntactic evidence for such items is forthcoming.

3.3. Semantic Content is Not Speech Act Content

It is a common move amongst minimalists to deny that semantic content is speech act content. Minimalists have to deny this equivalence since, even if there are such things as minimal propositions, it is clear that they are not what we take to be conveyed in most ordinary communicative exchanges. However, CL go further than simply denying that semantic content is speech act content, instead they make the stronger claim that semantic content is a proper part of

24 Of course, CL might bite the bullet here and deny that there are situations which make both sentences true (arguing that it is only more fine-grained speech act content, like *Jill is ready to go the party* and *Jill is not ready to take the exam*, which can be true together), but this seems a prima-facie difficult position to defend, raising as it does substantial further questions. For instance, we now need to know whether a situation in which Jill is ready to go to the party but not ready to take the exam is a situation which makes the sentence 'Jill is ready' true or one which makes the sentence 'Jill is not ready' true, and why this is so in either case. At this juncture, CL recommend philosophical quietude on behalf of the philosopher of language, instead passing the problems over to the metaphysician for resolution at some later date. However I would suggest that an account which didn't take us to this impasse would, *ceteris paribus*, be preferable to this.

25 It might be objected that this logical form is itself still underarticulated since, to get to a determinate relationship expressed by 'ready', we need to know exactly what Jill is ready to do. For instance is she ready *to take* an exam, ready *to invigilate* an exam, ready *to mark* an exam, etc. However, I, along with CL, would disagree with this, assuming that 'ready' is capable of expressing an entirely determinate relationship, though one which is quite liberal, in the sense of being made true by a number of divergent situations. The sentence 'Jill is ready' would, on the current minimalist proposal, be made true by any situation where there is something which Jill is ready for, though she may realize the relationship of readiness by standing in any number of more fine-grained relationships to objects. See Borg 2004: ch. 4, for further discussion.

speech act content.[26] They suggest that a speaker uttering a given sentence may express any number of propositions (hence they label their position 'speech act pluralism') and stress that often the proposition (or propositions) hearers are interested in will not be the minimal one. Nevertheless the semantic content of the sentence will *always* form part of this larger speech act content. CL make this move since they wish to avoid the claim that minimal propositions are otiose in an account of communication; instead minimal propositions are taken to have a unique role as 'fall-back' content in cases of ignorance or mistake, etc. Where one knows next to nothing about the speaker and their context one can still know that they asserted the proposition expressed by the sentence uttered.

However it is not obvious to me that minimalists should embrace the view that the semantic content of a sentence is the content common to all speech acts involving that sentence. For, first, there is reason to think that speakers in general do not assert such propositions, and that hearers in general don't grasp them. While, second, it seems that semantic content might play the kind of fall-back role envisaged *without* it being part of speech act content. On the first point: it seems that we would normally expect the content of an assertion to be determined at least in part by the contents of the speaker's mind; what does the person uttering S intend to assert? However, according to Speech Act Pluralism, the mind of the speaker is little or no guide to the content of an assertion, since speakers may well be entirely oblivious to the minimal propositions their sentences express.[27] It is likely that the speaker who looks in the fridge and says 'There is nothing to eat' would be surprised to learn that they had asserted the quite general proposition that *there is nothing to eat (in the universe)*. Nor will the speaker who utters 'I've eaten', in response to an invitation to lunch, be aware that they are asserting the general proposition that *I've eaten (at some point in my past)*. Furthermore, on at least some occasions, speakers may be aware of the literal meanings of their sentences but explicitly intend not to assert these meanings. So, for instance, a speaker who says ironically, of Jill, 'She was nice' absolutely does *not* want to assert the proposition that *Jill was nice*.[28] Yet, prima

[26] In Borg 2004*a* I advocated the weaker view that semantic content is simply distinct from speech act content. Speech act pluralism, on the other hand, is also endorsed by Soames 2002. We might also note here Sperber and Wilson's (1986: 9) suggestion that: 'The semantic representation of a sentence deals with a sort of common core meaning shared by every utterance of it'.

[27] The worry discussed in this paragraph follows the 'meaning-intention' problem for hidden-indexical theories of belief reports as raised by Stephen Schiffer. As Schiffer (1992: 514) writes, 'if the hidden-indexical theory is correct, then [a speaker] has no conscious awareness of what she means, or of what she is saying [in uttering a sentence] and this is a prima facie reason to deny that she means what the theory is committed to saying she means'.

[28] The same worry might hold for metaphorical utterances or for conditional assertions (the speaker who says 'If pigs can fly, I'll come to the seminar' would not want to be taken to be asserting that *pigs can fly*).

facie at least, if a speaker doesn't think they've asserted p this is a reason to treat them as not having asserted p.[29]

A second point to note here is that there is also experimental evidence to show that minimal propositions need not play a part in hearers' comprehension of communicative exchanges, since hearers sometimes progress to pragmatic interpretation at a local, rather than a sentential, level. So, for instance, there is evidence to suggest that a hearer may recognize the need to assign a metaphorical interpretation to a word or sub-sentential item *without* first processing the entire sentence in which the word occurs to recover the proposition literally expressed (Gibbs 2002 terms this the 'direct access' view). Or again, consider scalar terms: on at least some occasions hearers pragmatically enrich scalar terms, e.g. interpreting 'some' as containing an upper bound as well as a lower one. Thus an utterance of 'Some students passed' may be interpreted as conveying the pragmatically enriched proposition *at least one but not all students passed* (rather than the weaker proposition yielded by the lexical entry for 'some': *at least one student passed*). Yet there is evidence to suggest that sometimes this pragmatic strengthening takes place at a local level. That is to say, for instance, hearers do not wait for the entire sentence to be processed for literal meaning before strengthening 'some' to *some but not all*.[30] Yet, it seems, if communication can be shown to proceed without hearers processing the literal meaning of the sentence, i.e. without grasping minimal propositions, then the claim that minimal propositions have a unique role to play in actual communicative exchanges is undermined.

Finally, we might note that even if minimal propositions do not constitute a proper part of speech act content, and thus that both speakers and hearers can be unaware of them in communicative exchanges, they might still be available to play the kind of fall-back role CL envisage.[31] The thought would be that, in cases of ignorance or mistake, where one knows one is not in a position to offer a full (i.e. context-affected) account of what the speaker said when she uttered U in her original context of utterance, one can retreat to the literal meaning of the sentence produced. This is *not* because there is a guarantee that the speaker did in fact assert the minimal proposition (i.e. not because minimal propositions are a proper part of speech act content), but simply because minimal propositions are (and are known to be) the content any competent language user is guaranteed

29 We should note that CL are entirely aware of this point (*IS* 200–2) but they argue that the nature of reporting shows that it cannot be the case that speakers have the final say on what they assert. However, as Gross (2006) argues, we might question CL's motivation for this claim.

30 See the eye-tracking experiments of Storto and Tanenhaus 2005.

31 For a range of cases in which the fall back to the minimal proposition is useful, see Horn 2006. For further argument that CL are wrong to require semantic content to form a proper part of speech act content, see Elugardo (this volume). Note also, however, that the view to be defended above runs counter to the traditional Gricean model, whereby the content recovered via syntactic content plus disambiguation and reference determination (i.e. the Gricean notion of 'what is said') is required to be part of what was meant (asserted) by the speaker.

to be able to recover merely through exposure to the sentence uttered.[32] It is this fact, perhaps together with a general feature of communication (namely, that indirect speech reports involving content sentences which share a literal meaning with the speaker's original utterance are typically judged correct), which guarantees the role of minimal propositions as the content deferred to when information about the context of utterance is insufficient, unreliable, or in some way unstable.[33] So, if I know that you said 'Jill is tall' but I don't know what comparison class you had in mind, I can nevertheless report you as having said that *Jill is tall* (i.e. I can report you using the minimal proposition expressed by your sentence). I can do so because, even if I don't know much about the context, I know what your words meant. Furthermore, in this case, my report counts as accurate since you would be willing to accept this way of reporting you. On the other hand, if I hear you say 'She was nice', referring to Jill who has just left the room, but I don't realize that you were being ironic, my later report of you as having asserted that *Jill was nice* may turn out to be inaccurate, since in this case you are unlikely to accept this way of being reported.[34] In this situation, I've done the best job I could: I've accurately reported the literal meaning of your sentence (I've fallen back to the only content I am guaranteed to grasp as a competent language user), even though on this occasion that is not what you meant.

So far, then, I've suggested that minimalism is defined by its acceptance of (i) propositionalism and (ii) the Basic Set assumption, just as CL suggest. I've also suggested that all minimalists must envisage a divide between semantic content and speech act content (iii), even though I've also argued that the precise formulation of this divide which CL adopt (whereby semantic content is always a part of speech act content) is an unnecessary development of the strict commitments of minimalism. Now we come to the final feature which I take to be definitive of minimalism: the commitment to formalism. This is a feature

[32] One issue here concerns the semantic content of genuinely context-sensitive terms: can someone who is exposed only to the sentence 'I am here', without knowing who produced the sentence or where they were, really grasp the content it expresses? As I have argued elsewhere, I think they can grasp a rigidified reflexive content which does constitute the semantic (propositional) content of such a sentence (see Borg 2004: ch. 3, and n.d.). However, this is not a point which I can explore further in this chapter.

[33] It might be objected that reports that share literal meaning are *not* typically judged correct (see Leslie, this volume). However, even if this is right, I would suggest that it does not undermine the general point here, for the minimalist as I envisage them might explain the fall-back role of minimal propositions purely in terms of their role as the content a competent speaker is guaranteed to be able to recover. So that, in problem contexts, one resorts to interpreting a sentence in lieu of interpreting a speaker.

[34] Herman Cappelen has noted that, even in ironic cases, it is sometimes correct to report a speaker using the minimal proposition expressed by the sentence originally uttered. Thus it seems correct to say 'A said that Jill was nice, but she was being ironic'. Note, however, that the current view, which holds that reports utilizing such minimal propositions will typically count as correct, can accommodate this fact. What CL need to show is the much stronger claim that in cases of irony (and elsewhere) *all* such reports utilizing minimal propositions are in fact correct.

which, again, CL appear to tacitly endorse. However, I want to suggest that a full appreciation of the constraints which formalism places on a theory may serve to show that minimalism is a much more extreme position than CL envisage.

3.4. Formalism

As noted at the outset of this chapter, minimalism appears to be the natural descendant of formal theories of meaning. The aim, just as it was for previous formal theories, is to deliver a perfectly general, systematic theory of literal meaning. As CL note:

> Semanticists disagree on what the central semantic features are (truth conditions, intensions, extensions, prototypes, functions from worlds to truth values, stereotypes, situations, or whatever), but they do tend to agree that semantics is a discipline that aims to characterize systematically certain features of linguistic expressions and to do so in a way that captures general truths about languages, and not just truths about particular speakers in specific contexts.[35]

What I take this striving towards systematicity and generality to amount to is a commitment to formalism—the idea that there is an entirely formal (i.e. syntactic) route to semantic content.[36]

However, as it stands, this commitment is somewhat vague, for it seems that we might understand it in one of two ways:

(*a*) Every contextual contribution to semantic content is syntactically triggered.
(*b*) Every contextual contribution to semantic content is formally tractable.

CL are explicit in endorsing (*a*), indeed it forms the second condition of their initial statement of minimalism: 'all semantic context sensitivity is grammatically (i.e. syntactically or morphologically) triggered'.[37] Notice, however, that, by their definition, it looks as if all contextualists also agree on this condition, since CL construe contextualists as arguing that some (or in the limit case of the radical contextualist, all) expressions are context-sensitive, in which case context sensitivity remains something which is grammatically coded for. As noted in § 2, I disagree with CL over their definition of moderate and radical contextualists; thus I would argue that, while surprise or hidden indexical theorists (those I would classify as moderate contextualists) agree with the minimalist in endorsing (*a*), the

[35] *IS* 58.

[36] One motivation for the search for a systematic theory is that we might think that it alone could account for the compositionality of natural language, which in turn is required to account for the productivity and systematicity of linguistic comprehension.

[37] *IS* 2. Note that they claim that this condition follows from the Basic Set assumption. I would suggest this is only the case given the additional assumption that the kind of context dependency shown by members of the Basic Set is the only kind of context sensitivity there is. Specifically, then, only if there are no top–down pragmatic effects on semantic content.

true radical contextualists (Travis, Searle, Recanati, and the relevance theorists) actually reject (*a*). This was the argument of § 2; however, the commitment to formalism which I want to concentrate on now is (*b*).

CL (along with all contextualists of whatever stripe) reject (*b*), for they hold that speaker intentions play a role in determining semantic content. For CL speaker intentions figure at the semantic level to disambiguate ambiguous or polysemous expressions, to precisify vague expressions, and to determine reference assignments for indexicals and demonstratives.[38] Yet it seems that speaker intentions must constitute a non-formal aspect of a context of utterance. The argument for this claim emerges from what is known in AI circles as the Frame Problem.

The worry is that, *in principle*, any piece of information may turn out to be relevant in assigning an intentional state to an agent. So, imagine that you hear Jack say 'I would like that' while pointing at a cake. It might seem natural to assign him the intentional state of intending to refer to that cake. However, imagine that you also know that Jack is an avid collector of cake plates, then it might seem more natural to interpret him as intending to refer to the plate the cake is on. Or imagine that you know that Jack and Jill are playing a game in which various foodstuffs stand for various toys, then Jack's utterance of 'that' might be meant to refer to their toy truck. The point here is that assigning intentional states is a defeasible matter: no matter how good an intentional explanation looks to be it can always be defeated by the introduction of new evidence which would account for the agent's behaviour in some other way.[39] Thus there is simply no limit on the amount of contextual evidence which could turn out to be relevant in assigning an intentional state to another. On the other hand, however, it is clear that *in practice* there is a limit on the amount of information we take to be relevant in determining the intentional state of another. We don't laboriously check through *everything* we know when trying to work out to what Jack might be referring, rather we somehow settle on a tiny fraction of the relevant beliefs and proceed from there. Yet this kind of reasoning process (one which is potentially sensitive to anything one believes, but which in practice looks only to a tiny subset of those beliefs) is clearly a form of inference to the best explanation: it is driven by a consideration of the content of beliefs and representations, not by the syntax of those representations.[40] Assigning intentional states to others then is a matter of more than mere syntax. It is not a general computational process but one which is itself highly context-sensitive. It thus seems that appealing to current speaker intentions as an integral part of determining semantic content runs counter to the general, systematic, and computational aims of semantic theorizing.

At times, CL *seem* to agree with this point. For instance, as we saw in the last section, a key argument of minimalism is that intuitions about correct indirect

[38] *IS* 145. [39] See Recanati 2004: 54.

[40] See Fodor 2000: 31–7. The argument that current speaker intentions lie beyond the grasp of formal semantics is spelt out at greater length in Borg 2004*b*.

speech reports are irrelevant (or at least, are not directly relevant) to semantic theorizing. In support of this claim CL write:

[R]eporters are interested neither in systematicity nor in generality; they aim to convey something about a particular act in a particular context . . . Reporters draw on information about the specific intentions of, knowledge about, and the history of, a reported speaker . . . These are features one does *not* want to solicit when the aim is systematic and general.[41]

However, when Recanati raises the objection that incorporating speaker intentions in a minimalist theory of meaning is a form of cheating, they write that: 'We find this remark about "cheating" baffling. Why is it cheating?' (*IS* 149). The suggestion of this section is that Recanati is right to view it as a kind of cheating because, if one has in one's background motivation for minimalism an idea that a semantic theory will provide a general, systematic, and syntax-driven account of sentential content, then one cannot appeal to any formally intractable aspects of the context of utterance as an integral part of the determination of that content. This is why the division between what Bach has termed 'wide' and 'narrow' features of the context is more than a merely terminological matter (*IS* 147): incorporating wide features, i.e. speaker intentions, at the semantic level is, if the argument of this section is correct, beyond the scope of the kind of formal, syntax driven approach to meaning the semantic minimalist aims to deliver.[42] It seems to me then that a semantic minimalist who remains true to minimalist principles all the way down must eschew current speaker intentions as not semantically relevant. If this is right, then the true test for minimalism is (as it perhaps was all along) how it deals with the existence of those expressions for which it seems uncontroversial that their content is bound up with current speaker intentions. That is to say, the true test of minimalism is how it deals with overtly context-sensitive expressions like demonstratives and indexicals.[43]

[41] *IS* 58.

[42] One response I can envisage here is: 'what is wrong with a position (call it 'minimalism' or whatever you like) which endorses (*a*) but rejects (*b*)? Sure it wouldn't be an entirely systematic, general theory of meaning, but what is wrong with that?' Two worries present themselves here: if, like me, you have any background ideas about linguistic comprehension being underpinned by a computational cognitive module, then you need semantic content to be entirely computationally determined. Secondly, and more importantly, once you allow that current speaker intentions are relevant in at least some cases, it's not clear why they shouldn't be allowed to operate more generally. The semantic theorist who claims that speaker intentions are relevant to content only for obviously context-sensitive terms is committed to driving a massive wedge between semantic content and speech act content; what we say is (almost) never what our sentences mean. This is a pretty big bullet to bite. Once the door has been opened to speaker intentions at one point, and we assume that a semantic theory has the wherewithal to recover what a speaker has in mind, why not allow speaker intentions to influence content elsewhere and allow semantic content to cleave more closely to our intuitions about the content of utterances?

[43] The solution I would like to propose for this problem, which involves distinguishing issues of reference determination/identification on one hand and issues of semantic content itself on the other, is discussed in Borg 2004: ch. 3, and n.d.

4. CONCLUSION

It seems to me that CL are wrong to frame the debate between minimalists and contextualists in terms of the *range* of context-sensitive items each one posits, rather I think it should be seen as a debate about the *mechanisms* which operate within a semantic theory. According to the radical contextualist (as I construe her) pragmatic processes are endemic throughout semantic content, both when grammatically triggered and when only contextually triggered. Furthermore, the aspects of context which intrude on semantic content for the contextualist may take any form, they may include objective features (like who is speaking and when), and they may include features the hearer can only determine abductively (like speaker intentions). On the other hand, according to the minimalist (as I construe her) there is an entirely formal route to meaning. This means not only that every contextual contribution to semantic content must be grammatically marked but also that those features contributed by the context must themselves be formally tractable. This is a much more austere form of minimalism than that recommended by CL and it remains, of course, a moot point whether a theory with such a restricted base can really do the things required of it. Yet it seems to me that it is this austere theory which really carries the minimalist convictions to their proper conclusion.

Despite its many persuasive arguments against contextualism, then, I see *IS* as presenting a version of radical contextualism which is not radical enough and a version of minimalism which is not minimal enough. Even if this is right, *Insensitive Semantics* remains a very important book because it helps us to see that, for instance, contextualist arguments about the context sensitivity of 'red' are no more than red herrings, but it does not perhaps constitute the ultimate defence of minimalism it aims to provide. [44]

REFERENCES

Bach, K. (1994), 'Conversational Impliciture,' *Mind and Language*, 9: 124–62.

—— (forthcoming) 'The Excluded Middle: Semantic Minimalism without Minimal Propositions', *Philosophy and Phenomenological Research*.

Bezuidenhout, A. (2006), 'The Coherence of Contextualism', *Mind and Language*, 21: 1–10.

Borg, E. (2004*a*), *Minimal Semantics*. Oxford: Oxford University Press.

—— (2004*b*), 'Formal Semantics and Intentional States', *Analysis*, 64: 215–23

[44] Versions of this chapter were presented at University College Dublin, Reading, and Oxford. Thanks to the audiences on those occasions, especially Herman Cappelen, and to Kent Bach and Ray Elugardo for helpful comments and discussion. I'm also grateful to two readers for OUP for raising many useful points. This chapter was completed during AHRC-funded research leave.

____(n.d.) 'Referential Intentions, Minimal Semantics and Epistemic Behaviourism', typescript.

Cappelen, H., and E. Lepore (2005), *Insensitive Semantics: A Defense of Semantic Minimalism and Speech Act Pluralism.* Oxford: Blackwell.

Carston, R. (2002), *Thoughts and Utterances.* Oxford: Blackwell.

____(2005), Relevance Theory, Grice and the Neo-Griceans: A response to Laurence Horn's "Current Issues in Neo-Gricean Pragmatics" ', *Intercultural Pragmatics*, 2–3: 303–19

Fodor, J. (2000), *The Mind doesn't Work that Way.* Cambridge, Mass.: MIT Press.

Fodor, J., and E. Lepore (1991), 'Why Meaning (Probably) isn't Conceptual Role', *Mind and Language*, 6: 328–43.

Gibbs, R. (2002), 'A New Look at Literal Meaning in Understanding What is Said and Implicated', *Journal of Pragmatics*, 34: 457–86.

Gross, S. (2006), 'Can One Sincerely Say What One Doesn't Believe?', *Mind and Language*, 21: 11–20.

Horn, L. (2006), 'More Issues in Neo- and Post-Gricean Pragmatics: A Reply to Carston', *Intercultural Pragmatics*, 3: 81–93.

King, J., and J. Stanley (2005), 'Semantics, Pragmatics and the Role of Semantic Content', in Z. Gendler Szabó (ed.), *Semantics Versus Pragmatics.* Oxford: Oxford University Press.

Recanati, F. (2002), 'Unarticulated Constituents', *Linguistics and Philosophy*, 25: 299–345.

____(2004), *Literal Meaning.* Cambridge: Cambridge University Press.

Schiffer, S. (1992), Belief Ascription', *Journal of Philosophy*, 89: 499–521.

Soames, S. (2002), *Beyond Rigidity.* Oxford: Oxford University Press.

Sperber, D., and D. Wilson (1986), *Relevance: Communication and Cognition.* Oxford: Blackwell

Stanley, J. (2005*a*), 'Semantics in Context', in G. Preyer and G. Peter (eds.), *Contextualism in Philosophy: Knowledge, Meaning, and Truth*, pp. 221–54. Oxford: Oxford University Press.

____(2005*b*), 'Review of Recanati's *Literal Meaning*', *Notre Dame Philosophical Reviews*: http://ndpr.nd.edu/review.cfm?id=3841

____and Z. Szabó (2000), 'On Quantifier Domain Restriction', Mind and Language, 15: 219–61.

Storto, G, and M. Tanenhaus (2005), 'Are Scalar Implicatures Computed Online?', in E. Maeir, C. Bary, and J. Huitinle (eds.), Proceedings of *Sinn und Bedeutunng*, 9: 435–45. Nijmegen: Nijjmegen Centre for Semantics.

Travis, C. (1997), 'Pragmatics', in B. Blale and C. Wright (eds.), *Companion to the Philosophy of Language*, pp. 87–107. Oxford: Blackwell.

Index